Fodor's 7th Edition

Caribbean Ports of Call

The Guide
for All Budgets

Completely
Updated

Where to Shop, Eat,
and Explore

Cruise Lines,
Cruise Ships

Ports of
Embarkation

Maps, Travel Tips,
and Web Sites

Portions of this book appear in *Fodor's Caribbean*

Fodor's Travel Publications • New York, Toronto, London, Sydney, Auckland
www.fodors.com

II

Fodor's Caribbean Ports of Call

EDITOR: Douglas Stallings

Editorial Contributors: Isabel Abisláiman, Nancy Orr Athnos, Carol Bareuther, John Bigley, Gene Bourg, Sandra Davis-Taylor, Lisa Dunford, Kathy Foster, Suzanne Gordon, Paul A. Greenberg, Lynne Helm, Jennie Hess, John and Judy Ingrisano, Baty Landis, Lynda Lohr, Diane P. Marshall, Maribeth Mellin, Elise Meyer, JoAnn Milivojevic, Paris Permenter, Vernon Ramesar, Eileen Robinson Smith, Jordan Simon, Lan Sluder, Harriet Swift, Chelle Koster Walton, Jane E. Zarem

Editorial Production: David Downing

Maps: David Lindroth *cartographer;* Bob Blake and Rebecca Baer, *map editors*

Design: Fabrizio La Rocca, *creative director;* Guido Caroti, *art director;* Melanie Marin, *senior picture editor*

Cover Design: Pentagram

Production/Manufacturing: Angela L. McLean

Cover Photo: Norwegian Cruise Line (top photo), Angelo Cavalli/Age Fotostock (bottom photo)

Copyright

Special Sales

Fodor's Travel Publications are available at special discounts for bulk purchases for sales promotions or premiums. Special editions, including personalized covers, excerpts of existing guides, and corporate imprints, can be created in large quantities for special needs. For more information, contact your local bookseller or write to Special Markets, Fodor's Travel Publications, 1745 Broadway, New York, NY 10019. Inquiries from Canada should be directed to your local Canadian bookseller or sent to Random House of Canada, Ltd., Marketing Department, 2775 Matheson Boulevard East, Mississauga, Ontario L4W 4P7. Inquiries from the United Kingdom should be sent to Fodor's Travel Publications, 20 Vauxhall Bridge Road, London SW1V 2SA, England.

An Important Tip & An Invitation

Although all prices, opening times, and other details in this book are based on information supplied to us at press time, changes occur all the time in the travel world, and Fodor's cannot accept responsibility for facts that become outdated or for inadvertent errors or omissions. So **always confirm information when it matters,** especially if you're making a detour to visit a specific place. We follow up on all suggestions. Contact the Caribbean Ports of Call editor at editors@fodors.com or c/o Fodor's at 1745 Broadway, New York, New York 10019.

PRINTED IN THE UNITED STATES OF AMERICA

10 9 8 7 6 5 4 3 2 1

CONTENTS

Maps and Charts

HOW TO USE THIS BOOK

Up front is a **Cruise Primer,** with some basic information about cruising and cruise ships. **Cruising the Caribbean** gives you the low-down on the cruise lines and cruise ships that regularly ply the waters of the Caribbean. **Ports of Embarkation** gives you background on the most important ports for joining a cruise, including suggestions for where to stay and eat, and what you might want to do if you spend an extra day or two before or after your cruise. And finally, **Ports of Call** gives you our best advice on what to do in each major Caribbean cruise port, including some suggestions for activities, sightseeing, and lunch spots, not to mention a run-down of some of the better shore excursions offered by the ships.

Icons and Symbols

✕ Restaurant
🏨 Lodging establishment
🐤 Good for kids (rubber duck)
☞ Sends you to another section of the guide for more information
✉ Address
☎ Telephone number
🕙 Opening and closing times and tour durations

🎟 Admission prices (those we give apply to adults; substantially reduced fees are almost always available for children, students, and senior citizens)

Numbers in black circles ❸ that appear on the maps, in the margins, and within the tours correspond to one another.

For hotels, you can assume that all rooms have private baths, phones, TVs, and air-conditioning unless otherwise noted and that all hotels operate on the European Plan (with no meals) if we don't specify another meal plan. We always list a property's facilities but not whether you'll be charged extra to use them, so when pricing accommodations, do ask what's included. For restaurants, it's always a good idea to book ahead; we mention reservations only when they're essential or are not accepted. All restaurants we list are open daily for lunch and dinner unless stated otherwise; dress is mentioned only when men are required to wear a jacket or a jacket and tie.

1 CRUISE PRIMER

If you haven't cruised before, you may be anxious about choosing and booking a cruise. With the dozens of lines, hundreds of ships, and thousands of itineraries out there, the choices can seem mind-boggling. If you feel overwhelmed, what you need is a strategy. With a game plan, choosing a line, a ship, and itinerary becomes easy. Divide the work up into steps and forge ahead.

You have to know what you want in order to find it. You also have to be able to explain yourself to a travel agent or make your own decisions when booking a cruise yourself on-line. So take an inventory of your priorities: what sort of rhythm do you want—rest and relaxation at sea or excursions in new ports every day? Do you want a big, extravagant ship or a smaller, simpler one? Do you want all-out luxury or a barefoot and budget trip? Do you want to get dressed up for dinner every night, or do you want to dine as you are? Do you want to go to bed early or dance the night away? What do you want out of your days? Enrichment or entertainment? Roulette or relaxation? Maybe a little of both? No single ship has everything, but you can narrow down the field to a few that fit the bill.

The more you know, the easier it will be to make your choice. So get as much information as possible. Begin by getting recommendations from friends and coworkers who have taken cruises. What did or didn't they like about their ship? Would they take the same cruise again? Friends and family provide the best recommendations, because they're most likely to know what you would like.

Next, visit or call more than one cruise-only travel agency and ask for suggestions. CLIA (Cruise Line International Association) travel agents have information about all types of ships and are likely to know about ships that your friends and family may not be aware of. Ask each agent to send you brochures for the recommended ships. Be aware that many travel agents work exclusively with certain cruise lines. One agency may specialize in Carnival, NCL, and Holland America, another in Princess. But the agency that sells more Holland America cruises will usually be able to offer you better prices.

When leafing through brochures, take a good look at the photographs—not just the cabins and deck layout but the pictures of people. A cruise geared toward senior citizens won't be promoted with shots of twentysomethings in its brochure. For instance, Carnival shows lots of younger couples and families with children, while Royal Caribbean shows a mix of ages, often in the same shot. Celebrity shows chic people in stylish settings. Brochures and their video and electronic equivalents, along with Web sites, are the most useful tools for planning a cruise. All give you valuable information about what you will and won't find on board.

BEFORE YOU GO

Once you have chosen your cruise and signed on to go, it's time to get ready. Preparations for a cruise may involve many distinct tasks, but none of them are difficult, especially if broken down into manageable steps. Most important, allow plenty of time to get ready so you don't get harried in the last couple of weeks.

Tickets and Vouchers

After you make the final payment to your travel agent, the cruise line will issue your cruise tickets and vouchers for airport–ship transfers. Depending on the airline, and whether you have purchased an air-sea package, you may receive your plane tickets or charter-flight vouchers at the same time; you may also receive vouchers for any shore excursions, although most cruise lines issue these aboard ship. Should your travel documents not arrive when promised, contact your travel agent or cruise line. If you book late, tickets may be delivered directly to the ship.

Passports and Visas

In the past, cruise lines sailing from Florida ports to the Caribbean rarely asked to see American passengers' passports. A passport is now necessary. If you don't have one to show authorities, you may be asked to fill out a citizenship form—delaying your embarkation—and you can be denied entry to a country if you have no proof of citizenship. If you do not have a passport, take a certified copy of your birth certificate, which must have a raised seal, and your driver's license. Immigration regulations require every passenger boarding a cruise ship from a U.S. port to provide additional personal data, such as your current mailing address and telephone number, to the cruise operator in advance of embarkation. Failure to provide this information required by the U.S. government may result in denial of boarding.

If you are boarding a ship outside the United States, you'll need the appropriate entry requirements for that country. On cruises to or from some countries, you may be required to obtain a visa in advance. It is always the responsibility of the person traveling to obtain the necessary travel documents, including visas. Check with your travel agent or cruise line about specific requirements. If you do need a visa for your cruise, your travel agent should be able to help you obtain it, but there may be a charge of $25 or more for this service, in addition to the visa charge. Read your cruise documents carefully to see what documents you'll need for embarkation. You don't want to be turned away at the pier.

What to Pack

Certain packing rules apply to all cruises. Always take a sweater in case of cool evening ocean breezes or overactive air-conditioning. A rain slicker usually comes in handy, too, and make sure you bring at least one pair of comfortable walking shoes for exploring port towns. Men who want to participate in formal night activities should pack a dark suit, a tuxedo, or a white dinner jacket. Women should pack one long gown or cocktail dress for every two or three formal evenings on board. Life on board most ships is much more casual than it once was, but there's always a dress-up evening that you can attend or skip.

Generally speaking, plan on one outfit for every two days of cruising, especially if your wardrobe contains many interchangeable pieces. Ships often have convenient laundry facilities. Don't forget your toiletries and sundry items, but if you do, these are readily available in port shops or in the ship's gift shop (although usually at a premium price). Cabin amenities typically include soap and often shampoo, conditioner, and other lotions and potions.

Outlets in cabin bathrooms are usually compatible with U.S.-purchased appliances. This may not be the case on older ships or those with European registries; call ahead if this is a concern for you. Most cabin bathrooms are equipped with low-voltage outlets for electric shavers, and many newer ships have built-in hair dryers.

Take an extra pair of eyeglasses or contact lenses in your carry-on luggage. If you use a prescription drug, pack enough to last the duration of the trip or have your doctor write a prescription using the drug's generic name, since brand names vary from country to country. Always carry medications in their original packaging to avoid problems with customs officials. Don't pack them in luggage that you plan to check, so that you'll have them with you in case your bags go astray. Pack a list of the offices that supply refunds for lost or stolen traveler's checks. Make a copy of your passport and keep it separate from your actual passport. If you should lose your passport or it is stolen, having a copy of it can greatly facilitate replacement. Make copies, or write down the numbers, of your credit cards in case those should be lost or stolen.

FORMAL/SEMIFORMAL/CASUAL

Although no two cruises are quite the same, evening dress tends to fall into three categories.

Formal cruises celebrate the ceremony of cruising. Jackets and ties for men are the rule for dinner, tuxedos are not uncommon, and the dress code is observed faithfully throughout the evening.

Semiformal cruises are a bit more relaxed than their formal counterparts. Men wear jackets and ties most nights.

Casual cruises are the most popular. Shipboard dress and lifestyle are informal. Men wear sport shirts and slacks to dinner most nights and don jackets and ties only two or three evenings of a typical seven-day sailing.

In today's casual-Friday world, most cruise lines have reduced the focus on formal and semiformal dining and offer multiple dining options, including room service. However, it would be wise to ask the cruise line about its dining dress code so you know what to expect and what to pack.

Accessibility Issues

The latest cruise ships have been built with the needs of travelers with disabilities in mind, and many older ships have been modified to accommodate them. But several cruise lines operate older ships that have not been modified or do not have elevators: the tall sailing ships and explorer-type vessels are not the easiest ships to navigate if you are in a wheelchair. The key areas to be concerned about are public rooms, outer decks, and, of course, your cabin.

If you need a specially equipped cabin, book as far in advance as possible and ask specific questions of your travel agent or a cruise-line representative. Specifically, ask how your cabin is configured and equipped.

Is the entrance level or ramped? Are all doorways at least 30″ wide (wider if your wheelchair is not standard)? Are pathways to beds, closets, and bathrooms at least 36″ wide and unobstructed? In the bathroom, is there 42″ of clear space in front of the toilet and are there grab bars behind and on one side of it and in the bathtub and shower? Are elevators wide enough to accommodate wheelchairs?

The best cruise ship for passengers who use wheelchairs is one that ties up right at the dock at every port, at which time a ramp or even an elevator is always made available. Unfortunately, it's hard to ascertain this in advance, since a ship may tie up at the dock at one port on one voyage and, on the next, anchor in the harbor and have passengers transported to shore via tender. Ask your travel agent to find out which ships are capable of docking. If a tender is used, some ships will have crew members carry the wheelchair and passenger from the ship to the tender. Unfortunately, other ships will refuse to take wheelchairs on tenders, especially if the water is choppy.

ARRIVING AND DEPARTING

If you have purchased an air-sea package, you will be met by a cruise-company representative when your plane lands at the port city and then shuttled directly to the ship in a bus or minivan. Some cruise lines arrange to transport luggage between airport and ship so passengers don't have to hassle with baggage claim at the start of a cruise or with baggage check-in at the end. If you decide not to buy the air-sea package but still plan to fly, ask your travel agent if you can use the ship's transfer bus. Otherwise, you will have to take a taxi to the ship.

If you live close to the port of embarkation, bus transportation may be available. If you are part of a group that has booked a cruise together, this transportation may be part of your package. Another option for those who live close to their point of departure is to drive to the ship, an increasingly popular option. Major U.S. cruise ports all have parking facilities.

Embarkation

Check-In

On arrival at the dock, you must check in before boarding your ship. (A handful of smaller cruise ships handle check-in at the airport.) An officer will collect or stamp your ticket, inspect or even retain your passport or other official identification, ask you to fill out a tourist card, check that you have the correct visas, and collect any unpaid port or departure tax.

Seating assignments for the dining room are often handed out at this time, too, although most cruise ships are now offering you the opportunity to dine when and with whom you like in any of several restaurants aboard. You may also register your credit card to open a shipboard account, or that may be done later at the purser's office.

After this, you will be required to go through a security check and to pass your hand baggage through an x-ray inspection. These are the same machines in use at airports, so ask to have your photographic film inspected by hand.

Although it takes only 5 or 10 minutes per family to check in, lines are often long, so aim for off-peak hours. The worst time tends to be immediately after the ship begins boarding; the later it is, the less crowded. For example, if boarding is from 2 to 4:30, lines are shorter after 3:30.

Boarding the Ship

Before you walk up the gangway, the ship's photographer will probably take your picture; there's no charge unless you buy the picture (usually $7 to $8). On board, stewards may serve welcome drinks in souvenir glasses—for which you're usually charged between $3 and $5.

You will either be escorted to your cabin by a steward or, on a smaller ship, given your key—now usually a plastic card—by a ship's officer and directed to your cabin. Some elevators are unavailable to passengers during boarding, since they are used to transport luggage. You may arrive to find your luggage outside your cabin or just inside the door; if it hasn't arrived a half hour before sailing, contact the purser. If your luggage doesn't make it to the ship in time, the purser will have it flown to the next port.

Visitors' Passes

A few cruise ships permit passengers to invite guests on board prior to sailing, although nowadays most lines prohibit all but paying passengers from boarding for reasons of security and insurance liability. Cruise companies that allow visitors usually require that you obtain passes several weeks in advance; call the line for policies and procedures.

Most ships do not allow visitors while the ship is docked in a port of call. If you meet a friend on shore, you won't be able to invite him or her back to your stateroom.

Disembarkation

The last night of your cruise is full of business. On most ships you must place everything except your hand luggage outside your door, ready to be picked up by midnight or early in the morning. Color-coded tags, distributed to your cabin in a debarkation packet, should be placed on your luggage before the crew collects it. The color of your tag will determine when you leave the ship and help you retrieve your luggage on the pier.

Your shipboard bill is left in your room during the last day of a cruise or on the morning of your departure from the ship; to pay the bill (if you haven't already put it on your credit card) or to settle any questions, you must stand in line at the purser's office. Tips to the cabin steward and dining staff are distributed on the last night of the cruise or are automatically added to your onboard account. On many ships, you can review your account on your in-cabin television and change those tips in any way you like, up or down. You may also make changes to or discuss your bill at the purser's office at any time during the cruise. Some ships will deliver your account to your room the morning of your departure. If you have not already paid it by credit card or wish to dispute any charges on it, go to the purser immediately to settle or discuss your account. Do not wait until you're ready to get off the ship, as lines may be long and the wait could delay your departure and fray your nerves. Some lines close down their computer files for the cruise by 9 AM or 10 AM to prepare for the next cruise and may be unable to credit your account with any disputed charges, requiring you to contact your credit-card company or the cruise line later for a refund.

On the morning the cruise ends, in-room breakfast service may not be available because stewards are too busy, but you will usually find breakfast being served in both the formal dining room and at the ship's buffet dining area. Most passengers clear out of their cabins as soon as possible, gather their hand luggage, and stake out a chair in one of the public lounges to await the ship's clearance through customs. Be patient—it takes a long time to unload and sort thousands of pieces of luggage.

Passengers are disembarked in groups according to color-coded luggage tags; those with the earliest flights get off first. If you have a tight connection, notify the purser before the last day, and he or she may be able to arrange faster pre-clearing and debarkation.

Customs and Duties

U.S. Customs

Before a ship lands, each individual or family must fill out a customs declaration. If your purchases total less than the limit for your destination, you will not need to itemize them. Be prepared to pay whatever duties are owed directly to the customs inspector, with cash or check. Be sure to keep receipts for all purchases, and be ready to show curious officials what you've bought.

U.S. Customs pre-clears some ships sailing into and out of Miami and other ports—it's done on the ship before you disembark. In other ports you must collect your luggage from the dock, then stand in line to pass through the inspection point. This can take up to an hour.

ALLOWANCES

U.S. residents who have been out of the country for at least 48 hours may bring home, for personal use, $800 worth of foreign goods duty-free, as long as they haven't used the $800 allowance or any part of it in the past 30 days. However, this exemption applies to a few Caribbean countries, including Anguilla, the Cayman Islands, Guadeloupe, Martinique, Mexico, St. Barths, St. Martin (the French side only), and the Turks and Caicos Islands. This exemption may include 1 liter of alcohol (for travelers 21 and older), 200 cigarettes, and 100 non-Cuban cigars. Family members from the same household who are traveling together may pool their $800 personal exemptions. For fewer than 48 hours, the duty-free allowance drops to $200, which may include 50 cigarettes, 10 non-Cuban cigars, and 150 ml of alcohol (or perfume containing alcohol). The $200 allowance cannot be combined with other individuals' exemptions, and if you exceed it, the full value of all the goods will be taxed. Antiques, which the U.S. Customs Service defines as objects more than 100 years old, enter duty-free, as do original works of art done entirely by hand, including paintings, drawings, and sculptures.

While the above rules are generally applicable, allowances are less generous for many Caribbean and Central American countries. U.S. residents who have been out of the country for at least 48 hours may bring home only $600 worth of foreign goods duty-free, as long as they have not used the $600 allowance or any part of it in the past 30 days. This allowance, lower than the standard $800 exemption, applies to the 24 countries in the Caribbean Basin Initiative (CBI)—including Antigua and Barbuda, Aruba, Bahamas, Barbados, Belize, British Virgin Islands, Costa Rica, Dominica, Dominican Republic, El Salvador, Grenada, Guatemala, Guyana, Haiti, Honduras, Jamaica, Montserrat, the Netherlands Antilles (Bonaire, Curaçao, and St. Maarten—the Dutch side only), Nicaragua, Panama, St. Kitts and Nevis, St. Lucia, St. Vincent and the Grenadines, and Trinidad and Tobago. If you visit a CBI country and a non-CBI country, you may still bring in $800 worth of goods duty-free, but no more than $600 may be from the non-CBI country.

If you're returning from the U.S. Virgin Islands (USVI), the duty-free allowance is $1,200. If your travel included the USVI and another country—say, the Dominican Republic—the $1,200 allowance still applies, but at least $600 worth of goods has to be from the USVI.

ALCOHOL AND TOBACCO

U.S. residents 21 and older may bring back 2 liters of alcohol duty-free, as long as one of the liters was produced in a CBI country. In addition, regardless of your age, you are allowed 200 cigarettes and 100 non-Cuban cigars. Antiques, which the U.S. Customs Service defines as objects more than 100 years old, enter duty-free, as do original works of art done entirely by hand, including paintings, drawings, and sculptures. You may also send packages home duty-free, with a limit of one parcel per addressee per day (except alcohol or tobacco products or perfume worth more than $5). You can mail up to $200 worth of goods for personal use; label the package PERSONAL USE and attach a list of its contents and their retail value. If the package contains your used personal belongings, mark it PERSONAL GOODS RETURNED to avoid paying duties. You may send up to $100 worth of goods ($200 from the U.S. Virgin Islands) as a gift; mark the package UNSOLICITED GIFT. Mailed items do not affect your duty-free allowance on your return.

SENDING PACKAGES HOME

You may also send packages home duty-free, with a limit of one parcel per addressee per day (except alcohol or tobacco products or perfume worth more than $5). You can mail up to $200 worth of goods for personal use; label the package PERSONAL USE and attach a list of its contents and their retail value. If the package contains your used personal belongings, mark it PERSONAL GOODS RETURNED to avoid paying duties. You may send up to $100 worth of goods as a gift; mark the package UNSOLICITED GIFT. Mailed items do not affect your duty-free allowance on your return.

U.S. CUSTOMS FOR FOREIGNERS

If you hold a foreign passport and will be returning home within hours of docking, you may be exempt from all U.S. Customs duties. Everything you bring into the United States must leave with you when you return home. When you reach your own country, you will have to pay duties there.

Canadian Customs

Canadian residents who have been out of Canada for at least seven days may bring in C$750 worth of goods duty-free. If you've been away fewer than seven days but more than 48 hours, the duty-free allowance drops to C$200. If your trip lasts 24 to 48 hours, the allowance is C$50. You may not pool allowances with family members. Goods claimed under the C$750 exemption may follow you by mail; those claimed under the lesser exemptions must accompany you. Alcohol and tobacco products may be included in the seven-day and 48-hour exemptions but not in the 24-hour exemption. If you meet the age requirements of the province or territory through which you reenter Canada, you may bring in, duty-free, 1.5 liters of wine *or* 1.14 liters (40 imperial ounces) of liquor *or* 24 12-ounce cans or bottles of beer or ale. Also, if you meet the local age requirement for tobacco products, you may bring in, duty-free, 200 cigarettes and 50 cigars. Check ahead of time with the Canada Customs and Revenue Agency or the Department of Agriculture for policies regarding meat products, seeds, plants, and fruits.

You may send an unlimited number of gifts (only one gift per recipient, however) worth up to C$60 each duty-free to Canada. Label the package UNSOLICITED GIFT—VALUE UNDER $60. Alcohol and tobacco are excluded.

U.K. Customs

Caribbean nations—even those that are *départements* of France and use the euro as their official currency—are not part of the European

Union (EU) with regard to customs. From countries outside the European Union, including those in the Caribbean, you may bring home, duty-free, 200 cigarettes or 50 cigars; 1 liter of spirits or 2 liters of fortified or sparkling wine or liqueurs; 2 liters of still table wine; 60 ml of perfume; 250 ml of toilet water; plus @145 worth of other goods, including gifts and souvenirs. Prohibited items include meat products, seeds, plants, and fruits.

ON BOARD

The first thing to do upon arriving at your cabin or suite is to make sure that everything is in order. If there are twin beds instead of the double bed you wanted—or other problems—ask to be moved before the ship departs. Unless the ship is full, you can usually persuade the chief housekeeper or hotel manager to allow you to change cabins. It is customary to tip the stewards who help you move. In most modern ships, beds can be pushed together to create one single bed or moved apart for two. Ask your cabin steward to set the beds up the way you would like them or to move you to another room.

Since your cabin is your home away from home for a few days or weeks, everything should be to your satisfaction. Take a good look around: is the cabin clean and orderly? Do the toilet, shower, and faucets work? Check the telephone and television. Again, major problems should be addressed immediately. Minor concerns, such as a shortage of pillows, can wait until the frenzy of embarkation subsides.

Your dining-time and seating-assignment card may be in your cabin; now is the time to check it and immediately request any changes. The maître d' usually sets up shop in one of the public rooms specifically for this purpose.

Shipboard Accounts

Virtually all cruise ships operate as cashless societies. Passengers charge onboard purchases and settle their accounts at the end of the cruise with a credit card, traveler's checks, or cash. You can sign for wine at dinner, drinks at the bar, shore excursions, gifts in the shop—virtually any expense you may incur aboard ship. On some lines, an imprint from a major credit card is necessary to open an account. Otherwise, a cash deposit may be required and a positive balance maintained to keep the shipboard account open. Either way, you will want to open a line of credit soon after settling in, if an account was not opened for you at embarkation. This can easily be arranged by visiting the purser's office, in the central atrium or main lobby. On most ships, you can now view your account at any time on your in-cabin television. To make your stay aboard as seamless—and as cashless—as possible, many cruise lines now add dining-room gratuities at a set rate to your onboard account. Some lines offer access to personal records via Internet; you can alter automatic tips, for example, before your cruise begins.

Tipping

For better or worse, tipping is an integral part of the cruise experience. Most companies pay their cruise staff nominal wages and expect tips to make up the difference between this nominal amount and a living wage. Most cruise lines have recommended tipping guidelines, and on many ships "voluntary" tipping for beverage service has been replaced with a mandatory 15% service charge, which is added to every bar bill.

On the other hand, the most expensive luxury lines (such as Seabourn) include tips in the cruise fare and may prohibit crew members from accepting additional gratuities. On many small adventure ships, a collection box is placed in the dining room or lounge on the last full day of the cruise, and passengers contribute anonymously.

Some large cruise lines now add dining-room tips of $10 to $12 a person per day directly to your bill. That sum is intended to cover all your dining-room service, other than the wine steward and the maître d' if he provides special service to you (although both those may also be included in the daily tip that is automatically added to your account); it may also include your room steward. Ask the purser if tips are being added to your bill and which personnel will receive them—waiter, busboy, and room steward are all expecting tips. You may adjust tips up or down.

Dining

Ocean liners serve food nearly around the clock. There may be as many as four breakfast options: early-morning coffee and pastries on deck, breakfast in bed through room service, buffet-style in the cafeteria, and a more formal breakfast in the dining room. There may also be several lunch choices, midafternoon hors d'oeuvres, tea time, and late-night buffets. You may eat whatever is on the menu, in any quantity, at any meal. Room service is traditionally, but not always, free (☞ Shipboard Services, *below*).

Restaurants

The chief meals of the day are served in the main dining room, which on most ships can accommodate only half the passengers at once. Meals are therefore usually served in early (or main) and late (or second) seatings. Early seating for dinner is generally between 6 and 6:30, late seating between 8 and 8:30.

Most cruise ships have a buffet-style restaurant, usually near the swimming pool, where you can eat lunch and breakfast. On many of the newer ships, that room, nearly always located on the Lido Deck near the swimming pool, becomes a casual, waiter-service dining room at dinner. Those dining rooms, often featuring grilled specialties, are popular on nights when the ship has been in port all day. Many ships provide self-serve coffee or tea in their cafeteria around the clock, as well as midnight buffets.

Some ships, particularly newer ones, also have alternative specialty restaurants for which a reservation must be made. You might have to pay a fee for grilled steak or Asian cuisine. On-demand food shops may include pizzerias, ice cream parlors, and caviar or cappuccino bars; there may be an extra charge at these facilities, too.

Smoking is often banned in main dining rooms. At least one cruise line—Carnival—now has a nonsmoking ship. Smoking policies vary and change; contact your cruise line to find out what the situation will be on your cruise.

Seatings

When it comes to your dining-table assignment, you should have options on four important points: early or late seating; smoking or no-smoking section (if smoking is allowed in the dining room); a table for two, four, six, or eight; and special dietary needs. When you receive your cruise documents, you will usually receive a card asking for your dining preferences. Fill this out and return it to the cruise line, but remember that you will not get your seating assignment until you board the ship. Check it out immediately, and if your request was not met, see the maître d'—usually there is a time and place set up for changes in dining assignments.

On some ships, seating times are strictly observed. Ten to 15 minutes after the scheduled mealtime, the dining-room doors are closed, although this policy is increasingly rare. On other ships, passengers may enter the dining room at their leisure, but they must be out by the end of the seating. When a ship has just one seating, passengers may enter any time the kitchen is open.

Seating assignments often apply only to dinner. Most ships have open seating for breakfast or lunch, which means you may sit anywhere at any time the meal is served. Smaller or more luxurious ships offer open seating for all meals.

Several large cruise lines now offer several restaurant and dining options and have eliminated preassigned seating, so you can dine with whom you like at any table that's available and at any time the dining room is open.

CHANGING TABLES
Dining is a focal point of the cruise experience, and your companions at meals may become your best friends on the cruise. However, if you're traveling on a ship that assigns you to a table where you dine every night with the same people and you find you don't enjoy their company, the maître d' can usually move you to another table if the dining room isn't completely full—a tip helps. He will probably be reluctant to comply with your request after the first full day at sea, however, because the waiters, busboys, and wine steward who have been serving you won't receive their tips at the end of the cruise. Be persistent if you are truly unhappy.

Cuisine

Most ships serve food geared to the American palate, but there are also theme dinners featuring the cuisine of a particular country. Some European ships, especially smaller vessels, may offer a particular cuisine throughout the cruise—Scandinavian, German, Italian, or Greek, perhaps—depending on the ship's or the crew's nationality. The quality of cruise-ship cooking is generally good, but even a skilled chef is hard put to serve 500 or more extraordinary dinners per hour. Presentation is often spectacular, especially at gala midnight buffets.

There is often a direct relationship between the cost of a cruise and the quality of its cuisine. The food is very sophisticated on some (mostly expensive) lines, among them Crystal Cruises, Cunard Line, Seabourn Cruise Line, and Silversea Cruises. In the more moderate price range, Celebrity Cruises has gained renown for the culinary stylings of French chef Michel Roux, who acts as a consultant to the line.

Special Diets

With notification well in advance, many ships can provide kosher, low-salt, low-cholesterol, sugar-free, vegetarian, or other special menus. However, there's always a chance that the wrong dish will somehow be served. Especially when it comes to soups and desserts, it's a good idea to ask about the ingredients.

Large ships usually offer an alternative "light" or "spa" menu based upon American Heart Association guidelines, using leaner cuts of meat, low-cholesterol or low-sodium preparations, smaller portions, salads, fresh-fruit desserts, and healthy garnishes. Some smaller ships may not be able to accommodate special dietary needs. Vegetarians generally have no trouble finding appropriate selections.

Wine

Wine at meals costs extra on most ships; prices are usually comparable to those in shoreside restaurants and are charged to your shipboard account. A handful of luxury vessels include both wine and liquor. On some lines, you can also select the wines you might like for dinner before leaving home and they will appear at your table and on your bill at the end of the cruise.

The Captain's Table

It is both a privilege and an interesting experience to be invited to dine at the captain's table. Although some seats are given to celebrities, repeat passengers, and passengers in the most expensive suites, other invitations are given at random to ordinary passengers. You can request an invitation from the chief steward or the hotel manager, although there is no guarantee you will be accommodated. The captain's guests always wear a suit and tie or a dress, even if the dress code for that evening is casual. On many ships, passengers may be invited to dine at the other officers' tables, or officers may visit a different passenger table each evening.

Bars

Whether adjacent to the pool or attached to a lounge, a ship's bars tend to be its social centers. Except on a handful of luxury-class ships where everything is included in the ticket price, bars operate on a pay-as-it's-poured basis. Rather than demand cash after every round, however, most ships allow you to charge drinks to an account.

In international waters there are, technically, no laws against teenage drinking, but almost all ships require passengers to be over 18 or 21 to purchase alcoholic beverages. Many cruise ships have chapters of Alcoholics Anonymous (a.k.a. "Friends of Bill W.") or will organize meetings on request. Look for meeting times and places in the daily program slipped under your cabin door each night or delivered to the cabin by the steward.

Entertainment

Lounges and Nightclubs

On ocean liners, the main entertainment lounge or showroom schedules nightly musical revues, magic acts, comedy performances, and variety shows, all included in the price of the cruise. During the rest of the day the room is used for group activities, such as shore-excursion talks or bingo games. Generally, the larger the ship, the bigger and more impressive the productions. Newer ships have elaborate showrooms that often span two or three decks. Some are designed like an amphitheater while others have two levels—a main floor and a balcony. Seating is sometimes in clusters of armchairs set around cocktail tables. Other ships have more traditional theater-style seating.

Many larger ships have several showrooms and a variety of bars, ranging from sports bars to piano bars and mirrored-floors-and-strobe-light dance bars. Entertainment and ballroom dancing may go late into the night; adult midnight comedy shows are popular on many ships. Elsewhere, you may find a disco, nightclub, or cabaret, usually built around a bar and dance floor. Music is provided by a piano player, a disc jockey, or by performing ensembles such as a country-and-western duo, a harpist and violinist, or a jazz combo.

On smaller ships the entertainment options are more limited, sometimes consisting of no more than a piano around which passengers gather. There may be a main lounge where scaled-down revues are staged. Often talented crew members double as entertainers, and on many ships a crew night, featuring crew members performing dances and songs of their native lands, is a highlight.

Library

Many cruise ships have a library with up to 1,500 volumes, from the latest best-sellers to reference works. Many shipboard libraries also stock videotapes for in-cabin VCRs.

Movie Theaters

Most vessels have a room for screening movies. On older ships and some newer ones, this is often a genuine cinema-style movie theater, while on other ships it may be just a multipurpose room. Films are frequently one or two months past their first release date but not yet available on videotape or cable TV. Films rated "R" are edited to minimize sex and violence. Over the course of a weeklong voyage a dozen films may be screened, each repeated several times. Theaters are also used for lectures, religious services, and private meetings.

With a few exceptions, ocean liners equip their cabins with closed-circuit TVs showing movies (continuously on some newer ships), shipboard lectures, and regular programs (thanks to satellite reception). Ships with in-cabin VCRs usually provide a selection of movies on videocassette at no charge (a deposit is sometimes required).

Casinos

Once a ship is 12 mi off American shores, it is in international waters and gambling is permitted. (Some "cruises to nowhere," in fact, are little more than sailing casinos.) All ocean liners—except Disney Cruise Line ships—as well as many cruise yachts and motor-sailing ships have casinos. On larger vessels you'll usually find poker, baccarat, blackjack, roulette, craps, and slot machines. House stakes are much more modest than those in Las Vegas or Atlantic City. On most ships the maximum bet is $200; some ships allow $500. Payouts on the slot machines (some of which take as little as a nickel) are generally much lower, too. Credit is never extended, but many casinos have handy ATM machines that dispense cash for a hefty fee.

Children are officially barred from the casinos, but it's not uncommon to see them playing the slots rather than the adjacent video machines. Most ships offer free individual instruction and off-hours gambling classes. Casinos are usually open from early morning to late night, although you may find only unattended slot machines before evening. In adherence to local laws, casinos are always closed while a ship is in port.

Game Rooms

Most ships have a room with card tables and board games. These rooms are for serious players and are often the site of friendly round-robin competitions and tournaments. Most ships furnish everything for free (cards, chips, games, and so forth), but a few charge $1 or more for each deck of cards. Be aware that professional cardsharps and hustlers have been fleecing passengers almost as long as there have been ships. There are small video arcades on most medium and large ships. Family-oriented ships often have a computer learning center.

Bingo and Other Games

Daily high-stakes bingo games are often even more popular than casinos. You can play for as little as a dollar a card. Most ships have a snowball bingo game with a jackpot that grows throughout the cruise into hundreds or even thousands of dollars. Another popular cruise pastime is the so-called "horse races": fictional horses are auctioned off to "owners." Individual passengers can buy a horse or form "syndicates." Bids usually begin at around $25 and can top $1,000 per horse. Races are then "run" according to dice throws or computer-generated random numbers. Audience members can bet on their favorites.

Sports and Fitness

Swimming Pools

All but the smallest ships have at least one pool. Some are elaborate affairs with water slides or retractable roofs; hot tubs and whirlpools are quite common. Pools may be filled with fresh water or saltwater; some ships have one of each. While in port or during rough weather pools are usually emptied or covered with canvas. Many are too narrow or too short to allow swimmers more than a few strokes in any direction; none have diving boards, and not all are heated. Often there are no lifeguards. Wading pools are sometimes provided for small children.

Sundeck

The top deck is usually called the Sundeck or Sports Deck. On some ships this is where you'll find the pool or whirlpool; on others it is dedicated to volleyball, basketball, table tennis, shuffleboard, and other cruise-ship sports. A number of ships have paddle-tennis courts, and a few have golf driving ranges. Often, after the sun goes down, the Sundeck is used for social activities such as barbecues and dancing under the stars.

Exercise and Fitness Rooms

Most newer ships and some older ones have well-equipped fitness centers, and some have full-fledged spas, with elaborate exercise equipment, massage, sauna, whirlpools, and a wide range of spa treatments, from high-pressure water treatments to mud treatments. An upper-deck fitness center often has an airy and sunny view of the sea; an inside, lower-deck health club is often dark and small unless it is equipped with an indoor pool or beauty salon.

Many ships have full-service exercise rooms with elaborate body-building and cardiovascular equipment, aerobics classes, and individual fitness instruction. Some ships offer cruise-length physical-fitness programs, which may include lectures on weight loss or nutrition. These often are tied in with a spa menu. The more extensive programs are often sold on a daily or weekly basis. There is a charge for each of the spa treatments but no charge to use the exercise equipment or attend the exercise classes.

Promenade Deck

Many vessels designate certain decks for fitness walks and may post the number of laps per mile. Fitness instructors may lead daily walks around the Promenade Deck. A number of ships discourage jogging and running on the decks or ask that no one take fitness walks before 8 AM or after 10 PM, so as not to disturb passengers in cabins. With the advent of the megaship, walking and jogging have in many cases moved up top to tracks on the Sundeck or Sports Deck.

Shipboard Services

Room Service

A small number of ships have no room service at all, except when the ship's doctor orders it for an ailing passenger. Many offer only breakfast (Continental on some, full on others); most, however, have selections that you can order around the clock, although menus may be abbreviated at some hours. Many ships now offer unlimited round-the-clock room service. There usually is no additional charge other than for beer, wine, or spirits delivered to your room.

Minibars

An increasing number of cruise lines equip cabins with small refrigerators or minibars stocked with snacks, soda, beer, wine, and liquors. There is usually a small charge for these items, just as there would be in a hotel.

Laundry and Dry Cleaning

All but the smallest ships and shortest cruises offer laundry services—full-service, coin-operated self-service, or both. Use of machines is generally free, although some ships charge for detergent, use of the machines, or both. Valet laundry service includes cabin pickup and delivery and usually takes 24 hours. Some ships also offer dry-cleaning services, but a concern for the environmental effect of the chemicals used in dry-cleaning is beginning to limit those services, so don't count on it.

Hair Stylists

Even the smallest cruise liners have a hair stylist and manicurist on staff. Larger ships have complete beauty salons, and some have barbershops. Book your appointment well in advance, especially for days of such popular events as formal dinners.

Film Processing

Many ships offer overnight film processing. It's expensive but convenient.

Photographer

The staff photographer, a near-universal fixture on cruise ships, records every memorable, photogenic moment both on board and on shore. The thousands of photos snapped over the course of a cruise are displayed publicly in special cases every morning and are offered for sale, usually for $6 to $8 for a 5″ × 7″ color print or $12 to $15 for an 8″ × 10″. If you want a special photo or a portrait, the photographer is usually happy to oblige. Many passengers choose to have a formal portrait taken before the captain's farewell dinner—the dressiest event of the cruise. The ship's photographer usually anticipates this demand by setting up a studio with an attractive backdrop near the dining-room entrance.

Religious Services

Most ships provide nondenominational religious services on Sundays and religious holidays, and some offer Catholic masses daily and Jewish services on Friday evenings. The kind of service held depends upon the clergy the cruise line invites on board. You'll often find religious services in the library, the theater, or one of the private lounges, although a few ships have actual chapels—and some offer a wedding chapel and full wedding services. Travel agents and the ship's staff can provide details.

Communications

SHIPBOARD

Most cabins have loudspeakers and telephones. Generally, the loudspeakers cannot be switched off because they are used for broadcast of important notices. Telephones are used to call fellow passengers, order room service, summon a doctor, request a wake-up call, or speak with the ship's officers or departments.

SHIP TO SHORE

Sending e-mails can be an expensive proposition, with ships charging anywhere from 50¢ to $1.00 a minute for Internet access. You may also purchase a package with a onetime activation fee ranging from $3.95 to $10.95. Most cruise lines offer several plans that include blocks of time—either 100 minutes ranging from $55 to $75 or 250 minutes for $100 to $150. Norwegian Cruise Lines ships are among those with wireless internet capability, and you may bring along your own laptop with a wi-fi card or rent a laptop from the ship; you generally pay for a block of time or pay a fee for unlimited access.

Satellite facilities make it possible to call anywhere in the world from most ships. Most are also equipped with fax machines, and some provide credit card–operated phones. It may take as long as a half hour to make a connection, but unless a storm is raging outside, conversation is clear and easy. On older ships, voice calls must be put through on shortwave wireless or via the one phone in the radio room. Newer ships are generally equipped with direct-dial phones in every cabin for calls to shore. Be warned: the cost of communication, regardless of the method, can be quite expensive—up to $15 a minute. (On some ships, though, it's much cheaper, costing as little as $3.95 a minute.) If possible, wait until you go ashore to call home. Cell phones can be used on ships, although reception depends on your distance from shore and whether your cell phone provider has service to the area where you are cruising. Many cell phones do not work outside of the U.S.

Safety at Sea

Fire Safety

The greatest danger facing cruise-ship passengers is fire. All of the cruise lines reviewed in this book must meet international standards for fire safety, which require sprinkler systems, smoke detectors, and other safety features. These rules are designed to protect against loss of life. They do not guarantee that a fire will not happen; in fact, fire is relatively common on cruise ships. The point here is not to alarm but to emphasize the importance of taking fire safety seriously.

Fire safety begins with you, the passenger. Once settled into your cabin, locate life vests and review posted emergency instructions. Make sure vests are in good condition and learn to secure them properly. Make certain the ship's purser knows if you have a physical infirmity that may hamper a speedy exit from your cabin so that in an emergency he or she can quickly dispatch a crew member to assist you. If you are traveling with children, be sure that child-size life jackets are placed in your cabin.

Within 24 hours of embarkation, you will be asked to attend a mandatory lifeboat drill. Do so and listen carefully. If you are unsure of how to use your vest, now is the time to ask. Only in the most extreme circumstances will you need to abandon ship—but it has happened. The time you spend learning the procedure may serve you well in a mishap.

Health Care

Quality medical care at sea is another important safety issue. All big ships are equipped with medical infirmaries to handle minor emergencies. However, these should not be confused with hospitals. There are no international standards governing medical facilities or personnel aboard cruise ships, although the American Medical Association has recommended that such standards be adopted. If you have a preexisting medical condition, discuss your upcoming cruise with your doctor. Pack an extra supply of any medicines you might need. Once aboard, see the ship's doctor and alert him or her to your condition, and discuss treatments or emergency procedures before any problem arises. Passengers with potentially life-threatening conditions should consider signing up with a medical evacuation service, and all passengers should review their health insurance to make sure they are covered while on a cruise.

If you become seriously ill or injured and happen to be near a major city, you may be taken to a medical facility shoreside. But if you're farther afield, you may have to be airlifted off the ship by helicopter and flown either to the nearest American territory or to an airport where you can be taken by charter jet to the United States. Many standard health insurance policies, including Medicare plans, do not cover these or other medical expenses incurred outside the United States. You can, however, buy supplemental health insurance that is in effect only when you travel.

The most common minor medical problems confronting cruise passengers are seasickness and gastrointestinal distress. Modern cruise ships, unlike their transatlantic predecessors, are relatively motion-free vessels outfitted with computer-controlled stabilizers, and they usually sail in relatively calm waters. If you do feel queasy, you can get seasickness pills aboard ship. (Many ships give them out for free at the front desk.)

Outbreaks of food poisoning occasionally occur aboard cruise ships. Episodes are random; they can occur on ships old and new, big and small, budget and luxury. The Centers for Disease Control and Prevention (CDC) monitors cruise-ship hygiene and sanitation procedures, conducting voluntary inspections twice a year of all ships that sail regularly from U.S. ports (this program does not include ships that never visit the United States). A high score on the CDC report doesn't mean you won't get sick. Outbreaks have taken place on ships that consistently score very highly; conversely, some ships score very poorly yet passengers never get sick.

For a free listing of the latest cruise-ship sanitation scores, write to the CDC's **National Center for Environmental Health** (Vessel Sanitation Program, ✉ 1015 North America Way, Room 107, Miami, FL 33132 ☎ 888/232–3299 for fax-back service WEB www.cdc.gov). If you use the fax-back service, request publication 510051.

Crime on Ships

Crime aboard cruise ships has occasionally become headline news, thanks in large part to a few well-publicized cases. Most people never have any type of problem, but you should exercise the same precautions aboard ship that you would at home. Keep your valuables out of sight—on big ships virtually every cabin has a small safe in the closet. Don't carry too much cash ashore, use your credit card whenever possible, and keep your money in a secure place, such as a front pocket that's harder to pick. Single women traveling with friends should stick together, especially when returning to their cabins late at night. Be careful about whom you befriend, as you would anywhere, whether it's a fellow passenger or a member of the crew. Don't be paranoid, but do be prudent.

GOING ASHORE

Traveling by cruise ship presents an opportunity to visit many places in a short time. The flip side is that your stay in each port of call will be brief. For this reason cruise lines offer shore excursions, which maximize passengers' time. There are a number of advantages to shore excursions arranged by your ship: in some destinations, transportation may be unreliable, and a ship-packaged tour is the best way to see distant sights. Also, you don't have to worry about missing the ship. The disadvantage of a shore excursion is the cost—you pay more for the convenience of having the ship do the legwork for you. Of course, you can always book a tour independently, hire a taxi, or use foot power to explore on your own.

Arriving in Port

When your ship arrives in a port, it will tie up alongside a dock or anchor out in a harbor. If the ship is docked, passengers walk down the gangway to go ashore. Docking makes it easy to move between the shore and the ship.

Tendering

If your ship anchors in the harbor, you will have to take a small boat—called a launch or tender—to get ashore. Tendering is a nuisance. Passengers wishing to disembark may be required to gather in a public room, get sequenced boarding passes, and wait until their numbers are called. The ride to shore may take as long as 20 minutes. If you don't like waiting, plan to go ashore an hour or so after the ship drops its anchor.

Because tenders can be difficult to board, passengers with mobility problems may not be able to visit certain ports. The larger ships are more likely to use tenders. It is usually possible to learn before booking a cruise whether the ship will dock or anchor at its ports of call. (For more information about where ships dock and tender, *see* Chapter 4.)

Before anyone is allowed to walk down the gangway or board a tender, the ship must be cleared for landing. Immigration and customs officials board the vessel to examine passports and sort through red tape. It may be more than an hour before you're allowed ashore. You will be issued a boarding pass, which you'll need to get back on board.

Returning to the Ship

Cruise lines are strict about sailing times, which are posted at the gangway and elsewhere and announced in the daily schedule of activities. Be sure to be back on board at least a half hour before the announced sailing time or you may be stranded. If you are on a shore excursion that was sold by the cruise line, however, the captain will wait for your group before casting off. That is one reason many passengers prefer ship-packaged tours.

If you're not on one of the ship's tours and the ship sails without you, immediately contact the cruise line's port representative, whose phone number is often listed on the daily schedule of activities. You may be able to hitch a ride on a pilot boat, although that is unlikely. Passengers who miss the boat must pay their own way to the next port.

2 CRUISING THE CARIBBEAN

By Sandra
Davis-Taylor
More ships ply the waters of the Caribbean than any other spot on earth. Some are huge ships carrying more than 2,000 passengers; some are mid-size ships welcoming about 1,000 cruisers; and others are comparatively small ships on which you'll find yourself with 300 or fewer other passengers. There are fancy ships and party ships, ships with sails, ships that pride themselves on the numbers of ports they visit, and ships that provide so much activity right on board that you hardly have time or inclination to go ashore. In peak season, it's not uncommon for thousands of passengers to disembark from several ships into a small town on the same day—a phenomenon not always enjoyed by locals. With such an abundance of cruise ships in this area, however, you can choose the ship and the itinerary that suit you best.

CHOOSING YOUR CRUISE

Every ship has its own personality, depending on its size, the year it was built, and its intended purpose. Big ships are more stable and offer a huge variety of activities and facilities. Smaller ships feel intimate, like private clubs. For every big-ship fan there is somebody who would never set foot aboard one of these "floating resorts."

After giving some thought to your itinerary and where in the Caribbean you might wish to go, the ship you choose is the most important factor in your Caribbean cruise vacation, since it may determine which islands you will see and how you will see them. Big ships visit major ports of call such as St. Thomas, St. Maarten/St. Martin, Nassau, and San Juan; when they call at smaller islands with shallower ports, passengers must disembark aboard tenders (small boats that ferry a few dozen passengers to shore at a time). Or they may skip these smaller ports entirely. Small and mid-size ships can visit smaller islands, such as St. Barths, Canouan, or Tortola, more easily; passengers can usually disembark directly onto the pier without having to wait for tenders to bring them ashore.

Itineraries

You'll want to give some consideration to your ship's Caribbean itinerary when you are choosing your cruise. The length of the cruise will determine the variety and number of ports you visit, but so will the type of itinerary and the point of departure. **Loop cruises** start and end at the same point and usually explore ports close to one another; **one-way cruises** start at one point and end at another and range farther afield.

Most cruises to the Bahamas, the Mexican Riviera, and other points in the Caribbean are loop cruises. On Caribbean itineraries, you often have a choice of departure points. Ships sailing out of San Juan, Puerto Rico, can visit up to five ports in seven days, while loop cruises out of Florida can reach up to four ports in the same length of time. So-called "Caribazon" cruises combine a journey up or down the Amazon River with port calls in the Caribbean. The Panama Canal can also be combined with a Caribbean cruise: the 50-mi canal is a series of locks, which make up for the height difference between the Caribbean and the Pacific.

Eastern Caribbean Itineraries

Eastern Caribbean itineraries consist of two or three days at sea as well as stops at some of the Caribbean's busiest cruise ports. A typical cruise will usually take in three or four ports of call, such as St. Thomas or St. Croix in the U.S. Virgin Islands, San Juan, or St. Maarten/St. Martin, along with a visit to the cruise line's "private" island for beach time. Every major cruise line has at least two of the major islands on its itineraries. Additional itineraries might also add Dominica, Barbados, St. Kitts, or Martinique.

Western Caribbean Itineraries

Western Caribbean itineraries embarking from Galveston, Ft. Lauderdale, Miami, New Orleans, or Tampa might include Key West, Belize, Cozumel or Playa del Carmen in Mexico, the Cayman Islands, or Jamaica—all perfect choices for passengers who enjoy scuba diving, snorkeling, and visiting Maya ruins. Ships often alternate itineraries in the Western Caribbean with itineraries in the Eastern Caribbean on a weekly basis.

Southern Caribbean Itineraries

Southern Caribbean cruises tend to be longer in duration with more distant ports of call. They usually embark from a port that is not on the U.S. mainland. Embarking in San Juan, for example, allows you to reach the lower Caribbean on a seven-day cruise with three or four ports of call. Southern Caribbean itineraries might leave Puerto Rico for the Virgin Islands, Guadeloupe, Grenada, Curaçao, Barbados, Antigua, St. Lucia, Martinique, Venezuela, or Aruba. Smaller ships leave from ports as far south as St. George's, Grenada, and cruise through the Grenadines. Every major cruise line offers some Southern Caribbean itinerary, but these cruises aren't as popular as Western and Eastern Caribbean cruises.

Other Itineraries

In recent years, shorter itineraries have grown in their appeal to today's time-crunched and budget-constrained travelers. If you are planning your first cruise in the tropics, short cruises to the Bahamas let you test your appetite for cruising before you take a chance on a longer and more expensive cruise. Embarking at Fort Lauderdale, Miami, or Port Canaveral, you will cruise for three or four days, taking in at least one port of call (usually Nassau or Freeport in the Bahamas) and possibly a visit to a "private" island.

When to Go

Average year-round temperatures throughout the Caribbean are 78°F–85°F, with a low of 65°F and a high of 95°F; downtown shopping areas always seem to be unbearably hot. High season runs from December 15 to April 15. Many travelers make reservations months in advance for this most fashionable, most expensive, and most crowded time to go, but with the many new cruise ships that have entered the market, you can often book quite close to your departure date and still find plenty of room, although you may not get exactly the kind of cabin you would prefer. A low-season (summer) visit offers certain advantages: temperatures are virtually the same as in winter (cooler on average than in parts of the U.S. mainland), island flora is at its most dramatic, the water is smoother and clearer, and while there is always a breeze, winds are rarely strong enough to rock a ship. Some tourist facilities close down in summer, however, and many ships move to Europe, Alaska, or the northeastern United States.

Hurricane season runs from June 1 through November 30. Although cruise ships stay well out of the way of these storms, hurricanes and tropical storms—their less-powerful relatives—can affect the weather throughout the Caribbean for days, and damage to ports can force last-minute itinerary changes.

Cruise Costs

The average daily price for Caribbean itineraries will vary dramatically depending on several circumstances. The cost of a cruise on a luxury line such as Radisson Seven Seas or Seabourn may be five or more times the cost of a cruise on a mainstream line such as Carnival or Holland America. When you cruise will also affect your costs: published brochure rates are usually highest during the peak season. However, you can reduce this cost in several ways. If you shop around and/or book early you will undoubtedly pay less. If you take a cruise during the off-season, especially during hurricane season, you will generally pay less. Sometimes you can book a last-minute cruise at substantial savings if the ship hasn't booked all its cabins. Frequent cruisers also get discounts from their preferred cruise lines.

In addition to the cost of your cruise there are extra costs, such as airfare to the port city. Only the most expensive cruises include airfare, but virtually all cruise lines offer air add-ons, which may be less expensive than the current lowest airline fare. Shore excursions can be a substantial expense; the best shore excursions are not cheap. But if you skimp too much on your excursion budget you'll deprive yourself of an important part of the Caribbean cruising experience. Finally, there will be many extras added onto your shipboard account during the cruise, including drinks (both alcoholic and non-alcoholic), activity fees (you pay to use that onboard climbing wall), use of special restaurants, spa services, and even cappuccino and espresso.

Tipping is another extra. At the end of the cruise, it's customary to tip your room steward, server, and the person who buses your table. You should expect to pay an average of $7.50 to $11 per person per day in tips. Some lines are moving away from the traditional method of tipping. Norwegian Cruise Lines, for example, gives you the option of adding a flat $10 per day to your onboard account to cover tips; Radisson Seven Seas and Holland America have tipping-optional policies, though most passengers tip anyway. Each ship offers guidelines.

Solo travelers should be aware that there are few single cabins on most ships. Taking a double cabin can cost twice the advertised per-person rates (which are based on double occupancy). Some cruise lines will find same-sex roommates for singles; each then pays the per-person, double-occupancy rate.

CRUISE LINES AND CRUISE SHIPS

For each cruise line, we list the ships (grouped by similar configurations) that regularly cruise in the Caribbean. Not all ships cruise in the Caribbean all year; for example, some go to Alaska or the Mediterranean during the summer, while others spend part of the year in Hawaii. But we do not list ships that have no regular itineraries in the Caribbean. Thus, not all ships owned by the cruise lines are described below.

When two or more ships are substantially similar, their names are given at the beginning of a review and separated by commas. Passenger-capacity figures are given on the basis of two people sharing a cabin (basis-2); however, many of the larger ships have three- and four-berth cabins, which can increase the total number of passengers tremendously when all berths are occupied. When total occupancy figures differ from basis-2 occupancy, we give them in parentheses.

Luxury Cruise Lines

With less than 5% of the market, the ultraluxury cruise lines, which include Crystal, Radisson Seven Seas, Seabourn, Silversea, and Windstar, offer high staff-to-guest ratios for personal service, superior cuisine in a single seating (except Crystal), and a highly inclusive product with few on-board charges. These small and mid-size ships offer much more space per passenger than you will find on the mainstream lines' vessels. Lines differ in what they emphasize, with some touting luxurious accommodations and entertainment and others focusing on exotic destinations and onboard enrichment.

If you consider travel an entitlement rather than a luxury and frequent exclusive resorts, then you will appreciate the extra attention and the higher level of comfort that these luxury cruise lines can offer.

Itineraries on these ships often include the big casino and beach resorts, but luxury ships also visit some of the more uncommon Caribbean destinations. With a shallow draft and intimate size, the luxury ships can visit such ports as Anguilla, Guadeloupe and the Iles des Saintes, St. Barths, Tobago, and Jost Van Dyke and Virgin Gorda in the British Virgin Islands.

Crystal Cruise Line

Crystal's two mid-size ships stand out for their modern design, amenities, and spaciousness. The vessels were built to deliver the first-rate service of a luxurious, small ship, but they have many of the onboard facilities of a big ship. Crystal ships have long set standards for onboard pampering—one reason these vessels spend several days at sea rather than in port. White-glove service, stellar cuisine, and even air-conditioned tenders complete the effect of total luxury and comfort. To the typical litany of ocean-liner diversions, Crystal adds destination-oriented lectures and talks by scholars, political figures, and diplomats, plus luxe theme cruises emphasizing such topics as food and wine or the arts.

Crystal's target clientele is affluent and older but still active. On select cruises highly trained and experienced youth counselors are brought in to oversee activities for kids and teens. Staff are well trained, friendly, highly motivated, and thoroughly professional. However, alone among the luxury lines, Crystal's fares do not include tips, so the crew can be noticeably solicitous of gratuities. The line's casinos are operated by Caesars Palace at Sea.

Crystal Cruise's third ship, the *Crystal Serenity,* was due to depart on its inaugural cruise in July 2003. The 68,000-ton, 14-deck, 1,800-passenger ship is 36% larger than the line's first two ships, the *Crystal Harmony* and *Crystal Symphony,* but carries just 12% more passengers. Most *Serenity* staterooms have private verandahs.

Suggested tipping guidelines are as follows: steward, $4 per day (single travelers, $5 per day); waiter, $4 per day ($6 per day in alternative restaurants); assistant waiter, $2.50 per day; butler penthouse, $4 per day; 15% added to bar bills. Tips for other personnel are at your discretion. Gratuities may be charged to a shipboard account.

✉ *Crystal Cruise Line, 2049 Century Park E, Suite 1400, Los Angeles, CA 90067,* ☎ *800/446–6620 or 310/785–9300,* FAX *310/785–9201,* WEB *www.crystalcruises.com.*

THE SHIPS OF CRYSTAL CRUISE LINE

🐎 **Crystal Harmony, Crystal Symphony.** Crystal's sleek and sophisticated ships harbor classy, uncluttered interiors and understated decor. Best of all, they are roomy, with one of the highest ratios of passenger to space of any ships. Staterooms deliver space in abundance—the smallest measuring 183 square ft on *Harmony* and 246 square ft on *Symphony*—and more than half have private verandahs. Even the lowest-category staterooms have a separate sitting area (love seat with coffee table), a desk/vanity, and queen or twin beds—with space left over to comfortably move about. Large closets, ample drawer space, and bathtubs are standard. Cabins are equipped with voice mail, goose-down pillows, fine linens, and thick towels. Onboard amenities include grand lounges and Broadway-style entertainment. *408 cabins, 940 passengers, 8 passenger decks. 2 restaurants, dining room, café, grill, ice cream parlor, in-room safes, minibars, in-room VCRs, 2 pools, 1 lap pool, fitness classes, gym, hair salon, 2 outdoor hot tubs, sauna, spa, steam room, 7 bars (Harmony), 4 bars (Symphony), casino, cinema, dance club, showroom, video game room, children's programs (ages 3–16), dry cleaning, laundry facilities, laundry service, computer room, Internet, no kids under 3 months, no-smoking rooms. AE, D, MC, V.*

Seabourn Cruise Line

Ultraluxury cruise pioneer Seabourn Cruise Line has earned accolades from repeat guests, traveler polls, and consumer publications since its founding in 1987. Its fleet of three identical, all-suite ships, *Seabourn Pride, Seabourn Legend,* and *Seabourn Spirit,* the last based in Asia and the Pacific, is known as the "Yachts of Seabourn." The crowd tends to be older and affluent, and people tend to dress up. These sleek-lined 10,000-ton ships are celebrated for extraordinary levels of personalized service, sumptuous suites of 277 square ft or more—40% with balconies—and exceptional cuisine designed by famed chef-restaurateur Charlie Palmer. All drinks, including wine and alcohol, are complimentary throughout the voyage, and tipping is not allowed. Shore excursions often include privileged access to historic and cultural sites when they are not open to the public.

✉ *Seabourn Cruise Line, 6100 Blue Lagoon Dr., Suite 400, Miami, FL 33126,* ☎ *305/463–3000 or 800/929–9391,* FAX *305/463–3010,* WEB *www.seabourn.com.*

THE SHIPS OF SEABOURN CRUISE LINE

Seabourn Legend, Seabourn Pride. Striking and sleek, Seabourn's twin-funnel ships feel like swank private clubs—elegant, but not stifling. All cabins have a fresh daily fruit basket, stocked bar, thick terry robes and slippers, designer soaps and toiletries, aromatherapy bath menu, twin sinks, and large tub and shower. In rooms without balconies, the sitting area is next to a 5-ft-wide picture window; about 40% of the cabins have balconies. Cuisine is exceptional and prepared to order; service is unfailingly superb. Waterskiing, sailing, and windsurfing may be enjoyed directly from the ship's stern—when at anchor and weather permitting. A 30- by 30-ft submersible steel mesh tank is always set out for a protected saltwater swimming experience. *106 cabins, 208 passengers, 6 passenger decks. Restaurant, dining room, in-room safes, refrigerators, in-room VCRs, pool, fitness classes, gym, hair salon, 2 outdoor hot tubs, sauna, spa, steam room, 2 bars, casino, cinema, dance club, showroom, dry cleaning, laundry facilities, laundry service, computer room. AE, D, MC, V.*

Seven Seas Cruises

Seven Seas Cruises (*formerly* Radisson Seven Seas Cruises) is part of Carlson Hospitality Worldwide, one of the world's major hotel and travel companies. The cruise line was formed in December 1994 with the merger of the one-ship Diamond Cruises and Seven Seas Cruises lines. From these modest beginnings, SSC has now grown into a major luxury player in the cruise industry. With the launch of the line's fifth ship, the *Seven Seas Mariner,* in March 2001, SSC became the world's largest luxury line, with more than 2,000 berths in this category. The 700-passenger all–balcony suite *Seven Seas Voyager* entered service in April 2003.

The line's spacious ocean-view cabins have the industry's highest percentage of private balconies; you'll always find open seating at dinner (which includes complimentary wine); there's a strict no-tipping policy; and activities tend to be oriented toward exploring the destinations on the itinerary. Although passengers tend to be older and affluent they are still active, and SSC manages to provide a high level of service and sense of intimacy on mid-size ships, which have the stability of larger vessels.

✉ *Seven Seas Cruises, 600 Corporate Dr., Suite 410, Fort Lauderdale, FL 33334,* ☎ *954/776–6123, 800/477–7500, or 800/285–1835;* FAX *954/772–3763;* WEB *www.rssc.com.*

THE SHIPS OF SEVEN SEAS CRUISES

SSC Radisson Diamond. As wide as an ocean liner and as long as a mega-yacht, the *Diamond* is a futuristic catamaran perched over the sea. The twin-hull design cuts down on pitch and roll movements, making it one of the most stable cruise ships afloat. There are few organized events on board; passengers gather at their leisure for lectures and card games. Cabins, situated on three upper decks, are all outside suites, each with a large sitting area (243 to 486 square ft); 70% have a private verandah with teak decking, others a large bay window. Marble bathrooms have a vanity, bathtub, and shower. International cuisine is served in the Grand Dining Room—one of the prettiest afloat. *175 cabins, 350 passengers, 6 passenger decks. Restaurant, dining room, in-room safes, minibars, in-room VCRs, pool, fitness classes, gym, hair salon, outdoor hot tub, sauna, spa, steam room, 2 bars, casino, cinema, dance club, showroom, dry cleaning, laundry service, no-smoking rooms; no kids under 1. AE, D, MC, V.*

Seven Seas Navigator. The spacious *Navigator* is a mid-size ship with a big-ship feel. Every stateroom is a superbly appointed, ocean-view suite ranging from 300 to more than 1,000 square ft—90% with private teak balconies. All standard suites have walk-in closets and marble bathrooms with separate tub and shower, cotton bathrobes, hair dryers, TV/VCRs, refrigerators stocked with soft drinks, and en-suite bar set up upon embarkation. At 300 square ft, even the smallest stateroom is sufficiently roomy for comfortable en-suite dining—course by course, ordered from the Compass Rose dining room. There is 1 crew member for every 1.5 passengers. *251 cabins, 490 passengers, 8 passenger decks. Restaurant, dining room, in-room safes, minibars, in-room VCRs, pool, fitness classes, gym, hair salon, outdoor hot tub, sauna, spa, steam room, 4 bars, casino, cinema, dance club, showroom, dry cleaning, laundry service, no-smoking rooms; no kids under 1. AE, D, MC, V.*

☝ ***Seven Seas Mariner.*** The world's first and only all-suite, all-balcony ship is also Seven Seas' largest, with the highest space-per-passenger ratio in the fleet. All cabins are outside suites ranging from 301 square feet to 1,580 square ft including the verandah. The ship's dining rooms include Signatures, the only restaurant at sea staffed by chefs wearing the Blue Riband of Le Cordon Bleu of Paris, the famed culinary institute. On certain voyages the chefs offer Le Cordon Bleu "Classe Culinaire des Croisiers," workshops that offer a hands-on introduction to the art of French cooking. Passengers on SSC ships have consistently placed the Judith Jackson spas among their favorites on land or sea. *328 cabins, 700 passengers, 8 passenger decks. 3 restaurants, dining room, in-room safes, minibars, in-room VCRs, pool, fitness classes, gym, hair salon, outdoor hot tub, sauna, spa, steam room, 4 bars, casino, cinema, dance club, showroom, children's programs (ages 6–17), dry cleaning, laundry service, no kids under 1, no-smoking rooms. AE, D, MC, V.*

Silversea Cruise Line

Silversea Cruises straddles the line that separates ocean-liner and luxury-yacht cruising. Its ships have full-size showrooms, domed dining rooms, and a selection of bars and shops; yet all rooms are outside suites, most have private verandahs, and space- and crew-to-passenger ratios are among the best at sea. Unlike on Seabourn and Windstar ships, there is no retractable marina at the stern for water sports. Instead, the Silversea ships have larger swimming pools and more deck space than other cruise yachts. Another of the line's selling points is its all-inclusive packaging, which includes gratuities, port charges, transfers, some shore excursions, and all beverages. All packages include economy airfare to the port of embarkation and a complimentary pre-cruise hotel room. Perhaps more compelling than the line's low prices is its flair for originality. The pasta chef's daily special is a passenger favorite, as is the galley lunch, held just once each cruise, when the galley is transformed into a buffet restaurant.

✉ *Silversea Cruise Lines, 110 E. Broward Blvd., Fort Lauderdale, FL 33301, ☎ 954/522–4477 or 800/722–9955, WEB www.silversea.com.*

THE SHIPS OF SILVERSEA CRUISE LINE

Silver Cloud, Silver Wind, Silver Whisper. Silversea's ships have the feel of a private yacht but with much more spaciousness, including larger public rooms and a two-tier showroom with a movable stage. The sleek decor is meant to evoke the great steamships of the past. The restaurant has brass sconces, wood paneling, and brass-ringed portholes; diners sit in high-backed chairs at small tables adorned by crisp, white tablecloths and set with Cristofle silver, fine porcelain, and European crystal. All cabins are outside suites (larger on the Silver Whisper) with walk-in closets and marble baths, and most open onto a teak verandah with floor-to-ceiling glass doors. Creature comforts include fine bedding (Frette linens and down pillows), Bulgari toiletries, stocked fridges, and a daily-replenished fruit basket. *148/148/194 cabins (Silver Cloud/Silver Wind/Silver Whisper), 296/296/388 passengers, 6/6/7 passenger decks. Restaurant, dining room, in-room safes, refrigerators, in-room VCRs, pool, fitness classes, gym, hair salon, 2 hot tubs, sauna, spa, steam room, 3 bars, casino, showroom, dry cleaning, laundry facilities, laundry service, computer room. AE, D, MC, V.*

Windstar Cruises

Windstar's vessels cross a four-masted, 19th-century sailing ship with a 20th-century yacht. Hulls have the latest technological advances, and computers control the six sails. At the touch of a button, thousands of feet of sail unfurl—a spectacular sight to see. Diesel engines help to propel the ships when the wind does not provide enough sail power, but these are primarily sailing ships. Few modern vessels capture the feeling of being at sea the way these do. Although the ship's design may be reminiscent of sailing vessels of yore, the amenities and shipboard service are among the best at sea. Life on board is unabashedly sybaritic, attracting a sophisticated, relatively young crowd happy to sacrifice bingo and masquerade parties for the attractions of remote islands and water sports; even motorized water sports are included, and passengers pay extra only for scuba diving. A retractable marina at the stern allows water sports directly from the ship at anchor. These ships are especially popular with honeymooners, and you won't find many singles or children aboard. Service is comprehensive, competent, and designed to create an elite and privileged ambience. Tipping is not expected.

✉ *Windstar Cruises, 300 Elliott Ave., Seattle, WA 98119, ☎ 206/281–3535 or 800/258–7245, ⨺ 206/281–7110, ⟪WEB⟫ www.windstarcruises.com.*

THE SHIPS OF WINDSTAR CRUISES

Windspirit, Windstar, Windsurf. Inspired by the great sailing ships of a bygone era, the Windstar ships are white, long, and lean, with bow masts and brass-rimmed portholes. Though the hulls are steel, the interiors glow with wood paneling and teak trim—a look rare among modern cruise ships. Instead of the chrome-and-glass banisters so popular on other ships, the vessels feature iron banisters with teak handrails. Every cabin is an outside suite, appointed in burled maple veneer and outfitted with plentiful closet space and mirrors. Portholes are trimmed in brass, cabinetwork is accented with rich wood moldings, and bathroom floors are made of teak. Stocked refrigerators, CD players, hair dryers, and terry robes are standard accoutrements in all staterooms. *74/74/152 cabins (Windspirit/Windstar/Windsurf), 148/148/308 passengers, 4/4/7 passenger decks. Dining room (2 on Windsurf), in-room safes, minibars, in-room VCRs, saltwater pool (2 on Windsurf), fitness classes, gym, hair salon, 2 outdoor hot tubs, massage (Windspirit and Windstar), sauna, spa (Windsurf), 2 bars, casino, cinema, dance club, laundry service, computer room, no-smoking rooms. AE, D, MC, V.*

Mainstream Cruise Lines

More than 85% of the Caribbean is covered by nine mainstream cruise lines. They offer the advantage of something for everyone and nearly every available sports facility imaginable, including ice-skating rinks, 18-hole miniature golf courses, and rock-climbing walls.

Generally speaking, the mainstream lines have two sizes of ships—cruise liner and megaship—in their fleets. Cruise liners have plentiful outdoor deck space, and most have a wraparound outdoor promenade deck that allows you to stroll or jog the ship's perimeter. In the newest cruise liners, traditional meets trendy. You'll find atrium lobbies and expansive sun and sports decks, picture windows instead of portholes, and cabins that open onto private verandahs. The smallest cruise liners carry 500 passengers, while the largest accommodate 1,500 passengers and are stuffed with diversions.

If you're into big, bold, brassy and nonstop activity, these huge ships offer it all. The centerpiece of most megaships is a three-, five-, or seven-story central atrium. However, these giant vessels are most easily recognized by their profile: the hull and superstructure rise as many as 14 stories out of the water and are capped by a huge sun or sports deck with a jogging track and swimming pool, which may be Olympic-size. Some megaships have a wraparound promenade deck. Picture windows are standard equipment, and cabins in the top categories have private verandahs. From their casinos and discos to their fitness centers, everything is bigger and more extravagant than on other ships. You may want to rethink a cruise aboard one of these ships if you want a little downtime, since you'll be joined by 1,500 to 3,000 fellow passengers.

Carnival Cruise Lines

Carnival Cruise Lines is the largest and most successful cruise line in the world, carrying more passengers than any other. Today's Carnival is a vastly different company from the one launched in 1972 with one refitted transatlantic ocean liner by entrepreneur Ted Arison, who made a vacation experience once reserved for the very rich widely accessible. Carnival became the standard by which lower-price cruise lines are measured. Not even its critics can deny that the line delivers what it promises. Brash and sometimes rowdy, Carnival throws a great party. Activities and entertainment are nonstop, beginning just after sunrise and continuing well into the night. Food has been upgraded in recent years, and it is plentiful and fairly diverse, better tasting and well presented, with healthy options.

Cabins are spacious and comfortable, comparable with those on any ship in this price category. Carnival's ships are like floating theme parks, though each one has a personality. The effect is most exaggerated on the newer, bigger ships, including the Fantasy, Destiny, Spirit, and Conquest classes. The *Carnival Conquest,* the largest, at 110,000 tons, debuted in November 2002; other megaships will be added to the fleet through 2005.

Carnival cruises are popular with young, single cruisers as well as with those older than 55. The line's offerings also appeal to parents cruising with their children. Dinner in the main dining room is served at 6 PM and 8 PM seatings. While Carnival's "Total Choice Dining" is not really a meal plan, all ships offer something for everyone at all hours, including 24-hour room service.

Gratuities are customarily given on the last evening of the cruise, but they may be prepaid at a rate of $9.75 per passenger per day. Carnival recommends the following tips: cabin steward, $3.50 per day; dining-room team service, $5.50 per day; alternative dining service, 75¢ per day. A 15% gratuity is automatically added to bar and beverage tabs.

✉ *Carnival Cruise Lines, 3655 N.W. 87th Ave., Miami, FL 33178-2428,* ☎ *305/599–2600, 800/438–6744, or 800/327–9501,* WEB *www.carnival.com.*

THE SHIPS OF CARNIVAL CRUISE LINES

℃ *Fantasy, Fascination, Imagination, Inspiration, Paradise, Sensation.* The six Fantasy-class ships based in the Caribbean are not unlike Las Vegas casino-hotels afloat. Identical in layout, they share gaudy marble, brass, neon, and mirrored decor, though details differ. The *Sensation* is the most subtle in its design approach; the *Paradise* is still the world's only smoke-free cruise ship. A seven-deck atrium is the centerpiece of each ship, and each has a bustling promenade. Cabins are decorated in bright colors; each is fairly spacious, and some suites have private verandahs. Each has a Seaview Bistro for casual dining in addition to the main dining room. Activities tend to be nonstop. *1,022 cabins, 2,052 passengers (2,606 at full occupancy), 10 passenger decks. Restaurant, 2 dining rooms, food court, pizzeria, in-room safes, 3 pools, fitness classes, gym, hair salon, 6 outdoor hot tubs, spa, 10 bars, casino, cinema, dance club, showroom, video game room, children's programs (ages 2–15), laundry facilities, laundry service, computer room, no-smoking rooms (Paradise all no-smoking). AE, D, MC, V.*

🕑 ***Carnival Destiny, Carnival Triumph, Victory.*** Carnival's Destiny-class ships can carry a whopping 3,471 passengers when all their third and fourth berths are filled. In keeping with their size, everything on these ships is big: the atrium spans nine decks, the spa sits on two decks, an outdoor water slide stretches 200 ft, and the casino covers 9,000 square ft. There's a two-level dance floor and a three-story theater for the Las Vegas–style shows. The deck area has four swimming pools, two with swim-up bars and another with a retractable roof. More than half of the cabins have ocean views, and 60% of the standard outside cabins and all suites have private verandahs. Specially designed family staterooms, some with connecting cabins, are near the ship's children's facilities. Carnival has embraced the trend toward alternative restaurants, and you can get Italian and Chinese food, as well as pizza and pastries. *1,321 cabins, 2,642 passengers (3,471 at full occupancy), 12 passenger decks. 5 restaurants, dining room, pizzeria, in-room safes, 4 pools, fitness classes, gym, hair salon, 7 outdoor hot tubs, spa, 5 bars, casino, cinema, dance club, showroom, video game room, children's programs (ages 2–15), laundry facilities, laundry service, computer room, no-smoking rooms. AE, D, MC, V.*

🕑 ***Celebration, Jubilee, Holiday.*** Originally considered "superliners" when introduced in 1985, the Holiday-class ships are almost quaint by today's standards. These ships ushered in the age of boxy hulls and superstructures that rise straight out of the water. Inside, they have Carnival's trademark brassy art, brightly colored walls, neon lights, and spectacularly lighted ceilings and floors. Cabins are slightly larger than those on most lower-cost cruise ships. Outside cabins have picture windows; all cabins are furnished with twin beds convertible into kings, as well as ample closet and drawer space. The lower-price Holiday-class ships have the same menus as other Carnival ships, with two dining rooms serving three meals and a Lido-area food court for casual breakfasts and lunches. *743 cabins, 1,486 passengers (Celebration/Jubilee 1,896 at full occupancy, Holiday 1,800 at full occupancy), 9 passenger decks. 2 restaurants, 2 dining rooms, pizzeria, in-room safes, 3 pools, fitness classes, gym, hair salon, outdoor hot tubs, spa, 2 bars, casino, cinema, dance club, showroom, video game room, children's programs (ages 2–15), laundry facilities, laundry service, computer room, no-smoking rooms. AE, D, MC, V.*

🕑 ***Legend, Pride, Spirit.*** The first of Carnival's Spirit-class ships entered service in 2001 with notable design improvements over those of previous lines. For example, all staterooms aboard these superliners are located above ocean level, making for a more comfortable cruise. Cabins have ample drawer and closet space, and in-cabin TVs show first-run films. Other innovations include eye-popping 11-story atriums, two-level promenades, wide decks, shopping malls, and reservations-only supper clubs. Greater speed allows Spirit-class ships to visit destinations in a week that would take other ships 10 days or more. Most staterooms have ocean views, and of those 80% have balconies. *Carnival Pride* is fast, cruising at 22 knots. Terrific children's programs make this a good ship for any family vacation. *1,062 cabins, 2,124 passengers (2,667 at full occupancy), 13 passenger decks. 3 restaurants, dining room, pizzeria, in-room safes, 4 pools, fitness classes, gym, hair salon, 5 outdoor hot tubs, spa, 16 bars, casino, cinema, dance club, showroom, video game room, children's programs (ages 2–15), laundry facilities, laundry service, computer room, no-smoking rooms. AE, D, MC, V.*

☟ **Conquest.** The 110,000-ton *Conquest*, the first in Carnival's new Conquest class, debuted in 2002. Offering an enormous variety of entertainment areas, including an expanded kids' section and a teen club/video arcade, this huge ship sets new standards for family travel. Cabins are decorated in subdued peach tones and are among the largest offered in the cruise industry; standard interior cabins, the smallest, measure 185 square ft. Interior spaces are inspired by Impressionist painters. Among the couple-pleasing settings is the romantic reservations-only supper club. *1,487 cabins, 2,974 passengers (3,700 at full occupancy), 13 passenger decks. 3 restaurants, 2 dining rooms, pizzeria, in-room safes, 4 pools, fitness classes, gym, hair salon, 7 outdoor hot tubs, spa, 22 bars, casino, cinema, dance club, showroom, video game room, children's programs (ages 2–15), laundry facilities, laundry service, computer room, no-smoking rooms.*

Celebrity Cruises

Celebrity Cruises has made a name for itself based on sleek ships and superior food. Style and layout vary from ship to ship, lending each a distinct personality. In terms of size and amenities, Celebrity's vessels rival almost any in cruising, but with a level of refinement rare on bigger ships. In just a short time Celebrity has won the admiration of its passengers and its competitors—who have copied its occasional adults-only cruises, nouvelle cuisine, and cigar clubs and hired its personnel (a true compliment). Celebrity has risen above typical mass-market cruise cuisine by hiring chef Michel Roux as a consultant. Menus are creative; both familiar and exotic dishes have been customized to appeal to American palates. All food is prepared from scratch, using only fresh produce and herbs, aged beef, and fresh fish—even the ice cream on board is homemade. Entertainment choices range from Broadway-style productions, captivating shows, and lively discos to Monte Carlo–style casinos and specialty lounges.

Celebrity attracts everyone from older couples to honeymooners. Summertime children's programs are as good as those on any upscale cruise line. Service is friendly and first class—rapid and accurate in the dining rooms. Waiters, stewards, and bartenders are enthusiastic, take pride in their work, and try to please.

Tip your cabin steward/butlers $3.50 per day; chief housekeeper 50¢ per day; dining-room waiter $3.50 per day; assistant waiter $2 per day; and restaurant manager 75¢ per day, for a total of $10.25 per day. A 15% service charge is added to all beverage checks. For children under 12, or the third or fourth person in the stateroom, half of the above amounts is recommended. Gratuities are typically handed out on the last night of the cruise, or they may be charged to your shipboard account.

✉ *Celebrity Cruises, 1050 Caribbean Way, Miami, FL 33132-2096,* ☎ *305/539–6000 or 800/646–1456,* FAX *800/437–5111,* WEB *www.celebritycruises.com.*

THE SHIPS OF CELEBRITY CRUISES

☟ **Horizon, Zenith.** Big when they were built but just mid-size now, these sister ships offer a somewhat more intimate alternative to the expansive megaships. Interiors are indisputably gracious, airy, and comfortable; the design makes the most of natural light through strategically placed oversize windows. Wide corridors, broad staircases, seven elevators, and well-placed signs make it easy to get around. Nine passenger decks give ample breathing space. Cabins are modern and fairly roomy, with reasonably large closets and bathrooms. Food preparation receives as many accolades as presentation, and there are two seatings for breakfast, lunch, and dinner. Celebrity avoids themed nights for dinner—common on other lines—in favor of its popular themed midnight buffets, served four nights a week. *677/687 cabins (Horizon/Zenith), 1,374/1,374 passengers, 9/9 passenger decks. 2 restaurants, dining room, food court, ice cream parlor, pizzeria, in-room safes, minibars, 2 pools, fitness classes, gym, hair salon, 3 outdoor hot tubs, sauna, spa, steam room, 7/9 bars, casino, cinema, dance club, showroom, video game room, children's programs (ages 3–17), dry cleaning, laundry service, computer room, no-smoking rooms. AE, MC, V.*

☺ ***Century, Galaxy, Mercury.*** Celebrity's Century-class ships are larger than their Horizon-class predecessors, with glass-domed atriums and contemporary art throughout. Impressive two-story-high dining rooms and large theaters with full-size stages are notable improvements. The elaborate Elemis spas, which have enormous Thalassotherapy pools and the latest in treatments, are popular. The *Century* is high-tech and eclectically decorated, but the *Galaxy* is most impressive, with its aura of traditional elegance; the *Mercury* eschews eclectic decor for a more uniform look throughout. Standard cabins are intelligently appointed and apportioned, with few frills; space is well used, making for maximum elbow room in the bathrooms and good storage space in the closets. The *Century* has fewer private verandahs than its sister ships. *875/935/935 cabins (Century/Galaxy/Mercury), 1,750/1,870/1,870 passengers, 10/10/10 passenger decks. 2 restaurants, dining room, food court, ice cream parlor, pizzeria, in-room safes, minibars, 3 pools (2 on Century), fitness classes, gym, hair salon, 4 outdoor hot tubs (3 on Galaxy), sauna, spa, steam room, 6 bars, casino, cinema, dance club, showroom, video game room, children's programs (ages 3–17), dry cleaning, laundry service, computer room, no-smoking rooms. AE, MC, V.*

☺ ***Constellation, Infinity, Millennium, Summit.*** Dramatic exterior glass elevators, a glass-domed pool area, and a window-wrapped ship-top observation lounge keep the magnificence of the Caribbean well within the passenger's view aboard Millennium-class ships. These are the newest and largest in Celebrity's fleet, and each stocks plenty of premium amenities, including a flower-filled conservatory, music library, expansive spa, Internet café with 18 work stations, golf stimulator, and brand-name boutiques. Cabins are bright, spacious, and well appointed, and 80% have an ocean view (74% of those have private verandahs). *Infinity, Summit,* and *Constellation* have in-cabin Internet access. With a staff member for every two passengers, service is especially attentive. *975 cabins, 1,950 passengers, 11 passenger decks. Restaurant, dining room, food court, ice cream parlor, pizzeria, in-room safes, minibars, in-room VCRs, 3 pools, fitness classes, gym, hair salon, 3 outdoor hot tubs, sauna, spa, steam room, 6 bars, casino, cinema, dance club, showroom, video game room, children's programs (ages 3–17), dry cleaning, laundry service, computer room, Internet in some rooms, no-smoking rooms. AE, MC, V.*

Costa Cruise Lines

The Genoa-based Costa Crociere, parent company of Costa Cruise Lines, had been in the shipping business for more than 100 years and in the passenger business for almost 50 years when it was bought by Airtours and Carnival Cruises in 1997; Carnival gained sole ownership of the line in 2000, but the ships retain their Italian flavor. At this writing only two of the line's ships sailed from U.S. ports to the Caribbean, and during the winter season only. The ships are a combination of classic and modern design. The *CostaVictoria* entered service in 1996, followed by the somewhat larger *CostaAtlantica* in 2000. The *CostaMediterranea,* a sister ship to *CostaAtlantica,* was launched in summer 2003, and at this writing two much larger ships, the *CostaFortuna* and *CostaMagica,* were due in the fall of 2003 and late 2004, respectively. Passengers tend to be a little older—the average age is 54—and have an interest in all things Italian. You don't find a lot of first-time cruisers on Costa ships.

Suggested tipping guidelines are as follows: cabin steward, $3 per day; waiter, $3 per day; busboy, $1 per day; maître d' and head waiter, $2.50 per day. A 15% gratuity is added to beverage bills (including mineral water in the dining room). Gratuities are normally given out on the last night of the cruise and may be charged to your shipboard account.

☒ *Costa Cruise Lines, 200 S. Park Rd., Suite 200, Hollywood, FL 33021-8541,* ☎ *954/266-5600 or 800/462-6782,* FAX *954/266-2100,* WEB *www.costacruises.com.*

THE SHIPS OF COSTA CRUISE LINES

🐚 ***CostaAtlantica, CostaVictoria.*** These stylish ships embrace an ambience that is purely Italian, with marble floors and walls, wood cabinetry, and Italian art throughout. Cooking classes, Roman-toga theme nights, pizza, bocce ball games, and tarantella dance lessons reinforce the Italian feel. Staterooms are cheerfully decorated and fairly comfortable; 78% have an ocean view, and more than half the cabins on *CostaAtlantica* have private verandahs (*CostaVictoria* has none), though some have only small balconies. The Costa Kids Club is good, and all cruises allow parents to enjoy two evenings alone while their children are supervised by youth counselors. Both ships have a "Golf Academy at Sea," with PGA onboard clinics and golf excursions in most ports. The ships have Internet service in cabins and in an Internet café. *1,057/964 cabins (CostaAtlantica/CostaVictoria), 2,114/1,928 passengers, 12/12 passenger decks. 2 restaurants, dining room (2 on CostaVictoria), café, food court, pizzeria, in-room safes, 3 pools (1 indoor), fitness classes, gym, hair salon, 4 hot tubs, sauna, spa, steam room, 5 bars, casino, cinema, dance club, showroom, video game room, children's programs (ages 3–17), dry cleaning, computer room, no kids under 6 months. AE, D, MC, V.*

Disney Cruise Line

Disney Cruise Line launched its first ship, *Disney Magic,* in 1998, followed by her sister ship, *Disney Wonder,* in 1999. Dozens of the best ship designers, industry veterans, and Disney creative minds planned intensely for three years to produce these ships, which have impressed adults and children alike. Exteriors are reminiscent of the great ocean liners of the early 20th century, but interiors are technologically up-to-the-minute and full of novel development in dining, entertainment, cabin, and entertainment facilities. Three- and four-night cruises to the Bahamas are coupled with a stay at Walt Disney World, or you can opt for a weeklong Eastern Caribbean cruise on *Disney Magic.* Passengers represent a cross-section of North America and Europe, of all ages, but there are certainly more kids than on many other cruises, and plenty of activities to keep them occupied.

Disney suggests the following tips: for waiters $11 on a three-night cruise, $14.75 on a four-night cruise, and $25.75 on a seven-night cruise; for assistant waiters $8, $10.75, and $18.75; for cabin stewards $10.75, $14.50, and $25.25. A 15% service charge is added to bar, wine, and deck-service bills. Gratuities are normally given out on the last night of the cruise and may be charged to your shipboard account.

✉ *Disney Cruise Line, Box 10210, Lake Buena Vista, FL 32830,* ☎ *407/566–3500 or 800/325–2500,* WEB *www.disneycruise.com.*

THE SHIPS OF DISNEY CRUISE LINE

☾ *Disney Magic, Disney Wonder.* These sister ships offer family-friendly staterooms designed to offer maximum comfort. Cabins are among the largest in the industry, most accommodating two adults and two children—a bath-and-a-half, separating bath and toilet in different rooms—plus, 75% of all staterooms are outside, and 44% of those include private verandahs. The Disney dining plan is novel in its approach and inventive in its execution; passengers are rotated through three different themed restaurants, accompanied by their familiar waiters and tablemates. Adults also may opt to dine at Palo, a northern Italian restaurant with sweeping views. With nearly an entire deck designed just for kids, Disney's age-specific, supervised group activities for ages 3–7 and 8–12 give Mom and Dad some downtime. *877 cabins, 2,400 passengers, 11 passenger decks. Restaurant, 3 dining rooms, food court, ice cream bar, in-room safes, 3 pools, fitness classes, gym, hair salon, 2 hot tubs, sauna, spa, 6 bars, cinema, dance club, showroom, video game room, children's programs (ages 12 wks–17), dry cleaning, laundry facilities, computer room, no-smoking rooms; no kids under 3 months.*

Holland America Line

Founded in 1873, Holland America (HAL) is one of the oldest names in cruising. Steeped in the traditions of the transatlantic crossing, its cruises are classic, conservative affairs renowned for their grace and gentility. The line falls at the high end of the premium category and is deluxe by any standard. Service is taken seriously: the line maintains a school in Indonesia to train staff members, rather than hiring out of a union hall. Food is good by cruise-ship standards and served on Rosenthal china. In response to the challenge presented by its competitors, Holland America has gone "nouvelle" and introduced a lighter side to its menus, including many pastas and "heart-healthy" dishes. Holland America passengers tend to be older and less active than those traveling on the ships of its parent line, Carnival, although the age difference is getting narrower. As its ships attract a more youthful clientele, Holland America has taken steps to shed its "old folks" image, now offering stops at a private island in the Bahamas, trendier cuisine, and a "Club Hal" children's program. Still, these are not party cruises, and Holland America has managed to preserve the refined and relaxing qualities that have always been its hallmark.

Holland America is building three additional 85,000-ton Vista Class ships, to be introduced between 2003 and 2006.

In the 1970s, Holland America adopted a no-tips-required policy. Staff members perform their duties with great pride and professionalism. In turn, passengers don't feel the pressure or the discomfort of having crew members solicit tips. On the other hand, this is not a no-tipping policy, and most passengers give tips comparable to those recommended on other lines—entirely at their own discretion.

✉ *Holland America Line, 300 Elliott Ave., Seattle, WA 98119,* ☎ *206/ 281–3535 or 877/932–4259,* FAX *206/281–7110,* WEB *www. hollandamerica.com.*

THE SHIPS OF HOLLAND AMERICA LINE

☾ *Volendam, Zaandam.* These ships are structurally similar to HAL's other vessels, with the signature two-tier dining room and retractable roof over the main pool, but they are newer, entering service in 1999 and 2000, respectively. They are also slightly larger than the line's other ships and have Internet cafés and practice-size tennis courts. Priceless antiques and artwork line the halls; huge bouquets of fresh, fragrant flowers are everywhere (a Holland America trademark); and each ship has a teak promenade completely encircling the ship, which means there will always be room for you at the rail to watch the sunset. All standard outside cabins come with a bathtub, and all suites and minisuites have private verandahs. The "Passport to Fitness" encourages a healthy diet and exercise. *658/720 cabins (Volendam/Zaandam), 1,316/1,440 passengers (1,378/1,848 at full occupancy), 10/10 passenger decks. 2 restaurants, dining room, food court, in-room safes, refrigerators, in-room VCRs, 2 pools (1 indoor), fitness classes, gym, hair salon, 2 outdoor hot tubs, sauna, spa, steam room, 6 bars, casino, cinema, dance club, showroom, video game room, children's programs (ages 5–17), laundry facilities, laundry service, computer room, no-smoking rooms. AE, D, MC, V.*

🐚 **Rotterdam, Amsterdam.** The *Rotterdam*, Holland America's standard bearer, reflects the highest attainments of the shipbuilders' art. Everywhere you look, there are priceless antiques and original works of art, burnished brass, and sweeping staircases; a promenade completely encircles the ship with sleek and inviting teak deck chairs. Passengers are pampered, savoring cuisine in their choice of dramatic venues—a two-tiered dining salon, whose windows soar above the sea, or a candlelit Venetian-style villa. Cabins were designed with world cruising in mind, so they are larger than average; many outside cabins have sitting areas. *658/690 cabins (Rotterdam/Amsterdam), 1,316/1,380 passengers (1,442/1,776 at full occupancy), 10/10 passenger decks. 2 restaurants, dining room, food court, in-room safes, refrigerators, in-room VCRs, 2 pools (1 indoor), fitness classes, gym, hair salon, 2 outdoor hot tubs, sauna, spa, steam room, 6 bars, casino, cinema, dance club, showroom, video game room, children's programs (ages 5–17), laundry facilities, laundry service, computer room, no-smoking rooms. AE, D, MC, V.*

Noordam, Maasdam. A stunning three-deck atrium is just one of the welcoming public spaces; staterooms are restful, with understated elegance. From bow to stern, these ships are full of lounges and restaurants—14 in all—some cozy, some grand, and most with expansive floor-to-ceiling windows. Popular spaces include the Crow's Nest, a combined observation lounge and nightclub overlooking the bow; and the Lido Restaurant—the hallmark of every Holland America Line ship—which has an adjoining outdoor terrace and swimming pool. Antiques and artwork line the halls. The *Noordam*'s collection is largely from Asia, while the mostly Dutch paintings adorning the *Maasdam* depict the Age of Exploration. *605/633 cabins (Noordam/Maasdam), 1,214/1,266 passengers (1,378/1,590 at full occupancy), 9/10 passenger decks. 3 restaurants, dining room, food court, ice cream parlor, in-room safes, 2 pools, fitness classes, gym, hair salon, 2 hot tubs, sauna, spa, steam room, 9 bars, casino, cinema, dance club, showroom, video game room, children's programs (ages 5–17), dry cleaning, laundry facilities, laundry service, computer room, no-smoking rooms. AE, D, MC, V.*

🐚 **Zuiderdam, Osterdam.** With the highest space-to-passenger ratio in the fleet, HAL's Vista-class ships—forward-looking both in design and spirit—launched in December 2002. Innovative exterior elevators link 10 passenger decks, providing panoramic sea views. The ship also offers a range of understated, spacious accommodation categories, with Internet data ports in all staterooms, 85% of which have ocean views, most with private verandahs. The ships also have all the hallmarks of the Holland America brand—extensive art collections, numerous dining options, a covered promenade deck encircling the entire ship, two interior promenades, and a large Lido pool with a retractable dome. At this writing, the *Osterdam* was expected to enter service in summer 2003. *924 cabins, 1,848 passengers, (2,387 at full occupancy), 13 passenger decks. 3 restaurants, dining room, food court, ice cream parlor, in-room safes, 2 pools (1 indoor), fitness classes, gym, hair salon, 4 hot tubs, sauna, spa, steam room, 9 bars, casino, cinema, dance club, showroom, video game room, children's programs (ages 5–17), dry cleaning, laundry facilities, laundry service, computer room, Internet, no-smoking rooms. AE, D, MC, V.*

Norwegian Cruise Line

Norwegian Cruise Line (NCL) was established in 1966, when one of Norway's oldest and most respected shipping companies, Oslo-based Klosters Rederi A/S, acquired the *Sunward* and repositioned the ship from Europe to the then-obscure Port of Miami. With the formation of a company called Norwegian Caribbean Lines, the cruise industry was changed forever. NCL launched an entirely new concept with its regularly scheduled cruises to the Caribbean on a single-class ship, with an informal kind of luxury. No longer simply a means of transportation, the ship became a destination unto itself, offering guests an affordable alternative to land-based resorts. The *Sunward*'s popularity prompted other cruise lines to build ships to accommodate the burgeoning market, eventually turning Miami into the world's number one port of embarkation. NCL led the way with its fleet of sleek, new ships. In another bold move, NCL purchased the former *France* in 1979 and rebuilt the grand ocean liner in Bremerhaven, Germany, for Caribbean cruising. The rechristened *Norway* then assumed the honored position as flagship of the fleet. The late 1980s brought new ships and a new corporate name as Norwegian Caribbean Lines became Norwegian Cruise Line in 1987. NCL has continued its expansion by acquiring lines, stretching and refurbishing older ships, and building new megaships, including the line's newest, *Norwegian Dawn*.

As Princess did with its Personal Choice concept, NCL created a sensation in the industry with the concept of "Freestyle Cruising," which eliminates dinner-table and -time assignments and dress codes. The line has even loosened the rules on disembarkation, which means passengers can relax in their cabins until it's time to leave the ship (instead of gathering in a lounge to wait for their numbers to be called). NCL's passenger list usually includes senior citizens, families, and younger couples, mostly from the U.S. and Canada.

NCL applies a service charge to passengers' shipboard accounts: $10 per passenger per day for those 13 and older and $5 per day for children ages 3–12. These automatic tips can be increased, decreased, or removed. A 15% gratuity is added to bar tabs and spa bills.

✉ *Norwegian Cruise Line, 7665 Corporate Center Dr., Miami, FL 33126,* ☎ *305/436–4000 or 800/327–7030,* WEB *www.ncl.com.*

THE SHIPS OF NORWEGIAN CRUISE LINE

🌣 **Norwegian Sky, Norwegian Sun.** These ships come with all the bells and whistles, including a variety of dining options, specialty bars, and Internet access—both in a café and in cabins. A 24-hour health club has expansive ocean views, and the presence of the full-service Mandara Spa means you can turn your cruise into a spa vacation. Cabins are adequately laid out, with large circular windows and sitting areas, sufficient (but not generous) shelf and drawer space, and two lower beds that convert to a queen. But what makes Norwegian Cruise Line's ship different from other large ships is its relaxed onboard atmosphere and Free-Style Cruising concept, which means main dining rooms are smaller but there are more dining venues (some with an additional cost). *1,001/1,001 cabins (Sky/Sun), 2,002/2,002 passengers (2,400/2,400 at full occupancy), 12/11 passenger decks. 8/7 restaurants, 2 dining rooms, food court, in-room safes, refrigerators, 2 pools, fitness classes, gym, hair salon, 4 hot tubs, sauna, spa, steam room, 13/11 bars, casino, cinema, dance club, showroom, video game room, children's programs (ages 2–17), dry cleaning, laundry facilities, computer room, Internet; no kids under 6 months. AE, D, MC, V.*

Norwegian Sea. The *Norwegian Sea*, one of the older ships in Norwegian's lineup, completed a multimillion-dollar refurbishment project in January 2003. Enhancements include a new Le Bistro premium restaurant, new carpeting, upholstery, wood floors, and granite floors and countertops. All cabins were updated with new bedding, curtains, and towels. Standard cabins are small and awkwardly fitted with twin beds in an L-shape; tiny bathrooms have little counter space, though all now sport hair dryers. Service is friendly, warm, and efficient, as it is on all NCL ships, but there just aren't the kinds of extensive public amenities cruise goers are coming to expect. *763 cabins, 1,518 passengers, 9 passenger decks. 2 dining rooms, 2 restaurants, food court, ice cream parlor, in-room safes, 2 pools, fitness classes, gym, hair salon, 2 hot tubs, sauna, spa, 8 bars, casino, cinema, dance club, showroom, video game room, children's programs (ages 2–17), dry cleaning, laundry service, computer room; no kids under 6 months. AE, D, MC, V.*

☾ **Norwegian Majesty.** The *Norwegian Majesty* was lengthened in 1999 with the insertion of a prefab midsection that added 110 feet to its length and 203 cabins; about 71% are outside and many are no-smoking. Other additions included a second pool, an additional dining room, a coffee bar, a casino, another outdoor bar, and NCL's hallmark Le Bistro premium restaurant offering French classics and nouvelle cuisine. There's also significantly more deck space. During the conversion, all interiors were spruced up and refurbished. Some of the standard cabins are fairly small, and all have a shower only. Most ocean-view staterooms have refrigerators. Lower beds in most staterooms can be combined to form a queen-size bed. *731 cabins, 1,462 passengers, 9 passenger decks. 5 restaurants, dining room, food court, ice cream parlor, in-room safes, some refrigerators, 2 pools, fitness classes, gym, hair salon, 2 hot tubs, sauna, spa, 8 bars, casino, cinema, dance club, showroom, video game room, children's programs (ages 2–17), dry cleaning, laundry service, computer room, no-smoking rooms. AE, D, MC, V.*

☾ **Norway.** The former S/S *France*, one of the grandest of the classic ocean liners, is one of a kind, a legend in cruising, and the last of its kind. Bought by NCL in 1979, she was refurbished from stem to stern in 2002. All staterooms received new bedding, carpeting, linens, and curtains; the rare two-porthole views in the ocean-view staterooms were retained. All cabins are furnished with two lowers or one double bed. The *Norway* continues to sail in the traditional style, with two dinner seatings. *1,016 cabins, 2,032 passengers, 12 passenger decks. 2 restaurants, 2 dining rooms, in-room safes, refrigerators, 2 pools, fitness classes, gym, hair salon, hot tub, sauna, spa, steam room, 8 bars, casino, cinema, dance club, showroom, video game room, children's programs (ages 3–17), dry cleaning, laundry service, laundry facilities, computer room, no-smoking rooms; no kids under 6 months. AE, D, MC, V.*

☾ **Norwegian Dawn.** The line's newest and largest Freestyle Cruising ship, which is based in New York City, comes bedecked with one of the largest art collections afloat, including Andy Warhol prints in stairwells and originals by Matisse, Monet, and Renoir in the Le Bistro premium restaurant. A top speed of 25 knots allows the ship to do seven-night round-trips to the Bahamas and Florida. Cabins are reasonably large, with subdued decor and nice-looking cherry-veneer cabinetry; minisuites with private verandahs are especially nice. Most have separate toilet, sink, and shower facilities, and all have coffee makers. An extensive health club, wonderful children's facilities (including a small children's pool), and separate teen disco are definite pluses, as is wireless Internet access throughout the ship. *1,112 cabins, 2,224 passengers, 11 passenger decks. 5 restaurants, 3 dining rooms, café, food court, ice cream parlor, in-room safes, refrigerators, 2 pools, indoor lap pool, fitness classes, gym, hair salon, 5 hot tubs, 2 saunas, spa, 2 steam rooms, 9 bars, casino, cinema, dance club, showroom, video game room, children's programs (ages 2–17), dry cleaning, laundry facilities, laundry services, computer room, Internet, no-smoking rooms. AE, D, MC, V.*

Princess Cruise Line

Rising from modest beginnings in 1965, when it began with one ship cruising to Mexico, Princess has become one of the world's largest cruise lines. Its fleet goes to more destinations each year than any other major line, though many cruises depart from the west coast of the U.S. rather than the Caribbean. Princess was catapulted to stardom in 1977, when it became the star of *The Love Boat* television series, which introduced millions of viewers to the still-new concept of a seagoing vacation. The name and famous "seawitch" logo have remained synonymous with cruising ever since. Nearly everything about Princess is big, but the line doesn't sacrifice quality for quantity when it comes to building beautiful vessels. Decor and materials are top-notch, and service, especially in the dining rooms, is of a high standard. In short, Princess is refined without being pretentious.

Many Princess ships offer the line's innovative "Personal Choice Cruising" program, an individualized, unstructured style of cruising that gives passengers choice and flexibility in customizing their cruise experience—multiple dining locations, flexible entertainment, and affordable private balconies. It's the kind of program that has become important for the entire industry.

Princess passengers' average age is 45; you see a mix of younger and older couples on board.

Princess suggests tipping $10 per person, per day. On ships with "Personal Choice Cruising" gratuities are automatically added to accounts, which passengers can adjust at the purser's desk; 15% is added to bar bills.

✉ *Princess Cruise Line, 24305 Town Center Dr., Santa Clarita, CA 91355-4999,* ☎ *661/753–0000 or 800/774–6237,* 🌐 *www.princess.com.*

THE SHIPS OF PRINCESS CRUISE LINE

☾ ***Sun Princess, Dawn Princess, Sea Princess.*** Cabins in these sister ships offer an abundance of private balconies (more than 70% of outside cabins have them). All standard cabins are decorated in light colors and have a queen-size bed convertible to two singles, ample closet and bath space (with shower only), terry robes, and hair dryers. Several cabins on each ship are deemed fully accessible. Each subtly decorated vessel has two main showrooms and several dining rooms and restaurants (two with extra charges), from large to intimate. A wraparound teak promenade lined with canopied steamer chairs provides a peaceful setting for reading, napping, or daydreaming. *975 cabins, 1,950 passengers, 14 passenger decks. 5 restaurants, 3 dining rooms, café, food court, ice cream parlor, pizzeria, in-room safes, refrigerators, 5 pools, fitness classes, gym,* *hair salon, 9 hot tubs, sauna, spa, steam room, 12 bars, casino, cinema, dance club, showroom, video game room, children's programs (ages 3–17), dry cleaning, laundry facilities, laundry service, computer room, no-smoking rooms; no kids under 6 months. AE, D, MC, V.*

☙ ***Grand Princess, Golden Princess.*** These ultrasleek megaships are high-tech, stunning, and impressive, with several swimming pools, different entertainment venues, and three main dining rooms as well as other restaurants. Cabins, which are in a bewildering array of sizes, have generous closet and shelf space but few drawers. Even the smallest standard cabins are adequate for two people, and all rooms have terry robes and hair dryers; more than 700 outside cabins have spacious, private verandahs. Passengers can earn PADI scuba certification, participate in a customized fitness program, or mellow out in the Lotus spa—all on board during the cruise. Traditional touches include stepped-back decks in the back and the Wheelhouse Bar, which evokes the 160-year history of P. & O., Princess Cruise Line's parent company. *1,300 cabins, 2,600 passengers (1,910 at full occupancy), 13 passenger decks. 3 restaurants, 3 dining rooms, food court, ice cream parlor, pizzeria, in-room safes, refrigerators, 5 pools, fitness classes, gym, hair salon, 4 hot tubs, sauna, spa, steam room, 12 bars, casino, cinema, dance club, showroom, video game room, children's programs (ages 3–17), laundry facilities, computer rooms, no-smoking rooms; no kids under 6 months. AE, D, MC, V.*

Royal Caribbean Cruise Line

Imagine if the Mall of America were sent to sea. That's a fair approximation of what the megaships of Royal Caribbean Cruise Line (RCL) are all about. These giant vessels are indoor-outdoor wonders, with every conceivable activity in a resortlike atmosphere, including atrium lobbies, shopping arcades, large spas, and expansive sundecks. Several ships have such elaborate facilities as 18-hole miniature-golf courses, ice-skating rinks, and rock-climbing walls. These mammoth ships are quickly replacing the smaller vessels in Royal Caribbean's fleet, and passengers now have three generations of megaships to choose from, including the prototype, the *Sovereign of the Seas.*

The centerpiece of Royal Caribbean's megaships is the central atrium, a hallmark that has been duplicated by many other cruise lines. The brilliance of this design is that all the major public rooms radiate from this central point, so you can learn your way around these huge ships within minutes of boarding. Ships in the Vision series (*Legend of the Seas, Splendour of the Seas, Enchantment of the Seas, Grandeur of the Seas, Rhapsody of the Seas,* and *Vision of the Seas*) are especially big and airy, with sea views almost anywhere you happen to be. The main problem with its otherwise well-conceived vessels is that the line packs too many people aboard, making for an exasperating experience at embarkation, while tendering, and at disembarkation. However, Royal Caribbean is one of the best-run and most popular cruise lines.

While the line competes directly with Carnival for passengers—active couples and singles in their thirties to fifties, as well as a large family contingent—there are distinct differences of ambience and energy. Royal Caribbean is a bit more sophisticated and subdued than Carnival, even while delivering a good time on a grand scale.

Royal Caribbean suggests the following tips per passenger: dining-room waiter, $3.50 a day; stateroom attendant, $3.50 a day; assistant waiter, $2 a day. Gratuities for headwaiters and other service personnel are at your discretion. A 15% gratuity is automatically added to beverage and bar bills. All gratuities may be charged to your onboard account.

✉ *Royal Caribbean International, 1050 Caribbean Way, Miami, FL 33132,* ☎ *305/539–600 or 800/327–6700,* WEB *www.royalcaribbean.com.*

⛵ *Adventure of the Seas, Navigator of the Seas, Explorer of the Seas, Voyager of the Seas.* Royal Caribbean's enormous Voyager-class vessels are among the world's largest cruise ships and represent the highest space-per-guest ratio in the RCL fleet. Innovative and amazing features include ice-skating rinks, basketball courts, shopping promenades, in-line skating tracks, 18-hole miniature-golf courses, and rock-climbing walls. Spectacular three-story dining rooms have two dinner seatings, but there are other options, both casual and reservation-only (for an extra fee). Enhanced staterooms include larger-than-average beds, with rounded corners to leave more floor space, and larger closets; other cabins have twin beds convertible to a queen, and bathrooms with hair dryers and sizeable vanity areas; some inside staterooms have a view into the gigantic atrium. *1,557 cabins, 3,114 passengers (3,835/3,835/3,844/3,844 at full occupancy) (Adventure/Navigator/Explorer/Voyager), 15/15/14/14 passenger decks. 5 restaurants, dining room, food court, ice cream parlor, pizzeria, in-room safes, minibars, 2 pools, fitness classes, gym, hair salon, 2 hot tubs, sauna, spa, steam room, 14/16/12/10 bars, casino, cinema, dance club, showroom, video game room, children's programs (ages 3–17), dry cleaning, laundry service, computer room, no-smoking rooms. AE, D, MC, V.*

⛵ *Brilliance of the Seas, Radiance of the Seas.* Royal Caribbean's Radiance-class ships aren't the largest in the fleet, but they do offer great speed—allowing for longer itineraries—and the line's highest percentage of outside cabins. The central atrium spans 10 decks, and with its sea-facing elevators, you'll get to see more of the ocean. The coffeehouse-bookstore combination is a novel touch. The solarium, filled with lush foliage and cascading waterfalls, has an Indian theme on *Brilliance* and an African theme on *Radiance,* plus a retractable roof to make its indoor pool an outdoor pool. All cabins have two twin beds convertible into a queen, computer jack, vanity table with an extendable working surface, and bedside reading lights. *1,050/1,056 cabins (Brilliance/Radiance), 2,100/2,100 passengers (2,501/2,501 at full occupancy), 12/12 passenger decks. 5 restaurants, 3 dining rooms, food court, in-room data ports, in-room safes, refrigerators, 3 pools, fitness classes, gym, hair salon, 3 hot tubs, sauna, spa, steam room, 9 bars, casino, cinema, dance club, showroom, video game room, children's programs (ages 3–17), dry cleaning, laundry service, computer room, no-smoking rooms. AE, D, MC, V.*

⛵ *Majesty of the Seas, Monarch of the Seas, Sovereign of the Seas.* The first Sovereign-class ships entered service in 1988 and were the first of Royal Caribbean's floating-resort megaships—as tall as the Statue of Liberty and three football fields in length, with five-story atriums and signature glass elevators. These ships sail mostly on short itineraries to the Bahamas, though *Monarch of the Seas* does the Western Caribbean route. Dining rooms serve a different international menu each evening, and waiters dress accordingly. Relatively small 119-square-ft standard cabins make the most of limited space. Each is fitted with twin beds convertible to a queen, a large dressing table, large wardrobe closet, chair, and full-length mirror. Some have safes. *1,177/1,177/1,125 cabins (Majesty/ Monarch/Sovereign), 2,354/2,354/2,250 passengers (2,744/2,744/2,850 at full occupancy), 11/11/11 passenger decks. Dining room, food court, some in-room safes, 2 pools, fitness classes, gym, hair salon, 2 outdoor hot tubs, sauna, 9 bars, cinema, dance club, showroom, video game room, children's programs (ages 3–17), dry cleaning, laundry service, Internet, no-smoking rooms. AE, D, MC, V.*

Enchantment of the Seas, Grandeur of the Seas, Rhapsody of the Seas.
Launched in 1986, Vision-class vessels were the second line of Royal
Caribbean megaships. These vessels are full-featured, with seven-story
atriums, bi-level health clubs, and balconied showrooms. They are also
fast: passengers get four full days in port during a weeklong Caribbean
cruise. With touches of Jazz Age opulence, the *Grandeur of the Seas* is
one of the line's most elegant ships, and the *Enchantment* bears a striking resemblance to it but with Asian flourishes in key public spaces and
a Victorian formality in the colonnaded dining room. *Rhapsody* has a
cooler personality than the other Vision ships, most evident in the art
nouveau–inspired dining room. Cabins on all three ships are relatively
large and have 25% more balconies than previous megaship lines. *975/
1,000/1,000 cabins (Enchantment/Grandeur/Rhapsody), 1,830/2,000/
2,000 passengers (2,446/2,435/2,435 at full occupancy), 11/11/11 passenger decks. 2 restaurants, dining room, food court, ice cream parlor,
in-room safes, 2 pools (1 indoor), fitness classes, gym, hair salon, 6 hot
tubs, sauna, spa, 6 bars, casino, cinema, dance club, showroom, video
game room, children's programs (ages 3–17), dry cleaning, laundry facilities, computer room, no-smoking rooms. AE, D, MC, V.*

Nordic Empress. This distinctive-looking ship, with huge aft bay windows, was specifically designed for the short (three- to four-day) cruise
market and splits its year between Bermuda and the Caribbean. A simple design with a single main corridor makes it easy for passengers to
learn their way about. The interior, filled with large and festive public
rooms, is a glittering combination of art deco and futuristic designs; the
six-story atrium is dazzling and well lit, with lots of glass, chrome, and
cascading waterfalls. A triple-level casino and a sensational double-decker
dining room with a fantastic view of the sea round out a·very tidy ship.
Standard cabins are small at 117 square ft, and the bright decor can't
make them feel any larger; most have twin beds convertible to a queen.
*801 cabins, 1,602 passengers (2,020 at full occupancy), 12 passenger
decks. Restaurant, dining room, in-room safes, 2 pools, fitness classes,
gym, hair salon, 4 hot tubs, sauna, 4 bars, casino, cinema, dance club,
showroom, video game room, children's programs (ages 3–17), dry cleaning, laundry facilities, Internet, no-smoking rooms. AE, D, MC, V.*

Royal Olympia Cruises

Royal Olympia Cruises (formerly Royal Olympic Cruises) was created
by the merger of two well-known Greek cruise lines, Sun Line Cruises
and Epirotiki, in 1995. Since then, two new vessels, built in Germany,
have joined the fleet. In 2000 the line's new flagship, *Olympia Voyager,* was launched, followed by her sister ship, *Olympia Explorer* in
2002. Trips on these mid-size ships tend to be more oriented toward
exploring the culture of the ports visited. A cruise to the Maya Riviera, for example, might mix lectures by distinguished archaeologists
with traditional cruise activities, including bingo, card games, and
trivia contests, topped off with a sprinkling of Greek culture (language
and dance classes). All Royal Olympia ships offer buffets for breakfast and lunch, formal afternoon tea, and early and late dinner sittings.
Most officers and crew are Greek, so every cruise features a night where
passengers are entertained with songs and dances from Greece. The
passenger list tends to be a bit older and more interested in cultural
enrichment than nonstop activity, so shore excursions are tailored accordingly, and the ships do a higher proportion of two-week itineraries
than most other lines cruising in the Caribbean. Prices are toward the
top end of the mainstream category.

Royal Olympia suggests tips of $6 per day for dining-room staff (which
is equally distributed among the dining-room stewards, busboys, and

buffet stewards) and $3 per day for cabin attendants. A 10% service charge is added to bar bills. Gratuities can be charged to your shipboard account.

⊠ *Royal Olympia Cruises, 805 3rd Ave., New York, NY 10022-7513,* ☎ *212/688–7555 or 800/872–6400,* WEB *www.royalolympiacruises.com.*

THE SHIPS OF ROYAL OLYMPIA CRUISES

Olympia Explorer, Olympia Voyager. State-of-the-art propulsion technology enables these sleek, mid-size ships to reach speeds of 28 knots. The ships are attractive and subdued in their decor, with unusual and extensive art collections. Two-thirds of cabins are outside, and suites have unusual floor-to-ceiling bay windows with deep balconies. Entertainment varies from classical music concerts to cabaret-style shows performed in a fairly intimate showroom. Despite their relatively small size, these ships don't feel crowded, and they can visit smaller ports (Tortola, for example) that larger megaships can't. These ships aren't really suited to children, and there are no children's programs. *418 cabins, 836 passengers, 6 passenger decks. Restaurant, dining room, in-room safes, 2 pools, fitness classes, gym, hair salon, hot tub, sauna, steam room, spa, 2 bars, casino, cinema, dance club, laundry service, no-smoking rooms.*

Other Cruise Lines

There are a few small cruise lines sailing in the Caribbean, notably *Clipper Cruise Line, Star Clippers,* and *Windjammer,* that appeal to passengers who eschew mainstream cruises. Most of these cruises accommodate 150 or fewer passengers, and they focus on soft adventure, cruising between nearby ports and anchoring out so passengers can swim and snorkel directly from the ship. Itineraries usually leave plenty of time for exploring and other activities on- or offshore. Many of these cruises schedule casual enrichment talks that often continue on decks, at meals, and during trips ashore.

Clipper Cruise Line

The yachtlike *Nantucket Clipper* and *Yorktown Clipper* are small coastal cruisers. With their shallow drafts and inflatable, motorized landing craft, they are well suited to exploring remote and otherwise inaccessible tropical waters. Cruises are billed as soft adventure and educational, and all include a naturalist, historian, or other expert to lead lectures and field trips. Itineraries include a full range of organized shore excursions, but there are few other organized activities: there are no discos, casinos, or musical reviews aboard Clipper ships, and reading, socializing, and board games are the most popular activities. Sometimes local entertainers perform on board, and there may be movies in the dining room after dinner, but often passengers go ashore for nightlife. These cruises don't sacrifice aesthetics, however, and the line emphasizes such shipboard refinements as fine dining, though the service is not of the white-glove variety. Dinner is served in a single open seating. The line tries to maintain a sophisticated atmosphere, and there are two dressy evenings, where a jacket but no tie is appropriate for men. Passengers are typically older (often in their mid-sixties).

The line recommends $10 per day in gratuities, which are deposited in a box at cruise's end and divided equally among the crew. No service charges are added to wine or bar bills.

⊠ *Clipper Cruise Line, 11969 Westline Industrial Dr., St. Louis, MO 63146-3220,* ☎ *314/655–6700 or 800/325–0010,* WEB *www. clippercruise.com.*

Nantucket Clipper, Yorktown Clipper. The Clippers look more like boxy yachts than cruise ships. Their signature design is dominated by a large bridge and picture windows that ensure bright interior public spaces. As with all small ships, there are only two public rooms and deck space is limited. The glass-walled observation lounge does double duty as the ship's bar and lecture room. You'll only find outside cabins, but they are small and have tiny bathrooms, though the larger top-deck staterooms are quite spacious. Most cabins have a picture window, but a few have portholes. A fleet of inflatable Zodiac landing craft takes passengers ashore for independent exploration. *51/69 cabins (Nantucket/Yorktown), 102/138 passengers, 4 decks. Dining room, in-room safes, fitness classes, gym, hair salon, movies, no-smoking rooms; no room TVs. AE, MC, V.*

Star Clippers Cruise Line

Since 1991, Coral Gables, Florida-based Star Clippers Ltd. has offered sophisticated travelers the ultimate cruising alternative—cruises aboard authentic re-creations of 19th-century clipper ships. The brainchild of a Swedish entrepreneur, *Star Clippers* operates three of the largest full-rigged sailing ships in the world—offering the amenities, activities, and atmosphere of a private yacht at a price that is often less than you would pay on a mass-market cruise ship. Old-fashioned sailing is the key to Star Clipper's appeal. Passengers can help pitch the sails, steer the ship, and learn about navigational techniques from the captain. Most, however, opt to take in the nautical ambience as they lounge on the upper deck. While the line's laid-back philosophy is similar to Windjammer's, these vessels are geared toward a more upscale passenger. Public rooms are larger than those aboard a Windjammer ship, as are most cabins, which have hair dryers, televisions, and telephones. And ships have swimming pools. Amenities on Star Clippers vessels fall somewhere between those of a true sailing yacht and the high-tech Windstar ships. Prices, however, are much more affordable. But the differences are more than just in the level of luxury: Star Clippers are true sailing vessels, albeit with motors, while Windstar ships are ocean liners with masts and sails

Passengers are an international group: about half are European (mostly French, German, and Swedish), and nearly all are couples, from honeymooners to well-traveled retirees.

Star Clippers recommends the following gratuities: room steward, $3 per day; dining-room staff, $5 per day. A 15% gratuity is added to bar bills. Gratuities may be charged to your shipboard account.

✉ *Star Clippers, Inc., 4101 Salzedo Ave., Coral Gables, FL 33146,* ☏ *305/442–0550 or 800/442–0551,* WEB *www.starclippers.com.*

Royal Clipper, Star Clipper. These sleek, white ships have teak decks and trim and tapered steel masts rigged with 42 sails (Royal Clipper is only the second five-masted sailing ship in history). Fresh- and saltwater pools are surrounded by sunning areas. The pool on *Royal Clipper* has an unusual glass bottom, so patrons of the piano bar can view swimmers from below. Each handsomely appointed cabin has a vanity and tiny sitting area, but the tiniest cabins are truly that (107 square ft on *Royal Clipper,* and only 97 square ft on *Star Clipper*). Most outside cabins have portholes; a few have picture windows. Dinner is served at one seating. A marina platform lowers at the stern for diving and water sports. *114/85 cabins (Royal Clipper/Star Clipper), 228/170 passengers, 5/4 passenger decks. Dining room, in-room safes, 3/2 pools, fitness classes, gym, hair salon (Royal Clipper), 3 hot tubs, sauna, 2 bars, no-smoking rooms. AE, MC, V.*

Windjammer Barefoot Cruises

Windjammer Barefoot Cruises is the largest operator of tall ships in the world. Its five ships range in size from 327 to 1,740 tons and carry between 64 and 122 passengers. Each Windjammer ship has a distinctive and unique heritage, usually as the private yacht for some legendary financial mogul or European royal or in the service of a government for oceanographic and meteorological research.

Cruises combines the adventure of a traditional sailing voyage with a contemporary nod to comfort. With a relatively small number of passengers, the ships provide a totally laid-back cruise, and there are certainly no dress-up evenings. Windjammer's ships reach remote and exotic islands that are often inaccessible to larger cruise ships. The fleet sails the Caribbean year-round, offering affordable 6- and 13-day cruises.

Though Windjammer offers singles-only cruises, a typical cruise includes a diverse socioeconomic mix of passengers, who share a love of the sea and the tall ships. During winter holidays and the summer vacation period, Windjammer offers a supervised children's program called the "Junior Jammers Club," similar to a summer camp, so that parents can relax and enjoy their vacation time.

Windjammer recommends $60 per passenger per week in optional gratuities, which are shared equally by the entire crew, though not officers. Tips are usually extended on the last day of the cruise in cash.

✉ *Windjammer Cruises, Box 190120, Miami, FL 33119-0120,* ☎ *305/672–6453 or 800/327–2601,* FAX *305/674–1219,* WEB *www.windjammer.com.*

THE SHIPS OF WINDJAMMER BAREFOOT CRUISES

Legacy. The flagship in the Windjammer fleet is a four-masted Barquentine that was once a meteorological research and exploration vessel for the French government. She was acquired in 1989 by Windjammer and converted into a traditional tall ship. Expert craftsmanship is apparent in the hand-carved, exotic South American woods; custom-designed interiors; and relatively spacious accommodations. All cabins are air-conditioned and simply decorated and have either bunk, double, or twin beds; wooden wardrobes; and full-length mirrors. Baths have shower stalls. *Legacy* sails throughout the British and U.S. Virgin Islands during the winter months and the Bahamas during the summer season. *61 cabins, 122 passengers, 4 passenger decks. Dining room, in-room safes, fitness classes, bar, children's programs (ages 6–17), no-smoking rooms; no room TVs. D, DC, MC, V.*

Mandalay. Once considered the most luxurious yacht in the the world and the dream boat of financier E. F. Hutton, the former *Hussar* is the queen of the Windjammer fleet. From 1953, the ship functioned as a floating laboratory for Columbia University's geological observation team; nearly half the existing knowledge of the ocean floor was gathered by the vessel. In 1982, she joined Windjammer and was renamed *Mandalay.* While all cabins are air-conditioned and simply furnished, there are two larger cabins on the main deck—the Admiral Suite and the Captain's Cabin—that have large picture windows, refrigerators, and private sundecks. The *Mandalay* stops at unspoiled beaches with gentle waters as she sails the Windward and Leeward islands. *36 cabins, 72 passengers, 3 passenger decks. Dining room, in-room safes, fitness classes, bar, no-smoking rooms; no room TVs. D, DC, MC, V.*

Polynesia. Built in Holland in 1938, this four-masted schooner, originally named *Argus,* was the swiftest fishing schooner in the Portuguese Grand Banks fishing fleet. She was bought and extensively renovated by Windjammer in 1975 and was renamed *Polynesia*. The refurbishment added modern plumbing, a teak deck, two main-deck admiral suites, 12 main-deck cabins, and 40 standard cabins. All the simply furnished, double-occupancy accommodations have air-conditioning, exotic wood paneling, and tile floors; bathrooms have only showers. *Polynesia* also offers a specially designed family-style dining salon. It sails the Leeward and the Windward islands of the French West Indies. *57 cabins, 126 passengers, 4 passenger decks. Dining room, in-room safes, fitness classes, bar, no-smoking rooms; no room TVs. D, DC, MC, V.*

Yankee Clipper. Built in 1927 by industrialist Alfred Krup, the *Cressida* became the *Pioneer* when she was owned by the Vanderbilt family, who raced her from Newport Beach, California. Windjammer bought and rechristened her in 1984. Extensive refurbishments—conducted over a three-year period—restored her to her former majesty and beauty and also gave her three new masts of purpleheart and angelica woods, air-conditioned cabins, and a continuous upper deck. Passengers snorkel, scuba dive, sample exotic spices, and lounge on tranquil deserted beaches of the Grenadines. *32 cabins, 64 passengers, 3 passenger decks. Dining room, in-room safes, fitness classes, bar, no-smoking rooms; no room TVs. D, DC, MC, V.*

3 PORTS OF EMBARKATION

Miami is the world's cruise capital, and more cruise ships are based here year-round than anywhere else. Caribbean cruises depart for their itineraries from several ports on either of Florida's coasts, as well as other cities on the Gulf Coast. Generally, if your cruise is on an Eastern Caribbean itinerary, you'll depart from Miami, Fort Lauderdale, or Port Canaveral; short three- and four-day cruises to the Bahamas also depart from these ports. Most cruises on Western Caribbean itineraries depart from Tampa, New Orleans, or Galveston, though some depart from Miami as well. Cruises to the Southern Caribbean might depart from Miami if they are 10 days or longer, but more likely, they will depart from San Juan, Puerto Rico, or some other port deeper in the Caribbean.

Regardless of which port you depart from, air connections may prevent you from leaving home on the morning of your cruise or going home the day you return to port. Or you may wish to arrive early simply to give yourself a bit more piece of mind, or you may just want to spend more time in one of the these interesting port cities. Many people choose to depart from New Orleans just to have an excuse to spend a couple of days in the city before or after their cruise.

PORT ESSENTIALS

Car Rental

➤ MAJOR AGENCIES: **Alamo** (☎ 800/522–9696, WEB www.alamo.com). **Avis** (☎ 800/331–1084; 800/879–2847 in Canada; 0870/606–0100 in the U.K.; 02/9353–9000 in Australia; 09/526–2847 in New Zealand; WEB www.avis.com). **Budget** (☎ 800/527–0700; 0870/156–5656 in the U.K.; WEB www.budget.com). **Dollar** (☎ 800/800–6000; 0124/622–0111 in the U.K., where it's affiliated with Sixt; 02/9223–1444 in Australia; WEB www.dollar.com). **Hertz** (☎ 800/654–3001; 800/263–0600 in Canada; 0870/844–8844 in the U.K.; 02/9669–2444 in Australia; 09/256–8690 in New Zealand; WEB www.hertz.com). **National Car Rental** (☎ 800/227–7368; 0870/600–6666 in the U.K.; WEB www.nationalcar.com).

SURCHARGES

Before you pick up a car in one city and leave it in another, **ask about drop-off charges or one-way service fees,** which can be substantial.

Note, too, that some rental agencies charge extra if you return the car before the time specified in your contract. To avoid a hefty refueling fee, **fill the tank just before you turn in the car,** but be aware that gas stations near the rental outlet may overcharge. It's almost never a deal to buy the tank of gas that's in the car when you rent it; the understanding is that you'll return it empty, but some fuel usually remains. Surcharges may apply if you're under 25 or if you take the car outside the area approved by the rental agency. You'll pay extra for child seats (about $6 a day), which are compulsory for children under five, and usually for additional drivers (about $10 per day).

Dining

Unless otherwise noted, all prices are given in U.S. dollars. The following price categories are used in this book.

CATEGORY	COST*
$$$$	over $30
$$$	$20–$30
$$	$12–$20
$	$8–$12
¢	under $8

per person for a main course at dinner

Lodging

Whether you are driving or flying into your port of embarkation, it is often more convenient to arrive the day before or to stay for a day after your cruise. Thus, we offer lodging suggestions for each port.

The lodgings we list are convenient to the cruise port and the cream of the crop in each price category. We always list the facilities that are available, but we don't specify whether they cost extra; when pricing accommodations, always ask what's included. Properties are assigned price categories based on the range between their least expensive standard double room at high season (excluding holidays) and the most expensive. But if you find everything sold out or wish to find a more predictable place to stay, there are chain hotels at almost all ports of embarkation.

Assume that hotels operate on the **European Plan** (EP, with no meals) unless we specify that they use either the **Continental Plan** (CP, with a Continental breakfast), **Breakfast Plan** (BP, with a full breakfast), or the **Modified American Plan** (MAP, with breakfast and dinner). The following price categories are used in this book.

CATEGORY	COST*
$$$$	over $250
$$$	$175–$250
$$	$120–$175
$	$70–$120
¢	under $70

All prices are for a standard double room, excluding service and taxes.

MAJOR HOTEL CHAINS

Adam's Mark (☎ 800/444–2326, WEB www.adamsmark.com). **Baymont Inns** (☎ 800/428–3438, WEB www.baymontinns.com). **Best Western** (☎ 800/528–1234, WEB www.bestwestern.com). **Choice** (☎ 800/424–6423, WEB www.choicehotels.com). **Clarion** (☎ 800/424–6423, WEB www.choicehotels.com). **Comfort Inn** (☎ 800/424–6423, WEB www.choicehotels.com). **Days Inn** (☎ 800/325–2525, WEB www.daysinn.com). **Doubletree Hotels** (☎ 800/222–8733, WEB www.doubletree.com). **Embassy Suites** (☎ 800/362–2779, WEB www.embassysuites.com). **Fairfield Inn** (☎ 800/228–2800, WEB www.marriott.com). **Four Seasons** (☎ 800/332–3442,

WEB www.fourseasons.com). **Hilton** (☎ 800/445–8667, WEB www.hilton.com). **Holiday Inn** (☎ 800/465–4329, WEB www.sixcontinentshotels.com). **Howard Johnson** (☎ 800/654–4656, WEB www.hojo.com). **Hyatt Hotels & Resorts** (☎ 800/233–1234, WEB www.hyatt.com). **Inter-Continental** (☎ 800/327–0200, WEB www.intercontinental.com). **La Quinta** (☎ 800/531–5900, WEB www.laquinta.com). **Le Meridien** (☎ 800/543–4300, WEB www.lemeridien-hotels.com). **Marriott** (☎ 800/228–9290, WEB www.marriott.com). **Omni** (☎ 800/843–6664, WEB www.omnihotels.com). **Quality Inn** (☎ 800/424–6423, WEB www.choicehotels.com). **Radisson** (☎ 800/333–3333, WEB www.radisson.com). **Ramada** (☎ 800/228–2828, 800/854–7854 international reservations, WEB www.ramada.com or www.ramadahotels.com). **Renaissance Hotels & Resorts** (☎ 800/468–3571, WEB www.renaissancehotels.com). **Ritz-Carlton** (☎ 800/241–3333, WEB www.ritzcarlton.com). Sheraton (☎ 800/325–3535, WEB www.starwood.com/sheraton). **Sleep Inn** (☎ 800/424–6423, WEB www.choicehotels.com). **Westin Hotels & Resorts** (☎ 800/228–3000, WEB www.starwood.com/westin). **Wyndham Hotels & Resorts** (☎ 800/822–4200, WEB www.wyndham.com).

FORT LAUDERDALE

In the 1960s, Fort Lauderdale's beachfront was lined with T-shirt shops interspersed with quickie food outlets, and downtown consisted of a lone office tower, some dilapidated government buildings, and motley other structures waiting to be razed. Today the beach is home to upscale shops and restaurants, including the popular Beach Place retail and dining complex, while downtown has exploded with new office and luxury residential development. The entertainment areas, Las Olas Riverfront and Himmarshee Village, are thriving, while airport expansion and renovation continue. And busy Port Everglades is giving Miami a run for its money in the cruise-ship business.

A captivating shoreline with wide ribbons of sand for beachcombing and sunbathing makes Fort Lauderdale and Broward County a major draw for visitors and often tempts cruise-ship passengers to spend an extra day or two in the sun. Fort Lauderdale's 2-mi stretch of unobstructed beachfront has been further enhanced with a sparkling promenade designed more for the pleasure of pedestrians than vehicles.

The Cruise Port

Port Everglades, Fort Lauderdale's cruise port, is the second-largest in the world. The port is near downtown Fort Lauderdale, but it's spread out over a huge area.

If you are driving, to get to the main entrance take I–595 East straight into the Port (I–595 becomes Eller Drive once inside the Port). I–595 runs east–west with connections to the Fort Lauderdale–Hollywood International Airport, U.S. 1, I–95, State Road 7 (441), Florida's Turnpike, Sawgrass Expressway, and I–75.

➤ CONTACTS: **Port Everglades** (✉ 1850 Eller Dr., ☎ 954/523–3404, WEB www.broward.org/port.htm).

AIRPORT TRANSFERS

Fort Lauderdale–Hollywood International Airport is 2 mi (about 5 to 10 minutes) from the docks. If you haven't arranged an airport transfer with your cruise line, you'll have to take a taxi to the cruise-ship port. The ride in a metered taxi costs about $10.

PARKING

There are two enclosed parking facilities, called Northport and Midport (the former for 2,500 cars, the latter for 2,000 cars), close to the

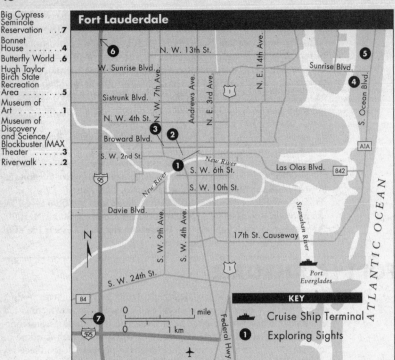

Fort Lauderdale

terminals. Use the Northport garage if your cruise leaves from Pier 1, 2, or 4; use Midport if your cruise leaves from Pier 18, 19, 21, 22/24, 25, 26, 27 or 29. The cost is $12 per day for either garage ($15 for RVs).

VISITOR INFORMATION
➤ CONTACTS: **Chamber of Commerce of Greater Fort Lauderdale** (⊠ 512 N.E. 3rd Ave., Fort Lauderdale 33301, ☎ 954/462–6000, WEB www. ftlchamber.com). **Greater Fort Lauderdale Convention & Visitors Bureau** (⊠ 1850 Eller Dr., Suite 303, Fort Lauderdale 33316, ☎ 954/765–4466, WEB www.broward.org). **Hollywood Chamber of Commerce** (⊠ 330 N. Federal Hwy., Hollywood 33020, ☎ 954/923–4000, WEB www.hollywoodchamber.org).

Where to Stay

Fort Lauderdale has a respectable variety of lodging options, from beachfront luxury suites to intimate B&Bs to chain hotels along the Intracoastal Waterway. If you want to be on the beach, be sure to mention this when booking your room, since many hotels advertise "waterfront" accommodations that are actually on the bay, not the beach.

For price categories, *see* Lodging at the beginning of this chapter.

$$$–$$$$ ⊡ **Hyatt Regency Pier Sixty-Six.** The trademark of this high-rise resort on the Intracoastal Waterway is its rooftop Pier Top Lounge, making one 360° revolution every 66 minutes. The 17-story tower dominates a 22-acre spread that includes the Spa 66, a full-service European-style spa. Each room has a balcony with views of the 142-slip marina, pool, ocean, or Intracoastal. Some guests prefer the ground-level lanai rooms. Lush landscaping and convenience to the beach, shopping, and restaurants add to the overall allure. Hail the water bus at the resort's dock for a three-minute trip to the beach. ⊠ 2301 S.E. 17th St. Causeway, 33316, ☎ 954/525–6666 or 800/327–3796, FAX 954/728–

3551, WEB *www.pier66.com. 380 rooms, 8 suites. 6 restaurants, 2 tennis courts, 2 pools, gym, hot tub, spa, snorkeling, boating, marina, parasailing, waterskiing, fishing, 3 bars. AE, D, DC, MC, V.*

$$$–$$$$ 🏨 **Marriott's Harbor Beach Resort.** Look down from the upper stories (14 in all) at night, and this 16-acre property south of the big public beach shimmers like a jewel. Spacious guest rooms have rich tropical colors, lively floral art prints, and warm woods. Part of the hotel's big-budget renovation is the addition of a European spa. No other hotel on the beach gives you so many activity options. ✉ *3030 Holiday Dr., 33316,* ☎ *954/525–4000 or 800/222–6543,* FAX *954/766–6152,* WEB *www.marriottharborbeach.com. 602 rooms, 35 suites. 3 restaurants, in-room data ports, room TVs with movies and video games, 5 tennis courts, 2 pools, gym, spa, beach, snorkeling, boating, parasailing, volleyball, 2 bars, children's programs (ages 5–12). AE, D, DC, MC, V.*

$$–$$$ 🏨 **Best Western Pelican Beach.** Directly on the beach and owned-managed by the hospitable Kruse family, this already lovely property has undergone a major transformation and now tries harder than ever to keep you on the premises with a new restaurant and lounge and a totally revamped pool area. ✉ *2000 N. Atlantic Blvd., 33305,* ☎ *954/568–9431 or 800/525–6232,* FAX *954/565–2622,* WEB *www.pelicanbeach.com. 10 rooms, 14 suites. Restaurant, lounge, 2 pools. AE, DC, MC, V.*

$–$$$ 🏨 **Riverside Hotel.** On Las Olas Boulevard, just steps from boutiques, restaurants, and art galleries, this charming hotel was built in 1936 and has taken on unprecedented luster with a $25 million renovation and expansion. The penthouse suites in the new 12-story executive tower have balconies offering sweeping views of Las Olas, New River, and the downtown skyline. Old Fort Lauderdale photos grace the hallways, and rooms are outfitted distinctively, with antique oak furnishings and framed French prints. Enjoy afternoon tea in the lobby and fine dining at Indigo, which has Southeast Asian cooking, or the elegant Grill Room. ✉ *620 E. Las Olas Blvd., 33301,* ☎ *954/467–0671 or 800/325–3280,* FAX *954/462–2148,* WEB *www.riversidehotel.com. 206 rooms, 11 suites. 2 restaurants, pool, dock, 2 bars, no-smoking rooms. AE, DC, MC, V.*

¢ 🏨 **Sea Chateau Resort.** A cozy two-story enclave about a block from the beach, this property has more going for it than affordability. Each room is done differently; many have canopy beds draped with gossamer fabric, and all have spacious closets and tub-showers. Efficiencies with kitchenettes anchor the corners. Rooms face the pool next to a quiet, shaded courtyard. Should you fall in love with the area, the owner is a licensed real estate agent. ✉ *555 N. Birch Rd., 33304,* ☎ *954/566–8331,* FAX *954/564–8411. 17 units. Pool, some kitchenettes, refrigerators. No credit cards.*

Where to Eat

For price categories, *see* Dining at the beginning of this chapter.

$$$–$$$$ ✕ **By Word of Mouth.** Unassuming but outstanding, this restaurant never advertises, hence its name. But word suffices, because locals consistently put it at the top of "reader's choice" restaurant polls. There is no menu; patrons are simply shown the day's specials. Count on a solid lineup of fish, fowl, beef, pasta, and vegetarian entrées. A salad is served with each dinner entrée. There's also an appealing selection of appetizers and desserts. ✉ *3200 N.E. 12th Ave.,* ☎ *954/564–3663. AE, MC, V.*

$$$–$$$$ ✕ **Shula's on the Beach.** It's only fitting that Don Shula, who coached the Miami Dolphins to that Perfect Season in 1972 and is the "winningest" coach in NFL history, should have a winning South Florida steak house. The good news for steak—and sports—fans is that the staff here turns out winners. Certified Angus beef is cut thick and grilled over a superhot fire for quick charring. Try Steak Mary Anne, named for Shula's wife, consisting of two sliced fillets covered in a savory sauce.

Seafood is available, too. Outside tables provide views of sand and ocean; inside seating provides access to sports memorabilia and large-screen TVs. ✉ *Sheraton Yankee Trader, 321 N. Fort Lauderdale Beach Blvd.,* ☎ *954/355–4000. AE, D, DC, MC, V.*

$–$$$$ ✕ **Casa D'Angelo.** Owner-chef Angelo Elia has refashioned his former Café D'Angelo into a gem of a Tuscan-style restaurant. Almost everything is made from scratch, and the oak oven turns out marvelous seafood and beef dishes. The pappardelle with porcini mushrooms takes pasta to pleasant heights. Another favorite from the pasta menu is linguine with arugula, shrimp, and scallops. Ask about the oven-roasted fish of the day. ✉ *1201 N. Federal Hwy.,* ☎ *954/564–1234. AE, D, DC, MC, V. No lunch.*

$$–$$$ ✕ **Rustic Inn Crabhouse.** Wayne McDonald started with a cozy one-room roadhouse in 1955, when this stretch was a remote service road just west of the little airport. Now, the plain, rustic place is huge. The ample menu includes steamed crabs seasoned with garlic and herbs, spices, and oil, opened with mallets on tables covered with newspapers, and peel-and-eat shrimp, served either with garlic and butter or spiced and steamed with Old Bay seasoning. A slice of pie or cheesecake is a nice finisher. ✉ *4331 Ravenswood Rd.,* ☎ *954/584–1637. AE, D, DC, MC, V.*

¢–$ ✕ **Floridian.** This Las Olas landmark has been around for as long as anyone can remember and serves up one of the best breakfasts around. Locals flock here for oversize omelets, sausage, bacon, and biscuits. Servers can be brisk, bordering on brusque, but chalk it up as part of the experience. It's open 24 hours every day of the year—even during hurricanes, count on savory sandwiches and hot platters for lunch and dinner. ✉ *1410 E. Las Olas Blvd.,* ☎ *954/463–4041. No credit cards.*

Beaches

Fort Lauderdale's **beachfront** offers the best of all possible worlds, with easy access not only to a wide band of beige sand but also to restaurants and shops. For 2 mi heading north, beginning at the Bahia Mar yacht basin, along Route A1A you'll have clear views, typically across rows of colorful beach umbrellas, to the sea and ships passing into and out of nearby Port Everglades. If you're on the beach, gaze back on an exceptionally graceful promenade.

Pedestrians rank above cars in Fort Lauderdale. Broad walkways line both sides of the beach road, and traffic has been trimmed to two gently curving northbound lanes, where in-line skaters skim past slow-moving cars. On the beach side, a low masonry wall doubles as an extended bench, separating sand from the promenade. At night the wall is accented with ribbons of fiber-optic color. The most crowded portion of beach is between Las Olas and Sunrise boulevards. Tackier aspects of this onetime strip—famous for the springtime madness spawned by the film *Where the Boys Are*—are now but a fading memory.

North of the redesigned beachfront is another 2 mi of open and natural coastal landscape. Much of the way parallels the Hugh Taylor Birch State Recreation Area, preserving a patch of primeval Florida.

Shopping

When you're downtown, check out the **Las Olas Riverfront** (✉ 1 block west of Andrews Ave. on the New River), a shopping, dining, and entertainment complex. **Vogue Italia** (✉ Las Olas Riverfront, 300 S.W. 1st Ave., ☎ 954/527–4568) is packed with trendy fashions by D&G, Ferre, Versus, Moschino, Iceberg, and others, at wholesale prices.

If only for a stroll and some window-shopping, don't miss **Las Olas Boulevard** (✉ 1 block off New River east of Andrews Ave.). The city's best boutiques plus top restaurants and art galleries line a beautifully landscaped street. **Atlantic Yard** (✉ 2424 E. Las Olas Blvd., ☎ 954/779–1191) has everything for the avant gardener from unique and unusual gardening goods to stylish teak furniture. **Casa Chameleon** (✉ 619 E. Las Olas Blvd., ☎ 954/763–2543) carries decorative items, including antiques, linens, and beautiful things to top your table. **Kilwin's of Las Olas** (✉ 809 E. Las Olas Blvd., ☎ 954/523–8338) lures pedestrians with the sweet smell of waffle cones to this old-fashioned confectionery with hand-paddled fudge and scoops of homemade ice cream. **Lily Pulitzer by Lauderdale Lifestyle** (✉ 819 E. Las Olas Blvd., ☎ 954/524–5459) specializes in the South Florida dress requisite—clothing and accessories in Lily Pulitzer's signature tropical colors and prints. **Pino Formica** (✉ 825 E. Las Olas Blvd., ☎ 954/522–2479) focuses on sleek shoes, handbags, and belts from Furla, Fendi, Prada, and other Italian labels. **Seldom Seen** (✉ 817 E. Las Olas Blvd., ☎ 954/764–5590) is a gallery of contemporary and folk art, including furniture, jewelry, ceramics, sculpture, and blown glass with a whimsical touch. **Zola Keller** (✉ 818 E. Las Olas Blvd., ☎ 954/462–3222) caters to those looking for special-occasion dresses—cocktail dresses, evening gowns, and even Miss Florida and Mrs. America pageant dresses.

Just north of Las Olas Boulevard on Route A1A is the happening **Beach Place** (✉ 17 S. Fort Lauderdale Beach Blvd. [A1A]). Browse through shops, have lunch or dinner at restaurants ranging from casual Caribbean to elegant American, or check out a selection of nightspots—all open late. The upscale eateries are on the lower level; upstairs prices are lower, and the ocean view is better.

Just west of the Intracoastal Waterway, the split-level **Galleria Mall** (✉ 2414 E. Sunrise Blvd.) has more than 1 million square ft of retail space, anchored by Neiman-Marcus, Dillard's, Burdines, and Saks Fifth Avenue, with 150 specialty shops for anything from cookware to sportswear and fine jewelry.

Nightlife

Café Iguana (✉ Beach Place, 17 S. Fort Lauderdale Beach Blvd., ☎ 954/763–7222) has a nightly DJ to keep the dance floor hopping. **Chili Pepper** (✉ 200 W. Broward Blvd., ☎ 954/525–0094) brings hot rock bands to the stage of this warehouse-size open-air venue. **Howl at the Moon Saloon** (✉ Beach Place, 17 S. Fort Lauderdale Beach Blvd., ☎ 954/522–5054) has dueling piano players and sing-alongs nightly. **Maguire's Hill 16** (✉ 535 N. Andrews Ave., ☎ 954/764–4453) highlights excellent bands in classic Irish-pub surroundings. **O'Hara's Jazz Café** (✉ 722 E. Las Olas Blvd., ☎ 954/524–1764) belts out live jazz, blues, R&B, and funk nightly. Its packed crowd spills onto this prettiest of downtown streets. **Rush Street** (✉ 220 S.W. 2nd St., ☎ 954/522–6900) is where hipsters line up around the corner to gain access to one of the best martini bars in Broward County. **Side Bar** (✉ 210 S.W. 2nd St., ☎ 954/524–1818) has a contemporary industrial feel and a polished professional crowd. **Tarpon Bend** (✉ 200 S.W. 2nd St., ☎ 954/523–3233) specialties—food, fishing gear and bait, and bands playing current covers—draw a casual, beer-drinking crowd. **Tavern 213** (✉ 213 S.W. 2nd St., ☎ 954/463–6213) is a small, no-frills club where cover bands play classic rock nightly. **Voodoo Lounge** (✉ 111 S.W. 2nd Ave., ☎ 954/522–0733) plays the latest in club music inside the nightclub and high hip-hop on the elegant outside deck. The scene here doesn't start until close to midnight.

Exploring Fort Lauderdale

Like its southeast Florida neighbors, Fort Lauderdale has been busily revitalizing for several years. In a state where gaudy tourist zones often stand aloof from workaday downtowns, Fort Lauderdale is unusual in that the city exhibits consistency at both ends of the 2-mi Las Olas corridor. The sparkling look results from efforts to thoroughly improve both beachfront and downtown. Matching the downtown's innovative arts district, cafés, and boutiques is an equally inventive beach area with its own share of cafés and shops facing an undeveloped shoreline.

Numbers in the margin refer to points of interest on the Fort Lauderdale map.

✪ ❼ **Big Cypress Seminole Reservation.** Some distance from Fort Lauderdale's tranquil beaches, but worth the one-hour drive, is an accessible part of the Everglades. At the **Billie Swamp Safari,** experience the majesty of the Everglades firsthand. Daily tours of the wetlands and hammocks, where wildlife abound, yield sightings of deer, water buffalo, bison, wild hogs, hawks, eagles, alligators, and occasionally the rare Florida panther. Tours are conducted aboard motorized swamp buggies—designed to provide you with an elevated view of the frontier. ✉ *19 mi north of I–75 Exit 14,* ☎ *863/983–6101 or 800/949–6101,* WEB *www.seminoletribe.com.* ✆ *Free; combined ecotour, show, airboat ride $38.* ☉ *Daily 8–5.*

Not far from the Billie Swamp Safari is the **Ah-Tha-Thi-Ki Museum,** whose name means "a place to learn, a place to remember." The museum honors the culture and tradition of the Seminoles through artifacts and reenactments of rituals and ceremonies. The site includes a living-history Seminole village, nature trails, and a boardwalk through a cypress swamp. ✉ *17 mi north of I–75 Exit 14,* ☎ *863/902–1113,* WEB *www.seminoletribe.com.* ✆ *$6.* ☉ *Tues.–Sun. 9–5.*

❹ **Bonnet House.** A 35-acre oasis in the heart of the beach area, this subtropical estate is a tribute to the history of Old South Florida. The charming home was the winter residence of the late Frederic and Evelyn Bartlett, artists whose personal touches and small surprises are evident throughout. Whether you're interested in architecture, artwork, or the natural environment, this is a special place. Be on the lookout for playful monkeys swinging from trees, a source of amusement during even some of the most solemn weddings performed on the grounds. ✉ *900 N. Birch Rd.,* ☎ *954/563–5393,* WEB *www.bonnethouse.org.* ✆ *$9.* ☉ *Wed.–Fri. 10–3, weekends noon–4.*

❻ **Butterfly World.** As many as 80 butterfly species from South and Central America, the Philippines, Malaysia, Taiwan, and other Asian nations are typically found within this 3-acre site inside Tradewinds Park. A screened aviary called North American Butterflies is reserved for native species. The Tropical Rain Forest Aviary is a 30-ft-high structure, with observation decks, waterfalls, ponds, and tunnels where thousands of colorful butterflies flutter about. ✉ *3600 W. Sample Rd., Coconut Creek,* ☎ *954/977–4400,* WEB *www.butterflyworld.com.* ✆ *$13.95.* ☉ *Mon.–Sat. 9–5, Sun. 1–5.*

❺ **Hugh Taylor Birch State Recreation Area.** Amid the tropical greenery of this 180-acre park, stroll along a nature trail, visit the Birch House Museum, picnic, play volleyball, pitch horseshoes, and paddle a rented canoe. Since parking is limited on A1A, park here and take a walkway underpass to the beach (between 9 and 5). ✉ *3109 E. Sunrise Blvd.,* ☎ *954/564–4521,* WEB *www.abfla.com/parks.* ✆ *$3.25 per vehicle with up to 8 people.* ☉ *Daily 8–sunset; ranger-guided nature walks Fri. at 10:30.*

❶ **Museum of Art.** In an Edward Larrabee Barnes–designed building that's considered an architectural masterpiece, this museum's permanent collection features 20th-century European and American art, including works by Picasso, Calder, Dalí, Mapplethorpe, Warhol, and

Stella, as well as a notable collection of works by celebrated Ashcan School artist William Glackens. Opened in 1986, the museum helped launch revitalization of the downtown district and nearby Riverwalk area. ✉ *1 E. Las Olas Blvd.,* ☎ *954/763–6464,* WEB *www.museumofart. org.* 🎫 *$7.* ☼ *Tues.–Sat. 10–5, Sun. noon–5.*

❸ **Museum of Discovery and Science/Blockbuster IMAX Theater.** The aim here is to show children—*and* adults—the wonders of science in an entertaining fashion. The 52-ft-tall Great Gravity Clock in the courtyard entrance lets arrivals know a cool experience awaits. Exhibits include Choose Health, about healthy lifestyle choices; Kidscience, encouraging youngsters to explore the world around them; and Gizmo City, a look at how gadgets work. Florida Ecoscapes has a living coral reef as well as live bees, bats, frogs, turtles, and alligators. The IMAX theater shows films (some 3-D) on a five-story screen. ✉ *401 S.W. 2nd St.,* ☎ *954/467–6637 for museum; 954/463–4629 for IMAX,* WEB *www.mods. org.* 🎫 *Museum $14, includes one IMAX show.* ☼ *Mon.–Sat. 10–5, Sun. noon–6.*

❷ **Riverwalk.** Fantastic views and entertainment prevail on this lovely, paved promenade on the New River's north bank. On the first Sunday of every month a jazz brunch attracts visitors. The walk has been extended 2 mi on both sides of the beautiful urban stream, connecting the facilities of the Arts and Science District.

BOAT TOURS
Water Taxi was started by longtime resident Bob Bekoff, who decided to combine the need for transportation with one of the area's most appealing features: miles of waterways that make the city known as the Venice of America. The taxi will pick you up at any of several hotels along the Intracoastal Waterway, and you can stop off at attractions like the Performing Arts Center or Beach Place. For lunch, enjoy a restaurant on Las Olas Boulevard or Las Olas Riverfront. In the evening, water taxis are a great way to go out to dinner or bar-hop, without the worry of choosing a designated driver. Water Taxi and Broward County Mass Transit have partnered to create Water Buses. These environmentally friendly electric ferries can carry up to 70 passengers. Ride either the water taxi or water bus unlimited from 6:30 AM to 12:30 AM for $5 (one-way adult fare is $4). The best way to use the water taxi or bus is to call about 20 minutes ahead of your desired pickup time, or check the schedule on the company's Web site. ☎ *954/467–6677,* WEB *www.watertaxi.com.*

GALVESTON

A thin strip of island in the Gulf of Mexico, Galveston is big sister Houston's beach playground—a year-round coastal destination just 50 mi away. Many of the first public buildings in Texas, including a post office, bank, and hotel, were built here, but most were destroyed in the Great Storm of 1900. Those that endured have been well preserved, and the Victorian character of The Strand shopping district and the neighborhood surrounding Broadway is still evident. On the Galveston Bay side of the island (northeast), quaint shops and cafés in old buildings are near the Seaport Museum, harborfront eateries, and the cruise-ship terminal. On the Gulf of Mexico side (southwest), resorts and restaurants line coastal Seawall Boulevard. The 17-ft-high seawall abuts a long ribbon of sand and provides a place for rollerblading, bicycling, and going on the occasional surrey ride.

Galveston is a port of embarkation for cruises on Western Caribbean itineraries; some Panama Canal cruises leave from here as well. It's an especially popular port of embarkation for people living in the south-eastern states who don't wish to fly to their cruise. Both Carnival and Royal Caribbean have made Galveston the homeport for two ships.

The Cruise Port

The relatively sheltered waters of Galveston Bay are home to the Texas Cruise Ship Terminal. It's only 30 minutes to open water from here. Driving south from Houston on I–45, you cross a long causeway before reaching the island. Take the first exit, Harborside Drive, left after you've crossed the causeway on to Galveston Island. Follow that for a few miles to the port. Turn left on 22nd Street (also called Kemper Street); there is a security checkpoint before you continue down a driveway. The drop-off point is set up much like an airport terminal, with pull-through lanes and curbside check-in.

➤ CONTACTS: **Port of Galveston** (✉ Harborside Dr. and 22nd St., ☎ 409/765–9321, WEB www.portofgalveston.com).

AIRPORT TRANSFERS

The closest airports are in Houston, 50 mi from Galveston. Houston has two major airports: Hobby Airport, 9 mi southeast of downtown, and George Bush Intercontinental, 15 mi northeast of the city.

Unless you have arranged airport transfers through your cruise line, you'll have to make arrangements to navigate the miles between the Houston airport you land at and the cruise-ship terminal in Galveston. Galveston Limousine Service provides scheduled transportation (return reservations required) between either airport and Galveston hotels or the cruise-ship terminal. Hobby is a shorter ride (1 hour, $50 round-trip), but Intercontinental (2 hours, $60 round-trip) is served by more airlines, including international carriers. Taking a taxi allows you to set your own schedule but can cost twice as much. Negotiate the price before you get in.

➤ CONTACTS: **Galveston Limousine Service** (☎ 800/640–4826, WEB www.galvestonlimousineservice.com).

PARKING

Parking is coordinated by the Port Authority. After you drop off your checked luggage and passengers at the terminal, you receive a color-coded parking pass from the attendant, with directions to the north or south lot, depending on which cruise you're taking. Both are approximately ½ mi back the way you came. Check-in, parking, and boarding are generally allowed four hours prior to departure. A shuttle bus (carry-on luggage only) runs back and forth between the lots and the ship every 7 to 12 minutes on cruise arrival and departure days (be sure to drop off your luggage *before* you park the car). The lot is closed other days. Port Authority security checks the well-lit, fenced-in lots every two hours. Parking for a 5-day cruise is $45, 7-day is $60, and 11-day is $80. Make sure to bring cash, because it's all that's accepted—and you have to pay in advance.

VISITOR INFORMATION

➤ CONTACTS: **Galveston Island Convention & Visitors Bureau** (✉ 2102 Seawall Blvd., 77550, ☎ 409/763–6564 or 888/425–4753, WEB www.galveston.com; Strand Visitors Center, ✉ 2016 Strand, ☎ 713/280–3907).

Where to Stay

For price categories, *see* Lodging at the beginning of this chapter.

$$–$$$$ ⊞ **San Luis Resort.** A long marble staircase alongside a slender fountain with sculpted dolphins welcomes you to the waterfront elegance of this resort. The upper-floor facade isn't much to look at, but don't

let that fool you; inside, the colors of the cool, cream marble and taupe stone in the lobby are echoed in the guest rooms. The sculptural lines of pink granite on the headboards and armchairs say Italian villa. All rooms have balconies facing the gulf, and prices rise with the floor height. Back on ground level, step into the meandering (and heated) grotto pool with a rock waterfall set amid coconut palms and bougainvillea; then have a Balinese massage (or a wildflower compress) at the Spa San Luis. ⊠ *5222 Seawall Blvd., 77551,* ☎ *409/744–1500 or 800/445–0090,* 🖹 *409/744–8452,* 🖥 *www.sanluisresort.com. 246 rooms. Restaurant, café, grill, room service, in-room data ports, cable TV, 2 tennis courts, 2 pools, health club, outdoor hot tub, spa, 2 bars, dry cleaning, business services, helipad, no-smoking rooms. AE, D, DC, MC, V.*

$$–$$$ 🏨 **Hotel Galvez.** This renovated six-story Spanish colonial hotel, built in 1911, was once called "Queen of the Gulf." Teddy Roosevelt and Howard Hughes were just two of the many well-known guests who have stayed here. Traditional dark wood and plush upholstery pieces furnish both the public and private areas. A pool, swim-up bar, and outdoor grill have been added to the tropical garden facing the sea. ⊠ *2024 Seawall Blvd., 77550,* ☎ *409/765–7721,* 🖹 *409/765–5780,* 🖥 *www.wyndham.com. 231 rooms. Restaurant, cable TV, pool, health club, hot tub, Internet, business services, meeting rooms, no-smoking rooms. AE, DC, MC, V.*

$$–$$$ 🏨 **Stacia Leigh.** Step aboard a 1906 two-story schooner for a harborside stay at a floating bed-and-breakfast near the *Elissa* and in sight of the port. White wicker furniture and multicolor quilts reflect the coastal Americana theme. Choose the Bradley or the Roosevelt Room for their bow-shaped, teak-paneled walls with small windows that provide 280° harbor views. There's a two-night minimum stay from May to October; ask about special packages and discounts. Free parking is available for guests going on cruises. ⊠ *Pier 22, Harborside Dr. and 22nd St., 77550,* ☎ *409/750–8858,* 🖥 *www.stacia-leigh.com. 11 rooms. Dining room, hot tub, recreation room; no room TVs, no-smoking rooms. AE, D, DC, MC, V. BP*

$–$$ 🏨 **Tremont House.** A four-story atrium lobby, with ironwork balconies and full-size palm trees, showcases an 1872 hand-carved rosewood bar in what was once a busy dry-goods warehouse. It is actually a historic place: Republic of Texas president Sam Houston presented his last speech at this hotel, both Confederate and Union soldiers bunked here, and Great Storm victims took refuge under this roof. Rooms have high ceilings and 11-ft windows. Period reproduction furniture and Victorian-pattern wallpapers add to the authenticity. It's the closest full-service lodging to the port, just a short walk from shopping on The Strand. ⊠ *2300 Ship's Mechanic Row, 77550,* ☎ *409/763–0300,* 🖹 *409/763–1539,* 🖥 *www.wyndham.com. 119 rooms. Restaurant, room service, cable TV with movies, golf privileges, bar, meeting rooms, no-smoking rooms. AE, D, DC, MC, V.*

Where to Eat

For price categories, *see* Dining at the beginning of this chapter.

$$–$$$ ✗ **Luigi's Ristorante Italiano.** One taste of the cannelloni with four cheeses or linguine *fruitti di mare* (with seafood) and you will think you walked into a trattoria in Florence instead of a converted 1895 bank building on The Strand. Northern Italian cuisine is served in Tuscan style amid muted sienna walls, a fruitwood-panel bar, and mural-size replicas of Italian art. Valet parking is complimentary. ⊠ *2318 Strand,* ☎ *409/ 763–6500. AE, D, DC, MC, V, No dinner Sun.*

$$–$$$ ✗ **Mosquito Café.** This chichi eatery in Galveston's historic East End serves fresh, contemporary food—some vegetarian—in a hip, high-ceilinged dining room and on an outdoor patio. Wake up to a fluffy egg frittata or a homemade scone topped with whipped cream, or try a large gourmet salad later on. The grilled snapper with Parmesan grits is a hit in the evening. ✉ *628 14th St.,* ☎ *409/763–1010. AE, D, DC, MC, V. No dinner Sun.–Wed.*

$–$$$ ✕ **Fisherman's Wharf.** New restaurants have sprung up to provide competition for the Landry's-owned harborside institution, but locals keep coming here for the reliably fresh seafood and reasonable prices. Dine indoors or watch the boat traffic (and waiting cruise ships) from the patio. Start with a cold combo, like boiled shrimp and grilled rare tuna. The fried fish, shrimp, and oysters are hard to beat as an entrée. ✉ *Pier 22, Harborside Dr. and 22nd St.,* ☎ *409/765–5708. AE, D, DC, MC, V.*

¢–$ ✕ **The Phoenix Bakery & Coffee House.** Every community needs a gathering place with the smell of fresh baked goods in the air. The New Orleans beignets, croissants, muffins, and other pastries at the Phoenix are impossible to resist. They also brew a flavorful cup of espresso and cook full breakfasts. Lunch is homemade soups, sandwiches, and maybe a slice of pie—old-fashioned apple, banana cream, bourbon pecan, or chocolate mousse, anyone? ✉ *221 Tremont St., at 23rd St.,* ☎ *409/ 763–4611. AE, D, DC, MC, V. No dinner.*

Beaches

The **Seawall** (✉ Seawall Blvd. from 61st St. to 25th St.) on the gulf-side waterfront attracts runners, cyclists, and rollerbladers. Just below it is a long, free beach near many big hotels and resorts. **Stewart Beach Park** (✉ 6th St. and Seawall Blvd., ☎ 409/765–5023) has a bathhouse, amusement park, bumper boats, miniature-golf course, and a water coaster in addition to saltwater and sand. It's open weekdays 9–5, weekends 8–6 from March to May; weekdays 8–6 and weekends 8–7 from June to September; and weekends 9–5 during the first two weekends of October. Admission is $5 per vehicle. **Galveston Island State Park** (✉ 3 Mile Rd., 10 mi southwest on Seawall Blvd., ☎ 409/737–1222), on the western, unpopulated end of the island, is a 2,000-acre natural beach habitat ideal for birding, walking, and renewing your spirit. It's open daily from 8 AM to 10 PM; admission is $3.

Shopping

The **Strand** is the best place to shop in Galveston. Old storefronts are filled with gift shops, antiques stores, and one-of-a-kind boutiques. The area is bounded by Strand and Postoffice Street (running east–west) and 25th and 19th streets (running north–south). More than 50 antiques dealers are represented at **Eiband's Gallery** (✉ 2001 Postoffice St., ☎ 409/ 763–5495), an upscale showroom filled with furniture, books, art, and jewelry. **Old Strand Emporium** (✉ 2112 Strand, ☎ 409/763–9445) is a charming deli and grocery reminiscent of an old-fashioned ice cream parlor and sandwich shop, with candy bins, packaged nuts, and more.

Nightlife

For a relaxing evening, choose any of the harborside restaurant-bars on Piers 21 and 22 to sip a glass of wine or a frozen Hurricane as you watch the boats go by.

The **Grand 1894 Opera House** (✉ 2020 Postoffice St., ☎ 409/765–1894 or 800/821–1894, 🆆🅴🅱 www.thegrand.com) stages musicals and hosts concerts year-round. It's worth visiting for the ornate architecture alone. Sarah Bernhardt and Anna Pavlova both performed on this storied stage.

Exploring Galveston

Broadway. The late 1800s were the heyday of Galveston's port (before Houston's was dug out). Victorian splendor is evident in the meticulously restored homes of this historic district, some of which are now museums. **Moody Mansion** (⊠ 2618 Broadway, ☎ 409/762–7668), the residence of generations of one of Texas's most powerful families, was completed in 1895. Tour its interiors of exotic woods and gilded trim filled with family heirlooms and personal effects. **Ashton Villa** (⊠ 2328 Broadway, ☎ 409/762–3933), a formal Italianate villa, was built in 1859 of brick. Look for the curtains that shielded the more modest Victorian guests from the naked Cupids painted on one wall. If you're in town the first two weekends of May, don't miss the **Galveston Historic Homes Tour.** In addition to visiting the neighborhood's museums, you can walk through privately owned homes dating from the 1800s. For more information about area house museums or the tour, contact the Heritage Visitors Center. ⊠ *2328 Broadway,* ☎ *409/765–7834.* ☞ *Visitor center free, museums $6 each, tour $20.* ☉ *Mon.–Sat. 10–4, Sun. noon–4.*

☾ **Moody Gardens** is a multifaceted entertainment and educational complex inside pastel-colored glass pyramid buildings. Attractions include the 13-story **Aquarium Pyramid,** showcasing marine life from four oceans in tanks and touch pools; **Rainforest Pyramid,** a 40,000-square-ft tropical habitat for exotic flora and fauna; **Discovery Pyramid,** a joint venture with NASA featuring more than 40 interactive exhibits; and two **IMAX theaters,** one of which has a space adventure ride. Outside, **Palm Beach** has white-sand beach, landscaped grounds, man-made lagoons, a kid-size water slide and games, and beach chairs. ⊠ *1 Hope Blvd.,* ☎ *409/741–8484 or 800/582–4673,* WEB *www.moodygardens.com.* ☞ *$8–$13 per venue, $30 day pass.* ☉ *Memorial Day–Labor Day, daily 10–9; Labor Day–Memorial Day, weekdays 10–6, weekends 10–8.*

Pier 21 Theater. At this theater on The Strand, watch the Great Storm of 1900 come back to life in a multimedia presentation that includes video clips of archival drawings, still photos, and narrated accounts from survivors' diaries. Also playing is a film about the exploits of pirate Jean Lafitte, who used the island as a base. ⊠ *Pier 21, Harborside Dr. and 21st St.,* ☎ *409/763–8808,* WEB *www.galvestonhistory. org/plc-pier21.htm.* ☞ *Great Storm $3.50, Pirate Island $2.50.* ☉ *Sun.–Thurs. 11–6, Fri.–Sat. 11–8.*

The Strand. This shopping area is defined by the architecture of its 19th- and early-20th-century buildings, many of which survived the storm of 1900 and are on the National Register of Historic Places. When Galveston was still a powerful port city—before the Houston Ship Channel was dug, diverting most boat traffic inland—this stretch, formerly the site of stores, offices, and warehouses, was known as the Wall Street of the South. As you stroll up The Strand, you pass dozens of shops and cafés. ⊠ *Between Strand and Postoffice St., 25th and 19th Sts.*

Texas Seaport Museum. Aboard the restored 1877 tall ship *Elissa* detailed interpretive signs provide information about the shipping trade in the 1800s, including the routes and cargos this ship carried into Galveston. Inside the museum building is a replica of the historic wharf and information about the ethnic groups that immigrated through this U.S. point of entry after 1837. ⊠ *Pier 21,* ☎ *409/763–1877,* WEB *www. tsm-elissa.org.* ☞ *$6.* ☉ *Daily 10–5.*

MIAMI

Miami is the busiest of Florida's very busy cruise ports. Because there's so much going on here, you might want to schedule an extra day or two before and/or after your cruise to explore North America's most Latin city. Downtown is a convenient place to stay if you are meeting up with a cruise ship, but at night, except for Bayside Marketplace, the American Airlines Arena, and a few ever-changing clubs in ware-

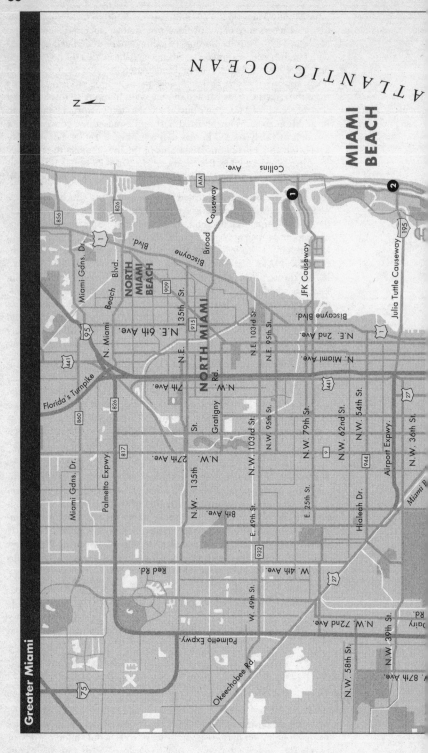

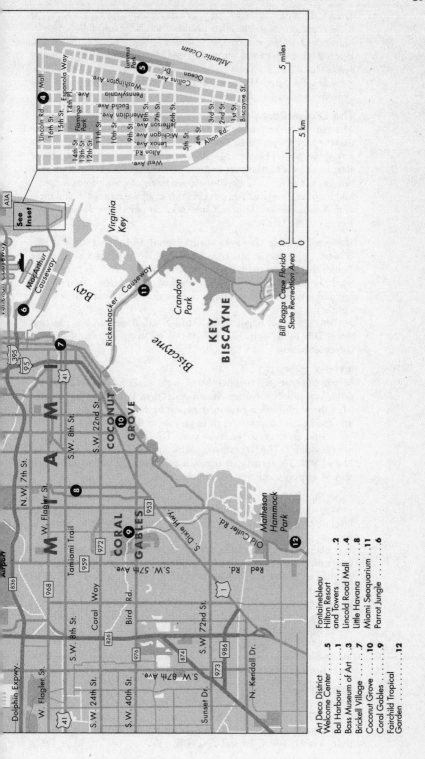

Inset:

Lincoln Rd. **4** Mall
16th St.
15th St.
14th Pl.
14th St.
13th St.
12th St.
Flamingo Park
Espanola Way
Ave.
Euclid Ave.
Pennsylvania Ave.
Meridian Ave.
Michigan Ave.
Jefferson Ave.
11th St.
10th St.
9th St.
8th St.
Lenox Ave.
Alton Rd.
West Ave.
Washington Ave.
Ocean Dr.
Collins Ave.
Lummus Park **5**
5th St.
4th St.
3rd St.
2nd St.
1st St.
Alton Rd.
Biscayne St.
Atlantic Ocean

5 miles
5 km

See Inset
A1A

MacArthur Causeway **6**
MIAMI
N.W. 7th St.
W. Flagler St. **8**
Dolphin Expwy.
W. Flagler St.
S.W. 8th St.
S.W. 24th St.
S.W. 40th St.
S.W. 57th Ave.
S.W. 72nd St.
S.W. 87th Ave.
Sunset Dr.
N. Kendall Dr.
Coral Way
Bird Rd.
Red Rd.
Tamiami Trail
CORAL GABLES **9**
S. Dixie Hwy.
Old Cutler Rd.
Matheson Hammock Park
COCONUT GROVE **10**
S.W. 22nd St.
S.W. 8th St.
7
Rickenbacker Causeway **11**
Virginia Key
Biscayne Bay
Crandon Park
KEY BISCAYNE
Bill Baggs Cape Florida State Recreation Area
12

Airport
836
968
976
874
973
986
959
972
953
826
41
395
95
41
A1A
1

Legend:

Art Deco District **5**
Welcome Center
Bal Harbour **1**
Bass Museum of Art ..**3**
Brickell Village **7**
Coconut Grove **10**
Coral Gables **9**
Fairchild Tropical **12**
Garden

Fontainebleau **2**
Hilton Resort
and Towers
Lincoln Road Mall **4**
Little Havana **8**
Miami Seaquarium ...**11**
Parrot Jungle **6**

houses, the area is deserted. Travelers spend little time here, since most tourist attractions are in other neighborhoods. Miami Beach, particularly the 1-square-mi Art Deco District in South Beach—the section below 24th–28th streets—is the heart of Miami's vibrant nightlife and restaurant scene. But you may also want to explore beyond the beach, including the Little Havana, Coral Gables, and Coconut Grove sections of the city.

The Cruise Port

The Port of Miami, in downtown Miami near Bayside Marketplace and the MacArthur Causeway, justifiably bills itself as the Cruise Capital of the World. Home to 18 ships and the largest year-round cruise fleet in the world, the port accommodates more than 3 million passengers a year. It has 12 air-conditioned terminals, duty-free shopping, and limousine service. You can get taxis at all the terminals, and there is an Avis location at the port, while other car-rental agencies offer shuttles to off-site lots.

If you are driving, take I–95 north or south to I–395. Follow the directional signs to the Biscayne Blvd. exit. When you get to Biscayne Boulevard, make a right. Go to 5th Street, which becomes Port Boulevard (look for the American Airlines Basketball Arena); then make a left and go over the Port bridge. Follow the directional signs to your terminal.

➤ CONTACTS: **Port of Miami** (⊠ 1015 North American Way, Miami, ☎ 305/371–7678 or 305/347–4860, WEB www.co.miami-dade.fl.us/portofmiami).

AIRPORT TRANSFERS

Miami International Airport (MIA), 6 mi west of downtown Miami, is the only airport in Greater Miami. More than 1,400 daily flights make MIA the ninth-busiest passenger airport in the world. If you have not arranged an airport transfer through your cruise line, you have a couple of options to get to the cruise port. The first is a taxi, and the fares are reasonable. The fare between MIA and the Port of Miami is a flat fare of $18. This fare is per trip, not per passenger, and includes tolls and $1 airport surcharge but not tip.

SuperShuttle vans transport passengers between MIA and local hotels, as well as the Port of Miami. At MIA the vans pick up at the ground level of each concourse (look for clerks with yellow shirts, who will flag one down). Drivers provide narration en route. Service from MIA is available around the clock on demand; for the return it's best to make reservations 24 hours in advance, although SuperShuttle can sometimes arrange pickups on as little as four hours' notice. The cost from MIA to downtown hotels runs $9–$13; to the beaches it can be $13–$17 per passenger, depending on how far north you go. Additional members of a party pay a lower rate for many destinations, and children under three ride free. There's a pet transport fee of $5 for a cat, $8 for a dog under 50 pounds in kennels.

➤ CONTACTS: **SuperShuttle** (☎ 305/871–2000 from MIA; 954/764–1700 from Broward [Fort Lauderdale]; 800/874–8885 from elsewhere).

PARKING

Street-level lots are right in front of each of the cruise terminals. The cost is $10 per day ($20 for RVs), payable in advance. You can pay with a credit card at most terminals (except for numbers 2 and 10), though it's MasterCard and Visa only.

VISITOR INFORMATION

➤ CONTACTS: **Greater Miami Convention & Visitors Bureau** (⊠ 701 Brickell Ave., Suite 2700, Downtown, 33131, ☎ 305/539–3063 or 800/

283–2707, WEB www.miamiandbeaches.com; Bayside Marketplace Visitor Center, ✉ 401 Biscayne Blvd., Bayside Marketplace, Miami 33132, ☎ 305/539–2980).

Where to Stay

Staying in downtown Miami will put you close to the cruise terminals, but there is little to do at night. South Beach is the center of the action in Miami Beach, but it's fairly distant from the port. Staying in Miami Beach, but north of South Beach's Art Deco District, will put you on the beach but nominally closer to the port.

For price categories, see Lodging at the beginning of this chapter.

$$$$ 🏨 **Hyatt Regency Miami.** The Hyatt is well positioned to enjoy the fruits of Miami's late-1990s renaissance—the Miami Avenue Bridge, the Port of Miami, and AmericanAirlines Arena seemed to sprout up around it—so if your vacation is based on boats, basketball, or business, you can't do much better. The distinctive public spaces are more colorful than businesslike, and guest rooms are done in an unusual combination of avocado, beige, and blond. Rooms also yield views of the river or port. The James L. Knight International Center is accessible without stepping outside, as are the downtown Metromover and its Metrorail connection. ✉ 400 S.E. 2nd Ave., Downtown, 33131, ☎ 305/358–1234 or 800/233–1234, FAX 305/358–0529, WEB www.miami.hyatt.com. 612 rooms, 51 suites. Restaurant, pool, health club, 2 bars, laundry service, concierge, business services, parking (fee). AE, D, DC, MC, V.

$$$$ 🏨 **Mandarin Oriental Miami.** Though it's a favorite of Wall Street tycoons and Latin American CEOs doing business with the Brickell Avenue banks, anyone who can afford to stay here won't regret it. The location is excellent, at the tip of Brickell Key in Biscayne Bay; rooms facing west have a panoramic view of the dazzling downtown skyline, while those facing east overlook Miami Beach and the blue Atlantic beyond. The Mandarin is fanatically picky about details, from the Bulova alarm clocks and hand-painted room numbers on rice paper to the recessed data ports on room desks that eliminate laptop cord clutter. ✉ 500 Brickell Key Dr., Brickell Key, 33131, ☎ 305/913–8288 or 866/888–6780, FAX 305/913–8300, WEB www.mandarinoriental.com. 329 rooms. Restaurant, in-room data ports, in-room safes, pool, spa, 2 bars, dry cleaning, laundry service, concierge, business services, meeting rooms, parking (fee). AE, D, DC, MC, V.

$$$–$$$$ 🏨 **Loews Miami Beach Hotel.** Unlike other neighborhood properties that are renovations of older hotels, this 18-story, 800-room gem was built from the blueprints up. Not only did Loews manage to snag 99 ft of beach, it also took over the vacant St. Moritz next door and restored it to its original 1939 art deco splendor, adding another 100 rooms to the complex. The resort has kids' programs, a health spa, 85,000 square ft of meeting space, and an enormous ocean-view grand ballroom. Dining, too, is a pleasure, courtesy of the Argentine-inspired Gaucho Room, Preston's South Beach Coffee Bar, and Hemisphere Lounge. ✉ 1601 Collins Ave., South Beach, Miami Beach 33139, ☎ 305/604–1601, FAX 305/531–8677, WEB www.loewshotels.com. 740 rooms, 50 suites. 4 restaurants, pool, spa, beach, 2 bars, lobby lounge, children's programs (ages 4–12), meeting room. AE, D, DC, MC, V.

$$$–$$$$ 🏨 **Wyndham Miami Beach Resort.** Of the great Miami Beach hotels, this 18-story modern glass tower is a standout. Its polished staff provides exceptional service, from helping you find the best shopping to bringing you an icy drink on the beach. The bright rooms have a tropical blue color scheme and are filled with attentive details: minirefrigerators, three layers of drapes (including blackout curtains), big closets, and bathrooms with high-end toiletries and magnifying mirrors. Two presidential suites were designed in consultation with the Secret Service, and a rooftop meeting room offers views of bay and ocean. ⊠ *4833 Collins Ave., Mid-Beach, Miami Beach 33140,* ☎ *305/532–3600 or 800/203–8368,* FAX *305/534–7409,* WEB *www.wyndham.com. 378 rooms, 46 suites. 2 restaurants, tennis court, pool, gym, massage, beach, 2 bars, meeting room. AE, D, DC, MC, V.*

$–$$$ 🖪 **Royal Hotel.** *Austin Powers* meets *2001: A Space Odyssey* in this avant-garde hotel, which doesn't take itself too seriously. Each room really has only two pieces of furniture: a "digital chaise longue" and a bed, both molded white plastic contortions from designer Jordan Mozer. The bed's projecting wings hold a phone and alarm clock. The headboard arcs back like a car spoiler and doubles as a minibar, filled to your taste. The chaise longue holds a TV/Web TV and keyboard for surfing the Net. A wild shag carpet and rainbow-paisley bathrobes remind you you're here to have fun—*Yeah, baby.* ⊠ *758 Washington Ave., South Beach, Miami Beach 33139,* ☎ *305/673–9009 or 888/394–6835,* FAX *305/673–9244,* WEB *www.royalhotelsouthbeach.com. 38 rooms, 4 suites. In-room data ports, laundry service, business services, meeting room. AE, D, DC, MC, V.*

¢–$$$ 🖪 **Days Inn Oceanside/Beach Front.** Pets are allowed at this eight-story budget hotel not far from the renowned and much more expensive Eden Roc and Fontainebleau resorts. North of the protected Art Deco District, this lodging survives in an area where older hotels are fast giving way to the wrecking ball and high-rise resorts. Expect to pay the top price for rooms with an ocean view, but all rooms are just steps from the beach and the tiki bar, where you can conjure dreams of Margaritaville. The rooms, however, are no-nonsense, with two double beds or one king and a color TV. ⊠ *4299 Collins Ave., Mid-Beach, Miami Beach 33141,* ☎ *305/673–1513 or 800/825–6800,* FAX *305/538–0727,* WEB *www.daysinn.com. 143 rooms. 2 restaurants, in-room safes, pool, bar, dry cleaning, laundry facilities, parking (fee). AE, DC, MC, V.*

Where to Eat

Restaurants listed here have passed the test of time, but you might double-check by phone before you set out for the evening. At many of the hottest spots, you'll need a reservation to avoid a long wait for a table. And when you get your check, note whether a gratuity is included; most restaurants add 15% (ostensibly for the convenience of, and protection from, Latin-American and European tourists who are used to this practice in their homelands), but you can reduce or supplement it depending on your opinion of the service.

For price categories, *see* Dining at the beginning of this chapter.

$$$–$$$$ ✗ **Nemo.** The open-air setting, bright colors, copper fixtures, and tree-shaded courtyard lend casual comfort, but it's the menu that earns the raves. Caribbean, Asian, Mediterranean, and Middle Eastern influences blend boldly, and succeed. Popular appetizers include garlic-cured salmon rolls with Tabiko caviar and wasabi mayo, and crispy prawns with spicy salsa *cruda.* Main courses might include wok-charred salmon or Indian-spice pork chop. Hedy Goldsmith's funky pastries are exquisite. ⊠ *100 Collins Ave., South Beach, Miami Beach,* ☎ *305/532–4550. AE, DC, MC, V.*

$$$–$$$$ ✗ **Pacific Time.** Packed nearly every night, chef-proprietor Jonathan Eismann's superb eatery has a high blue ceiling, banquettes, plank floors, and an open kitchen. The brilliant American-Asian food includes such masterpieces as Sizzling Local Yellowtail Hot & Sour Tempura, a crisp, ginger-stuffed whole fish served filleted over ribbon vegetables with herbs and a dipping sauce, and dry-aged Colorado beef grilled with shiitake mushrooms and bok choy. Diners can start with a spicy coconut curry of local pink shrimp and end with a soothing tropical sorbet. ✉ *915 Lincoln Rd., South Beach, Miami Beach,* ☎ *305/534–5979. Reservations essential. AE, DC, MC, V.*

$$–$$$$ ✕ **Azul.** This sumptuous eatery has conquered the devil in the details. In addition to chef Michelle Bernstein's exquisite French-Caribbean cuisine, the thoughtful touches in service graciously anticipate your needs. Does your sleeveless top mean your shoulders are too cold to properly appreciate the poached eggs with lobster-knuckle hollandaise? Ask for one of the house pashminas. Forgot your reading glasses and can't decipher the hanger steak with foie gras sauce? Request a pair from the host. Want to see how the other half lives? Descend the staircase to Cafe Sambal, the all-day casual restaurant. ✉ *Mandarin Oriental Hotel, 500 Brickell Key Dr., Brickell Key,* ☎ *305/913–8288. Reservations essential. AE, MC, V. Closed Sun. No lunch Sat.*

$–$$$$ ✕ **Tony Chan's Water Club.** An outstanding Chinese restaurant, this dining room, just off the lobby of the Doubletree Grand Hotel, overlooks a bayside marina. On the menu of more than 200 appetizers and entrées are minced quail tossed with bamboo shoots and mushrooms wrapped in lettuce leaves. Indulge in a seafood spectacular of shrimp, conch, scallops, fish cakes, and crabmeat tossed with broccoli in a bird's nest, or go for pork chops sprinkled with green pepper in a black bean-garlic sauce. A lighter favorite is steamed sea bass with ginger and garlic. ✉ *1717 N. Bayshore Dr., Downtown,* ☎ *305/374–8888. AE, D, DC, MC, V. No lunch weekends.*

¢–$$$ ✕ **Los Ranchos.** This steak-house chain sustains the tradition of Managua's original Los Ranchos by serving Argentine-style beef—lean, grass-fed tenderloin served with three Nicaraguan sauces. There are *chimichurri* (a thick sauce of olive oil, vinegar, cayenne, and herbs), a tomato-based marinara, and a fiery *cebollitas encurtidas* (with jalapeño and pickled onion). In addition to churrasco steak, specialties include spicy chorizo and an appetizer of fried cheese and plantain chips with a spicy dipping sauce. Don't look for veggies or elaborate salads—that's just not the Latin way—but there is live entertainment. ✉ *Bayside Marketplace, 401 Biscayne Blvd., Downtown,* ☎ *305/375–8188 or 305/375–0666;* ✉ *CocoWalk, 3015 Grand Ave., Coconut Grove,* ☎ *305/461–8222;* ✉ *125 S.W. 107th Ave., Sweetwater,* ☎ *305/221–9367;* ✉ *2728 Ponce de León Blvd., Coral Gables,* ☎ *305/446–0050;* ✉ *The Falls, 8888 S.W. 136th St., Suite 303, Kendall, Miami,* ☎ *305/238–6867 AE, DC, MC, V.*

¢–$$ ✕ **Café Prima Pasta.** One of Miami's many signatures is this exemplary Argentine-Italian spot, which rules the emerging North Beach neighborhood. Service can be erratic, but you forget it all on delivery of fresh-made bread with a bowl of spiced olive oil. Tender carpaccio and plentiful antipasti are a delight to share, but the real treat here is the hand-rolled pasta, which can range from crab-stuffed ravioli to simple fettuccine with seafood. If overexposed tiramisu hasn't made an enemy of you yet, try this legendary one in order to add espresso notes to your unavoidable garlic breath. ✉ *414 71st St., North Beach, Miami Beach,* ☎ *305/867–0106. MC, V.*

Beaches

The **beach on Ocean Drive from 1st to 22nd Street**—primarily the 10-block stretch from 5th to 15th Street—is one of the most talked-about beachfronts in America. The beach is wide, white, and bathed by warm aquamarine waves. Separating the sand from the traffic of Ocean Drive is palm-fringed Lummus Park, with its volleyball nets and chickee huts for shade. The beach also has some of the funkiest lifeguard stands you'll ever see, pop stars shooting music videos, and visitors from all over the world. Popular with gays is the beach at **12th Street.** Because much of South Beach has an adult flavor—women are often casually topless—many families prefer the beach's quieter southern reaches, especially **3rd Street Beach** (✉ Ocean Dr. and 3rd St., South

Beach). Unless you're parking south of 3rd Street, metered spaces near the waterfront are rarely empty. Instead, opt for a public garage and walk; you'll have lots of fun people-watching, too. ☎ *305/673–7714*

Haulover Beach Park. At this county park, far from the action of SoBe, you can see the Miami of 30 years ago. Pack a picnic, use the barbecue grills, or grab a snack at the concession stand. If you're into fitness, you may like the tennis and volleyball courts or paths designed for exercise, walking, and bicycling. The beach is nice for those who want water without long marches across hot sand, and a popular clothing-optional section at the north end of the beach lures people who want to tan every nook and cranny. Other offerings are kite rentals, kayak rentals, charter-fishing excursions, and a par-3, 9-hole golf course. ⊠ *10800 Collins Ave., Sunny Isles Beach, Miami Beach,* ☎ *305/947–3525,* WEB *www.miami-dade.fl.us/parks.com.* ☞ *$4 per vehicle.* ☉ *Daily dawn–dusk.*

North Shore Park Open Space. At this beach park between 79th and 87th streets on Collins Avenue, you'll find plenty of picnic tables, rest rooms, and healthy dunes. An exercise trail, concrete walkways, a playground, and lifeguards compromise or enhance the otherwise natural scene, depending on your point of view. You can park at a meter or in one of the pay lots across Collins Avenue. ⊠ *7901 Collins Ave., south of Surfside, Miami Beach,,* ☎ *305/993–2032.* ☞ *$1.* ☉ *Daily 7–6.*

Shopping

In Greater Miami you're never more than 15 minutes from a major commercial area that serves as both a shopping and entertainment venue for tourists and locals. The shopping is great on a two-block stretch of **Collins Avenue** between 6th and 8th Aves. Club Monaco, Polo Sport, Intermix, Nike, Kenneth Cole, Sephora, Armani Exchange, and Banana Republic are among the high-profile tenants, and a parking garage is just a block away on 7th. The busy **Lincoln Road Mall** is just a few blocks from the beach and convention center, making it popular with locals and tourists. There's an energy to shopping here, especially on weekends, when the pedestrian mall is filled with locals. You'll find a Victoria's Secret, Pottery Barn, Gap, and a Williams-Sonoma, as well as smaller emporiums with unique personalities. Creative merchandise, galleries, and a Sunday-morning antiques market can be found among the art galleries and cool cafés. An 18-screen movie theater anchors the west end of the street.

In a tropical garden setting, **Bal Harbour Shops** (⊠ 9700 Collins Ave., Bal Harbour, Miami Beach) is a swank collection of 100 shops, boutiques, and department stores, such as Chanel, Gucci, Cartier, Gianfranco Ferre, Hermès, Neiman-Marcus, and Saks Fifth Avenue. If it's luxe, it's here. **Bayside Marketplace** (⊠ 401 Biscayne Blvd., Downtown), the 16-acre shopping complex on Biscayne Bay, has more than 150 specialty shops, entertainers, tour-boat docks, a food court, and a Hard Rock Cafe. It's open late (until 10 during the week, 11 on Friday and Saturday), but its restaurants stay open even later. It's a great place to browse, buy, or simply relax by the bay with a tropical drink.

Base (⊠ 939 Lincoln Rd., Miami Beach, ☎ 305/531–4982) has good karma and great eclectic island wear for men and women. Stop here and you may run into the often-present designer. **El Credito Cigars** (⊠ 1100 S.W. 8th St., Little Havana, ☎ 305/858–4162) seems to have been transported from the Cuban capital lock, stock, and stogie. Rows of workers at wooden benches rip through giant tobacco leaves, cut them with rounded blades, wrap them tightly, and press them in vises. Dedicated smokers come here to pick up $90 bundles or peruse the *gigantes,* *supremos,* panatelas, and Churchills available in natural or maduro wrappers. The **Indies Company** (✉ 101 W. Flagler St., Downtown, ☎ 305/375–1492), the Historical Museum of Southern Florida's gift shop, offers artifacts and books reflecting regional history, including some inexpensive reproductions. In the Shore Club Hotel, **Scoop** (✉ 1901 Collins Ave., Miami Beach, ☎ 305/695–3297) is a small but spaciously arranged store carrying all the latest fashion requirements by Helmut Lang, Marc Jacobs, Earl, and Seven.

Nightlife

For information on what's happening around town, Greater Miami's English-language daily newspaper, the *Miami Herald,* publishes reliable reviews and comprehensive listings in its "Weekend" section on Friday and in the "IN South Florida" section on Sunday. It also publishes a free tabloid, *Street,* with entertainment listings. Call ahead to confirm details. *El Nuevo Herald* is the paper's Spanish version.

The best, most complete source of information on the performing arts and nightlife is *New Times,* a free newspaper distributed throughout Miami-Dade County each Thursday. Also worth consulting is the calendar in *Miami Today,* another free paper published Thursdays that's available in downtown Miami, Coconut Grove, and Coral Gables. Tabloids reporting on Deco District entertainment and the Miami social scene come and go. *Wire* reports on the gay community.

Most of the nightlife in Greater Miami is in Miami Beach. South Beach is headquarters for nightclubs that start late and stay open until the early morning. The clientele includes freak-show rejects, sullen male models, and sultry women.

The **Coconut Grove Playhouse** (✉ 3500 Main Hwy., Coconut Grove, ☎ 305/442–4000 or 305/442–2662) is now a serious regional theater owned by the State of Florida. If you're interested in high culture, the **Miami City Ballet** (✉ 2200 Liberty Ave., South Beach, Miami Beach, ☎ 305/929–7000) is internationally renowned; its season runs from September to March. The **New World Symphony** (✉ 555 Lincoln Rd., South Beach, Miami Beach, ☎ 305/673–3331 or 305/673–3330) performs in the Lincoln Theater on Lincoln Road Mall from October to May.

The Rose Bar at the **Delano** (✉ 1685 Collins Ave., Miami Beach, ☎ 305/672–2000) is dramatic and chic, with long gauzy curtains and huge pillars creating conversation nooks around the outdoor infinity pool. Inside, the cool, chic lounge area creates a glamorous space for the modelesque crowd. Offering more character than chic, the **Marlin** (✉ 1200 Collins Ave., Miami Beach, ☎ 305/673–8770) gleams with the high-tech look of stainless steel. DJs spin different music every night for the 25-to-40 crowd. For South Beach fabulousness, the glass-topped bar at the **Tides** (✉ 1220 Ocean Dr., Miami Beach, ☎ 305/604–5000) is the place to go for martinis and piano jazz.

In the northern reaches of downtown, **Cactus Nightclub** (✉ 2041 Biscayne Blvd., at 20th St., Downtown, ☎ 305/438–0662) is the gay place to head if you don't want to stay up 'til 4 AM to get some nightlife in. Special events include drag nights, male strippers, and a very popular Noche Latina on Saturday. Want 24-hour partying? **Club Space** (✉ 142 N.E. 11th St., Downtown, ☎ 305/375–0001), created from four warehouses downtown, has three dance rooms, an outdoor patio, a New York industrial look, and a 24-hour liquor license. It's open on weekends only, and you'll need to look good to be allowed past the velvet ropes.

The **Bermuda Bar & Grille** (✉ 3509 N.E. 163rd St., Miami Beach, ☎ 305/945–0196) is way north of SoBe but worth the drive if you want to hang with the locals. The vibe and crowd, though, are stylish, and there's a big tropical-forest scene, booths you can hide in, and pool tables to dive into, but it's closed from Sunday through Tuesday. One of several high-profile venues to hit South Beach, **Billboardlive** (⊠ 1501 Collins Ave., South Beach, Miami Beach, ☎ 305/538–2251) is four dazzling floors of fun with a performance stage, restaurants, bars, dance floors, private rooms, and a skybox. Expect to find world-class DJs here, too. You can dine as you watch the show at the Fontainebleau Hilton's **Club Tropigala** (⊠ 4441 Collins Ave., Miami Beach, ☎ 305/ 672–7469), which tries to blend modern Vegas with 1950s Havana. The four-tier round room is decorated with orchids, banana leaves, and philodendrons to create an indoor tropical jungle. Some of the performances are stellar, with a Latin flavor—Ricky Martin, Julio Iglesias, and Jose Feliciano have appeared here. Hotel guests are comped, but others pay a $20 cover. Reservations are suggested. **Honey** (⊠ 645 Washington Ave., Miami Beach, ☎ 305/604–8222) has soft lighting, cozy couches, and chaise longues, and vibey music that goes down as smoothly as its trademark honey-dipped apples. **Jazid** (⊠ 1342 Washington Ave., at 13th St., South Beach, Miami Beach, ☎ 305/673–9372), a stylishly redecorated standout on the strip, is sultry and candlelighted; the music is jazz, with blues and R&B. Popular with casually chic twenty- and thirtysomethings, **Opium Garden** (⊠ 136 Collins Ave., at 1st St., South Beach, Miami Beach, ☎ 305/674–8360) has a lush waterfall, an Asian temple motif with lots of candles, dragons and tapestries, and a restaurant next door. **Twist** (⊠ 1057 Washington Ave., at 10th St., South Beach, Miami Beach ☎ 305/538–9478), a longtime gay hot spot and local favorite with an outdoor patio and a game room, is crowded from 8 PM on, especially on Monday, Thursday (2-for-1), and Friday nights.

Exploring Greater Miami

Forty years ago Miami was best known for alligator wrestlers and you-pick strawberry fields or citrus groves. Well, things have changed. While Disney sidetracked families in Orlando, Miami was developing a grown-up attitude, courtesy of *Miami Vice,* European fashion photographers, and historic preservationists. Today, the wildest ride is the city itself.

Climb aboard and check out the different sides of Greater Miami. Miami, on the mainland, is South Florida's commercial hub, while its sultry sister, Miami Beach (America's Riviera), encompasses 17 islands in Biscayne Bay. But there's more to Miami Beach than the bustle of South Beach and its Deco District. There are quieter areas to the north, with names like Sunny Isles Beach, Surfside, and Bal Harbour. During the day downtown Miami is the lively hub of the mainland city, now more accessible thanks to the Metromover extension, which connects downtown sights with Metrorail's Government Center and Brickell stations. Other major attractions include Coconut Grove, Coral Gables, Little Havana, and, of course, the South Beach/Art Deco District, but since these areas are spread out beyond the reach of public transportation, you'll have to drive.

Numbers in the margin correspond to points of interest on the Greater Miami map.

❺ **Art Deco District Welcome Center.** Run by the Miami Design Preservation League, the center provides information about the buildings in the district. A gift shop sells deco memorabilia, posters, and books on Miami's history. Several tours—covering Lincoln Road, Espanola Way, North Beach, the entire Art Deco District—start here. You can rent audiotapes for a self-guided tour, join the Saturday-morning or Thursday-evening walking tours, or take a bicycle tour—all of the options provide detailed histories of the art deco hotels. Don't miss the special boat tours during Art Deco Weekend in early January. ⊠ *1001 Ocean Dr., at Barbara Capitman Way (10th St.), South Beach,* ☎ *305/531–3484 or 305/672–2014.* ⊑ *Tours $10–$15.* ☉ *Sun.–Thurs. 10–10, Fri.–Sat. 10* AM*–midnight.*

❶ **Bal Harbour.** Known for its upscale shops, this affluent community has a stretch of prime beach real estate where wealthy condominium owners cluster during the winter. Look close, and you may spy Bob Dole sunning himself outside his condo. ⊠ *Collins Ave. between 96th and 103rd Sts., Bal Harbour.*

❸ **Bass Museum of Art.** A diverse collection of European art is the focus of this impressive museum in Collins Park, a short drive north of SoBe's key sights. Works on display include *The Holy Family,* a painting by Peter Paul Rubens; *The Tournament,* one of several 16th-century Flemish tapestries; and works by Albrecht Dürer and Henri de Toulouse-Lautrec. An $8 million, three-phase expansion by architect Arata Isozaki added another wing, cafeteria, and theater, doubling the museum's size to nearly 40,000 square ft. ⊠ *2121 Park Ave., South Beach,* ☎ *305/673–7530,* WEB *www.bassmuseum.org.* ⊑ *$5.* ☉ *Tues.–Wed. and Fri.–Sat. 10–5, Thurs. 10–9, Sun. 11–5.*

❼ **Brickell Village.** Brickell (rhymes with fickle) is an up-and-coming downtown area with new low- and high-rise condos, a shopping area, Brickell Park, and plenty of popular restaurants. **Hardaway's Firehouse Four** (⊠ 1000 S. Miami Ave., Brickell Village), underwritten by NBA star Tim Hardaway, has a legendary happy hour and good burgers (including a tuna burger) in an old firehouse. **Perricone's Marketplace and Café** (⊠ 15 S.E. 10th St., Brickell Village), in a 120-year-old Vermont barn, is the biggest and most popular of the area's many Italian restaurants. The cooking is simple and good. Buy your wine from the on-premises deli and bring it to your table for a small corking fee. ⊠ *Between Miami River and S.W. 15th St., Brickell Village.*

❿ **Coconut Grove.** South Florida's oldest settlement, "The Grove" was inhabited as early as 1834 and established by 1873, two decades before Miami. Its early settlers included Bahamian blacks, "Conchs" (white Key Westers, many originally from the Bahamas), and New England intellectuals, who built a community that attracted artists, writers, and scientists, who established winter homes. Coconut Grove still reflects its pioneers' eclectic origins. Posh estates mingle with rustic cottages, modest frame homes, and stark modern dwellings, often on the same block. The historic center of the Village of Coconut Grove went through a hippie period in the 1960s, a laid-back funkiness in the 1970s, and a teenybopper invasion in the early 1980s. Today the tone is upscale and urban, with a mix of galleries, boutiques, restaurants, bars, and sidewalk cafés. On weekends the Grove is jam-packed with both locals and tourists—especially teenagers—shopping at the Streets of Mayfair, CocoWalk, and small boutiques. Parking can be a problem, especially on weekend evenings, when police direct traffic and prohibit turns at some intersections to prevent gridlock.

Of the 10,000 people living in Miami between 1912 and 1916, about 1,000 of them were gainfully employed by Chicago industrialist James Deering to build the **Vizcaya Museum and Gardens** (⊠ 3251 S. Miami Ave., Coconut Grove, ☎ 305/250–9133, WEB www.vizcayamuseum.com), a $20 million Italian Renaissance–style winter residence. Once comprising 180 acres, the grounds now cover a still-substantial 30-acre tract, including a native hammock and more than 10 acres of formal gardens and fountains overlooking Biscayne Bay. The house, open to the public, contains 70 rooms, 34 of which are filled with paintings, sculpture, antique furniture, and other decorative arts dating from the 15th through the 19th centuries and representing the Renaissance, baroque, rococo, and neoclassical styles. The house is open daily from 9:30 to 4:30, the garden from 9:30 to 5:30. Admission is $10.

❾ Coral Gables. If not for George E. Merrick, Coral Gables would be just another suburb. Merrick envisioned an American Venice, with canals and gracious homes spreading across the community. Today Coral Gables has a population of about 43,000. In its bustling downtown, more than 150 companies maintain headquarters or regional offices, and the University of Miami campus in the southern part of Coral Gables brings a youthful vibrancy: the median age of residents is 38. Like much of Miami, Coral Gables has realized the aesthetic and economic importance of historic preservation and has passed a Mediterranean design ordinance, rewarding businesses for maintaining their buildings' architectural styles. Even the street signs (ground-level markers that are hard to see in daylight, impossible at night) are preserved. They're worth the inconvenience, if only to honor the memory of Merrick. The upscale yet neighborly stretch of retail stores along the so-called **Miracle Mile** (⊠ Coral Way between S.W. 37th Ave. [Douglas Rd.] and S.W. 42nd Ave. [LeJeune Rd.], Coral Gables) is actually only ½ mi long. After years of neglect, it's been updated and upgraded and now offers a delightful mix of owner-operated shops and chain stores, bridal shops, art galleries and bistros, and enough late-night hot spots to keep things hopping.

⓬ Fairchild Tropical Garden. Comprising 83 acres, this is the largest tropical botanical garden in the continental United States. Eleven lakes, a rain forest, and lots of palm trees, cycads, and flowers, including orchids, mountain roses, bellflowers, coral trees, and bougainvillea, make it a garden for the senses—and there's special assistance for the hearing-impaired. Take the free guided tram tour, which leaves on the hour. Spicing up the social calendar are garden sales (like the Ramble in November and the International Mango Festival in July), moonlight strolls, and symphony concerts. An attractive gift shop in the new visitor center is a popular source for books on gardening and horticulture. ⊠ *10901 Old Cutler Rd., Coral Gables,* ☏ *305/667–1651,* WEB *www.fairchildgarden.org.* ☞ *$8.* ☉ *Daily 9:30–4:30.*

❷ Fontainebleau Hilton Resort and Towers. For a sense of what Miami was like during the Fabulous '50s, take a drive north to see the finest example of Miami Beach's grandiose architecture. By the 1950s smaller deco-era hotels were passé, and architects like Morris Lapidus got busy designing free-flowing hotels that affirmed the American attitude of "bigger is better." Wander through the lobby and spectacular pool area just to feel the energy generated by an army of bellhops, clerks, concierges, and travelers. ⊠ *4441 Collins Ave., between 44th and 45th Sts., South Beach,* ☏ *305/538–2000,* WEB *www.fontainebleau.hilton.com.*

❹ Lincoln Road Mall. The Morris Lapidus–renovated Lincoln Road is fun, lively, and friendly for people old, young, gay, and straight—and their dogs. Folks skate, scoot, bike, or jog here, past the electronics stores at the Collins Avenue end toward the chichi boutiques and outdoor cafés heading west. The best times to hit the road are during Sunday-morning farmers' markets and on weekend evenings, when cafés are bustling; art galleries, like Romero Britto's Britto Central, schedule opening; street performers take the stage; and bookstores, import shops, and clothing stores are open for late-night purchases. ⊠ *Lincoln Rd. between Collins Ave. and Alton Rd., South Beach.*

8 **Little Havana.** More than 40 years ago the tidal wave of Cubans flee-ing the Castro regime flooded into an older neighborhood west of down-town Miami. Don't expect a sparkling and lively reflection of 1950s Havana, however. What you will find are ramshackle motels and clut-tered storefronts. With a million Cubans and other Latinos—who make up more than half the metropolitan population—dispersed throughout Greater Miami, Little Havana and neighboring East Lit-tle Havana remain magnets for Hispanics and Anglos alike, who come to experience the flavor of traditional Cuban culture. That culture, of course, functions in Spanish. Many Little Havana residents and shop-keepers speak little or no English. In Little Havana's commercial heart, **Calle Ocho** (⊠ S.W. 8th St., Little Havana), experience such Cuban favorites as hand-rolled cigars or sandwiches piled with meats and cheeses. Although the entire area deserves exploring, if time is limited, try the stretch from Southwest 14th to 11th Avenue. In **Plaza de la Cuban-idad** (⊠ W. Flagler St. and S.W. 17th Ave., Little Havana) redbrick side-walks surround a fountain and monument with the words of José Martí, a leader in Cuba's struggle for independence from Spain and a hero to Cuban refugees and immigrants in Miami. The quotation, LAS PALMAS SON NOVIAS QUE ESPERAN (The palm trees are waiting brides), counsels hope and fortitude to the Cubans.

11 **Miami Seaquarium.** This old-fashioned attraction has six daily shows, starring sea lions, dolphins, and Lolita, a killer whale. (Lolita's tank is small for seaquariums—just three times her length—and so some wildlife advocates are trying to get her back to sea.) Exhibits include a shark pool, a 235,000-gallon tropical-reef aquarium, and manatees. Glass-bottom boats make tours of Biscayne Bay. Want to get your feet (and everything else) wet? The Water and Dolphin Exploration (WADE) program enables you to swim with dolphins during a two-hour ses-sion. Reservations are required. ⊠ *4400 Rickenbacker Causeway, Vir-ginia Key,* ☎ *305/361–5705,* WEB *www.miamiseaquarium.com.* ☞ *$24.45, WADE $140, parking $4.* ☉ *Daily 9:30–6 (last admission at 4:30); WADE Wed.–Sun. at noon and 3:30.*

6 **Parrot Jungle.** One of South Florida's original tourist attractions, Par-rot Jungle opened in 1936 and has relocated to Watson Island, linked by the MacArthur Causeway (Interstate 395) to Miami and Miami Beach. In addition to a thousand exotic birds, the attraction will in-clude a 17-ft Asian crocodile, 9-ft albino alligators, a serpentarium filled with venomous snakes, a petting zoo, and a two-story-high aviary with more than 100 free-flying macaws. A restaurant with indoor and out-door seating will overlook a lake where 60 postcard-perfect Caribbean flamingos hang out. Orchids and ferns and even trees from the origi-nal site are being transplanted along a Disneyesque jungle river that will meander through the park. The original site on Southwest 57th Avenue has been purchased by the Village of Pinecrest, which promises to preserve its popular trails, massive oaks, and bald cypress and add improvements. ⊠ *1111 Parrot Jungle Trail, Watson Island,* ☎ *305/ 666–7834,* WEB *www.parrotjungle.com.* ☞ *$23.95.* ☉ *Daily 10–6 (last admission at 4:30, later in season).*

NEW ORLEANS

Tucked beyond miles of marsh and isolated from the surrounding area, New Orleans sometimes seems closer in spirit to the Caribbean than to Our Town, USA. The European, African, and Caribbean cul-tures that settled here are intact and even thriving—often, as during Mardi Gras, exuberantly. Creole cuisine, the continuing legacy of New Orleans jazz, and the unabashed prioritizing of pleasure that define life

New Orleans

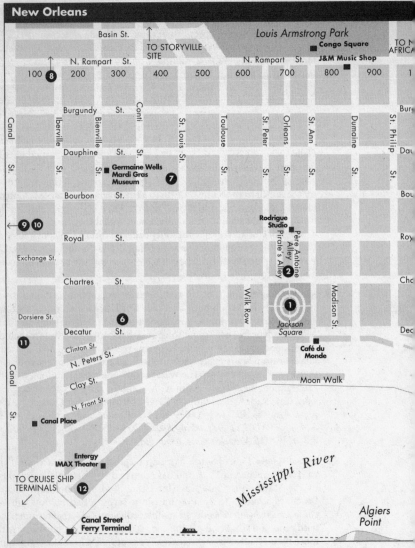

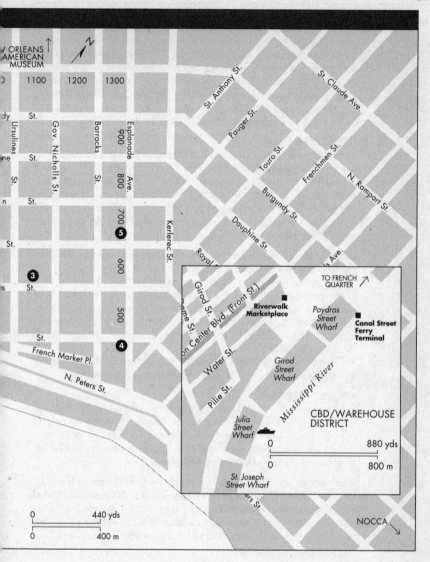

NEW ORLEANS
AMERICAN MUSEUM

N

1100   1200   1300

dy   St.
Ursulines
ne   St.
n   St.

Gov. Nicholls St.

Barracks   St.

Esplanade Ave.
900
800
700 **5**
600
500

Kerlerec St.

St. Anthony St.

Pauger St.

Touro St.

Burgundy St.

Dauphine St.

Royal

St. Claude Ave.

Frenchmen St.

N. Rampart St.

Ave.

3
St.

s
St.

4
St.
French Market Pl.

N. Peters St.

Girod St.

on Center Blvd. (Front St.)

Dame St.

Water St.

Pilie St.

Julia
Street
Wharf

St. Joseph
Street Wharf

ers St.

Riverwalk
Marketplace

Poydras
Street
Wharf

Girod
Street
Wharf

Mississippi River

TO FRENCH
QUARTER

Canal Street
Ferry
Terminal

CBD/WAREHOUSE
DISTRICT

0   880 yds
0   800 m

NOCCA

0   440 yds
0   400 m

here are all part of a culture that is by geographical dictate self-contained. Visitors are treated to that oh-so-rare mixture of modernity and true individuality, found in the frank indifference of leisure-seeking locals no less than in the raucous revelry of the French Quarter. No wonder the city is a favorite of cruise goers, who enjoy strolling the narrow streets of the French Quarter and partaking in its culinary and atmospheric pleasures. Most who embark here on one of the Western Caribbean cruises that leave from the city's cruise-ship terminal will spend a day or so either pre- or post-cruise taking it all in.

The Cruise Port

The Julia Street Cruise Terminal is at the end of Julia Street on the Mississippi River, in front of the Ernest M. Morial Convention Center. You can walk to the French Quarter from here in about 10 minutes; it's a short taxi ride to the Quarter or nearby hotels. Carnival, Norwegian, and Royal Caribbean base ships here at least part of the year, and the *Delta Queen* river steamboat leaves from the Robin Street Wharf, just south of the Julia Street terminals.

If you are driving, you'll probably approach New Orleans on I–10. Take the Business 90W/Westbank exit, locally known as Pontchartrain Expressway, and proceed to the Tchoupitoulas St./South Peters St. exit. Continue to Convention Center Boulevard, where you will take a right turn. Continue to Henderson Street, where you will turn left, and then continue to Port of New Orleans Place. Take a left on Port of New Orleans Place to Julia Street Terminals 1 and 2, or take a right to get to the Robin Street Wharf.

➤ CONTACTS: **Port of New Orleans** (✉ Port of New Orleans Pl., at the foot of Julia St., ☎ 504/522–2551 WEB www.portno.com).

AIRPORT TRANSFERS

Shuttle-bus service to and from the airport and the cruise port is available through New Orleans Tours Airport Shuttle. Buses leave regularly from the ground level near the baggage claim. To return to the airport, call 24 hours in advance of flight time. The cost one-way is $10 per person, and the trip takes about 40 minutes.

A cab ride to or from the airport from uptown or downtown New Orleans costs $28 for the first two passengers and $12 for each additional passenger. At the airport, pickup is on the lower level, outside the baggage claim area. There may be an additional charge for extra baggage.

➤ CONTACTS: **New Orleans Tours Airport Shuttle** (☎ 504/522–3500).

LONG-TERM PARKING

There is a lighted, outdoor parking lot at the cruise port, which charges $70 a week for cruise-ship passengers only. You will have to show your ticket and pay cash in advance. Several private parking lots and garages in the area will also allow cruise goers to park for $10 a day; some of these, including the garage at the Hilton Hotel on Convention Center Drive and the WTC Lot on Poydras Street, adjacent to the Hilton, offer covered parking. (You'll have to negotiate the few blocks to the cruise port on your own.) If you're going to park in one of the private lots, it's probably best to drop off your luggage first.

VISITOR INFORMATION

You can get information about visiting New Orleans from the Louisiana Office of Tourism and the New Orleans Metropolitan Convention & Visitors Bureau.

➤ CONTACTS: **Louisiana Office of Tourism** (✉ Box 94291, Baton Rouge, LA 70804-9291, ☎ 800/633–6970, FAX 225/342–8390, WEB www.louisianatravel.com). **New Orleans Metropolitan Convention & Vis-**

itors Bureau (✉ 1520 Sugar Bowl Dr., 70112, ☎ 504/566–5011 or 800/672–6124, ℻ 504/566–5021, WEB www.neworleanscvb.com).

Where to Stay

You can stay in a large hotel near the cruise-ship terminal or in more intimate places in the French Quarter. Hotel rates in New Orleans tend to be on the high end, though deals abound.

For price categories, *see* Lodging at the beginning of this chapter.

$$$$ 🏨 **New Orleans Hilton Riverside.** This sprawling, multilevel complex is smack on the Mississippi, and the riverfront streetcar stops out front. Guest rooms have French provincial furnishings; the 180 rooms that share a concierge have fax machines. The health club is one of the best in the Gulf South, and there is an excellent business center. Veteran jazz clarinetist Pete Fountain has a nightclub in the hotel. Adjacent to Riverwalk Shopping Center and Aquarium of the Americas, and directly across the street from Harrah's casino, the hotel has a resident golf pro and a 4-hole putting green. ✉ *Poydras St. at the Mississippi River, CBD, 70140,* ☎ *504/561–0500 or 800/445–8667,* ℻ *504/568–1721,* WEB *www.hilton.com. 1,600 rooms, 67 suites. 4 restaurants, putting green, 8 tennis courts, 2 pools, aerobics, health club, hair salon, outdoor hot tub, massage, sauna, racquetball, squash, 7 lounges, business services, parking (fee), no-smoking floor. AE, D, DC, MC, V.*

$$$$ 🏨 **New Orleans Marriott Hotel.** The Marriott has a fabulous view of the Quarter, the CBD, and the river. It's an easy walk from Riverwalk, the Canal Place mall, and the convention center. The rooms are comfortable, the service is friendly, and jazz enlivens the lobby and the Riverview Restaurant, which has one of the best views of New Orleans anywhere in the city. The room is ideal for Sunday brunch. ✉ *555 Canal St., French Quarter, 70130,* ☎ *504/581–1000 or 800/228–9290,* ℻ *504/523–6755,* WEB *www.marriott.com. 1,290 rooms, 54 suites. 3 restaurants, pool, health club, sauna, bar, lobby lounge, business services, meeting room, parking (fee). AE, D, DC, MC, V.*

$$$–$$$$ 🏨 **Monteleone Hotel.** The grande dame of French Quarter hotels, with its ornate baroque facade, liveried doormen, and shimmering lobby chandeliers, was built in 1886 and has been kept fresh through renovations. It's the Quarter's oldest hotel. Rooms are extralarge and luxurious, with rich fabrics and a mix of four-poster beds, brass beds, and beds with traditional headboards. Junior suites are spacious, and sumptuous VIP suites come with extra pampering. The slowly revolving Carousel Bar in the lobby is a local landmark. Chef Randy Buck prepares superb food in the Hunt Room Grill, one of the city's best-kept culinary secrets. ✉ *214 Royal St., French Quarter, 70130,* ☎ *504/523–3341 or 800/535–9595,* ℻ *504/528–1019,* WEB *www.hotelmonteleone.com. 598 rooms, 28 suites. 3 restaurants, pool, gym, bar, concierge, business services, meeting room. AE, D, DC, MC, V.*

$$–$$$ 🏨 **Holiday Inn–French Quarter.** Close to Canal Street, this modern hotel is a good home base for walking into the heart of the French Quarter or the CBD or for boarding the St. Charles streetcar line. The hotel's restaurant is a T. G. I. Friday's. ✉ *124 Royal St., French Quarter, 70130,* ☎ *504/529–7211 or 800/447–2830,* ℻ *504/566–1127,* WEB *www.sixcontinentshotels.com. 374 rooms. Restaurant, indoor pool, gym, parking (fee) AE, D, DC, MC, V.*

$–$$$ 🏨 **Le Richelieu in the French Quarter.** Close to the Old Ursuline Convent and the French Market, Le Richelieu combines the friendly, personal charm of a small hotel with luxe touches (upscale toiletries, hair dryers) at a moderate rate. Some rooms have mirrored walls and large walk-in closets, and all have brass ceiling fans, irons, and ironing boards. Balcony rooms have the same rates as standard rooms. An intimate bar and café is off the courtyard, with tables on the terrace by the pool. Many regular customers would never stay anywhere else. ⊠ *1234 Chartres St., French Quarter, 70116,* ☎ *504/529–2492 or 800/ 535–9653,* FAX *504/524–8179,* WEB *www.lerichelieu.com. 69 rooms, 17 suites. Café, some kitchenettes, some refrigerators, pool, bar, concierge, free parking. AE, D, DC, MC, V.*

Where to Eat

For price categories, *see* Dining at the beginning of this chapter.

$$$–$$$$ ✗ **Commander's Palace.** No restaurant captures New Orleans's gastronomic heritage and celebratory spirit as well as this one. The upstairs Garden Room's glass walls have marvelous views of the giant oak trees on the patio below, and other rooms promote conviviality with their bright pastels. The menu's classics include poached oysters in a seasoned cream sauce; a spicy and meaty turtle soup; terrific crab cakes in an oyster sauce; and a wonderful sautéed trout coated with crunchy pecans. Among the addictive desserts are the bread pudding soufflé and chocolate Sheba, a wonderful Bavarian cream. Weekend brunches are less ambitious but also less costly. ⊠ *1403 Washington Ave., Garden District,* ☎ *504/899–8221. Reservations essential. Jacket required. AE, D, DC, MC, V.*

$$$–$$$$ ✗ **Peristyle.** Some of the most creative cooking in New Orleans emanates from the kitchen of this smartly turned-out yet very approachable little restaurant on the French Quarter's edge. Chef Anne Kearney takes a thoroughly modern and personal approach to Continental cooking with a superb sauté of Gulf shrimp and fennel in a white-wine sauce, fork-tender lamb loin with a puree of garlicky white beans, and a whole, boned white trout filled with mussels, crab, and potatoes. The main dining room is swathed in pale-lavender walls and lined with sleek, tufted banquettes. A bucolic old painting serves as a backdrop to the cozy bar. ⊠ *1041 Dumaine St., French Quarter,* ☎ *504/593–9535. Reservations essential. MC, V. Closed Sun.–Mon. No lunch Tues.–Thurs. or Sat.*

$$–$$$$ ✗ **Galatoire's.** Galatoire's has always epitomized the old-style French-creole bistro. Many of the recipes date back to 1905. Fried oysters and bacon en brochette are worth every calorie, and the brick-red rémoulade sauce sets a high standard. Others on the list of winners include veal chops in béarnaise sauce and seafood-stuffed eggplant. The setting downstairs is a single, narrow dining room lit with glistening brass chandeliers, with bentwood chairs at the white-cloth tables adding to the timeless atmosphere. However, the din of the restaurant's regulars often fills the downstairs room, sometimes inhibiting conversation elsewhere. Upstairs are dining rooms and a bar for those awaiting tables. ⊠ *209 Bourbon St., French Quarter,* ☎ *504/525–2021. Reservations essential. Jacket required. AE, DC, MC, V. Closed Mon.*

$$$ ✗ **Nola.** Fans of chef Emeril Lagasse who can't get a table at Emeril's in the Warehouse District have this sassy and vibrant French Quarter restaurant as an alternative. Lagasse has not lowered his sights with Nola's menu, which is as lusty and rich as any in town. The kitchen stews *boudin* (blood sausage) with beer, onions, cane syrup, and creole mustard before ladling it all onto a sweet-potato crouton. Redfish is swathed in a horseradish-citrus crust before it's plank-roasted in a wood oven. Duck arrives glistening with a whisky-caramel glaze. The combinations seem endless. At dessert time, try the coconut cream or apple-buttermilk pie. ⊠ *534 St. Louis St., French Quarter,* ☎ *504/522– 6652. AE, D, DC, MC, V. No lunch Sun.*

$$–$$$ ✗ **Herbsaint.** Upscale food and downscale prices are among Herbsaint's assets. Chef Donald Link turns out food that sparkles with robust flavors and top-grade ingredients. "Small plates" and side dishes such as charcuterie, a knock-'em-dead shrimp bisque, gumbos, and cheese- or nut-studded salads are mainstays. More substantial appetites are courted with pork tenderloin, beef short ribs, and salmon in a mustard-seed crust. For dessert, go for the chocolate beignets, filled with molten chocolate. The plates provide most of the color in these rather somber, greenish-walled spaces, which are often noisy. The wine list is expertly compiled and reasonably priced, and the staff's suggestions are reliable. ⊠ *701 St. Charles Ave., CBD,* ☎ *504/524–4114. Reservations essential. AE, D, DC, MC, V. Closed Sun. No lunch Sat.*

$–$$ ✕ **Acme Oyster and Seafood Restaurant.** A rough-edged classic in every way, this no-nonsense eatery at the entrance to the French Quarter is a prime source of cool and salty raw oysters on the half shell; great shrimp, oyster, and roast-beef po'boys; and state-of-the-art red beans and rice. Table service, once confined to the main dining room out front, is now provided in the rear room as well. Expect lengthy lines at the marble-top oyster bar. Crowds lighten in the late afternoon. ⊠ *724 Iberville St., French Quarter,* ☎ *504/522–5973. Reservations not accepted. AE, DC, MC, V.*

$–$$ ✕ **Central Grocery.** This old-fashioned Italian grocery store produces authentic muffulettas, one of the gastronomic gifts of the city's Italian immigrants. Good enough to challenge the po'boy as the local sandwich champ, they're made by filling round loaves of seeded bread with ham, salami, mozzarella, and a salad of marinated green olives. Each sandwich, about 10 inches in diameter, is sold in wholes and halves. You can eat your muffuletta at a counter, but some prefer to take theirs out to a bench on Jackson Square or the Moon Walk along the Mississippi riverfront. The grocery closes at 5:30 PM. ⊠ *923 Decatur St., French Quarter,* ☎ *504/523–1620. No credit cards.*

$ ✕ **Café du Monde.** For most visitors, no trip to New Orleans would be complete without a cup of chicory-laced café au lait and a few sugar-dusted beignets in this venerable Creole institution. The tables are jammed at almost any hour with locals and tourists feasting on the views of Jackson Square. The magical time to go is just before dawn, when the bustle subsides and you can almost hear the birds in the crepe myrtles across the way. Four satellite locations (the New Orleans Centre, Riverwalk Marketplace in the CBD, Lakeside Shopping Center in Metairie, Esplanade Mall in Kenner) are convenient but lack the character of the original. ⊠ *800 Decatur St., French Quarter,* ☎ *504/525–4544. No credit cards.*

Shopping

The fun of shopping in New Orleans is in the regional items available throughout the city, in the smallest shops or the biggest department stores. You can take home some of the flavor of the city: its pralines (pecan candies), seafood (packaged to go), Louisiana red beans and rice, coffee (pure or with chicory), and creole and Cajun spices (cayenne pepper, chili, and garlic). There are even packaged mixes of such local favorites as jambalaya, gumbo, beignets, and the sweet red local cocktail called the Hurricane. Cookbooks also share the secrets of preparing distinctive New Orleans dishes. The French Quarter is well known for its fine antiques shops, located mainly on Royal and Chartres streets.

The main shopping areas in the city are the French Quarter, with its narrow streets lined with specialty, gift, and antiques shops and art galleries; the Central Business District (CBD), which has department stores and clothing, specialty, and jewelry shops; Magazine Street, known for its antiques shops and galleries; the Warehouse District, popular for Julia Street's contemporary arts galleries; and Uptown, with its neighborhood and specialty shops in several fashionable shopping areas.

Canal Place (✉ 333 Canal St., CBD, ☎ 504/587–0739) draws fashionable shoppers to 60 shops that include Saks Fifth Avenue, Gucci, Williams-Sonoma, Pottery Barn, Laura Ashley, and Brooks Brothers. **Jackson Brewery Corporation** (✉ 600 Decatur St., French Quarter, ☎ 504/566–7245) operates three indoor malls that house a mix of local shops and national chains. The Brewhouse, on Decatur Street across from Jackson Square, occupies a building in which Jax beer was brewed. A Virgin Megastore loaded with books and CDs occupies considerable square footage in the Brewhouse. Adjacent to the Brewhouse, and connected by indoor and outdoor walkways, is the Millhouse. **New Orleans Centre** (✉ 1400 Poydras St., CBD, ☎ 504/568–0000), a shopping complex between the Superdome and the Hyatt Regency hotel, houses Macy's and Lord & Taylor. **Riverwalk Marketplace** (✉ 1 Poydras St., Warehouse District, ☎ 504/522–1555), along the riverfront, has a ½-mi-long marketplace with 180 local and nationally known shops and restaurants, including Café du Monde.

Bayou Trading Company (✉ 622 Loyal St., French Quarter, ☎ 504/523–4200) offers an artistic look at Louisiana with bayou-inspired art, hand-painted and embroidered clothing, antique maps, pottery, ceramics, and glass. **Bergen Galleries** (✉ 730 Royal St., French Quarter, ☎ 504/523–7882, WEB www.bergengalleries.com) showcases collectibles and the city's largest display of posters, including ones for Mardi Gras and Jazz Fest, by local artists. The **Black Art Collection** (✉ 309 Chartres St., French Quarter, ☎ 504/529–3080) focuses on the works of major local and national black artists; inventory includes posters, jazz images, and antique African artifacts. **Currents . . .** (✉ 305 Royal St., French Quarter, ☎ 504/522–6099) is a chic store in which Terry and Sylvia Weidert create their own designs in 14- and 18-karat gold and platinum. Stop by **Jean Braly** (✉ 918 Royal St., French Quarter, ☎ 504/524–3208) if you're seeking tastefully unusual pieces. A compelling collection of jewelry, masks, clothing, and accessories awaits. **Louisiana Music Factory** (✉ 210 Decatur St., French Quarter, ☎ 504/586–1094) showcases regional music and carries videos, posters, books, and T-shirts. There's also the occasional jam session. **Louisiana Products** (✉ 618 Julia St., French Quarter, ☎ 504/524–7331) showcases Cajun and creole foods, Mardi Gras beads, local crafts, and novelties. Gift boxes of food items can be shipped anywhere. **Michalopoulos** (✉ 617 Bienville St. French Quarter, ☎ 504/558–0505) presents New Orleans architecture and street scenes as captured in the oil paintings and lithographs of James Michalopoulos. **Rodrigue Gallery** (✉ 721 Royal St., French Quarter, ☎ 504/581–4244 or 800/899–4244) showcases the work of internationally known Cajun artist George Rodrigue. His "blue dog" paintings are especially popular. **Serendipitous Masks** (✉ 831 Decatur St., French Quarter, ☎ 504/522–9158) has an excellent selection of feather masks and ornate Mardi Gras headdresses. The masks, which are crafted on the premises, can be made to order. **Sigle's Historic New Orleans Metal Craft** (✉ 935 Royal St., French Quarter, ☎ 504/522–7647) sells cast-iron wall planters, handcrafted since 1938; these are often seen on Quarter balconies and patios. **Violets** (✉ 808 Chartres St., French Quarter, ☎ 504/569–0088) is bound to steal your heart with an incomparable collection of ruffles, lace, bangles, and crystal beads—in the form of dresses, boudoir wear, chapeaux, jewelry—and plain old-fashioned romance.

Nightlife

No American city places such a premium on pleasure as New Orleans. From the well-appointed lounges of swank hotels to raucous French Quarter bars and sweaty dance halls to funky dives and rocking clubs in far-flung neighborhoods, this city is serious about frivolity—and about its music.

Bars tend to open in the early afternoon and stay open into the morning hours; live music, though, follows a more restrained schedule. Some jazz spots and clubs in the French Quarter stage evening sets around 6 PM or 9 PM; at a few clubs, such as the Palm Court, the bands actually finish by 11 PM. But this is the exception: for the most part, gigs begin between 10 and 11 PM, and locals rarely emerge for an evening out before 10. Keep in mind that the lack of legal closing time means that shows advertised for 11 may not start until after midnight.

The Beaux Arts–style **Harrah's New Orleans Casino** (⊠ 4 Canal St., CBD, ☎ 504/533–6000 or 800/427–7247, WEB www.harrahs.com), at the foot of Canal Street, is the largest casino in the South. Its 100,000 square ft hold 2,900 slots and 120 gaming tables. Valet parking is available.

At **Arnaud's Cigar Bar** (⊠ 813 Bienville St., French Quarter, ☎ 504/ 523–5433), sophistication awaits in the form of rich cigars and fine liquor served up in posh surroundings where no detail goes unobserved— even the air is filtrated and refined. After a round or two, venture upstairs to the quirky Germaine Wells Mardi Gras Museum, a showcase for many ball gowns worn by a relation of the owners, who was the queen of various Carnival balls. Those partial to the cocktail, be it shaken or stirred, will appreciate the extensive selection of vodkas, single-malt scotches, ports, and cognacs at the **Bombay Club** (⊠ 830 Conti St., French Quarter, ☎ 504/586–0972.), where the martinis approach high art. The plush, paneled interior creates a comfort zone for anyone nostalgic for the glory days of the British Empire. This bar in the Prince Conti Hotel features soft, live music nightly. The convivial **Crescent City Brewhouse** (⊠ 527 Decatur St., French Quarter, ☎ 504/522–0571) is known for its extensive menu of micro- and specialty brews; Abita Amber is a local favorite, but be sure to ask your server what's good—many of the selections are brewed on the premises. Live music is a dinnertime staple here. The river view from the second-floor balcony is worth a stop. **El Matador** (⊠ 504 Esplanade Ave., French Quarter, ☎ 504/ 569–8361) belongs more to the Marigny than to the French Quarter in spirit, sitting as it does at the beginning of Frenchmen Street. The horseshoe-shape bar is a favorite perch among local and visiting musicians and film types and the otherwise hip. Most nights see live music. **Napoleon House Bar and Cafe** (⊠ 500 Chartres St., French Quarter, ☎ 504/524–9752), a vintage watering hole, has long been popular with writers, artists, and other free spirits; locals who wouldn't be caught dead on Bourbon Street come here often. It is a living shrine to the New Orleans school of decor: faded grandeur. Murmuring ceiling fans, diffused light, and a lovely patio create a timeless, escapist mood. The house specialty is a Pimm's Cup cocktail; a menu including sandwiches, soups, salads, and cheese boards is also available. This is the perfect place for late-afternoon people-watching, an evening nightcap, or the beginning of an up-'til-dawn bender. **Pat O'Brien's** (⊠ 718 St. Peter St., French Quarter, ☎ 504/525–4823), one of the biggest tourist spots in town, is also the home of the oversize alcoholic beverage known as the Hurricane. Many people like to take their glass home as a souvenir; be wary of a deposit that is charged at the time of purchase and should be refunded if you don't take the glass with you. Actually five bars in one, Pat O's claims to sell more liquor than any other establishment in the world. The bar on the left through the entrance is popular with Quarterites, the patio in the rear draws the young (and young at heart) in temperate months, and the piano bar on the right side of the brick corridor packs in raucous celebrants year-round.

For many years, **Café Brasil** (⊠ 2100 Chartres St., Faubourg Marigny, ☎ 504/949–0851) ruled over Frenchmen Street, on most nights overflowing with sweaty dancers in spite of the spacious quarters. Things have slowed down a bit these days, as a wave of competition along the strip has diffused the crowds, but Brasil commands an established aura, and when a popular band is playing, it still throbs. Modern jazz and experimental theater draw smaller crowds of serious listeners who sit at comfortably spaced tables. At the **Chris Owens Club** (✉ 500 Bourbon St., French Quarter, ☎ 504/523–6400), the reluctantly aging Chris Owens is still an energetic female dancer and entertainer with a slightly risqué act. The late Al Hirt often played here. **Donna's Bar & Grill** (✉ 800 N. Rampart St., French Quarter, ☎ 504/596–6914) is a great place to hear traditional jazz, R&B, and the city's young brass bands in an informal neighborhood setting. On Monday night, musicians stop by after their gigs to sit in with drummer Bob French, and free red beans and rice are served at midnight. **Funky Butt at Congo Square** (✉ 714 N. Rampart St., French Quarter, ☎ 504/558–0872), named after jazz pioneer Buddy Bolden's signature tune and housed in art deco splendor, is a top spot for contemporary jazz. Local talent and local connoisseurs are both in plentiful supply; Jason Marsalis, of the musical dynasty, often plays here. Across the street from the Convention Center, **Mulate's** (✉ 201 Julia St., Warehouse District, ☎ 504/522–1492) seats 400, and the dance floor quickly fills with couples twirling and two-stepping to authentic Cajun bands. Regulars love to drag first-timers to the floor for impromptu lessons. The home-style Cajun cuisine is quite good, and the bands play until 10:30 or 11 PM. The renowned Dixieland clarinetist plays on a sporadic schedule in the plush **Pete Fountain's** (✉ 2 Poydras St., at the river, CBD, ☎ 504/523–4374 or 504/561–0500), which is on the third floor of the Hilton. Be sure to call ahead, and wear your good duds. **Preservation Hall** (✉ 726 St. Peter St., French Quarter, ☎ 504/522–2841 or 504/523–8939), the jazz tradition that flowered in the 1920s, is enshrined in this cultural landmark by a cadre of distinguished musicians, most of whom were schooled by an ever-dwindling group of elder statesmen who actually played with Louis Armstrong et al. There is limited seating on benches— many patrons end up squatting on the floor or standing in back—and no beverages are served or allowed. Nonetheless, legions of satisfied customers regard an evening here as an essential New Orleans experience. The original **Tipitina's** (✉ 501 Napoleon Ave., Uptown, ☎ 504/895–8477) was founded in the mid-1970s as the home base for Professor Longhair, the pioneering rhythm-and-blues pianist and singer who died in 1980; the club takes its name from one of his most popular songs. A bust of "Fess" stands prominently near the front door; first-timers should place their hand upon his bald head upon entering, in a onetime homage. As the multitude of concert posters on the walls indicates, Tip's hosts a wide variety of local and global acts. For about a decade Bruce Daigrepont has played a weekly Cajun dance on Sunday 5 PM–9 PM; free red beans and rice are served.

Exploring New Orleans

The **French Quarter,** the oldest part of the city, lives up to all you've heard: it's alive with the sights, sounds, odors, and experiences of a major entertainment hub. At some point, ignore your better judgment and take a stroll down **Bourbon Street,** past the bars, restaurants, music clubs, and novelty shops that have given this strip its reputation as the playground of the South. With its beautifully landscaped gardens surrounding elegant antebellum homes, the **Garden District** is mostly residential, but most homeowners do not mind you enjoying the sights from outside the cast-iron fences surrounding their magnificent properties.

Numbers in the margin refer to points of interest on the New Orleans map.

🖐 ⑫ **Audubon Aquarium of the Americas.** In this marvelous family attraction, more than 7,000 aquatic creatures swim in 60 displays filled with 500 to 500,000 gallons of water. Each of the four major exhibit areas—the Amazon Rainforest, the Caribbean Reef, the Mississippi River, and the Gulf Coast—has fish and animals native to that environment. A fun exhibit called Beyond Green focuses on frogs; it houses more than 25 frog species and features complementary informative displays. The aquarium's spectacular design allows you to feel part of the watery worlds displayed by providing close-up encounters with inhabitants. Package tickets for the aquarium and a river cruise are available outside the aquarium. You can also combine tickets for the aquarium and the **Entergy IMAX Theater** or for the aquarium, a river cruise, and the **Audubon Zoo.** Note that the zoo cruise halts operation for several weeks around December for maintenance. ☒ *1 Canal St., French Quarter,* ☎ *504/ 581–4629,* WEB *www.auduboninstitute.org.* ▭ *Aquarium $14; combination ticket with IMAX $18; combination ticket for aquarium, zoo, and round-trip cruise $32.50.* ☉ *Aquarium Sun.–Thurs. 9:30–6 (last ticket sold at 5), Fri.–Sat. 9:30–7 (last ticket sold at 6).*

③ **Beauregard-Keyes House.** This stately 19th-century mansion with period furnishings was the temporary home of Confederate general P. G. T. Beauregard. The house and grounds had severely deteriorated in the 1940s when the novelist Frances Parkinson Keyes moved in and helped restore it. Her studio at the back of the large courtyard remains intact, complete with family photos, manuscripts, and her doll and teapot collections. Keyes wrote 40 novels in this studio, all in longhand, among them the local favorite *Dinner at Antoine's.* If you do not have time to tour the house, take a peek through the gates at the beautiful walled garden at the corner of Chartres and Ursulines streets, or enter the garden through the driveway alongside the house, where you will find the gate unlocked during open hours. Landscaped in the same sun pattern as Jackson Square, the garden is in bloom throughout the year. ☒ *1113 Chartres St., French Quarter,* ☎ *504/523–7257.* ▭ *$5.* ☉ *Mon.–Sat. 10–3, tours on the hr.*

⑪ **Customs House.** Since it was built in 1849, this massive building has served as the customs house for the Port of New Orleans. It occupies an entire city block and replaces what had been Fort St. Louis, which guarded the old French city. The building has identical entrances on all four sides, because at the time it was completed no decision had been made as to which side would be the main entrance. You are welcome to look around, but no tours of the building are given. The Customs House will house thousands of bugs, dead and alive, when the **Audubon Insectarium** opens in 2004. Contact the institute for a progress report. ☒ *423 Canal St., French Quarter,* ☎ *504/581–4629,* WEB *www.auduboninstitute.org.*

⑩ **Garden District.** The Garden District is divided into two sections by Jackson Avenue. Upriver from Jackson is the wealthy **Upper Garden District,** where the homes are meticulously upkept. Below Jackson, the **Lower Garden District** is considerably rougher. Though the homes here are often just as structurally beautiful, most of them lack the recent restorations of those of the Upper Garden District. The streets are also less well patrolled; wander cautiously. **Magazine Street,** lined with antiques shops and coffeehouses (ritzier along the Upper Garden District, hipper along the Lower Garden District), serves as a southern border to the Garden District. St. Charles Avenue forms the northern border, and the **St. Charles Avenue streetcar** is a convenient way to get here from downtown. Several companies offer walking tours.

⑤ **Gauche House.** One of the most distinctive houses in the French Quarter, this mansion and its service buildings date to 1856. The cherub design of the effusive ironwork is the only one of its kind. It was once the estate of businessman John Gauche and is still privately owned. This house is not open to the public. *704 Esplanade Ave., French Quarter*

☞ ❼ **Hermann-Grima House.** One of the largest and best-preserved examples of American architecture in the Quarter, this Georgian-style house has the only restored private stable and the only working 1830s creole kitchen in the Quarter. Architect William Brand built the house in 1831. Cooking demonstrations on the open hearth are held here all day Thursday from October through May. You'll want to check the gift shop, which sells crafts and books. ⊠ *820 St. Louis St., French Quarter,* ☎ *504/525–5661,* WEB *www.gnofn.org˜hggh.* 🎫 *$6, combination ticket with Gallier House $10.* ⏰ *Tours weekdays 10–3:30.*

❶ **Jackson Square.** Surrounded by historic buildings and filled with plenty of the city's atmospheric street life, the heart of the French Quarter is a beautifully landscaped park with walkways set like rays streaming out of the center. Originally called the Place d'Armes, the square was founded in 1718 as a military marching ground. It was also the site of public executions carried out in various styles, including burning at the stake, beheading, breaking on the wheel, and hanging. A **statue of Andrew Jackson,** victorious leader of the Battle of New Orleans in the War of 1812, commands the center of the square; the park was renamed for him in the 1850s.

The Spanish-colonial **Cabildo** (☎ 504/568–6968, WEB lsm.crt.state.la. us), which dates from 1799, is where the Louisiana Purchase was made final in 1803. It later served as the city hall and then the state supreme court. It's now a museum open Tuesday to Sunday 9–5; admission is $5. **The Presbytère** (☎ 504/568–6968) now holds an outstanding exhibit on Mardi Gras. It's open Tuesday to Sunday, from 9 to 5; admission is $5. By day, dozens of artists hang their paintings on the park fence and set up outdoor studios where they work on canvases or offer to draw portraits of passersby. These artists are easy to engage in conversation and are knowledgeable about many aspects of the Quarter and New Orleans. You can also be entertained here, day or night, by street performers. ⊠ *French Quarter.* ⏰ *Park daily 8–at least 6 PM.*

❻ **Jean Lafitte National Park Visitor Center.** This center has free visual and sound exhibits on the customs of the state's ethnic groups, as well as information-rich daily history tours of the French Quarter. The one-hour tours leave at 9:30 AM and 11 AM and are free; tickets are handed out one per person (you must be present to get a ticket), beginning at 9 AM, for that day's tours only. Arrive at least 15 minutes before tour time to be sure of a spot. The office also supervises and provides information on Jean Lafitte National Park Barataria Unit across the river from New Orleans, and the Chalmette Battlefield, where the Battle of New Orleans was fought. ⊠ *419 Decatur St., French Quarter,* ☎ *504/589–2636,* WEB *www.nps.gov/jela.* ⏰ *Daily 9–5.*

❾ **Lafayette Cemetery #1.** Begun around 1833, this was the first planned cemetery in the city, with symmetrical rows, roadways for funeral vehicles, and lavish aboveground vaults and tombs for the wealthy families who built the surrounding mansions. In 1852, 2,000 yellow fever victims were buried here. The cemetery and environs figure in Anne Rice's popular series, *The Vampire Chronicles,* and movies such as *Interview with the Vampire* have exploited the eerie beauty of this walled graveyard. You can wander the grounds on your own or take an organized tour. One guided tour is arranged by **Save Our Cemeteries.** ⊠ *1400 block of Washington Ave., Garden District,* ☎ *504/525–3377* *for Save Our Cemeteries.* 🖾 *Cemetery free, tour $6.* ⊙ *Weekdays 7–2:30, Sat. 7–noon. Tours Mon., Wed., and Fri.–Sat. at 10:30.*

❹ Old Mint. Minting began in 1838 in this ambitious Ionic structure, the project of President Andrew Jackson. The New Orleans mint was built to provide currency for the South and the West, which it did until the Confederacy began minting its own currency here in 1861. When supplies ran out, the building served as a barracks, then a prison, for Confederate soldiers; the production of U.S. coins recommenced only in 1879 and stopped again, for good, in 1909. After years of neglect, the federal government handed the Old Mint over to Louisiana in 1966; the state now uses the quarters to exhibit collections of the Louisiana State Museum. The principal exhibit here is the **New Orleans Jazz Collection,** a brief but evocative tour through the history of jazz. Across the hall from the jazz exhibit are several rooms filled with Newcomb pottery and crafts, representing the respected arts practices that emerged from Newcomb Women's College in Uptown New Orleans during the late 19th and early 20th centuries. The **Louisiana Historical Center** holds the French and Spanish Louisiana archives. At the Barracks Street entrance, notice the one remaining sample of the mint's old walls—it'll give you an idea of the building's deterioration before its restoration. 🖾 *400 Esplanade Ave., French Quarter,* ☎ *504/568–6968,* WEB *lsm. crt.state.la.us.* 🖾 *$5.* ⊙ *Tues.–Sun. 9–5.*

❷ St. Louis Cathedral. The oldest active cathedral in the United States dominates Jackson Square on the north side. The austere interior is brightened by murals covering the ceiling and stained-glass windows along the first floor. 🖾 *Jackson Sq., French Quarter,* ☎ *504/525–9585,* WEB *www.saintlouiscathedral.org.* 🖾 *Free.* ⊙ *Mon.–Sat. 9–4:30, Sun. 1–4:30.*

❽ St. Louis Cemetery #1. "Cities of the dead," with rows of crypts like little houses, are one of the New Orleans's most enduring images. This cemetery, the oldest in the city, is an example of the aboveground burial practices of the French and Spanish. Because of the high water level, it was difficult to bury bodies underground without having the coffin float to the surface after the first hard rain. Modern-day burial methods permit underground interment, but many people prefer these ornate family tombs and vaults, which have figured in several movies, among them *Easy Rider.* Although the cemetery is open to the public, it is dangerous to enter it alone because of frequent muggings inside; group tours are a rational option. **Save Our Cemeteries** leads tours every Sunday at 10 AM, or by group appointment, departing from Royal Blend Coffee House at 621 Royal Street. Reserve by Friday afternoon to be sure of a spot on the tour. 🖾 *Basin and Conti Sts., Treme,* ☎ *504/525–3377 for Save Our Cemeteries.* 🖾 *Cemetery free, tours $12.* ⊙ *Cemetery daily 9–3, tours Sun. at 10 AM.*

SIGHTSEEING TOURS

Several companies offer three- to four-hour city tours by bus that include the French Quarter, the Garden District, Uptown New Orleans, and the lakefront. Prices range from $25 to $40 per person. Both Gray Line and New Orleans Tours offer a longer, seven-hour city tour by bus that includes a steamboat ride on the Mississippi River. Gray Line also operates a narrated loop tour by bus with 13 drop-off and pick-up points around the city. The cemeteries of New Orleans fascinate many people because of their unique aboveground tombs. The most famous, St. Louis Cemetery #1, is just outside the French Quarter; Magic Walking Tours, Hidden Treasures Tours, and Save Our Cemeteries offer guided walking tours. Reservations are generally required.

➤ TOUR OPERATORS: **Gray Line** (☎ 504/587–0861, WEB www. graylineneworleans.com). **Hidden Treasures Tours** (☎ 504/529–

4507). **Magic Walking Tours** (☎ 504/588–9693, WEB www. neworleansmagicwalkingtours.com). **New Orleans Tours** (☎ 504/592–1991 or 800/543–6332, WEB www.notours.com). **Save Our Cemeteries** (☎ 504/525–3377, WEB www.saveourcemeteries.org).

PORT CANAVERAL

Port Canaveral is located at the top of the barrier island that includes Cocoa Beach, sister to the town of Cocoa, on the mainland. Cocoa Beach is a popular year-round escape for Central Floridians, and it's just 10 minutes from the Kennedy Space Center. It's a busy port, by some accounts even busier than Port Everglades in Fort Lauderdale, and the embarkation point for many three- and four-day cruises to the Bahamas, as well as a few seven-day cruises. Many cruisers combine a short cruise with a stay at one of Orlando's popular theme parks, which are about an hour away.

The Cruise Port

Port Canaveral has six cruise terminals and is the home port of the two Disney Cruise Line ships. Carnival and Royal Caribbean also base ships here, as do some smaller lines.

In Brevard County, Port Canaveral is on State Road (S.R.) 528, also known as the Beeline Expressway, which runs straight to Orlando, which has the nearest airport. To drive to Port Canaveral from there, take the north exit out of the airport, staying to the right, to S.R. 528 (Beeline Expressway) East. Take S.R. 528 directly to Port Canaveral; it's about a 45-minute drive.

➤ CONTACTS: **Canaveral Port Authority** (✉ 9150 Christopher Columbus Dr., ☎ 321/783–7831 or 888/767–8226, WEB www.portcanaveral.org).

AIRPORT TRANSFERS

The Orlando airport is 45 minutes away from the docks. If you have not arranged airport transfers with your cruise line, then you will need to make your own arrangements. Taxis are expensive, but several companies offer minivan shuttles to Port Canaveral. For example, you can rent an entire van from Art's Shuttle for your group (about $50 for up to three people and then $10 for each additional person). Busy Traveler Transportation has scheduled trips to Port Canaveral from Orlando International Airport; parties of less than three might opt for Cocoa Beach Shuttle, which charges $20 per person. But you will need to make a reservation in advance regardless of which service you use.

➤ CONTACTS: **Art's Shuttle** (☎ 371/783–2112 or 800/567–5099). **Busy Traveler Transportation, Inc.** (☎ 321/453–5278 or 800/496–7433). **Cocoa Beach Shuttle** (☎ 888/784–4144).

PARKING

Outdoor, gated lots are near the terminals and cost $10 a day, which must be paid in advance, either in cash or by major credit card (MasterCard and Visa only).

VISITOR INFORMATION

➤ CONTACTS: **Cocoa Beach Area Chamber of Commerce** (✉ 400 Fortenberry Rd., Merritt Island 32952, ☎ 321/459–2200, WEB www. cocoabeachchamber.com).

Where to Stay

For price categories, *see* Lodging at the beginning of this chapter.

$$–$$$$ 🏨 **Inn at Cocoa Beach.** The finest accommodations in Cocoa Beach are in this charming oceanfront inn. Each spacious room is decorated differently, but all have some combination of reproduction 18th- and 19th-

Port Canaveral Area

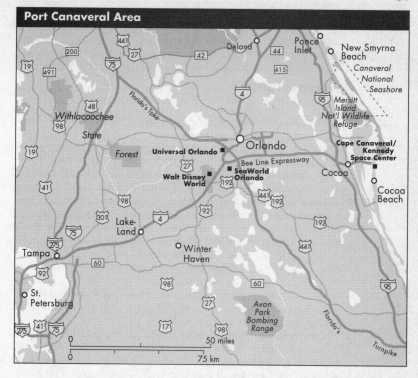

century armoires, four-poster beds, and comfortably upholstered chairs and sofas. There are several suites, some with whirlpool baths. All units have balconies or patios and views of the ocean. Included in the rate are an evening spread of wine and cheese and a sumptuous Continental breakfast with delicious homemade muffins and breads, served in the sunny breakfast room. ✉ *4300 Ocean Beach Blvd., Cocoa Beach 32931,* ☎ *321/799–3460; 800/343–5307 outside Florida,* FAX *321/ 784–8632,* WEB *www.theinnatcocoabeach.com. 50 rooms. In-room safes, some in-room hot tubs, cable TV, pool, fitness room, beach, bicycles, shuffleboard, bar, dry cleaning, meeting rooms, free parking; no kids under 12. AE, D, MC, V. CP.*

$$–$$$ ⊞ **Cocoa Beach Hilton Oceanfront.** It's easy to pass by the Hilton, since its sign is sometimes hidden by the dense foliage that grows right out to the edge of Route A1A. Once you turn into the parking lot, however, it's impossible to miss. At seven stories, it's one of the tallest buildings in Cocoa Beach. Just a small strip of sand dunes separates this resort from a wide stretch of excellent beach. Most rooms have ocean views, but for true drama get a room on the east end directly facing the water. The floor-to-ceiling windows really show off the scenery. ✉ *1550 N. Atlantic Ave., Cocoa Beach 32931,* ☎ *321/799–0003 or 800/526–2609,* FAX *321/799–0344,* WEB *www.cocoabeachhilton.com. 296 rooms, 11 suites. 2 restaurants, room service, in-room data ports, cable TV with movies, pool, fitness room, beach, volleyball, bars, video game room, dry cleaning, laundry facilities, Internet, convention center, meeting rooms, free parking, no-smoking rooms. AE, D, DC, MC, V.*

$–$$$ ⊞ **Wakulla Resort.** There's nothing fancy about these two-bedroom suites. They attract families because they're clean and comfortable, are just two blocks from the beach, and are convenient to NASA's attractions as well as those in Orlando. The five-room suites, designed to sleep six, include two bedrooms, a living room, dining room, and fully equipped kitchen.

Outdoor grills are available. ⊠ *3550 N. Atlantic Ave., Cocoa Beach 32931,* ☎ *321/783–2230 or 800/992–5852,* FAX *321/783–0980,* WEB *www. wakulla-suites.com. 116 suites. Kitchens, cable TV with movies and video games, pool, shuffleboard, dry cleaning, laundry facilities, business services, free parking, no-smoking rooms. AE, D, DC, MC, V.*

Where to Eat

For price categories, *see* Dining at the beginning of this chapter.

$$–$$$$ ✕ **Mango Tree Restaurant.** Dine in elegance at tables discretely spaced amid orchid gardens, with piano music playing in the background. House favorites include fresh grouper with shrimp and scallops glazed in hollandaise sauce, Indian River crab cakes, coq au vin, and veal Chandlier (scallopini seared with scallops and cognac). ⊠ *118 N. Atlantic Ave., Cocoa Beach,* ☎ *321/799–0513. AE, MC, V. Closed Mon. No lunch.*

$$–$$$ ✕ **Black Tulip.** Two cozy rooms yield some of Cocoa Village's finest food. Starters include island conch fritters served with a spicy mango dipping sauce or a three-cheese baked French onion soup. The chef's signature dish is roast duckling served with a sauce made of apples, cashews, and red wine. Or try the filet mignon medallions with a tangy mustard and artichoke sauce. Seafood lovers will go for the baked mahi-mahi topped with sliced bananas and served with a lemon-dill sauce. Lunch selections are lighter and include sandwiches and salads. ⊠ *207 Brevard Ave., Cocoa,* ☎ *321/631–1133. AE, DC, MC, V. Closed Sun.*

$$–$$$ ✕ **Cafe Margaux.** Choose a table outside in a charming courtyard or indoors in a flower-decorated dining room at this intimate Cocoa Village spot. If wild game suits your palate, try the pan-seared pheasant breast or the Long Island duckling. Seafood lovers may want to try the phyllo-encased Norwegian salmon medallions stuffed with French goat cheese or the sesame-seared ahi tuna over Japanese cucumbers. ⊠ *220 Brevard Ave., Cocoa,* ☎ *321/639–8343. AE, D, DC, MC, V. Closed Sun. and Tues.*

¢–$ ✕ **Lone Cabbage Fish Camp.** The natural habitat of wildlife and local characters, this one-of-a-kind spot sits on the St. Johns River, 9 mi north of the Cocoa city limits and 4 mi west of Interstate 95. Catfish, country ham, and fried turtle and alligator make the drive worthwhile. You can also fish from a dock here or take an airboat ride. Check out the gator souvenirs behind the bar and the Swamp Monster, stuffed and mounted on the wall; it was "caught" by one of the owners, Charlie Jones. ⊠ *8199 Rte. 520, Cocoa,* ☎ *321/632–4199. AE, MC, V.*

Beaches

Thirty-five-acre **Jetty Park** (⊠ 400 E. Jetty Park Dr., ☎ 321/783–7111) is right at the port. There's a fishing pier, nice beach area, campground, rest rooms with showers, and even a little store. Admission is $3 per car. North of Cocoa, **Playalinda Beach** (⊠ Rte. 402, Titusville, ☎ 321/267–1110), part of the **Canaveral National Seashore,** is the longest undeveloped stretch on Florida's Atlantic coast—hundreds of giant sea turtles come ashore here between May and August to lay their eggs. The park's extreme northern area is favored by nude sunbathers. There are no lifeguards, but park rangers patrol. Take Exit 80 from Interstate 95 and follow Route 406 east across the Indian River, then Route 402 east for another 12 mi. It's open daily from 6 to 6, and admission is $5 per vehicle. **Sydney Fisher Park at Cocoa Beach** (⊠ 2100 block of Rte. A1A) has showers, playgrounds, changing areas, picnic areas with grills, snack shops, and plenty of well-maintained, inexpensive, surfside parking lots. Beach vendors carry necessities for sunning and swimming. The parking fee is $3 for cars and $5 for RVs.

Shopping

In downtown Cocoa, cobblestone walkways wend through **Olde Cocoa Village,** a cluster of restored turn-of-the-20th-century buildings now occupied by restaurants and specialty shops purveying crafts, fine art, and clothing. **Ron Jon Surf Shop** (⊠ 4151 N. Atlantic Ave., Cocoa Beach, ☎ 321/799–8888) is an attraction in its own right—a castle that's purple, pink, and glittery as an amusement park, plunked down in the middle of the beach community. The multilevel store is packed with swimwear and surfboards and is open around the clock. It's worth a stop just to see what all those billboards are about.

Exploring the Cape Canaveral Area

With the Kennedy Space Center just 10 minutes away, there is plenty to do in and around Cocoa Beach, though many folks opt to travel the extra hour into Orlando to visit the popular theme parks.

Astronaut Memorial Planetarium and Observatory. One of the largest public-access observatories in Florida has a 24-inch telescope through which you can view objects in the solar system and deep space. The planetarium also has two theaters. One shows such films as *Deep Space Frontiers, Hubble Vision,* and *Planet Safari.* The other showcases planetarium and laser-light shows. The Science Quest Hall has an exhibit of scales calibrated to other planets. Travel 2½ mi east of Interstate 95 Exit 201 on Route 520, and take Route 501 north for 1¾ mi. ⊠ *1519 Clearlake Rd., Cocoa,* ☎ *321/634–3732,* WEB *www.brevard.cc.fl.us.* ⊠ *Observatory and exhibit hall free; film or planetarium show $6, both $10; laser show $6; Triple Combination (planetarium, movie, laser show) $14.* ☉ *Wed. 1:30–4:30, Fri.–Sat. 6:30–10:30; call for current shows and schedules.*

☾ **Brevard Museum of History and Natural Science.** Don't overlook the hands-on discovery rooms and the Taylor Collection of Victorian memorabilia at this fine science museum. Its nature center has 22 acres of trails encompassing three distinct ecosystems—sand pine hills, lake lands, and marshlands. ⊠ *2201 Michigan Ave., Cocoa,* ☎ *321/632–1830,* WEB *www.brevardmuseum.com.* ⊠ *$5.* ☉ *Tues.–Sat. 10–4, Sun. 1–4.*

☾ **Kennedy Space Center Visitor Complex.** Exhibits include **Astronaut Encounter,** where you can question a real astronaut, and **Exploration in the New Millennium,** a journey through time from the early Vikings' discoveries of Greenland and Iceland to 1976, when the first U.S. probe landed on Mars. You have an opportunity to touch a piece of Mars and to sign up for a future space flight. **Robot Scouts** is a walk-through exhibit of unmanned planetary probes; **Early Space Exploration** highlights the Mercury and Gemini programs; and the **Rocket Garden** contains a collection of authentic rockets. The **Apollo Saturn V Center** has multimedia shows as well as the 363-ft *Saturn V* rocket, and the **International Space Station Center** displays a detailed re-creation of a space-station module. Twin 5½-story-tall IMAX theaters with awesome sound systems can make you think you're at a launch (note that the center closes for some launch dates). There are two IMAX movies: *The Dream Is Alive,* narrated by Walter Cronkite, takes you through astronaut training and into the cabins where the astronauts live while in space. The latest film, *Space Station,* narrated by Tom Cruise, leads you on a journey to the International Space Station, 220 mi above Earth. The 3-D technology lets you see a space walk and navigate the Space Station as an astronaut does. You must purchase tickets for all exhibits and areas of the space complex. ⊠ *Rte. 405, Kennedy Space Center,* ☎ *321/449–4444 or 800/572–4636,* WEB *www.kennedyspacecenter.com.* ⊠ *$26 all-inclusive.* ☉ *Daily 9–5:30 (last tour at 2:45); call ahead regarding launch date closures.*

Merritt Island National Wildlife Refuge. Examine wildlife and rivers of grass at the 140,000-acre preserve adjacent to the Canaveral National Seashore. Wander along nature trails at this habitat for wintering migratory waterfowl, and take a self-guided, 7-mi driving tour along Black Point Wildlife Drive. On the Oak Hammock Foot Trail, learn about the plants of a hammock community. ⊠ *Rte. 402, across Titusville causeway,* ☎ *321/861–0667.* ☒ *Free.* ☉ *Daily sunrise–sunset; visitor center Nov.–Mar. daily 8–4:30, Apr.–Oct. Mon.–Sat. 8–4:30.*

United States Astronaut Hall of Fame. At the entrance to the Kennedy Space Center Visitor Complex, the hall of fame focuses not only on the milestones of the space program but also on the personal stories of the astronauts. Highlights of the interactive **Astronaut Adventure** include a mock lift-off with a take-your-breath-away g-force simulator and a hair-raising re-creation jet-aircraft dogfight complete with 360° barrel rolls. For a quiet interlude, view videotapes of historic moments in the space program. The **First on the Moon** exhibit focuses on the crew selection for *Apollo 11* and the Soviet Union's role in the space race. Also here is **U.S. Space Camp,** with budding astronauts in a hands-on learning environment. ⊠ *6225 Vectorspace Blvd., off Rte. 405, Kennedy Space Center, Titusville,* ☎ *321/269–6100,* ⴱ *www.astronauts.org.* ☒ *$13.95.* ☉ *Sept.–May, daily 9–5; June–Aug., daily 9–6.*

ORLANDO THEME PARKS

SeaWorld Orlando. In the world's largest marine adventure park, every attraction is devoted to demonstrating the ways that humans can protect the mammals, birds, fish, and reptiles that live in the ocean and its tributaries. The presentations are gentle reminders of our responsibility to safeguard the environment, and you'll find that SeaWorld's use of humor plays a major role in this education. The park is small enough that, armed with a map that lists show times, you can plan a chronological approach that flows easily from one attraction to the next. Near the intersection of I–4 and the Beeline Expressway; take I–4 to Exit 71 or 72 and follow signs. ⊠ *7007 Sea Harbor Dr., International Drive Area, Orlando,* ☎ *407/351–3600 or 800/327–2424,* ⴱ *www. seaworld.com.* ☒ *$55.33.* ☉ *Daily 9–6 or 7, until as late as 11 summer and holidays; educational programs daily, some beginning as early as 6:30 AM.*

Universal Orlando. The resort consists of **Universal Studios** (the original movie theme park), **Islands of Adventure** (the second theme park), and **CityWalk** (the dining-shopping-nightclub complex). Although it's bordered by residential neighborhoods and thickly trafficked International Drive, Universal Orlando is surprisingly expansive, intimate, and accessible, with two massive parking complexes, easy walks to all attractions, and a motor launch that cruises to the hotels. While Universal Orlando emphasizes "two parks, two days, one great adventure," you may find the presentation, creativity, and cutting-edge technology bringing you back for more. ⊠ *1000 Universal Studios Plaza, Orlando 32819-7610,* ☎ *407/363–8000 or 888/331–9108,* ⴱ *www. universalorlando.com.* ☒ *One-day, one-park ticket $52.95, two-day pass $100.65; parking $8, $10 for RVs.* ☉ *Usually 9–9, but hrs vary seasonally; CityWalk restaurants and bars have individual open hrs.*

Walt Disney World. Walt Disney World is a huge complex of theme parks and attractions, each of which is worth a visit. Parks include the **Magic Kingdom,** a family favorite and the original here; **Epcot,** Disney's international, educational park; **Disney–MGM Studios,** a movie-oriented theme park; and **Disney's Animal Kingdom,** which is much more than a zoo. Beyond these, there are water parks, elaborate minigolf courses, a sports center, resorts, restaurants, and nightlife. If you have only one day, you'll have to concentrate on a single park; Disney–MGM Studios or Animal Kingdom are easiest to do in a day, but arrive early and expect to stay until park closing, which might be as early as 5 PM for Animal Kingdom or as late as 11 PM during busy seasons at the Magic Kingdom. The most direct route to the Disney Parks from Port Canaveral is S.R. 528 (the Beeline Expressway) to I–4; when you get through Orlando, follow the signs to Disney and expect traffic. ⊠ *Lake Buena Vista,* ☎ *407/824–4321.* ▣ *One-day, one-park pass $53, parking $7 per day.* ☉ *Most parks open by 9 AM; closing hrs vary, but usually 5 PM for Animal Kingdom and 6–11 PM for other parks, depending on season.*

SAN JUAN, PUERTO RICO

In addition to being a major port of call, San Juan is one of the preeminent ports of embarkation for cruises on Southern Caribbean itineraries. For information on dining, shopping, nightlife, and sightseeing *see* San Juan, Puerto Rico *in* Chapter 4.

The Cruise Port

Cruise ships dock within a couple of blocks of Old San Juan. The Paseo de la Princesa, a tree-lined promenade beneath the city wall, is a nice place for a stroll—you can admire the local crafts and stop at the refreshment kiosks. A tourist information booth is in the cruise-terminal area. Major sights in the Old San Juan area are mere blocks from the piers, but be aware that the streets are narrow and steeply inclined in places. Even if you have only a few hours before your cruise, you'll have time to do a little sightseeing.

AIRPORT TRANSFERS

The ride from the Luis Muñoz Marín International Airport, east of downtown San Juan, to the docks in Old San Juan takes about 20 minutes. The white "taxi turistico" cabs, marked by a logo on the door, have a fixed rate of $16 to the cruise-ship piers; there is a small fee for luggage. Other taxi companies charge by the mile, which can cost a little more. Be sure the driver starts the meter, or agree on a fare beforehand.

VISITOR INFORMATION

➤ CONTACTS: **Puerto Rico Tourism Company** (Box 902-3960, Old San Juan Station, San Juan, PR 00902-3960, ☎ 787/721–2400, WEB www. gotopuertorico.com; ⊠ 666 Fifth Ave., New York, NY 10103 ☎ 800/ 223–6530; ⊠ 3575 W. Cahuenga Blvd., Suite 560, Los Angeles, CA 90068, ☎ 213/874–5991; ⊠ 901 Ponce de León Blvd., Suite 101, Coral Gables, FL 33134, ☎ 305/445–9112; ⊠ Plaza Dársenas, near Pier 1, Old San Juan, ☎ 787/722–1709; ⊠ Aeropuerto Internacional Luis Muñoz Marín, ☎ 787/791–1014 or 787/791–2551).

Where to Stay

If you are planning to spend one night in San Juan before your cruise departs, you'll probably find it easier to stay in Old San Juan, where the cruise-ship terminals are. But if you want to spend a few extra days in the city, there are other possibilities near good beaches a bit further out.

For price categories, *see* Lodging at the beginning of this chapter.

$$$$ 🏨 **Ritz-Carlton San Juan Hotel, Spa & Casino.** The Ritz's signature elegance won't undermine the feeling that this is a true beach getaway. The hotel's sandy stretch is lovely, as is the free-form pool, which is surrounded by a garden overlooking the ocean. Works by local artists adorn the lobby lounge and the hallways leading to the well-equipped business center. A full-service spa begs to pamper you with aloe body wraps and *parcha* (passion-fruit juice) massages. Though most room

windows are sealed shut to muffle airport noise, many suites open onto terraces. ⊠ *Av. Las Gobernadores (Rte. 187), Isla Verde 00979,* ☎ *787/253–1700 or 800/241–3333,* FAX *787/253–0700,* WEB *www. ritzcarlton.com. 403 rooms, 11 suites. 3 restaurants, in-room data ports, minibars, cable TV, 2 tennis courts, pool, gym, hair salon, health club, hot tub, massage, spa, beach, 3 bars, casino, nightclub, shop, children's programs (ages 4–12), concierge floor, business services, meeting rooms, parking (fee), no-smoking floor. AE, D, DC, MC, V. EP.*

$$$–$$$$ 🏨 **Caribe Hilton San Juan.** Beyond the lobby, your eyes are gently led to the Atlantic blue past the edge of the infinity pool. The beach, the only private one in San Juan, has been expanded. The open-air lobby's sunken bar looks out over the gentle cascades of a tri-level pool, which is adjacent to a wading pool and an area with whirlpool tubs. Rooms have ocean or lagoon views, and those on the executive floor include such services as private check-in and check-out and free Continental breakfast and evening cocktails. Local businesspeople frequent the on-site Morton's of Chicago restaurant. ⊠ *Calle Los Rosales, San Gerónimo Grounds, Puerta de Tierra, 00901,* ☎ *787/721–0303 or 800/468–8585,* FAX *787/725–8849,* WEB *www.caribehilton.com. 602 rooms, 44 suites. 3 restaurants, 3 tennis courts, pool, wading pool, health club, hot tub, spa, beach, 2 bars, shops, children's programs (ages 4–12), business services, meeting rooms, parking (fee). AE, D, DC, MC, V. BP.*

$$$–$$$$ 🏨 **El Convento Hotel.** Once a Carmelite convent, this 350-year-old building is a prime example of the right way to blend old-world gentility with modern luxury. Much of the original architecture is intact, including a colonial interior courtyard. Rooms have a Spanish-deco look, with dark woods, wrought-iron lamps, and ornate furniture. Complimentary wine and hors d'oeuvres are served before dinner, and there's an honor bar that's open until 4 AM. The courtyard's Café del Níspero and street-side Café Bohemio are among the dining choices. ⊠ *Calle Cristo 100, Old San Juan. Box 1048, 00902* ☎ *787/723–9020 or 800/ 468–2779,* FAX *787/721–2877,* WEB *www.elconvento.com. 54 rooms, 4 suites. 4 restaurants, in-room safes, minibars, pool, gym, massage, 2 bars, library, shops, meeting room, parking (fee). AE, D, DC, MC, V. CP.*

$$$ 🏨 **Wyndham Old San Juan Hotel & Casino.** The gleaming Wyndham blends classic Spanish colonial lines with a modern, triangular shape that subtly echoes the cruise ships docked nearby. The lobby, adjacent to the casino, shines with multihued tiles and mahogany. Each standard room—with honey-colored rugs, floral prints, and light woods—has a two-line phone, a coffeemaker, and a hair dryer. Spacious suites also have sitting rooms and extra TVs. On the ninth floor you'll find a small patio pool and whirlpool bath; the seventh-floor concierge level provides hassle-free check-ins, Continental breakfasts, and evening hors d'oeuvres. ⊠ *Calle Brumbaugh 100, Old San Juan 00901,* ☎ *787/ 721–5100 or 800/996–3426,* FAX *787/721–1111,* WEB *www.wyndham. com. 185 rooms, 55 suites. Restaurant, some minibars, cable TV, pool, gym, hot tub, massage, 2 bars, casino, concierge floor, business services, meeting rooms, parking (fee). AE, D, DC, MC, V. CP.*

¢–$ 🏨 **Hostería del Mar.** Condado's high-rises are far to the west of this small, white inn on the beach in Ocean Park. Rooms are attractive and simple, with tropical prints and rattan furniture. Many rooms have ocean views, and four apartments have kitchenettes. The staff is courteous and helpful, and the ground-floor restaurant, which serves vegetarian dishes and fruit shakes as well as seafood and steaks, faces the trade winds and has breathtaking beach views. ⊠ *Calle Tapia 1, Ocean Park 00911,* ☎ *787/727–3302 or 800/742–4276,* FAX *787/268–0772,* WEB *www.prhtasmallhotels.com. 8 rooms, 4 apartments, 1 suite. Restaurant, some kitchenettes, beach, free parking. AE, D, DC, MC, V. EP.*

TAMPA

Although glitzy Miami seems to hold the trendiness trump card and Orlando is the place your kids want to visit annually until they hit middle school, the Tampa Bay area has that elusive quality that many attribute to the "real Florida." The state's second-largest metro area is less fast-lane than its biggest (Miami), or even Orlando, but its strengths are just as varied, from broad cultural diversity to a sunset-worshiping beach culture. Florida's third-busiest airport, a vibrant business community, world-class beaches, and superior hotels and resorts—many of them historic—make this an excellent place to spend a week or a lifetime. Carnival and Royal Caribbean base several ships in Tampa for cruises to the Western Caribbean, Holland America one ship, and several other lines base ships here seasonally.

The Cruise Port

Tampa is the largest shipping port in the state of Florida, and it's becoming ever more important to the cruise industry. In Tampa's downtown area, the port is linked to nearby Ybor City and the rest of the Tampa Bay Area by a new streetcar line.

To reach the port by car, take I–4 West to Exit 1 (Ybor City), and go south on 21st Street. To get to Terminals 2 and 6, turn right on Adamo Drive (Highway 60), then left on Channelside Drive. To get to Terminal 7, continue beyond Adamo Drive, where 21st Street merges with 22nd Street, and turn right on Maritime Boulevard, then left on Guy N. Verger to Hooker's Point.
➤ CONTACTS: **Tampa Port Authority** (✉ 1101 Channelside Dr., Tampa, ☎ 813/905–7678 or 800/741–2297, WEB www.tampaport.com).

AIRPORT TRANSFERS

Bay Shuttle provides van-shuttle service from Tampa International Airport to the cruise-ship terminals for a fee of $10 for the first passenger, $8 for each additional passenger. You need to make a reservation.
➤ CONTACTS: **Bay Shuttle** (☎ 813/259–9998, WEB www.tampabayshuttle.com).

PARKING

Parking is available at the port directly across from the terminals. For Terminals 2 and 3 (Carnival and Royal Caribbean), parking is in a garage across the street. For Terminal 6 (Holland America), parking is outdoors in a guarded, enclosed lot. The cost is $10 a day, payable in advance by credit card (MasterCard or Visa) or in cash.

VISITOR INFORMATION

➤ CONTACTS: **St. Petersburg/Clearwater Area Convention & Visitors Bureau** (✉ 14450 46th St. N, Suite 108, St. Petersburg 33762, ☎ 727/464–7200 or 877/352–3224, WEB www.floridasbeach.com). **Tampa Bay Convention and Visitors Bureau** (✉ 400 N. Tampa St., Suite 2800, Tampa 33602, ☎ 800/368–2672 or 813/223–1111, WEB www.visittampabay.com).

Where to Stay in the Tampa Bay Area

If you want to be close to the cruise-ship terminal, then you'll have to stay in Tampa, but if you want to spend more time in the area and perhaps stay on the beach, St. Petersburg and the beaches are close by.

For price categories, *see* Lodging at the beginning of this chapter.

$$$$ 🏨 **Don CeSar Beach Resort.** A favorite of Scott and Zelda Fitzgerald, this sprawling, sybaritic beachfront "Pink Palace" has long been a Gulf Coast landmark because of its remarkable architecture. Steeped in turn-of-the-last-century elegance, the hotel claims a rich history, com-

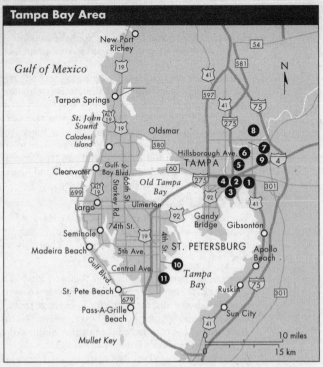

Tampa Bay Area

plete with a resident ghost. The restaurant, Maritana Grille, specializes in Florida seafood and is lined with huge fish tanks. The more casual Don CeSar Beach House, less than ½ mi from the main building,
has one-bedroom condos and a great little beach bar. ⊠ *3400 Gulf
Blvd., St. Pete Beach 33706,* ☎ *727/360–1881 or 800/282–1116,* FAX
727/367–3609, WEB *www.doncesar.com. 234 rooms, 43 suites at resort;
70 condos at Beach House. 3 restaurants, ice cream parlor, room service, in-room data ports, some kitchens, 2 pools, health club, hair salon,
spa, beach, boating, jet skiing, parasailing, volleyball, 2 bars, lobby
lounge, shops, baby-sitting, children's programs (ages 5–12), dry cleaning, laundry service, concierge, business services, meeting room, airport shuttle. AE, DC, MC, V.*

$$$–$$$$ 🏨 **Tampa Marriott Waterside.** Across from the Tampa Convention Cen-
ter, this downtown hotel was built for conventioneers but is also con-
venient to popular tourist spots such as the Florida Aquarium, the St.
Pete Times Forum hockey arena, and shopping and entertainment dis-
tricts Channelside, Hyde Park, and Ybor City. At least half of the rooms
and most of the suites overlook the channel to Tampa Bay; the bay it-
self is visible from the higher floors of the 27-story resort. The lobby
coffee bar overlooks the water. Il Terrazzo is the hotel's formal, Italian
dining room. The three golf courses at which the hotel offers privileges
are about 20 minutes away. ⊠ *700 S. Florida Ave., Downtown, Tampa
33602,* ☎ *813/221–4900,* FAX *813/221–0923* WEB *www.tampawaterside.
com. 681 rooms, 36 suites. 3 restaurants, grill, room service, in-room
data ports, in-room safes, golf privileges, pool, gym, hair salon, spa, boat-
ing, marina, bar, lobby lounge, baby-sitting, laundry facilities, laundry
service, business services, car rental. AE, D, DC, MC, V.*

$$$–$$$$ 🏨 **Tradewinds Resort.** Most rooms have a view of the beach at this
sprawling gulf-front property, which is actually three resorts in one.
The place has some of the showmanship of an Orlando hotel, with a

huge man-made lagoon inside, complete with gondolas on its labyrinthine waterways. The resort's own kids' character, Beaker the Toucan, makes appearances at kids' programs and can even tuck your child into bed at night for a fee. There are on-site swimming lessons for kids and adults. ✉ *5500 Gulf Blvd., St. Pete Beach 33706,* ☎ *727/562–1212 or 800/ 237–0707,* FAX *727/562–1214,* WEB *www.tradewindsresort.com. 644 rooms, 473 suites (Island Grand: 378 rooms, 200 suites; Sandpiper: 56 rooms, 103 suites; Sirata Beach: 210 rooms, 170 suites). 11 restaurants, ice cream parlor, pizzeria, in-room data ports, in-room safes, some kitchenettes, some minibars, refrigerators, some in-room VCRs, putting green, 4 tennis courts, 10 pools, outdoor hot tubs, health club, spa, beach, boating, jet skiing, volleyball, 4 bars, sports bar, video game room, shops, children's programs (ages 4–11), laundry facilities, laundry service, Internet, business services, meeting rooms. AE, D, DC, MC, V.*

$$$ 🏨 **Wyndham Harbour Island Hotel.** Even though this 12-story hotel is on a 177-acre island in Tampa Bay, it's just an eight-minute walk and short drive from downtown Tampa. Many units have terrific views of the water or the downtown skyline. The lobby has light-wood paneling and fashionable furniture. Service is attentive. There is a marina, and you may use the extensive health and fitness center and 20 tennis courts at the Harbour Island Athletic Club, next door, for a fee. This is a good choice for those who want to be downtown without actually being in the midst of the action. ✉ *725 S. Harbour Island Blvd., Harbour Island, Tampa 33602,* ☎ *813/229–5000,* FAX *813/229–5322,* WEB *www.wyndham.com. 279 rooms, 20 suites. Restaurant, room service, in-room data ports, minibars, pool, dock, boating, fishing, bar, lobby lounge, laundry service. AE, DC, MC, V.*

$$–$$$ 🏨 **Don Vicente de Ybor Historic Inn.** This boutique hotel is in a carefully restored building constructed in 1895 by Vicente Martinez Ybor, the founder of Ybor City. From the pink stucco exterior to the white marble staircase in the main lobby, the hotel is an architectural tour de force. Rooms have antique furnishings, Persian rugs, and four-poster canopied beds. Most rooms have wrought-iron balconies. The clubs and shops of Ybor City are within a short walk. ✉ *1915 Republica de Cuba, Ybor City, Tampa 33605,* ☎ *813/241–4545,* FAX *813/241–6104,* WEB *www. donvicenteinn.com. 16 suites. Restaurant, in-room data ports, bar, dry cleaning, laundry service. AE, D, DC, MC, V.*

$$–$$$ 🏨 **Hilton Garden Inn Tampa Ybor Historic District.** Architecturally, this property pales when compared to the century-old classic structures around it in Ybor City, but it is convenient: just across the street from the Centro Ybor complex, 2 mi from downtown Tampa, and 5 mi from Tampa International Airport. The hotel restaurant has a full breakfast buffet and doesn't try to compete with the culinary heavyweights in a six-block radius. Rooms are business traveler–friendly, with dual phone lines, large desks, and ergonomic chairs. ✉ *1700 E. 9th Ave., Ybor City, Tampa 33605,* ☎ *813/769–9267,* FAX *813/769–3299,* WEB *www. tampayborhistoricdistrict.gardeninn.com. 8 rooms, 11 suites. Restaurant, in-room data ports, microwaves, refrigerators, pool, exercise equipment, laundry facilities, laundry service, business services. AE, D, DC, MC, V.*

$–$$$ 🏨 **Island's End Cottages.** These simply decorated one- and three-bedroom cottages have water views. Outdoors, attractive wooden walkways lead to latticework sitting areas and peaceful gazebos. The grounds are nicely landscaped, and you can walk to the beach, restaurants, and shops. Grills are available if you want to barbecue. This small resort is a great place for families who want to enjoy the beach life. ✉ *1 Pass-A-Grille Way, St. Pete Beach 33706,* ☎ *727/360–5023,* FAX *727/367–7890,* WEB *www.islandsend.com. 6 cottages. Kitchens, in-room VCRs, pool, fishing, laundry facilities. MC, V.*

Where to Eat in the Tampa Bay Area

For price categories, *see* Dining at the beginning of this chapter.

$$–$$$$ ✕ **Bern's Steak House.** Fine mahogany paneling and ornate chandeliers define the elegance at legendary Bern's, which many feel is Tampa's best restaurant. Chef-owner Bern Lexer ages his own beef, grows his own organic vegetables, roasts his own coffee, and maintains his own saltwater fish tanks. Cuts of topmost beef are sold by weight and thickness. The wine list includes some 7,000 selections (with 1,800 dessert wines). After dinner, take a tour of the kitchen and wine cellar before having dessert upstairs in a cozy booth. ✉ *1208 S. Howard Ave., Hyde Park, Tampa,* ☎ *813/251–2421; 800/282–1547 in Florida,* WEB *www. bernsteakhouse.com. AE, DC, MC, V. No lunch.*

$$–$$$$ ✕ **Big City Tavern.** The name makes the place sound like it's merely a bar, but it's far more than that. In the ballroom of a historic Cuban social club, with an ornate tin ceiling and dark wood furniture, this classy dining room serves well-prepared dishes, ranging from veal saltimbocca with potato lasagna to a tasty pan-fried Carolina trout. A great starter is the lobster-and-carrot soup. There's a good selection of wines by the glass and imported beers from Ireland, Australia, and in between. The tavern is relatively quiet and removed from the frenzied crowds at street level. ✉ *Centro Ybor, 1600 E. 8th Ave., 2nd floor, Ybor City, Tampa,* ☎ *813/247–3000. AE, D, MC, V. No lunch weekends.*

$$–$$$ ✕ **Columbia.** A fixture since 1905, this magnificent structure with spacious dining rooms and a sunny courtyard takes up an entire city block. The paella is possibly the best in Florida, and the Columbia 1905 salad—with ham, olives, cheese, and garlic—is legendary. The menu has Cuban classics such as *ropa vieja* and *arroz con pollo.* There's flamenco dancing most nights. You can buy and smoke hand-rolled cigars in the bar. ✉ *2117 E. 7th Ave., Ybor City, Tampa,* ☎ *813/248–4961,* WEB *www.columbiarestaurant.com. AE, D, DC, MC, V.*

$–$$$ ✕ **Gratzzi.** This warm northern Italian eatery hits local critics' short lists of best restaurants, attesting to its prowess with tasty classics such as veal saltimbocca and osso buco with pan-seared polenta. While the *zuppa de pesce* (fish soup) is a pricey dish at $16.50 a bowl, it's also one of the best, with expertly prepared mussels, clams, shrimp, scallops, and whitefish in a red sauce on pasta. Other dishes on the extensive menu are more affordable and include rotisserie-cooked meat and seafood. ✉ *199 2nd Ave. N, BayWalk, St. Petersburg,* ☎ *727/822–7769. AE, D, DC, MC, V. No lunch.*

$–$$$ ✕ **Marchand's Grill.** Once the Pompeii Room in the former Vinoy Hotel, opened in 1925, this wonderful eatery has frescoed ceilings and a spectacular view of Tampa Bay and the nearby boat docks. The food is impressive as well. The imaginative, changing menu lists temptations such as asparagus ravioli, roasted eggplant soup, browned gnocchi with wild mushrooms and pinot grigio broth, and seafood bouillabaisse. The wine list is extensive, including a number of by-the-glass selections. There is live music Tuesday through Saturday nights. ✉ *Renaissance Vinoy Resort, 501 5th Ave. NE, St. Petersburg,* ☎ *727/894–1000. AE, DC, MC, V.*

¢–$ ✕ **Ovo Cafe.** The eclectic menu at this sophisticated restaurant pleases just about any palate. Of the excellent soups, a good shrimp bisque and a Mexican corn soup with roasted pimientos are successes. A house specialty is stuffed pasta pillows (similar to ravioli, but larger), with such fillings as steak Stroganoff and chicken-fennel sausage. An unusual twist is a selection of waffles as a main dish or a dessert. One of the best is the Ybor Republic, topped with chocolate ice cream and a splash of coffee liqueur. The café offers about a dozen martinis, including a tasty version with Godiva white chocolate liqueur and crème de menthe. ⊠ *1901 E. 7th Ave., Ybor City, Tampa,* ☎ *813/248–6979,* WEB *www.ovocafe.com. AE, D, DC, MC, V. Closed Sun.*

Beaches

Spread over six small islands, or keys, 900-acre **Fort De Soto Park** (⊠ 3500 Pinellas Bayway S, Tierra Verde, ☎ 727/866–2484) lies at the mouth of Tampa Bay. It has 7 mi of beaches, two fishing piers, picnic and camping grounds, and a historic fort. The fort was built on the southern end of Mullet Key to protect sea lanes in the gulf during the Spanish-American War. Roam the fort or wander the beaches and the islands. **Pass-A-Grille Beach** (⊠ off Gulf Blvd. [Rte. 699], St. Pete Beach), at the southern end of St. Pete Beach, has parking meters, a snack bar, rest rooms, and showers. **St. Pete Beach** (⊠ 11260 Gulf Blvd., St. Pete Beach, ☎ 727/549–6165) is a free beach on Treasure Island. There are dressing rooms, metered parking, and a snack bar.

Shopping

For bargains stop at the **Big Top** (⊠ 9250 Fowler Ave., Northeast Tampa, Tampa), open weekends 8–5, where vendors hawk new and used items at 1,000-plus booths. The new **Channelside** shopping and entertainment complex (⊠ 615 Channelside Dr., Downtown, Tampa) offers movie theaters, shops, restaurants, clubs, and Pop City, a glorified games arcade. If you want to grab something at Neiman-Marcus on your way home, the upscale **International Plaza** (⊠ 2223 N. Westshore Blvd., Airport Area, Tampa) mall is immediately south of the airport. **Old Hyde Park Village** (⊠ Swan Ave. near Bayshore Blvd., Hyde Park, Tampa) is a gentrified shopping district like the ones you find in every other major American city. Williams-Sonoma and Brooks Brothers are mixed in with bistros and sidewalk cafés. More than 120 shops, department stores, and eateries are found in one of the area's biggest market complexes, **Westfield Shopping Town at Brandon** (⊠ Grand Regency and Rte. 60, Brandon), an attractively landscaped complex near Interstate 75, about 20 minutes from downtown by car. If you are shopping for hand-rolled cigars, a Tampa specialty, head for 7th Avenue in **Ybor City,** where a few hand-rollers practice their craft in small shops.

Nightlife

The biggest concentration of nightclubs, as well as the widest variety, is found along 7th Avenue in Ybor City. It becomes a little like Bourbon Street in New Orleans after the sun goes down. Popular **Adobe Gilas** (⊠ 1600 E. 8th Ave., Ybor City, Tampa, ☎ 813/251–0558) has live music on weekends, karaoke on Wednesday, and a balcony overlooking the crowds on 7th Avenue. There's a large selection of margaritas and 65 brands of tequila. Crowds tend to wear black leather at the **Castle** (⊠ 16th St. at 9th Ave., Ybor City, Tampa, ☎ 813/247–7547, WEB www.castle-ybor.com). It's no fetish club or biker bar, just a cavernous dance club with a medieval castle–style interior. Considered something of a dive—but a lovable dive—by a loyal local following that ranges from esteemed jurists to nose ring–wearing night owls, the **Hub** (⊠ 719 N. Franklin St., Downtown, Tampa, ☎ 813/229–1553) is known for one of Tampa's best martinis and one of its most eclectic juke boxes. **Improv Comedy Theater** (⊠ Centro Ybor, 1600 E. 8th Ave., Ybor City, Tampa, ☎ 813/864–4000, WEB www.tampaimprov.com) stars top comedians in performances Wednesday–Saturday. At the **Pleasure Dome** (⊠ 1430 E. 7th Ave., Ybor City, Tampa, ☎ 813/247–2711), men onstage wear women's clothes and sing Streisand songs. This big dance club is actually predominately hetero—DJs crank out techno, dance, and hip-hop music until the female-impersonator show begins at 12:30 AM. **Pop City** (⊠ 615 Channelside Dr., Downtown, Tampa, ☎ 813/223–4250, WEB www.popcitytampa.com) has a DJ blasting tunes and a game room with extreme-video games, billiards, and a rock-climbing wall. **Stumps Supper Club** (⊠ 615 Channelside Dr., Downtown, Tampa, ☎ 813/226–2261) serves southern food and lively dance music.

Exploring the Tampa Bay Area

The west coast's crown jewel as well as its business and commercial hub, Tampa has high-rises and heavy traffic. Amid the bustle is the region's greatest concentration of restaurants, nightlife, stores, and cultural events.

Numbers in the margin refer to points of interest on the Tampa Bay Area map.

⑦ Adventure Island. Water slides, pools, and artificial-wave pools create a 30-acre wonderland at this water park, a corporate cousin of Busch Gardens. Rides such as the Key West Rapids and Tampa Typhoon are creative, if geographically incorrect. (There are no rapids in Key West and *typhoon* is a term used only in Pacific regions—Tampa Hurricane just wouldn't have had the same alliterative allure.) The park's planners took the younger kids into account, with offerings such as Fabian's Funport, which has a scaled-down wave pool and interactive water gym. Along with a championship volleyball complex and a surf pool, you'll find cafés, snack bars, changing rooms, and video games. ⊠ *10001 Malcolm McKinley Dr., less than 1 mi north of Busch Gardens, Central Tampa, Tampa,* ☎ *813/987–5660,* WEB *www.adventureisland.com.* ☎ *Ages 10–adult $28; ages 3–9 $26; under 3 free.* ☉ *Mid-Mar.–late Oct., daily 10–5.*

⑥ Busch Gardens. More than 2,700 animals are just part of the attraction at this sprawling, carefully manicured theme park. Themed sections attempt to capture the spirit of 19th-century Africa, and the Skyride simulates an African safari—taking in free-roaming zebras, giraffes, rhinos, lions, and other animals. The 335-acre park also has live entertainment, animal exhibits, shops, restaurants, games, and thrill rides, including six roller coasters. The pulse-pumping lineup includes **Kumba** and **Montu,** both reaching speeds of more than 60 mph; **Gwazi,** a 7,000-ft-long wooden coaster; and **Python** and **Scorpion,** 360 degree–loop coasters with 60-ft drops. Passenger vans take you on a Serengeti safari in **Rhino Rally,** where you view Asian elephants, rhinos, and zebras. At one point, a bridge breaks away and passengers spend a few minutes on a rapids ride. You can also take a beer-tasting class—after all, Anheuser-Busch owns the park. Allow from six to eight hours to do Busch Gardens. This is not the ideal destination for small children. There are a few kid-oriented attractions, such as **Land of the Dragons,** a cool playground, and children's ride area, but most of the park is geared toward teens or adults. ⊠ *3000 E. Busch Blvd., 8 mi northeast of downtown Tampa and 2 mi east of I–275 Exit 50, Central Tampa, Tampa,* ☎ *813/987–5082,* WEB *www.buschgardens.com.* ☎ *Ages 10–adult $50; ages 3–9 $41; under 3 free.* ☉ *Daily 9–6, later in summer.*

① Florida Aquarium. The $84 million aquarium is no overpriced fishbowl; it's a dazzling architectural landmark with an 83-ft-high multitiered glass dome. It has more than 4,800 specimens of fish, other animals, and plants, representing 550 species native to Florida. Five major exhibit areas reflect the diversity of the state's natural habitats—wetlands, bays, beaches, and coral reefs. Creature-specific exhibits are the No Bone Zone (lovable invertebrates) and Sea Hunt, with predators ranging from sharks to exotic lion fish. The most impressive single exhibit is the living coral reef, in a 500,000-gallon tank ringed with viewing windows, including an awesome 43-ft-wide panoramic opening. Part of the tank is a walkable tunnel, almost giving the illusion of venturing into underwater depths. There you see a thicket of elk-horn coral teeming with tropical fish. A dark cave reveals sea life you would normally see only on night dives, and shark-feeding shows include divers chumming from the safety of a cage. If you have three hours, try the DolphinQuest Eco-Tour, which takes up to 50 passengers onto Tampa's bays in a 64-ft catamaran for an up-close look at bottlenose dolphins and other wildlife. ⊠ *701 Channelside Dr., Downtown, Tampa,* ☎ *813/273–4000,* WEB *www.flaquarium.net.* 🎟 *Aquarium $15, DolphinQuest $18.* ◷ *Daily 9:30–5.*

❹ Henry B. Plant Museum. This museum is one part architectural time capsule and one part magic carpet ride to gilded-era America. Originally a luxury hotel, built by railroad magnate Henry B. Plant in 1891, the building is filled with the furnishings it held when Colonel Theodore Roosevelt made it his U.S. headquarters during the Spanish-American War. Plant spared no expense in constructing this classic Moorish revival building. The museum displays the finer things of life from the 1890s, including 19th-century artwork and furniture brought from Europe when the hotel opened. On Sunday afternoons, get a glimpse into the time period through "Upstairs/Downstairs," in which actors play the parts of hotel staff and guests. At periodic Saturday antiques appraisals, you can bring up to three personal treasures for expert evaluation. ⊠ *401 W. Kennedy Blvd., off I–275 Exit 44, Downtown, Tampa,* ☎ *813/254–1891,* WEB *www.plantmuseum.com.* 🎟 *$5.* ◷ *Tues.–Sat. 10–4, Sun. noon–4.*

🖐 ❺ Lowry Park Zoo. In Tampa's 24-acre zoo, exotic creatures from four continents live in their natural habitats. Check out the Asian Domain and its primates, from chimpanzees to woolly monkeys. Spot some fancy flying in the free-flight bird aviary, and come face to face with alligators, panthers, bears, and red wolves at the Florida Wildlife Center, a sanctuary for indigenous animals. There's also a walk-in lorikeet aviary where you can feed and pet the colorful birds, as well as a stringray touch tank, and Manatee and Aquatic Center, one of the most extensive in the state. Gentle animals such as sheep and goats are the primary residents of the children's petting zoo. To get a look at a gentle creature that is quintessentially part of Florida, visit the Manatee Amphitheater. This zoo is particularly attuned to night events: parties range from food and beer tastings for adults to chaperoned sleepovers for children ages 6–14. Adjacent to the zoo, the Fun Forest at Lowry Park has rides and an arcade. ⊠ *7530 North Blvd., Central Tampa, Tampa,* ☎ *813/935–8552,* WEB *www.lowryparkzoo.com.* 🎟 *$9.50.* ◷ *Daily 9:30–5.*

❿ Museum of Fine Arts. Outstanding examples of European, American, pre-Columbian, and Far Eastern art are at St. Petersburg's major art museum. There are also photographic exhibits. Staff members give narrated gallery tours two to five times a day. ⊠ *255 Beach Dr. NE, St. Petersburg,* ☎ *727/896–2667,* WEB *www.fine-arts.org.* 🎟 *$6.* ◷ *Tues.–Sat. 10–5, Sun. 1–5. Tours Tues.–Fri. at 10, 11, 1, 2, and 3; Sat. at 11, 1, 2, and 3; Sun. at 1 and 2.*

❽ Museum of Science and Industry (MOSI). This fun and stimulating scientific playground is a place where you learn about Florida weather, anatomy, flight, and space by seeing *and* by doing. At the Gulf Coast Hurricane Exhibit you can experience what a hurricane and its 74-mph winds feel like (and live to write home about it). The Bank of America BioWorks Butterfly Garden is a 6,400-square-ft engineered ecosystem project that not only serves as a home for free-flying butterflies but also demonstrates how wetlands can clean water. The Verizon *Challenger*

Learning Center gives simulated flights, and the 100-seat Saunders Planetarium—Tampa Bay's only planetarium—has afternoon and evening shows, one of them a trek through the universe. For adventurous spirits, there's a high-wire bicycle ride 30 ft above the floor. Don't worry, you're strapped to the bike, which is attached to the wire and can't fall. There's also an IMAX theater, where films are projected on a hemispherical 82-ft dome. ⊠ *4801 E. Fowler Ave., 1 mi north of Busch Gardens, Northeast Tampa, Tampa,* ☎ *813/987–6300 or 800/995–6674,* WEB *www.mosi.org.* ⌨ *$14.* ☉ *Weekdays 9–5, weekends 9–7.*

Riverwalk. Downtown Tampa's waterside walkway connects such entities as the Marriott Waterside, the Channelside shopping and entertainment complex, and the Florida Aquarium. New Fort Brooke Park will include a wall of bronze plaques telling the story of Tampa's Seminole War fort from the Seminole perspective. The landscaped walkway extends 4 mi along the cruise-ship channel and along the Hillsborough River in the downtown area.

⓫ Salvador Dalí Museum. The world's most extensive collection of originals by the Spanish surrealist Salvador Dalí is found here. Valued at more than $125 million, the collection includes 94 oils, more than 100 watercolors and drawings, and 1,300 graphics, sculptures, photographs, and objets d'art, including floor-to-ceiling murals. Frequent tours are led by well-informed docents. How did the collection end up here? A rich northern industrialist and friend of Dalí, Ohio magnate A. Reynolds Morse, was looking for a museum site after his huge personal Dalí collection began to overflow his mansion. The people of St. Petersburg vied admirably for the collection, and the museum was established here as a result. ⊠ *1000 3rd St. S, St. Petersburg,* ☎ *727/823–3767 or 800/ 442–3254,* WEB *www.salvadordalimuseum.org.* ⌨ *$10.* ☉ *Mon.–Wed. and Fri.–Sat. 9:30–5:30, Thurs. 9:30–8, Sun. noon–5:30.*

❾ Seminole Indian Casino. If you've brought your body to Tampa but your heart's in Vegas, you can satisfy that urge to hang around a poker table at 4 AM here. The casino has poker tables, high-stakes bingo, and gaming machines. Coffee and doughnuts are free for gamblers, and the casino lounge serves drinks until 2:15 AM. ⊠ *5223 N. Orient Rd., Northeast Tampa, Tampa,* ☎ *813/621–1302 or 800/282–7016,* WEB *www. casino-tampa.com,* ⌨ *Free.* ☉ *Daily.*

❸ Tampa Museum of Art. The 35,000-square-ft museum has an impressive permanent collection of Greek and Roman antiquities, along with five galleries that host traveling exhibits. A 124,000-square-ft space, designed by internationally renowned architect Rafael Viñoly, will be under construction until about 2005; until then, the museum will remain open at its current location next to the new building. It will close for a short time when exhibits are moved. ⊠ *600 N. Ashley Dr., Downtown, Tampa,* ☎ *813/274–8130,* WEB *www.tampamuseum.com.* ⌨ *$5.* ☉ *Tues.–Wed. and Fri.–Sat. 10–5, Thurs. 10–8, Sun. 11–5.*

❷ Ybor City. One of only three National Historic Landmark districts in Florida, Tampa's lively Cuban enclave has brick streets and wrought-iron balconies. Cubans brought their cigar-making industry to Ybor (pronounced *ee*-bore) City in 1866, and the smell of cigars—hand-rolled by Cuban immigrants—still wafts through the heart of this east Tampa area, along with the strong aroma of roasting coffee. These days the neighborhood is emerging as Tampa's hot spot as empty cigar factories and social clubs are transformed into boutiques, galleries, restaurants, and nightclubs that rival those in Miami's sizzling South Beach. Take a stroll past the ornately tiled **Columbia** restaurant and the stores lining 7th Avenue. Guided walking tours of the area ($5) enable you to see artisans hand-roll cigars following time-honored methods. Step back into the past at **Centennial Park** (⊠ 8th Ave. and 18th St., Tampa), which re-creates a period streetscape and hosts a fresh market every Saturday. Ybor City's destination within a destination is the dining and entertainment palace **Centro Ybor** (⊠ 1600 E. 7th Ave., Tampa). It has shops, trendy bars and restaurants, a 20-screen movie theater, and GameWorks, an interactive playground developed by Steven Spielberg.

A visit to the **Ybor City State Museum** provides a look at the history of the cigar industry. Admission includes a tour of La Casita, one of the "shotgun" houses occupied by cigar workers and their families in the late 1890s. ⊠ *1818 9th Ave., between Nuccio Pkwy. and 22nd St., from 7th to 9th Ave., Tampa,* ☎ *813/247–6323,* WEB *www.ybormuseum. org.* ⊠ *$2.* ◷ *Tues.–Sat. 9–5; tours Sat. at 10:30.*

4 PORTS OF CALL

Nowhere in the world are conditions better suited to cruising than in the Caribbean Sea. Tiny island nations, within easy sailing distance of one another, form a chain of tropical enchantment that curves from Cuba in the north all the way down to the coast of Venezuela. There's far more to life here than sand and coconuts, however. The islands are vastly different, with a variety of cultures, topographies, and languages represented. Colonialism has left its mark, and the presence of the Spanish, French, Dutch, Danish, and British is still felt. Slavery, too, has left its cultural legacy, blending African overtones into the colonial/Indian amalgam. The one constant, however, is the weather. Despite the islands' southerly latitude, the climate is surprisingly gentle, due in large part to the cooling influence of the trade winds.

The Caribbean is made up of the Greater Antilles and the Lesser Antilles. The former consist of those islands closest to the United States: Cuba, Jamaica, Hispaniola (Haiti and the Dominican Republic), and Puerto Rico. (The Cayman Islands lie south of Cuba.) The Lesser Antilles, including the Virgin, Windward, and Leeward islands and others, are greater in number but smaller in size, and constitute the southern half of the Caribbean chain.

CARIBBEAN ESSENTIALS

Currency

The U.S. dollar is the official currency on Puerto Rico and in the USVI, as well as the British Virgin Islands. On Grand Cayman you will usually have a choice of Cayman or U.S. dollars when you take money out of an ATM, and you may even be able to get change in U.S. dollars. On most other islands, U.S. paper currency (not coins) is usually accepted, but you may need to change a few dollars into local currency for phone calls, tips, and taxis. When you pay in dollars you'll almost always get change in local currency, so it's best to carry bills in small denominations. Canadian dollars and British pounds are occasionally accepted. If you need local currency (say, for a trip to one of the French islands), change money at a local bank or use an ATM for the best rate. Most major credit cards are accepted all over the Caribbean, except at local market stalls and small establishments.

Where to Eat

Cuisine on the Caribbean's islands is as varied as the islands themselves. The region's history as a colonial battleground and ethnic melting pot creates plenty of variety and adds lots of unusual tropical fruit and spices. In fact, the one quality that defines most Caribbean cooking is its spiciness, acquired from nutmeg, mace, allspice, peppers, saffron, and many other seasonings grown in the islands. Dress is generally casual, although throughout the islands, beachwear is inappropriate most anywhere except on the beach. Unless otherwise noted, prices are given in U.S. dollars. The following price categories are used in this book.

CATEGORY	COST*
$$$$	over $30
$$$	$20–$30
$$	$12–$20
$	$8–$12
¢	under $8

*per person for a main course at dinner

Passports and Visas

On most Caribbean islands, U.S., Canadian, or British citizens must have either a valid passport or prove citizenship with a birth certificate (with a raised seal) and a government-issued photo I.D. Visitors from other countries must present a valid passport. It is always best to bring a passport. If you are not a U.S., British, or Canadian citizen, never make cruise reservations without first checking the immigration requirements of the ports of call on the ship's itinerary. Children must also have appropriate identification (usually an original birth certificate with a raised seal); if both parents are not traveling with the child, then a notarized letter of permission signed by the absent parent is usually required. Always ask about the requirements of traveling with children before you leave for a cruise.

Shore Excursions

Typical excursions include an island or town bus tour, a visit to a beach or rum factory, a boat trip, snorkeling or diving trip, and charter fishing. In recent years, however, shore excursions have gotten more adventurous with mild river rafting, parasailing, jet skiing, hiking, and biking added to the mix. It's always safest to take a ship-arranged excursion, but it's almost never the cheapest option.

If you prefer to break away from the pack, find a knowledgeable taxi driver or tour operator—they're usually within a stone's throw of the pier—or wander around on your own. A group of four to six people will find this option more economical and practical than will a single person or a couple.

Renting a car is also a good option on many islands—again, the more people, the better the deal. But get a good island map before you set off, and be sure to find out how long it will take you to get around.

Conditions are ideal for water sports of all kinds—scuba diving, snorkeling, windsurfing, sailing, waterskiing, and fishing excursions abound. Your shore-excursion director can usually arrange these activities for you if the ship offers no formal excursion.

The Caribbean

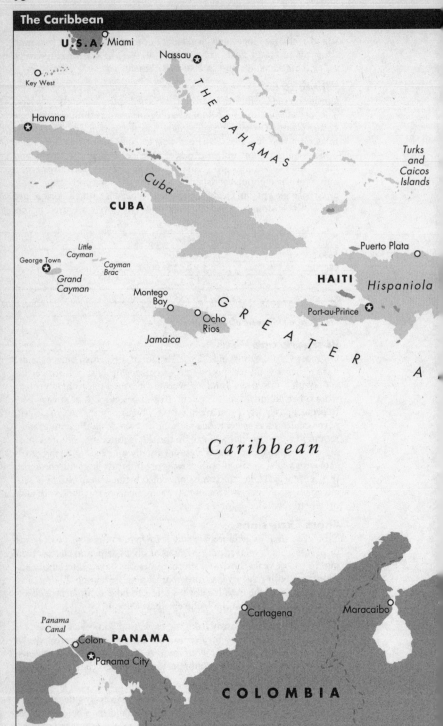

U.S.A. Miami

Key West

Nassau

THE BAHAMAS

Havana

Cuba

CUBA

Turks and Caicos Islands

Little Cayman

Cayman Brac

George Town

Grand Cayman

Puerto Plata

HAITI

Hispaniola

Montego Bay

Ocho Rios

GREATER A

Port-au-Prince

Jamaica

Caribbean

Cartagena

Maracaibo

Panama Canal

Colon

PANAMA

Panama City

COLOMBIA

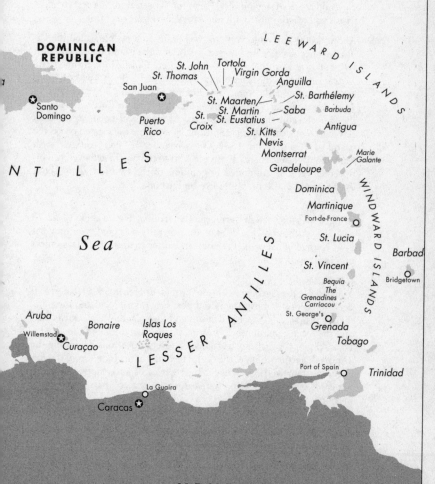

ATLANTIC OCEAN

DOMINICAN
REPUBLIC

LEEWARD ISLANDS

St. John
St. Thomas
Tortola
Virgin Gorda
Anguilla
San Juan
St. Barthélemy
St. Maarten
St. Martin
Saba
Barbuda
Santo
Domingo
St.
Croix
St. Eustatius
Antigua
Puerto
Rico
St. Kitts
Nevis
Montserrat
Marie
Galante
Guadeloupe
NTILLES
Dominica
Martinique
Fort-de-France
WINDWARD ISLANDS
St. Lucia
Sea
Barbad
St. Vincent
Bridgetown
Bequia
The
Grenadines
Carriacou
St. George's
Aruba
Bonaire
Islas Los
Roques
Grenada
Willemstad
LESSER ANTILLES
Tobago
Curaçao
Port of Spain
Trinidad
La Guaira
Caracas

VENEZUELA

PORTS OF CALL

Antigua

Some say Antigua has so many beaches that you could visit a different one every day for a year. Most have snow-white sand, and many are backed by lavish resorts that offer sailing, diving, windsurfing, and snorkeling.

The larger of the British Leeward islands, Antigua was the headquarters from which Lord Horatio Nelson (then a mere captain) made his forays against the French and pirates in the late 18th century. You may wish to explore English Harbour and its carefully restored Nelson's Dockyard, as well as tour old forts, historic churches, and tiny villages. Appealing aspects of the the island's interior include a small tropical rain forest ideal for hiking, ancient Native American archaeological digs, and restored sugar mills. Due to time constraints, it's best to make trips this far from port with an experienced tour operator.

About 4,000 years ago Antigua was home to a people called the Ciboney. They disappeared mysteriously, and the island remained uninhabited for about 1,000 years. When Columbus sighted the 173-square-km (108-square-mi) island in 1493, the Arawaks had already set up housekeeping. The English moved in 130 years later, in 1623. Then a sequence of bloody battles involving the Caribs, the Dutch, the French, and the English began. Africans had been captured as slaves to work the sugar plantations by the time the French ceded the island to the English in 1667. On November 1, 1981, Antigua, with Barbuda, its sister island 30 mi (48 km) to the north, achieved full independence. The combined population of the two islands is about 70,000, only 1,200 of whom live on Barbuda.

CURRENCY

Antigua uses the Eastern Caribbean (E.C.) dollar. Figure about EC$2.70 to US$1. Although U.S. dollars are generally accepted, you may get your change in beewees. Prices given below are in U.S. dollars unless otherwise indicated.

TELEPHONES

You can use the Caribbean Phone Card (available in $5, $10, and $20 denominations in most hotels and post offices) for local and long-distance calls. To call the United States and Canada, dial 1, the area code, and the seven-digit number, or use a phone card or one of the "CALL USA" phones, which are available at several locations, including the airport departure lounge, the cruise terminal at St. John's, and the English Harbour Marina. These take credit cards and, supposedly, calling cards (though Cable & Wireless, the phone company in Antigua, tacks on a fee).

SHORE EXCURSIONS

The following are good choices in Antigua. They may not be offered by all cruise lines. Times and prices are approximate.

Hiking Safari. You hike about 2 mi (3km) through a rain forest up Signal Hill, one of the highest points on the island. Then you can enjoy the views, which on a clear day will include Guadeloupe and Nevis. Juice and water are provided. ☉ *3 hrs,* 🖻 *$50.*

Historical Tour. Get a sense of Antigua's British-colonial history with great views along the way. The highlight is a visit to Nelson's Dockyard, a gem of Georgian British maritime architecture and a must for history buffs and Anglophiles. Tours usually include a stop for a drink. ☉ *3–4 hrs,* 🖻 *$40.*

Island Jeep Safari. You'll be given an insider's look via four-wheel drive at the whole island, complete with deserted plantation houses, rainforest trails, ruined sugar mills and forts. Some tours visit Fort George, and most include a stop for a swim at one of the island's beaches. Most tours include soft drinks. ☉ *3 hrs,* ▭ *$66.*

Jolly Roger Pirate Cruise. Cruise on a replica pirate ship along the coast, enjoying an open bar, games, dancing, and sometimes live music. When the ship anchors, it's possible to swim. The tour ends with a West Indian jump-up. ☉ *3 hrs,* ▭ *$40*

Coming Ashore

Though some ships dock at the deep-water harbor in downtown St. John's, most use Heritage Quay, a multimillion-dollar complex with shops, condominiums, a casino, and a food court. Most St. John's attractions are an easy walk from Heritage Quay; the older part of the city is eight blocks away. A tourist information booth is in the main docking building.

If you intend to explore beyond St. John's, consider hiring a taxi driver-guide. Taxis meet every cruise ship. They're unmetered; fares are fixed, and drivers are required to carry a rate card. Agree on the fare before setting off, and plan to tip drivers 10%. Some cabbies may take you from St. John's to English Harbour and wait for a "reasonable" amount of time (about a half hour) while you look around, for about $40; you can usually arrange an island tour for around $25 per hour. Renting your own car isn't usually practical, since you must purchase a $20 temporary driving permit in addition to the car-rental fee, which is usually about $50 per day in the high season.

Exploring Antigua

Numbers in the margin correspond to points of interest on the Antigua map.

➍ **English Harbour.** The most famous of Antigua's attractions lies on the coast, just south of Falmouth. When the Royal Navy abandoned the station at English Harbour in 1889, it fell into a state of decay. The Society of the Friends of English Harbour began restoring it in 1951, and November 14, 1961—now celebrated as Dockyard Day—Nelson's Dockyard was reopened with much fanfare. Today it's reminiscent, albeit on a much smaller scale, of Williamsburg, Virginia. Within the compound are crafts shops, restaurants, and two splendidly restored 18th-century hotels, the Admiral's Inn and the Copper and Lumber Store Hotel. (The latter, occupying a supply store for Nelson's Caribbean fleet, is a particularly fine example of Georgian architecture, with warm brick, hardwood floors, timber ceilings, sailing prints, nautical maps, burgundy leather armchairs and sofas, and an interior courtyard evoking Old England.) The Dockyard National Park also includes serene nature trails accessing beaches, rock pools, and crumbling plantation ruins and hilltop forts.

The **Admiral's House Museum** displays ship models, a model of English Harbour, silver regatta trophies, maps, prints, and Nelson's very own telescope and tea caddy. ⊠ *Nelson's Dockyard,* ☎ *268/463–1053 or 268/463–1379.* ▭ *$2 suggested donation.* ☉ *Daily 8–6.*

➌ **Falmouth.** This town sits on a lovely bay backed by former sugar plantations and sugar mills. The most important historic site here is St. Paul's Church, which was rebuilt on the site of a church used by troops during the Nelson period.

➋ **Fort George.** East of Liberta—one of the first settlements founded by freed slaves—on Monk's Hill, this fort was built from 1689 to 1720.

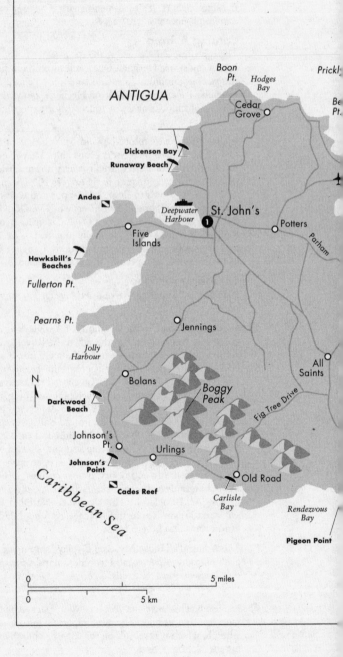

Antigua

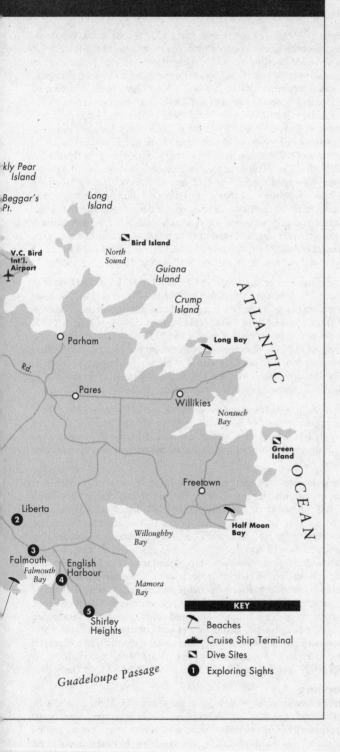

kly Pear
Island

Beggar's
Pt.

Long
Island

V.C. Bird
Int'l.
Airport

North
Sound

Bird Island

Guiana
Island

Crump
Island

Parham

Rd.

Pares

Willikies

Long Bay

Nonsuch
Bay

ATLANTIC

Green
Island

Freetown

OCEAN

Liberta

2

3

Falmouth

Falmouth
Bay

English
Harbour

4

Willoughby
Bay

Half Moon
Bay

Mamora
Bay

5

Shirley
Heights

KEY

Beaches

Cruise Ship Terminal

Dive Sites

1 Exploring Sights

Guadeloupe Passage

Among the ruins are the sites for 32 cannons, water cisterns, the base of the old flagstaff, and some original buildings.

❶ **St. John's.** Antigua's capital, with some 45,000 inhabitants (approximately half the island's population), lies at sea level at the inland end of a sheltered northwestern bay. Although it has seen better days, a couple of notable historic sights and some good waterfront shopping areas and restaurants make it worth a visit. Signs at the **Museum of Antigua and Barbuda** say PLEASE TOUCH, encouraging visitors to explore Antigua's past. Try your hand at the educational video games or squeeze a cassava through a *matapi* (a grass sieve). Exhibits interpret the nation's history, from its geological birth to its political independence in 1981. There are 34-million-year-old fossil and coral remains; models of a sugar plantation and a wattle-and-daub house; an Arawak canoe; and a wildly eclectic assortment of objects, from cannonballs to 1920s telephone exchanges. The colonial building that houses the museum is the former courthouse, which dates from 1750. The superlative museum gift shop carries such unusual items as calabash purses, seed earrings, and lignum vitae pipes, as well as historic maps and local books. ✉ *Church and Market Sts.,* ☎ *268/462–1469.* 💲 *$2 suggested donation.* ☉ *Weekdays 8:30–4, Sat. 10–1.*

At the south gate of the **Anglican Cathedral of St. John the Divine** are figures of St. John the Baptist and St. John the Divine said to have been taken from one of Napoléon's ships and brought to Antigua. The original church was built in 1681, replaced by a stone building in 1745, and destroyed by an earthquake in 1843. The present structure was completed in 1845. With an eye to future earthquakes, the parishioners had the interior completely encased in pitch pine, hoping to forestall heavy damage. The church was elevated to the status of a cathedral in 1848. ✉ *Between Long and Newgate Sts.,* ☎ *268/461–0082.*

Redcliffe Quay, at the water's edge just south of Heritage Quay, is the most appealing part of St. John's. Attractively restored and superbly re-created buildings in a riot of cotton-candy colors house shops, restaurants, and boutiques and are linked by courtyards and landscaped walkways.

❺ **Shirley Heights.** This bluff affords a spectacular view of English Harbour. The heights are named for Sir Thomas Shirley, the governor who fortified the harbor in 1787. At the top is Shirley Heights Lookout, a restaurant built into the remnants of the 18th-century fortifications. Most notable for its boisterous Thursday and Sunday barbecues that often continue well into the night with live music and dancing, it serves dependable burgers, pumpkin soup, grilled meats, and rum punches. Not far from Shirley Heights is the **Dows Hill Interpretation Centre,** where observation platforms provide still more sensational vistas of the whole English Harbour area. There's a multimedia sound-and-light presentation on the island's history and culture, in which illuminated displays, incorporating lifelike figures and colorful tableaux, are presented with running commentary and music—resulting in a cheery, if bland, portrait of Antiguan life since the days of the Amerindians. ☎ *268/460–2777 (National Parks Authority).* 💲 *EC$15.* ☉ *Daily 9–5.*

Shopping

Redcliffe Quay, on the waterfront at the south edge of St. John's, is by far the island's the most appealing shopping area. Several restaurants and more than 30 boutiques, many with one-of-a-kind wares, are set around landscaped courtyards shaded by colorful trees. **Heritage Quay,** in St. John's, has 35 shops—including many that are duty-free—that cater to the cruise-ship crowd, since many ships dock here. Outlets here include

Benetton, the Body Shop, Sunglass Hut, Dolce & Gabbana, and Oshkosh B'Gosh. There are also shops along **St. John's, St. Mary's, High,** and **Long streets.** The tangerine-and-lilac-hued four-story **Vendor's Mall** at the intersection of Redcliffe and Thames streets gathers the pushy, pesky vendors that once clogged the narrow streets. It's jammed with stalls; air-conditioned indoor shops sell some higher-priced, if not higher-quality, merchandise. On the west coast the Mediterranean-style, arcaded **Jolly Harbour Villa Resort and Marina** holds interesting galleries and shops.

The **Gazebo** (⌧ Redcliffe Quay, St. John's, ☎ 268/460–2776) is a vast, bilevel jumble of Mexican pottery and ceramics, Indonesian furnishings, gorgeous blue-glaze plates that rival delftware in both beauty and craftsmanship, hand-painted rocking horses, basketry, hammocks, and more. The **Goldsmitty** (⌧ Redcliffe Quay, St. John's, ☎ 268/462–4601) is Hans Smit, an expert goldsmith who turns gold, black coral, and precious and semiprecious stones into one-of-a-kind works of art. **Isis** (⌧ Redcliffe Quay, St. John's, ☎ 268/462–4602) sells island and international bric-a-brac, such as antique jewelry, hand-carved walking sticks, and glazed pottery. **Jacaranda** (⌧ Redcliffe Quay, St. John's, ☎ 268/462–1888) sells batik, sarongs, and swimwear, as well as Caribbean food and local artwork. **Kate Designs** (⌧ Redcliffe Quay, St. John's, ☎ 268/460–5971) sells acclaimed St. Kitts artist Kate Spencer's distinctive work—lovely silk-screen scarves and sarongs, vividly colored place mats, paintings, prints, note cards—as well as Liza Kirwan's delicate, hand-painted silk scarves and former fashion designer Heike Petersen's whimsical "ethnic dolls." **Noreen Phillips** (⌧ Redcliffe Quay, St. John's, ☎ 268/462–3127) creates glitzy appliquéd and beaded evening wear—inspired by the colors of the sea and sunset—in sensuous fabrics ranging from chiffon and silk to Italian lace and Indian brocade.

Map Shop (⌧ St. Mary's St., St. John's, ☎ 268/462–3993) stocks a "must" buy for those interested in Antiguan life: the paperback *To Shoot Hard Labour: The Life and Times of Samuel Smith, an Antiguan Workingman*. Also check out the books of Jamaica Kincaid, whose writing about her native Antigua has won international acclaim. The shop also offers a fine assortment of books on Caribbean cuisine, flora, fauna, and history.

Abbott's (⌧ Heritage Quay, St. John's, ☎ 268/462–3108) sells pricey items, from Baume and Mercier watches to Belleek china to Kosta Boda art glass, in a luxurious, air-conditioned showroom. **La Casa Habana** (⌧ Heritage Quay, St. John's, ☎ 268/462–2677) sells Cuban cigars (just remember that it's illegal to take them into the United States).

The delightfully whimsical **Sofa** (⌧ English Harbour, ☎ 268/463–0610) carries some of the quirkier creations of island artisans, including hand-painted furniture, mosaic vases, and recycled-paper books—justifying the name (an acronym for Sculpture, Objects, Functional Art). Owner Fiona Jade will happily direct you to the studios of such intriguing Antiguan artists as Gilly Gobinet, Gramma Aki, Freeston Williams, and Yolanda Woodberry.

Outdoor Activities & Sports

GOLF

Cedar Valley Golf Club (⌧ Friar's Hill, ☎ 268/462–0161), northeast of St. John's, has a 6,100-yard, 18-hole course. The bland, not terribly well-maintained terrain offers some challenge with its tight, hilly fairways and numerous doglegs. Greens fees are $35, including cart.

SCUBA DIVING

With all the wrecks and reefs, there are lots of undersea sights to explore, from coral canyons to sea caves. The most accessible wreck is the schooner *Andes,* not far out in Deep Bay, off the Five Islands Peninsula. Among the favorite sites are **Green Island, Cades Reef,** and **Bird Island** (a national park). **Big John's Dive Antigua** (⊠ Rex Halcyon Cove Beach Resort, Dickenson Bay, ☏ 268/462–3483) offers certification courses and day and night dives closer to St. John's. **Dockyard Divers** (⊠ Nelson's Dockyard, English Harbour, ☏ 268/460–1178), owned by British ex-merchant seaman Captain A. G. Fincham, is one of the island's longest-established outfits and offers diving and snorkeling trips, PADI courses, and dive packages with accommodations.

Beaches

Antigua's beaches are public, and many are dotted with resorts that have water-sports outfitters and beach bars. Most hotels have taxi stands, so getting back to the ship isn't usually a problem. Sunbathing topless or in the buff is strictly illegal except on one of the small beaches at Hawksbill Beach Hotel on the Five Islands Peninsula. Most cruise-ship beach excursions go to the beaches on the west coast.

Dickenson Bay is a lengthy stretch of powder-soft white sand and exceptionally calm water, where you'll find small and large hotels, water sports, concessions, and beachfront restaurants. **Half Moon Bay,** a ¾-mi (1-km) crescent, is a prime snorkeling and windsurfing area. On the Atlantic side of the island the water can be quite rough (the eastern end is calmer). **Johnson's Point** is a series of connected, deliciously deserted beaches of bleached white sand on the southwest coast overlooking Montserrat. You can explore a ruined fort at one end; notable beach bars are OJ's (try the snapper) and Turner's. **Pigeon Point,** near Falmouth Harbour, has two fine white-sand beaches; the leeward side is calmer, while the windward side is rockier, with sensational views and snorkeling around the point. Several restaurants and bars are nearby. **Runaway Beach,** a stretch of glittering sand, is still rebuilding after years of hurricane erosion. Both the water and the scene are relatively calm, and beach bars such as Lashings and Amigo's (the surprisingly good Mexican restaurant at Barrymore Beach Hotel) offer cool shade and cold beer.

Where to Eat

In restaurants, a 10% service charge and 7% tax are usually added to the bill.

$$–$$$ ✕ **Admiral's Inn.** This English Harbour tavern in the Admiral's Inn hotel is a must for Anglophiles and mariners. Soak up the centuries at the inside bar under dark timbers (sailors from Nelson's fleet carved their names into the bar top). Most diners sit on the terrace under shady Australian gums to enjoy the views of the harbor complex. Specialties include curried conch, fresh snapper with equally fresh limes, and lobster thermidor. The pumpkin soup is not to be missed. ⊠ *Admiral's Inn, Nelson's Dockyard, English Harbour,* ☏ *268/460–1027. Reservations essential. AE, MC, V.*

$$–$$$ ✕ **Commissioner Grill.** White-tile floors, powder-blue chairs, floral tablecloths, glass buoys, Antiguan pottery, conch shells, and historic maps give this converted 19th-century tamarind warehouse a timeless island feel. Specials might include whelks in garlic butter, bacon-wrapped plantains in mustard sauce, snapper in lobster sauce, or mahi-mahi creole. Local seafood is the obvious choice, although beef and poultry are also reliable. Lunch is considerably cheaper and more authentic. ⊠ *Commissioner Alley and Redcliffe St., St. John's,* ☏ *268/462–1883. AE, DC, MC, V.*

$–$$ ✕ **Big Banana–Pizzas in Paradise.** This tiny, often-crowded spot is tucked into one side of a restored warehouse which has broad plank floors, wood beams, and stone archways. Cool Benetton-style photos of lo-

cals and jamming musicians adorn the brick walls. It serves some of
the island's best pizza (try the lobster or the seafood variety) as well
as such tasty specials as conch salad. There's live entertainment some
nights, and sports nuts congregate at the bar's huge satellite TV. ⊠ *Redcliffe Quay, St. John's,* ☎ *268/480–6985. AE, MC, V. Closed Sun.*

Aruba

Though the "A" in the ABC (Aruba, Bonaire, Curaçao) Islands is
small—only 31 km (19 mi) long and 10 km (6 mi) at its widest—the
island's national anthem proclaims "the greatness of our people is their
great cordiality," and this is no exaggeration. Once a member of the
Netherlands Antilles, Aruba became a quasi-independent "separate en-
tity within the Kingdom of the Netherlands" in 1986, with its own roy-
ally appointed governor, a democratic government, and a 21-member
elected parliament. Long secure in a solid economy—with good education, housing, and health care—the island's population of nearly
95,000 treats visitors as welcome guests. English is spoken everywhere.

The island's distinctive beauty lies in the stark contrast between the
sea and the countryside: rocky deserts, cactus jungles, secluded coves,
and aquamarine panoramas with crashing waves. But it's best-known
for its duty-free shops, the glorious 11-km (7-mi) strand of Palm and
Eagle beaches, and casinos.

CURRENCY

Arubans accept U.S. dollars readily, so you need only acquire Aruban
florins (AFl) for pocket change. Note that the Netherlands Antilles florin
used on Bonaire and Curaçao is not accepted on Aruba.

TELEPHONES

When making calls to anywhere in Aruba, simply dial the seven-digit
number. AT&T customers can dial 800–8000 from special phones at
the cruise dock and in the airport's arrival and departure halls. Otherwise dial 121 to contact the international operator to place a an international call.

SHORE EXCURSIONS

The following are good choices on Aruba. They may not be offered
by all cruise lines. Times and prices are approximate.

Aruba Town and Countryside Drive. A comprehensive town-and-coun-
try bus tour takes in the major island sights, including the island's most
popular attraction, the limestone Natural Bridge; the California Lighthouse, set amid vanilla sand dunes; the desolate Alto Vista Chapel; boulder formations that resemble abstract sculptures; and caves stippled
with petroglyphs and filled with stalactites and stalagmites. After the
tour, you can be dropped off in town or at the cruise-ship terminal.
⊙ *3 hrs,* 🖼 *$35*

Atlantis Submarine Tour. Explore an underwater reef teeming with
marine life without getting wet aboard a 65-ft air-conditioned sub, *Atlantis VI,* that takes 48 passengers 95–150 ft (29–46 m) below the surface along Barcadera Reef. During the 30-minute cruise out to the dive
site, you can have a drink on deck; the dive itself lasts about an hour.
⊙ *2 hrs,* 🖼 *$80.*

***Kukoo Kunuku* Bar Hop and Dinner Tour.** One uniquely Aruban insti-
tution is a psychedelically painted 1957 Chevy bus called the *Kukoo
Kunuku.* You start with a champagne toast followed by dinner, then
you travel to several bars to enjoy Aruban nightlife. The fee includes
dinner, your first drink at each bar stop, and transportation. ⊙ *4–5
hrs,* 🖼 *$69.*

Sailing and Snorkeling Tour. Take a motorized catamaran to a shallow coral reef and the wreck of the German freighter *Antilla*, which was sunk during World War II. ☼ *3 hrs,* ☼ *$40.*

Coming Ashore

Ships tie up at the Aruba Port Authority cruise terminal; inside are a tourist information booth and duty-free shops. From here, you're a five-minute walk from various shopping districts and downtown Oranjestad. Just turn right as you leave the cruise terminal.

The "real" Aruba—what's left of its wild, untamed beauty—can only be experienced on a drive through the countryside (though be aware that there are no public bathrooms except for those in a few restaurants). Your valid driver's license will work in Aruba, so you can rent a car or a four-wheel-drive vehicle if you want to explore on your own. If you haven't made reservations, be aware that the car rental agencies are slow at processing walk-up rental applications. And the island's roads aren't always clearly marked. Your best bet may be to hire a taxi (you can flag one in the street). There are no meters, but rates are fixed; just confirm the fare before setting off. It should cost about $30 an hour for up to four people.

Exploring Aruba

Numbers in the margin correspond to points of interest on the Aruba map.

❻ Butterfly Farm. Hundreds of butterflies from around the world flutter about this spectacular garden. Guided 20- to 30-minute tours (included in the price of admission) provide an entertaining look into how these insects complete their life cycle: from egg to caterpillar to chrysalis to butterfly. There's a special deal offered here: after your initial visit, you can return as often as you like for free. ✉ *J. E. Irausquin Blvd., Palm Beach,* ☎ *297/58–63656,* WEB *www.thebutterflyfarm.com.* ✆ *$10.* ☼ *Daily 9–4:30; last tour at 4.*

❷ Hooiberg. Named for its shape (*hooiberg* means "haystack" in Dutch), this 541-ft (165-m) peak lies inland just past the airport. If you have the energy, climb the 562 steps to the top for an impressive view of the city.

❺ Natural Bridge. Centuries of raging wind and sea sculpted this coral-rock bridge in the center of the windward coast. To reach it, drive inland along Hospitalstraat and then follow the signs. Just before you reach the geological wonder, you'll pass the massive stone ruins of the Bushiribana Gold Smelter, an intriguing structure that resembles a crumbling fortress, and a section of surf-pounded coastline called Boca Mahos. Near Natural Bridge are a souvenir shop and a café overlooking the water.

❶ Oranjestad. Aruba's charming capital is best explored on foot. The palm-lined thoroughfare in the center of town runs between pastel-painted buildings, old and new, of typical Dutch design. There are many malls with boutiques and shops.

At the **Archaeological Museum of Aruba** you'll find two rooms chock-full of fascinating Indian artifacts, farm and domestic utensils, and skeletons. ✉ *J. Irausquinplein 2A,* ☎ *297/58–28979.* ✆ *Free.* ☼ *Weekdays 8–noon and 1–4.*

One of the island's oldest edifices, **Fort Zoutman** was built in 1796 and played an important role in skirmishes between British and Curaçaon troops in 1803. The Willem III Tower, named for the Dutch monarch of that time, was added in 1868 to serve as a lighthouse. The fort has been used as a government office building, a police station, and a prison. Its historical museum displays Aruban artifacts in an 18th-century house. ✉ *Zoutmanstraat*, ☎ *297/58–26099.* 🎫 *Free.* ⊙ *Weekdays 8–noon and 1–4.*

The tiny **Numismatic Museum of Aruba**, next to St. Francis Roman Catholic Church, displays coins and paper money—including some salvaged from shipwrecks in the region. Some of the coins on display circulated during the Roman Empire, the Byzantine Empire, and the ancient Chinese dynasties; a few date as far back as the 5th century BC. The museum had its start as one Aruban's private collection and is now run by a family. ✉ *Zuidstraat 7*, ☎ *297/58–28831.* 🎫 *Free.* ⊙ *Weekdays 7:30–noon and 1–4:30.*

❹ Rock Formations. The massive boulders at Ayo and Casibari are a mystery, as they don't match the island's geological makeup. You can climb to the top for fine views of the arid countryside. On the way you'll doubtless pass Aruba whip-tail lizards—the males are cobalt blue, the females blue with dots. The main path to Casibari has steps and handrails (except on one side), and you must move through tunnels and along narrow steps and ledges to reach the top. At Ayo you'll find ancient pictographs in a small cave (the entrance has iron bars to protect the drawings from vandalism). You may also encounter a boulder climber, one of many who are increasingly drawn to Ayo's smooth surfaces. Access to Casibari is via Tanki Highway 4A to Ayo via Route 6A; watch carefully for the turnoff signs near the center of the island on the way to the windward side.

❸ San Nicolas. During the heyday of the oil refineries, Aruba's oldest village was a bustling port; now its primary business is tourism. The main promenade is full of interesting kiosks, and the whole district is undergoing a revitalization project that will bring parks, a cultural center, a central market, a public swimming pool, and an arts promenade.

Shopping

Caya G. F. Betico Croes in Oranjestad is Aruba's chief shopping street. Several malls—gabled, pastel-hued re-creations of traditional Dutch colonial architecture—house branches of such top names as Tommy Hilfiger, Little Switzerland, Nautica, and Benetton; the ritziest are the **Royal Plaza** and **Seaport Village** malls, both right near the cruise-ship pier. The stores are full of Dutch porcelains and figurines. Also consider the Dutch cheeses (you're allowed to bring up to 10 pounds of hard cheese through U.S. Customs), hand-embroidered linens, and any product made from the native aloe vera plant. There's no sales tax, and Arubans consider it rude to haggle.

Art and Tradition Handicrafts (✉ Caya G. F. Betico Croes 30, Oranjestad, ☎ 297/58–36534; ✉ Royal Plaza Mall, L. G. Smith Blvd. 94, Oranjestad, ☎ 297/58–27862) sells intriguing items that look handpainted. Buds from the *mopa mopa* tree are boiled to form a resin colored by vegetable dyes. Artists then stretch the resin by hand and mouth. Tiny pieces are cut and layered to form intricate designs—truly unusual gifts. For perfumes, cosmetics, men's and women's clothing, and leather goods, stop in at **Aruba Trading Company** (✉ Caya G. F. Betico Croes 12, Oranjestad, ☎ 297/58–22602), which has been in business since 1930. **Gandelman Jewelers** (✉ Royal Plaza Mall, L. G. Smith Blvd. 94, Oranjestad, ☎ 297/58–34433) sells Gucci and Rolex watches at reasonable prices, as well as gold bracelets, and a full line of Lladró figurines. **Wulfsen & Wulfsen** (✉ Caya G. F. Betico Croes 52, Oranjestad, ☎ 297/58–23823) has been one of the most highly regarded clothing stores in the Netherlands Antilles for three decades.

Aruba

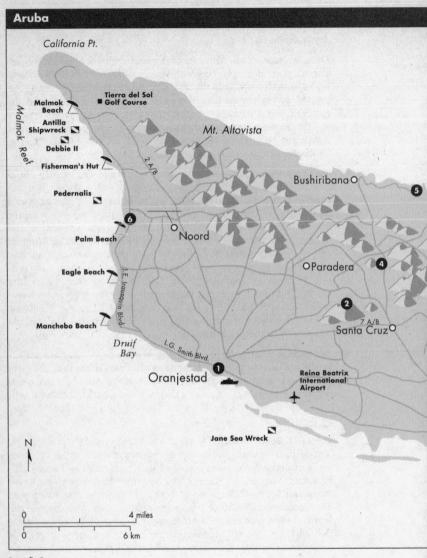

California Pt.

Malmok Reef

Tierra del Sol
Golf Course

Malmok
Beach

Antilla
Shipwreck

Debbie II

Fisherman's Hut

Pedernalis

2 A/B

Mt. Altovista

Bushiribana

5

6

Palm Beach

Noord

Eagle Beach

J.E. Irausquin Blvd.

Paradera

4

Manchebo Beach

2

Druif
Bay

L.G. Smith Blvd.

7 A/B

Santa Cruz

N

Oranjestad

1

Reina Beatrix
International
Airport

Jane Sea Wreck

0   4 miles

0   6 km

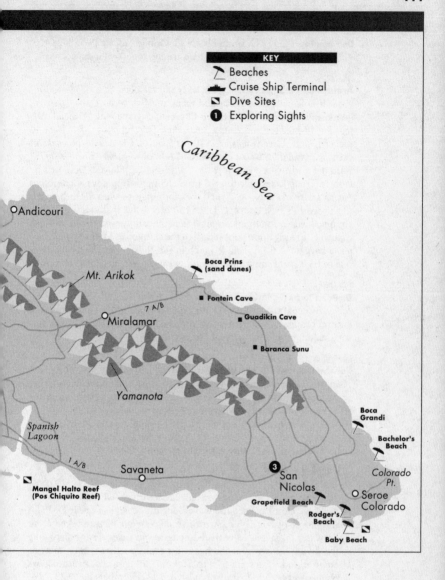

KEY

Beaches
Cruise Ship Terminal
Dive Sites
Exploring Sights

Caribbean Sea

Andicouri

Boca Prins
(sand dunes)

Mt. Arikok

Fontein Cave

7 A/B

Guadikin Cave

Miralamar

Baranca Sunu

Yamanota

Boca
Grandi

*Spanish
Lagoon*

Bachelor's
Beach

1 A/B

*Colorado
Pt.*

Savaneta

San
Nicolas

Seroe
Colorado

Mangel Halto Reef
(Pos Chiquito Reef)

Grapefield Beach

Rodger's
Beach

Baby Beach

Outdoor Activities & Sports

FISHING

De Palm Tours (⊠ L. G. Smith Blvd. 142, Oranjestad, ☎ 297/58–24400, WEB www.depalm.com) runs deep-sea fishing tours seven days a week.

GOLF

Aruba Golf Club (⊠ Golfweg 82, near San Nicolas, ☎ 297/58–42006) has a 9-hole course with 20 sand traps and five water traps, roaming goats, and lots of cacti. There are 11 greens covered with artificial turf, making 18-hole tournaments a possibility. The clubhouse has a bar and locker rooms. Greens fees are $10 for 9 holes, $15 for 18 holes. Golf carts are available. **Tierra del Sol** (⊠ Malmokweg, ☎ 297/58–60978) is on the northwest coast near the California Lighthouse. Designed by Robert Trent Jones, Jr., this 18-hole championship course combines Aruba's native beauty—cacti and rock formations—with the lush greens of the world's best courses. The $130 greens fee includes a golf cart equipped with a communications system that allows you to order drinks that will be ready upon your return to the clubhouse. Half-day golf clinics, a bargain at $45, include lunch in the clubhouse. The pro shop is one of the Caribbean's most elegant, with an extremely attentive staff.

HIKING

De Palm Tours (⊠ L. G. Smith Blvd. 142, Oranjestad, ☎ 297/58–24400, WEB www.depalm.com) offers a guided three-hour trip to sites of unusual natural beauty that are accessible only on foot. The fee is $25 per person, including refreshments and transportation.

HORSEBACK RIDING

Rancho Daimari (⊠ Plantage Daimari, ☎ 297/58–60239, WEB www.visitaruba.com/ranchodaimari) will lead your horse to water—either at Natural Bridge or Natural Pool—in the morning or afternoon for $55 per person. **Rancho Notorious** (⊠ Boroncana, Noord, ☎ 297/58–60508, WEB www.ranchonotorious.com) will take you to the beach to snorkel for $55, on a tour of the countryside for $50, or on a three-hour ride up to the California Lighthouse for $65.

WATER SPORTS

De Palm Tours (⊠ L. G. Smith Blvd. 142, Oranjestad, ☎ 297/58–24400) is one of the best options for novice divers who don't want to be certified. Don a helmet and walk along the ocean floor near De Palm Island, home of huge blue parrot fish. Have your picture taken at an underwater table loaded with champagne and roses. Try Snuba—like scuba diving but without the heavy air tanks—either from a boat or from an island. Rates are $79 to $99, including meals. **Pelican Tours & Watersports** (⊠ J. E. Irausquin Blvd. 232, Palm Beach, ☎ 297/58–72302, WEB www.pelican-aruba.com) has snorkeling tours for around $30, brunch tours or sunset cruises for around $50. **Red Sail Sports** (⊠ J. E. Irausquin Blvd. 83, Oranjestad, ☎ 297/58–61603, 877/733–7245 in the U.S., WEB www.aruba-redsail.com), with courses for children and others new to scuba diving, is especially good for beginners. It also offers snorkeling tours.

Beaches

Beaches in Aruba are beautiful and clean. On the north side the water is too choppy for swimming, but the views are great. **Baby Beach,** on the island's eastern tip, is a semicircle bordering a bay that's as placid and just about as deep as a wading pool—perfect for tots and terrible swimmers. Thatched shaded areas are good for cooling off. Just down the road is the island's unusual pet cemetery. You may see some shore divers here. Stop by the nearby snack shop for chicken legs, burgers, hot dogs, beer, and soda. **Eagle Beach,** on the southwestern coast, is across the highway from what is known as Time-Share Lane. This beach, which is more than a mile long, has been designated one of the 10 best in the world by *Travel & Leisure* magazine. **Manchebo Beach (Punta Brabo)** is impressively wide. The shoreline in front of the Manchebo Beach Resort is where officials turn a blind eye to the occasional top-less sunbather. **Palm Beach,** the center of Aruban tourism, offers the best in swimming, sailing, and other water sports. It runs from the Wyndham Aruba Beach Resort to the Aruba Marriott Resort.

Where to Eat

Restaurants usually add a 10% to 15% service charge.

$$$–$$$$ ✕ **Chez Mathilde.** This elegant restaurant occupies one of Aruba's last 19th-century houses. Ask to sit in the greenhouse atrium, which some say has the feel of Paris. The outstanding French-style menu is constantly re-created by the Dutch chef, who has a deft touch with sauces. Feast on baked escargots, roasted breast of duck with tamarind sauce, ostrich fillet, or quail stuffed with calves' sweetbreads in a bell-pepper sauce. Crepes suzette and chocolate layer cake with *ponche crema* (Venezuelan brandied eggnog) sauce will also win you over. ✉ *Havenstraat 23, Oranjestad,* ☎ *297/58–34968. Reservations essential. AE, DC, MC, V. No lunch Sun.*

$$$ ✕ **Jakarta.** The abundant use of flavorful Indonesian spices brings this restaurant's cuisine to life. The signature *rijsttafel,* which consists of 20 miniature meat, fish, vegetable, and fruit dishes, jumps off the page of the straw-faced, banana-leaf-covered menu. Vegetarians can order egg rolls, vegetable soup, or meat-free rijsttafel. Sample the java juice (blue Curaçao, vodka, Cointreau, banana liqueur, and orange and pineapple juice) at the bamboo bar on the back patio, which is adorned with wind chimes, big clay pots, and tiki torches. ✉ *Wilhelminastraat 64, Oranjestad,* ☎ *297/58–38737. AE, D, DC, MC, V. Closed Tues.*

$$–$$$$ ✕ **Hostaria Da' Vittorio.** Part of the fun at this family-oriented lunch and dinner spot is watching chef Vittorio Muscariello prepare regional specialties in the open kitchen. Try the *branzino al sale* (sea bass baked in a hard salt shell). Exciting presentations and warm service reflect the management's stated desire to honor the essence of Italy: "ancient, but always young." As you leave, pick up some limoncello liqueur or olive oil at the door. A 15% gratuity is automatically added to your bill. ✉ *L. G. Smith Blvd. 380, Palm Beach,* ☎ *297/58–63838. AE, MC, V.*

Barbados

Barbadians (Bajans) are a warm, friendly, and hospitable people, who are genuinely proud of their country and culture. Tourism is the island's number one industry; but with a sophisticated business community and stable government, life here doesn't skip a beat after passengers return to the ship. A resort island since the 1700s, Barbados has cultivated a civilized attitude toward tourists.

Under uninterrupted British rule for 340 years—until independence in 1966—Barbados retains a very British atmosphere. Afternoon tea is a ritual, and cricket is the national sport. The atmosphere, though, is hardly stuffy. This is still the Caribbean, after all.

Beaches along the island's south and west coasts are picture-perfect, and all are open to cruise passengers. On the rugged east coast, where Bajans have their vacation homes, the Atlantic Ocean attracts world-class surfers. The northeast is dominated by rolling hills and valleys; the interior of the island is covered by acres of sugarcane and dotted with small villages. Historic plantations, a stalactite-studded cave, a wildlife preserve, rum factories, and tropical gardens are among the island's attractions. Bridgetown, the capital, is a busy city with more traffic than charm.

CURRENCY

The currency of Barbados is the Barbados dollar (BDS$), and the exchange rate is set at about two Barbados dollars to one U.S. dollar. Either currency is accepted almost everywhere on the island, as are major credit cards and traveler's checks, so you may not need to exchange money. Always ask which currency is being quoted. Prices given below are in U.S. dollars unless otherwise indicated.

TELEPHONES

You can purchase phone cards at the cruise-ship terminal. Direct-dialing to the United States, Canada, and other countries is efficient and reasonable, but some toll-free numbers cannot be accessed from Barbados. To charge your overseas call on a major credit card without incurring a surcharge, dial 800/744–2000 from any pay phone.

SHORE EXCURSIONS

The following are popular choices on Barbados. They may not be offered by all cruise lines. Times and prices are approximate.

Atlantis Submarine. A 50-ft mini-submarine dives as deep as 150 ft below the surface for an exciting view of Barbados's profuse marine life. Most passengers find this trip to the depths—without getting wet—to be thrilling. ⊗ 2½ hrs, ⊠ $90.

Island Tour and Harrison's Cave. After a bus tour of the island, which includes historic Holetown, the picturesque interior of the island, and the rugged Atlantic coast, passengers arrive at the island's most popular attraction. An electric tram winds through this limestone cave. A highlight of the one-hour excursion is a 40-ft underground waterfall. The tour usually includes a visit to the Flower Forest or Orchid World. ⊗ 4 hrs, ⊠ $60.

Malibu Beach Break. Tour the Malibu Rum Distillery, enjoy a refreshing rum drink, and then relax at the beach, where there are changing rooms, showers, lockers, and beach chairs. ⊗ 4 hrs, ⊠ $25.

Coming Ashore

Up to eight ships at a time can dock at Bridgetown's Deep Water Harbour, on the northwest side of Carlisle Bay. The cruise-ship terminal has duty-free shops, handicraft vendors, a post office, a telephone station, a tourist information desk, and a taxi stand. To get downtown, follow the shoreline to the Careenage. It's a 15-minute walk or a $3 cab ride.

Taxis await ships at the pier. Drivers accept U.S. dollars and appreciate a 10% tip. Taxis are unmetered and operate at a fixed hourly rate of $20 per carload (up to three passengers). Most drivers will cheerfully narrate an island tour. You can rent a car with a valid driver's license, but rates are steep—during the high season, up to $100 per day.

Exploring Barbados

Numbers in the margin correspond to points of interest on the Barbados map.

BRIDGETOWN

This bustling capital city is a major duty-free port with a compact shopping area. The principal thoroughfare is Broad Street, which leads west from National Heroes Square. Bridgetown, surprisingly enough, has both rush hours and traffic congestion.

❶ National Heroes Square. Across Broad Street from the Parliament Buildings and bordered by High and Trafalgar streets, this triangular area (formerly called Trafalgar Square) marks the center of town. Its monument to Lord Horatio Nelson—who was in Barbados briefly, as a 19-year-old navy lieutenant—predates Nelson's Column in London's Trafalgar Square by 36 years. Also here are a war memorial and a fountain that commemorates the advent of running water on Barbados in 1865.

2 Parliament Buildings. Overlooking National Heroes Square, these Victorian buildings house the British Commonwealth's third-oldest parliament. Stained-glass windows depict British monarchs from James I to Victoria. There are twice-daily tours when parliament is not sitting (call to confirm). ⊠ *Broad St., St. Michael,* ☎ *246/427–2019.* ▨ *Donations welcome.* ☉ *Tours weekdays (when parliament isn't in session) at 11 and 2.*

3 St. Michael's Cathedral. George Washington, on his only visit outside the United States, is said to have worshiped here in 1751. The original structure was then nearly a century old. Destroyed twice by hurricanes, it was rebuilt in 1784 and again in 1831. ⊠ *Spry St., east of National Heroes Sq., St. Michael.*

CENTRAL BARBADOS AND THE WEST COAST

4 Barbados Museum. This intriguing museum, in the former British military prison in the historic Garrison area, has artifacts from Arawak days (around 400 BC) and galleries that depict 19th-century military history and everyday life. You can see cane-harvesting tools, wedding dresses, ancient (and frightening) dentistry instruments, and slave sale accounts kept in a spidery copperplate handwriting. The museum's Harewood Gallery showcases the island's flora and fauna; its Cunard Gallery has a permanent collection of 20th-century Barbadian and Caribbean paintings and engravings; and its Connell Gallery features European decorative arts. Along with other galleries, including one for children, the museum also has a gift shop and a café. ⊠ *Hwy. 7, Garrison Savannah, St. Michael,* ☎ *246/427–0201 or 246/436–1956,* ᴡᴇʙ *www.barbmuse.org.bb.* ▨ *$6.* ☉ *Mon.–Sat. 9–5, Sun. 2–6.*

9 Flower Forest. It's a treat to meander among fragrant flowering bushes, canna and ginger lilies, puffball trees, and more than 100 other species of tropical flora in a cool, tranquil forest of flowers and other plants. A ½-mi-long (1-km-long) path winds through the 50 acres of grounds, a former sugar plantation; it takes 30–45 minutes to follow the path, or you can wander freely for as long as you wish. Seats, where you can pause and reflect, are located throughout the forest. There is also a snack bar, gift shop, and beautiful view of Mt. Hillaby. ⊠ *Hwy. 2, Richmond Plantation, St. Joseph,* ☎ *246/433–8152.* ▨ *$7.* ☉ *Daily 9–5.*

6 Folkestone Marine Park & Visitor Centre. This park just north of Holetown has both an onshore and offshore component. Onshore, the museum and aquarium illuminate some of the island's marine life; offshore, there's an underwater snorkeling trail around Dottin's Reef (glass-bottom boats are available for nonswimmers). A barge sunk in shallow water is home to myriad fish, making it a popular dive site. ⊠ *Church Point, Holetown, St. James,* ☎ *246/422–2314.* ▨ *Free.* ☉ *Weekdays 9–5.*

10 Gun Hill Signal Station. The 360° view from Gun Hill, 700 ft (215 m) above sea level, was what made this location strategically important to the 18th-century British Army. Using lanterns and semaphores, soldiers based here could communicate with their counterparts at The Garrison, on the south coast, and at Grenade Hill in the north. Time moved slowly in 1868, and Captain Henry Wilkinson whiled away his off-duty hours by carving a huge lion from a single rock—which is on the hillside just below the tower. Come for a short history lesson but

116

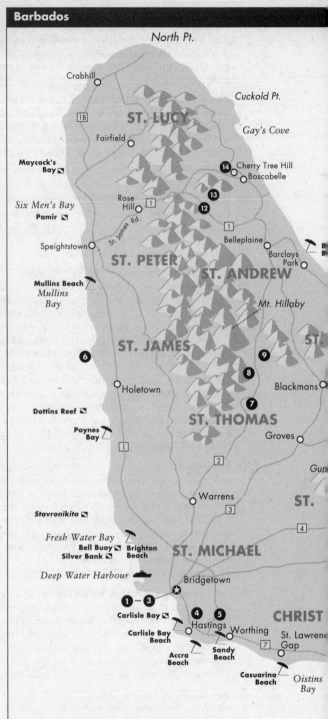

Barbados

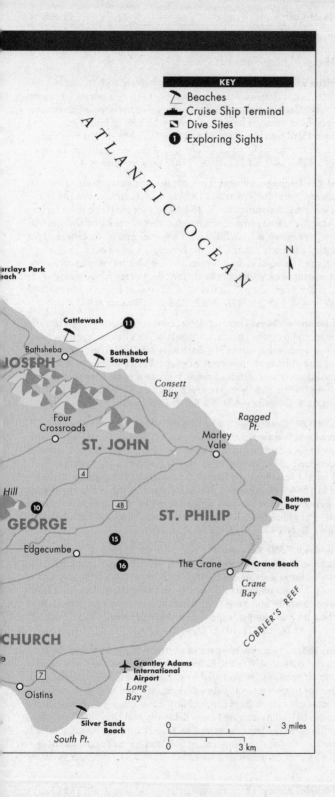

KEY

🏖 Beaches
🚢 Cruise Ship Terminal
◨ Dive Sites
❶ Exploring Sights

ATLANTIC OCEAN

N

Barclays Park
Beach

Cattlewash   ⓫

Bathsheba

Bathsheba
Soup Bowl

Consett
Bay

JOSEPH

Four
Crossroads

Ragged
Pt.

Marley
Vale

ST. JOHN

Hill

⓾

4

4B

GEORGE

ST. PHILIP

Bottom
Bay

Edgecumbe

⓯

⓰

The Crane

Crane Beach

Crane
Bay

COBBLER'S REEF

CHURCH

Grantley Adams
International
Airport

7

Oistins

Long
Bay

Silver Sands
Beach

South Pt.

0   3 miles

0   3 km

mainly for the view; it's so gorgeous, military invalids were sent here to convalesce. ⊠ *Gun Hill, St. George,* ☎ *246/429–1358.* 🖅 *$5.* ⊙ *Weekdays 9–5.*

👆 **❼ Harrison's Cave.** This limestone cavern, complete with stalactites, stalagmites, subterranean streams, and a 40-ft (12-m) waterfall, is a rare find in the Caribbean—and one of Barbados's most popular attractions. The one-hour tours are on electric trams, which fill up fast; reserve ahead of time. Hard hats are required and provided, but all that may fall on you is a little dripping water. ⊠ *Hwy. 2, Welchman Hall, St. Thomas,* ☎ *246/438–6640.* 🖅 *$12.50.* ⊙ *Daily 9–6; last tour at 4.*

👆 **❺ Tyrol Cot Heritage Village.** This coral-stone cottage just south of Bridgetown was constructed in 1854 and has been preserved as an example of period architecture. In 1929 it became the home of Sir Grantley Adams, the first premier of Barbados. Part of the Barbados National Trust, the cottage is now filled with antiques and memorabilia of Sir Grantley and Lady Adams. It's the centerpiece of an outdoor "living" museum of colorful chattel houses, each with a traditional artisan or craftsman at work inside. Crafts are for sale, and refreshments are available at the "rum shop." ⊠ *Rte. 2, Codrington Hill, St. Michael,* ☎ *246/424–2074 or 246/436–9033.* 🖅 *$6.* ⊙ *Weekdays 9–5.*

❽ Welchman Hall Gully. This 1-mi-long (2-km-long) natural gully is really a collapsed limestone cavern, once part of the same underground network as Harrison's Cave. The Barbados National Trust protects the peace and quiet here, making it a beautiful place to hike past acres of labeled flowers and stands of trees. You can see and hear some native birds and, with luck, a native green monkey. ⊠ *Welchman Hall, St. Thomas,* ☎ *246/438–6671.* 🖅 *$6.* ⊙ *Daily 9–5.*

NORTHERN BARBADOS AND THE EAST COAST

⓫ Andromeda Gardens. An intriguing collection of unusual and beautiful plant specimens from around the world is cultivated in 6 acres of gardens nestled between streams, ponds, and rocky outcroppings overlooking the sea above the Bathsheba coastline. The gardens were created in 1954 with flowering plants collected by the late horticulturist Iris Bannochie. They're now administered by the Barbados National Trust. The Hibiscus Café serves snacks and drinks. ⊠ *Bathsheba, St. Joseph,* ☎ *246/433–9261.* 🖅 *$6.* ⊙ *Daily 9–5.*

👆 **⓭ Barbados Wildlife Reserve.** The reserve is the habitat of herons, land turtles, screeching peacocks, shy deer, elusive green monkeys, brilliantly colored parrots (in a large walk-in aviary), a snake, and a caiman. The animals run or fly freely, except for the snake and caiman, so step carefully and keep your hands to yourself. Late afternoon is the best time to glimpse a green monkey. ⊠ *Farley Hill, St. Peter,* ☎ *246/422–8826.* 🖅 *$11.50.* ⊙ *Daily 10–5.*

⓬ Farley Hill. At this national park in northern St. Peter, across the road from the Barbados Wildlife Reserve, the imposing ruins of a plantation great house are surrounded by gardens and lawns, along with an avenue of towering royal palms and gigantic mahogany, whitewood, and casuarina trees. Partially rebuilt for the filming of *Island in the Sun,* the 1957 film starring Harry Belafonte and Dorothy Dandridge, the structure was later destroyed by fire. Behind the estate, there's a sweeping view of the region called Scotland for its rugged landscape. ⊠ *Farley Hill, St. Peter,* ☎ *246/422–3555.* 🖅 *$1.50 per car; walkers free.* ⊙ *Daily 8:30–6.*

⓮ St. Nicholas Abbey. There's no religious connection at all. The island's oldest great house (circa 1650) was named after the British owner's hometown, St. Nicholas parish near Bristol, and Bath Abbey nearby. Its stone-and-wood architecture makes it one of only three original Jacobean-style houses still standing in the Western Hemisphere. It has Dutch gables, finials of coral stone, and beautiful grounds. The first floor, fully furnished with period furniture and portraits of family members, is open to the public. Home movies, shot by the current owner's father, record Bajan life in the 1930s. The Calabash Café, in the rear, serves snacks, lunch, and afternoon tea. ⊠ *Cherry Tree Hill, St. Lucy,* ☎ *246/422–8725.* ⬚ *$5.* ⊙ *Weekdays 10–3:30.*

SOUTHERN BARBADOS

☞ ⑯ **Rum Factory and Heritage Park.** A long road through acres of cane fields brings you to the first rum distillery built in Barbados in the 20th century. Situated on a 350-year-old sugar plantation, the spotless, environmentally friendly, high-tech distillery produces ESA Field white rum and premium Alleyne Arthur varieties. Adjacent is the 7-acre Heritage Park, which showcases Bajan skills and talents in its Art Foundry and Cane Pit Amphitheatre; a row of shops and vendor carts is filled with local products, crafts, and foods. ⊠ *Foursquare Plantation, St. Philip,* ☎ *246/420–1977.* ⬚ *$5.* ⊙ *Daily 9–5.*

⑮ **Sunbury Plantation House & Museum.** Lovingly rebuilt after a 1995 fire destroyed everything but the thick flint-and-stone walls of this 300-year-old plantation house, Sunbury offers an elegant glimpse of the 18th and 19th centuries on a Barbadian sugar estate. Period furniture, old prints, and a collection of horse-drawn carriages lend an air of authenticity. Luncheon is served in the back garden. ⊠ *Off Hwy. 5, Six Cross Roads, St. Philip,* ☎ *246/423–6270,* WEB *www.barbadosgreathouse.com.* ⬚ *$6.* ⊙ *Daily 10–5.*

Shopping

Duty-free shopping is found in Bridgetown's Broad Street department stores and their branches in Holetown and at the cruise-ship terminal. (Note that to purchase items duty-free, you must show your passport). Stores are generally open weekdays 8:30–4:30 and Saturdays 8:30–1.

The **Best of Barbados** (⊠ Worthing, Christ Church, ☎ 246/421–6900), which has seven locations, offers high-quality artwork and crafts in both "native" style and modern designs; everything is made or designed on Barbados. **Del Sol** (⊠ Galleria Mall, Broad St., Bridgetown, St. Michael, ☎ 246/431–0678) has unique shirts, hats, other apparel, and accessories. The designs appear black and white indoors but change to bright colors when exposed to the sun. **Earthworks Pottery** (⊠ No. 2, Edgehill Heights, St. Thomas, ☎ 246/425–0223) is a family-owned and -operated workshop and retail outlet where you can purchase anything from a dish or knickknack to a complete dinner service or one-of-a-kind art piece. Earthworks's products are sold in gift shops throughout the island, but the biggest selection is available here, where you also can watch the potters work. **Greenwich House Antiques** (⊠ Greenwich Village, Trents Hill, St. James, ☎ 246/432–1169) fills an entire plantation house with Barbadian mahogany furniture, crystal, silver, china, books, and pictures; it's open daily 10:30–5:30. **Pelican Craft Centre** (⊠ Harbour Rd., Bridgetown, St. Michael, ☎ 246/427–5350) is a cluster of workshops halfway between the cruise-ship terminal and downtown Bridgetown, where craftspeople create and sell "100% Barbadian-made" leather goods, batik, basketry, carvings, jewelry, glass art, paintings, pottery, and other items. It's open weekdays 9–6 and Saturday 9–2, with extended hours during holidays or to accommodate cruise-ship arrivals.

Outdoor Activities & Sports

FISHING

Billfisher II (☎ 246/431–0741) is a 40-ft Pacemaker that can accommodate up to six people; trips include drinks and transportation to and from the boat. Full-day charters include a full lunch and guaranteed fish (or a 25% refund on a full-day charter). ***Blue Jay*** (☎ 246/429–2326) is a fully equipped 45-ft Sport Fisherman, with a crew that knows where blue marlin, sailfish, barracuda, and kingfish play. Four to six people can be accommodated—it's the only charter boat on the island with four chairs. Drinks, snacks, bait, tackle, and transfers are provided.

GOLF

Barbados Golf Club (⊠ Hwy. 7, Durants, Christ Church, ☎ 246/434–2121), the first public golf course on Barbados, is a par-72, 18-hole championship course designed by Ron Kirby. Greens fees are $119 for 18 holes and $70 for 9 holes, plus a cart fee. Unlimited three-day and seven-day passes are available. Several hotels offer golf privileges, with preferential tee-time reservations and reduced rates. Club and shoe rentals are available. **Club Rockley Barbados** (⊠ Golf Club Rd., Rockley, Christ Church, ☎ 246/435–7873), on the southeast coast, has a challenging 9-hole course that can be played as 18 from varying tee positions. It's open to the public daily, and club rentals are available. Greens fees in high season are $50 for 18 holes and $37.50 for 9 holes. At the venerable **Country Club at Sandy Lane** (⊠ Hwy. 1, Paynes Bay, St. James, ☎ 246/432–2829), golfers can play on the Old Nine or on either of two 18-hole championship courses: the Tom Fazio–designed Country Club Course or the Green Monkey Course, which opened in 2003. Greens fees in high season are $50 for 9 holes or $140 for 18 holes. The **Royal Westmoreland Golf Club** (⊠ Westmoreland St. James, ☎ 246/422–4653) has a world-class Robert Trent Jones, Jr., par-72, 18-hole championship course that meanders through the former 500-acre Westmoreland Sugar Estate. Greens fees ($190 for visitors in high season) include use of an electric cart; club rental is available.

HORSEBACK RIDING

The **Caribbean International Riding Center** (⊠ Cleland Plantation, St. Andrew, ☎ 246/422–7433) offers 1½-hour rides through the Scotland District and 2½-hour treks that continue on to Morgan Lewis Beach, on the Atlantic coast. Prices range from $60 to $90; helmets are compulsory and provided.

WATER SPORTS

Waterskiing, snorkeling, and parasailing are available on most beaches along the west and south coasts. Windsurfing is best at **Silver Sands Beach,** near the southern tip of the island, where the winds are strongest. For scuba divers, Barbados is a rich and varied underwater destination. On the south coast, **Dive Boat Safari** (⊠ Grand Barbados Beach Resort, Aquatic Gap, St. Michael, ☎ 246/427–4350) offers three dives daily and full instruction. **Dive Shop, Ltd.** (⊠ Aquatic Gap, St. Michael, ☎ 246/426–9947; 888/898–3483 in the U.S.; 888/575–3483 in Canada), the island's oldest dive shop, offers three dives daily, beginner dives, and certification. Underwater camera rentals are available.

On the west coast, **Dive Barbados** (⊠ Mount Standfast, St. James, ☎ 246/422–3133) offers all levels of PADI instruction, reef and wreck dives, underwater camera rental, and free transportation. **Hightide Watersports** (⊠ Coral Reef Club, Holetown, St. James, ☎ 246/432–0931 or 800/513–5763) offers one- and two-tank dives, night reef/wreck/drift dives, PADI instruction, equipment rental, and free transportation.

Beaches

All beaches in Barbados are open to cruise-ship passengers. The west coast has the stunning coves and white-sand beaches dear to the hearts of postcard publishers, plus calm, clear water for snorkeling, scuba diving, and swimming. Popular **Accra Beach,** in Rockley, has gentle surf and a lifeguard. There are plenty of places to eat and drink and to rent water-sports equipment. There's also a convenient parking lot. **Casuarina Beach,** at the east end of the St. Lawrence Gap area, always has a nice breeze and a fair amount of surf. Public access is from Maxwell Coast Road. Refreshments are available at the Casuarina Beach Hotel. The exquisite crescent of pink sand at **Crane Beach** is protected by steep cliffs. As attractive as this location is now, it was named not for the elegant long-legged wading birds but for the crane used for hauling and loading cargo when this area was a busy port. Protected by a reef, the rolling surf is great for bodysurfing. A lifeguard is usually on duty. Changing rooms are available at Crane Beach Hotel for a small fee (which you can apply toward drinks or a meal at the restaurant). Beach access is through the hotel and down about 200 steps. South of Holetown, **Paynes Bay** is lined with luxury hotels. It's a very pretty area, with plenty of beach to go around and good snorkeling. Parking areas and public access are available opposite the Coach House. You can grab a bite to eat or a cold drink at Bomba's Beach Bar. Close to the southernmost tip of the island, **Silver Sands/Silver Rock Beach** is a beautiful strand of white sand that always has a stiff breeze, which attracts intermediate and advanced windsurfers.

Where to Eat

A 15% V.A.T. (value-added tax) is in effect in Barbados. Most restaurant prices are V.A.T.-inclusive. A 10% service charge is added to most restaurant bills; if no service charge is added, tip waiters 10% to 15%.

$$–$$$ ✕ **The Crane.** Perched on an oceanfront cliff, the Crane in the Crane Beach Hotel is an informal luncheon spot by day. Enjoy seafood chowder—prepared with lobster, shrimp, dolphinfish, local vegetables, and a dash of sherry—or a light salad or sandwich while absorbing the breathtaking view. In the evening, candlelight and a softly strummed guitar enhance grilled Caribbean lobster seasoned with herbs, lime juice, and garlic butter and served in its shell. Landlubbers can order a perfect filet mignon. Sundays are really special, with a gospel brunch at 10 AM and a Bajan buffet at 12:30 PM. ⊠ *Crane Beach Hotel, Crane Bay, St. Philip,* ☎ *246/423–6220. Reservations essential. AE, D, DC, MC, V.*

$$ ✕ **Atlantis Hotel.** People have enjoyed lunch with a view at this hotel's restaurant for more than 40 years—especially on Sunday, when an enormous Bajan buffet includes pumpkin fritters, spinach cake, pickled breadfruit, fried-flying fish, roast chicken, pepper-pot stew, and fried okra and eggplant. Homemade coconut pie tops the dessert list. The Atlantis is a lunch stop for many day tours. ⊠ *Atlantis Hotel, Tent Bay, Bathsheba, St. Joseph,* ☎ *246/433–9445. AE.*

$$ ✕ **Waterfront Cafe.** This friendly bistro beside the Careenage is the perfect place to enjoy a drink, snack, or meal—and to people-watch. Locals and tourists gather for alfresco all-day dining on sandwiches, salads, fish, pasta, pepper-pot stew, and tasty Bajan snacks such as buljol, fish cakes, or plantation pork (plantains stuffed with spicy minced pork). The pan-fried flying fish sandwich is especially popular. In the evening you can gaze through the arched windows while savoring nouvelle creole cuisine, enjoying cool trade winds, and listening to live jazz. There's a Carib buffet and steel-pan music Tuesday nights from 7 to 9. ⊠ *Bridge House, The Careenage, Bridgetown, St. Michael,* ☎ *246/427–0093. AE, DC, MC, V. Closed Sun.*

$-$$ ✕ **Baku Beach Bar.** Whether you're going to the beach, coming from the beach, or just wanting to be near the beach, this is a great place for lunch or an informal dinner. Tables spill into the courtyard, through tropical gardens, and onto a boardwalk by the sea. Try a Caesar salad, a burger, spareribs, or grilled fish served with the salsa of your choice: fruit, pesto, herb lemon, or ginger soy. On the side, have garlic bread, sautéed onions, rice pilaf, or spicy potato wedges. Got room for crème brûlée, lemon tart, or a brownie with ice cream? Maybe dawdling over cappuccino is enough. ✉ *Hwy. 1, Holetown, St. James,* ☎ *246/432–2258. AE, MC, V.*

Belize

A sliver of land wedged between Guatemala and the Caribbean Sea, Belize is only 109 km (68 mi) wide at its broadest point. Belize probably has the greatest variety of flora and fauna of any country of its size in the world. Because Belize is so small, even if you are in port only a few hours, with careful planning you can experience a good deal of its glorious diversity. Until 1973, the country was known as British Honduras, so English, the official language here, aligns the nation more with the British Caribbean than with the rest of Central America.

Belize City, the country's business, cultural, and transportation hub, has a population of around 50,000, but it is not really representative of the rest of the country. Where Belize City is crowded and uncharming, elsewhere in Belize you'll often find more iguanas or howler monkeys than humans. A few miles off the mainland is the Belize Barrier Reef, a great wall of coral stretching the entire 333 km (200 mi) length of the coast. Dotting the reef like punctuation marks are more than 200 cayes (pronounced keys), and farther out to sea are three coral atolls—all superb for diving and snorkeling. Many, like Ambergris Caye (pronounced Am-*bur*-griss Key) and Caye Caulker, which are jolly resort islands with ample supplies of bars, restaurants, and inns, are reachable on day trips from Belize City.

The main choice you'll have to make is whether to stay in Belize City for a little shopping, a little walking, and perhaps lunch or a dram at one of the Fort George hotels or restaurants, or alternatively to head out by boat, rental car, taxi, or tour on a more active adventure. Alas, poor Belize's tourist infrastructure, used to handing small numbers of international visitors, is not always up to the task of dealing with 2,000-some cruise-ship passengers at one time. Some popular spots, such as Belize Zoo or cave tubing sites, are swamped on cruise-ship days. Even the nurse sharks at Shark-Ray Alley in Hol Chan Marine Reserve get stuffed with chum by early afternoon and often disappear for a little shark nap.

CURRENCY

The Belize dollar ($) is the official currency of Belize. For years, it's been pegged to the United States dollar at a rate of 2 to 1. Since the U.S. dollar is universally accepted, there's no need to acquire Belize currency. Prices quoted throughout this chapter are in U.S. dollars unless otherwise indicated.

TELEPHONES

Calling locally or internationally is easy, but rates are high; around 90¢ a minute for calls to the U.S. To call the United States, dial 001 plus the area code and number. Pay phones accept only pre-paid phone cards, available in shops in denominations from $2.50 to $25. To place a call using your own calling card, use your long-distance carrier's access code or call the operator by dialing 114.

SHORE EXCURSIONS

The following are good choices in Belize. They may not be offered by all cruise lines. Times and prices are approximate.

Cave Tubing and Jungle Walk. After a one-hour bus ride, you'll be given an inner tube. Then you walk 45 minutes through the jungle to the entrance of the caves on the Branch River. After an hour of tubing on the underground river, you'll have lunch and be given a chance to rest and explore. ⏱ 6½ hrs, 🚌 $96.

Maya Ruins at Altun Ha. An hour away from Belize City by bus, these Maya ruins are the most thoroughly excavated in the country. After a one-hour tour, you'll have time to enjoy lunch or a cool drink or to explore the Belize Tourism Village. ⏱ 4 hrs, 🚌 $45.

Shark-Ray Alley Snorkel and Sightseeing. You take a speedboat trip to one of the offshore cayes, where you snorkel among rays and nurse sharks. This is followed by a beach barbecue near the resort town of San Pedro. ☎ 7½ hrs, 🚌 $90.

Wildlife Adventure Tour. After a motor-launch trip up the Belize River, you will stop for lunch, then board a bus for the Belize Zoo, which includes only animals indigenous to Belize. ⏱ 6 hrs, 🚌 $81.

Coming Ashore

Because Belize City's harbor is shallow, passengers are tendered in. If you're going the independent route, try to get in line early for the tenders, as it sometimes takes an hour and a half or more for all the passengers to be brought ashore. The Fort Pointe Tourist Village opened in 2002 and is a clean but antiseptic collection of gift shops, restaurants, and tour operators nicely situated along the harbor.

Taxis, tour guides, and car rental desks are readily available. Taxi trips—official taxis have green license plates—within Belize City's small downtown area are supposed to be set at $2.50 plus 50¢ for each additional passenger, although drivers meeting the cruise ships try to charge whatever the traffic will bear. Taxis don't have meters, so settle on the fare in advance; you shouldn't have to pay more than $5 to go anywhere in the city. By the hour, expect to pay $40–$50. There's no need to tip cab drivers.

It's also possible to rent a car and explore on your own. Crystal, a local company, has a branch at the Tourist Village, but rates can be high (around $65 per day). Downtown streets are narrow and often one-way. You can take two major roads out of Belize City—the Northern Highway, which leads to the Mexican border, 102 mi (164 km) away, and the Western Highway, which runs 81 mi (130 km) to Guatemala. Both are paved and in good condition. Recently installed signs point you to nearby destinations such as the Belize Zoo.

By and large, Belizeans are the friendliest folks you'll meet in any port in the Caribbean. Give them respect rather than just a tip, a smile rather than a command, and you'll enjoy a delightful side of the Caribbean that's long lost in many other destinations.

Belize City

Numbers in the margins correspond to points of interest on the Belize map.

Many Belize hands will tell you the best way to see Belize City is through a rear-view window. But, with an open mind to its peculiarities, and with a little caution (the city has a crime problem, though this rarely affects visitors since the areas usually frequented by cruise-ship

124

passengers are closely watched by tourist police), you may decide Belize City has a raffish, atmospheric charm rarely found in other Caribbean ports of call. You might even see the ghost of Graham Greene at a hotel bar.

A 5- to 10-minute stroll from the perky Tourist Village brings you into the other worlds of Belize City. On the north side of Haulover Creek is the colonial-style world of the Fort George section, where large old homes, stately but sometimes down at the heels, take the breezes off the sea and share their space with hotels and restaurants. On the south side is the bustling world of the Albert Street, the main commercial thoroughfare. But don't stroll too far. Parts of Belize City are unsafe by night or day. During the daylight hours, as long as you stay within the main commercial district and the Fort George area—and ignore the street hustlers—you should have no problem. Nearly all the sights worth seeing in Belize City are in this part of town.

2 Fort George Lighthouse. Towering over the entrance to Belize Harbor, this lighthouse stands guard on the tip of Fort George Point. It was designed and funded by the country's greatest benefactor, Baron Bliss. A memorial to him is nearby. ⊠ *Fort St.*

4 House of Culture. The finest colonial structure in the city is said to have been designed by the illustrious British architect Sir Christopher Wren. Built in 1812, it was once the residence of the governor general, the queen's representative in Belize. After he and the rest of government moved to Belmopan in the wake of Hurricane Hattie in 1961, the house became a venue for social functions and a guest house for visiting VIPs. Queen Elizabeth stayed here in 1985, Prince Philip in 1988. ⊠ *Regent St. at Southern Foreshore,* ☎ *501/227–3050.* ☞ *$2.50.* ☉ *Weekdays 8:30–4:30.*

3 Museum of Belize. This new museum, in the Central Bank of Belize building complex, is one of the highlights of Belize City. It has displays on Belize history and culture ranging from ancient Maya artifacts to a cell from the old jail built in 1853. ⊠ *Gabourel La.,* ☎ *501/223–4524.* ☞ *$5.* ☉ *Tues.–Fri. 10–6, Sat. 10–3.*

5 St. John's Cathedral. At the south end of Albert Street, this lovely structure is the oldest Anglican church in Central America and the only one outside England where monarchs were crowned. From 1815 to 1845 four kings of the Mosquito Coast (a British protectorate along the coast of Honduras and Nicaragua) were crowned here. ⊠ *Albert St.* ☎ *501/227–2137.*

1 Swing Bridge. Each day at 5:30 AM and 5:30 PM, four men hand-winch the bridge a quarter-revolution so a bevy of waiting boats can continue their journeys upstream. The bridge, made in England, opened in 1923; it was renovated and upgraded in 1999. It's the only one of its kind left. Before the Swing Bridge arrived, cattle were "hauled over" the creek in a barge. ⊠ *Haulover Creek where Queen and Albert Sts. meet.*

INDEPENDENT TOURS

Several Belize City–based tour guides and operators offer custom trips for ship passengers. Tour guide Reginald Tripp, of **Reggie's Tours** (⊠ 29 Clinic Rd., Ladyville, ☎ 501/225–2195), has carved out a profitable niche running independent trips for cruise passengers to Sibun River for cave tubing, to Goff Caye for snorkeling, and elsewhere. Katie Valk of **Maya Travel Services** (⊠ 42 Cleghorn St., ☎ 501/223–1623), a New Yorker with attitude (softened by some 15 years' residency in Belize), can organize a custom trip to just about anywhere in the country.

Shopping

Belize does not have the crafts tradition of its neighbors, Guatemala and Mexico, and imported goods are expensive due to high duties, but hand-carved items of Zircote or other local woods make good souvenirs. The **Fort Pointe Tourist Village,** where the ship tenders come in, is a collection of bright and clean gift shops selling T-shirts and Belizean and Guatemalan crafts. Beside the Tourist Village is an informal **Street Vendor Market,** with funkier goods and performances by a "Brukdown" band or a group of Garifuna drummers.

The ground floor of the **Commercial Center** (⊠ Market Square, ☎ 501/227–2117) has herbalists and traditional healers. The **Image Factory** (⊠ 91 N. Front St., ☎ 501/223–4151) is a gallery featuring Belize's hippest artists.

Outdoor Activities & Sports

GOLF

Caye Chapel Golf Resort (⊠ Caye Chapel, 16 mi northeast of Belize City, ☎ 501/226–8250) is a beautiful 18-hole seaside course occupying much of Caye Chapel, a privately owned island. Some water taxis to Caye Caulker will drop you here, or you can fly the 12 minutes to the island's private airstrip, by prior arrangement with the resort, for about $100 round-trip. Challenges include brisk prevailing winds and the occasional crocodile. Unlimited golf, with clubs and cart rental and a poolside lunch, costs $200. If you've ever wanted to play golf in the jungle, **Roaring River Golf Club** (⊠ Mile 50¼, Western Hwy., 2 mi west of Belmopan, ☎ 501/820–3031), a new 9-hole course near Belize's little capital, Belmopan, is your chance to do it. Don't expect a country club setting, but it's fun. The setting on the pristine Roaring River is ideal, and you can even take a dip. The cost is $20, including club rental.

Beaches

There are no beaches of note within easy driving distance of Belize City. For beaches, you'll have to pop over to Ambergris Caye or Caye Caulker.

Where to Eat

Whether it's local creole fare like stew chicken or a succulent spiny lobster (in season mid-June through mid-February), you can enjoy Belizean cuisine in Belize City and on the islands. Tap water (pipe water as it's called here) is safe to drink in Belize City and San Pedro; on Caye Caulker, it's best to drink bottled water.

$$–$$$ ✕▥ **The Smoky Mermaid.** On the ground floor of the Great House is one of the best restaurants in the city. In a large courtyard shaded by breadfruit and sapodilla trees, amiable servers bring Caribbean-influenced seafood dishes, inventive pasta, and savory barbecues. At lunch, a shrimp burger costs $9 and the piña colada pie is $6. ⊠ *13 Cork St.,* ☎ *501/223–4759, AE, MC, V.*

$$ ✕ **Wet Lizard.** For a casual, fun lunch, this spot next to the Tourist Village is unbeatable. Try the conch fritters and jerk chicken sandwich, both around $7. ⊠ *1 N. Front St.,* ☎ *501/223–2664. MC, V.*

$ ✕ **Macy's Café.** This is the best place for creole food. A filling plate of stewed chicken, rice and beans, and plantains costs about $5. You can also get more exotic fare, including armadillo, brocket deer, gibnut, and, by request, stewed iguana, known locally as bamboo chicken. The proprietor proudly displays a photo of Harrison Ford, who commandeered the table by the door during the making of *The Mosquito Coast.* ⊠ *18 Bishop St.,* ☎ *501/207–3419. No credit cards.*

Side Trips by Road from Belize City

Numbers in the margins correspond to points of interest on the Belize map.

6 **Altun Ha.** If you've never visited an ancient Maya site, make a trip to Altun Ha, 45 km (28 mi) north of Belize City. It's not the most dramatic site in the country, but it is the most thoroughly excavated and the most accessible from Belize City. The first inhabitants settled here before 900 BC, and their descendants abandoned the site around AD 900. At its height the city was home to 10,000 people. ⊠ ☎ *No phone.* ⊠ *$2.50.* ☉ *Daily 9–5.*

9 **Belize Zoo.** One of the smallest, but arguably one of the best, zoos in the world, this park houses only animals native to Belize. As you stroll the trails on a self-guided tour, you visit several Belizean ecosystems—rain forest, lagoons, and riverine forest—and spot more than 125 species. Besides spotted and rare black jaguars, you'll also see the country's four other wild cats; the puma, margay, ocelot, and jaguarondi. Probably the most famous resident of the zoo is named April. She's a Baird's tapir, the national animal of Belize. This relative of the horse and rhino is known to locals as the mountain cow. ⊠ *Western Hwy., 30 mi (48 km) west of Belize City,* ☎ *501/220–8004,* WEB *www. belizezoo.org.* ⊠ *$7.50.* ☉ *Daily 9–4:30.*

8 **Community Baboon Sanctuary.** One of the country's most interesting wildlife conservation projects, the Community Baboon Sanctuary is actually a haven for black howler monkeys, agile bundles of black fur with deafening roars. The reserve, encompassing a 35 km (20 mi) stretch of the Belize River, was established in 1985 by a group of local farmers. Today there are nearly 1,000 black howler monkeys in the sanctuary, as well as numerous other species of birds and mammals. Exploring the sanctuary is made easy by about 5 km (3 mi) of trails that start near a small museum. ⊠ *Bermudian Landing Village, 45 km (28 mi) northwest of Belize City—turn left off Northern Hwy. at Mile 14,* ☎ *501/227–7369.* ⊠ *$5.* ☉ *Dawn–dusk.*

7 **Crooked Tree Wildlife Sanctuary.** A paradise for animal lovers, this sanctuary encompasses a chain of inland waterways covering more than 3,000 acres. You're likely to see iguanas, crocodiles, coatis, and turtles. The sanctuary's most prestigious visitor, however, is the jabiru stork. With a wingspan of up to 9 ft, it is the largest flying bird in the Americas. At the center of the reserve is Crooked Tree, one of the oldest inland villages in Belize. There are a number of excellent guides in the village, including Sam Tillet. ⊠ *Turn west off Northern Hwy. at Mile 30.8, then drive 3 km (2 mi),* ☎ *501/223–4987 for Belize Audubon Society.* ⊠ *$4.*

10 **Hummingbird Highway.** Belmopan, Belize's little capital, a town of 8,000 civil servants and their families and nondescript government buildings about 80 km (50 mi) southwest of Belize City, isn't really worth a special trip. But the road that begins near Belmopan, the Hummingbird Highway, is. Once a potholed nightmare, this 78-km (49-mi) paved two-lane, which turns south off the Western Highway, is now the best road in Belize, if not in all of Central America. It's also the country's most scenic route. As you go south toward Dangriga Town, on your right rise the jungle-covered Maya Mountains, largely free of signs of human habitation except for the occasional field of corn or beans. Closer to Dangriga are large citrus groves and banana plantations.

Less than half an hour south of Belmopan on the Hummingbird is the **Blue Hole,** a natural turquoise pool surrounded by mosses and lush vegetation, excellent for a cool dip. The Blue Hole is actually part of an underground river system. On the other side of the hill is St. Herman's Cave, once inhabited by the Maya. A path leads up from the highway, near the Blue Hole. ⊠ *Hummingbird Hwy.* ⊠ *$4.*

Ambergris Caye and Caye Caulker

If you would rather spend your time in Belize on an island instead of the mainland, you have two main choices: Ambergris Caye or Caye Caulker.

Ambergris Caye, also known as San Pedro, after its only town, is a laid-back Caribbean-style resort island that's the most popular tourist destination in Belize. Once a sleepy fishing village, San Pedro still has streets of sand, and the tallest building is only three stories high. Caye Caulker is Ambergris Caye's little-sister island—smaller, less developed, and cheaper.

Once on Ambergris or Caulker, you can laze on a beach, shop, ride around on a golf cart (there are no rental cars on the islands, but golf carts rent for around $35 for eight hours), have lunch in a seaside bistro, or take a boat out to the barrier reef for some of the Caribbean's best snorkeling.

It's usually possible to get to either island (but not both) during the typical ship's stop, either by scheduled water taxi or by puddle-jumper airplane.

GETTING TO AMBERGRIS CAYE AND CAYE CAULKER

➤ AIR TRAVEL: Especially if you are going to Ambergris Caye, you may prefer to fly, or you can water taxi over and fly back. There are hourly flights on two airlines. The flight to Caulker takes about 15 minutes and that to San Pedro about 25 minutes. The cost is $52 round-trip to either island. A taxi between the Tourist Village and the Municipal Airport is around $3. On Ambergris, the airstrip is at the south end of town, within easy walking distance of restaurants and shops. Be sure you fly out of Belize City's Municipal, not out of the international airport north of the city. Flights from International are about twice as costly, plus you'll have a $20 cab fare each way to the airport. **Maya Island Air** (☎ 501/226–2435 or 800/225–6732 in the U.S., WEB www.mayaislandair.com) has hourly flights, and you can make a reservation on the company Web site. **Tropic Air** (☎ 501/226–2012 or 800/422–3435 in the U.S., WEB www.tropicair.com) has frequent flights, and you can make reservations by e-mail.

➤ BOAT AND FERRY TRAVEL: To go by water taxi—fast open boats with twin outboard engines—turn left from the Tourist Village and walk about five minutes to the Marine Terminal, which is next to the Swing Bridge. Boats to both islands are operated by the Caye Caulker Water Taxi Association. There are at least six trips a day to each island, beginning at 8 AM. The trip to or from Caulker takes 45 minutes and costs $7.50 one-way or $12.50 round-trip. The trip to or from San Pedro takes 75 minutes and costs $12.50 one-way or $22.50 round-trip. In San Pedro, these water taxis dock at Shark's Pier in the middle of town. For information on schedules, contact the **Caye Caulker Water Taxi Association** (☎ 501/226–0992 WEB www.gocayecaulker.com).

EXPLORING AMBERGRIS CAYE AND CAYE CAULKER

Numbers in the margins correspond to points of interest on the Belize map.

⑫ **Ambergris Caye.** Ambergris is the queen of the cayes. With a population around 4,400, the island's only town, San Pedro, remains a small, friendly, and prosperous village. It has one of the highest literacy rates in the country and an admirable level of awareness about the fragility of the reef. The large number of substantial private houses being built on the edges of town is proof of how much tourism has enriched San Pedro.

Hol Chan Marine Reserve (Maya for "little channel"), 6 km (4 mi) from San Pedro at the southern tip of Ambergris, is a 20-minute boat ride from the island. Hol Chan is a break in the reef about 100 ft wide and 20 ft–35 ft deep, through which tremendous volumes of water pass with the tides. Varying in depth from 50 ft to 100 ft, Hol Chan's canyons lie between buttresses of coral running perpendicular to the reef, separated by white, sandy channels. Because fishing is forbidden, snorkelers and divers can see teeming marine life, including spotted eagle rays, squirrel fish, butterfly fish, parrot fish, and queen angelfish as well as Nassau groupers, barracuda, and large shoals of yellowtail snappers. Shark-Ray Alley, a sandbar where you can snorkel with nurse sharks and rays (which gather here to be fed) and even larger numbers of day-trippers, was added to the reserve in 1999. Sliding into the water is a feat of personal bravery, as sight of the sharks and rays brushing past you is daunting yet spectacular. You need above-average swimming skills, as the current is often strong. ⊠ *Off southern tip of Ambergris Caye.* 🕾 *$5.*

⑪ **Caye Caulker.** On Caye Caulker, where the one village is home to around 800 people, brightly painted houses on stilts line the coral sand streets. Flowers outnumber cars 10 to 1 (golf carts, bicycles, and bare feet are the preferred means of transportation). The living is easy, as you might guess from all the NO SHIRT, NO SHOES, NO PROBLEM signs at the bars. This is the kind of place where most of the listings in the telephone directory give addresses like "near football field."

SHOPPING

At **Belizean Arts** (⊠ Fido's Courtyard, off Barrier Reef Dr., Ambergris Caye ☎ 501/226–2638) you'll find a selection of works by local painters. Also on display—and for sale—are handicrafts from the region. At **Sea Gal Boutique** (⊠ Barrier Reef Dr., in Holiday Hotel, Ambergris Caye, ☎ 501/226–2431) the owner has an artist's eye. Everything is beautiful, even the T-shirts.

Annie's Boutique (⊠ Front St., north end of island, near the Split, Caye Caulker, ☎ 501/226–0151) has some of the best women's and children's clothes in Belize. Here you'll find dresses and sarongs made with fabrics from Bali, unique silver jewelry, and Guatemalan bags that somehow don't make you look like a backpacker.

OUTDOOR ACTIVITIES & SPORTS

➤ SCUBA DIVING AND SNORKELING: If you get to Ambergris Caye early enough, you'll have time for a quick dive or snorkel trip out to the reef. More than a dozen dive and snorkel shops line the beachfront downtown, offering about the same trips at similar prices. Speedboats take divers and snorkelers out to their destinations, usually to Hol Chan Marine Reserve south of Ambergris or Mexico Rocks off North Ambergris. Dives off Ambergris are usually single-tank dives at depths of 50 ft–80 ft, giving you approximately 35 minutes of bottom time. Most companies offer morning and afternoon single-tank dives. Snorkeling costs $20 to $25 per person for two or three hours, including equipment and admission to Hol Chan. Most snorkel trips begin mid-morning or early afternoon. If your schedule requires a different time, you may have to pay a little more. Diving trips run around $40 for a single-tank dive, $50–$65 for a double-tank dive, plus equipment rental.

Dive and snorkeling trips to Hol Chan that originate in Caye Caulker are a bit cheaper. Snorkeling costs $15 to $20 per person for two or three hours, including equipment and admission to Hol Chan. If you arrive on the island after the first wave of boats go to the reef, usually around 10:30 am, you may have to pay more for a "custom" trip. Diving trips run around $35 for a single-tank dive, $45–$60 for a double-tank dive, plus equipment rental.

Amigos del Mar (✉ off Barrier Reef Dr., near Mayan Princess Hotel, Ambergris Caye, ☎ 501/226–2706, WEB amigosdive.com) is probably the most consistently recommended dive operation on the island. It offers a range of local dives and snorkel trips. The well-regarded **Gaz Cooper's Dive Belize** (✉ 5 mi north of town at Playa Blanca Resort, Ambergris Caye, ☎ 501/226–3202, WEB www.divebelize.com) boasts about having the smallest dive operation on the island.

On Caye Caulker, if you're looking for someone to take you out to the reef, **Frenchie's Diving Services** (✉ Front St., Caye Caulker ☎ 501/226–0234) is a well-regarded local operator.

Among the top guides in the entire country is **Captain Chocolate Heredia** (✉ Front St., Caye Caulker ☎ 501/226–0151), who with several employees runs terrific manatee spotting and snorkel trips.

BEACHES

Although the barrier reef just offshore limits the wave action, which, over eons, builds classic wide sandy beaches, and there is a good deal of seagrass on the shore bottom, Ambergris Caye's beaches are among the best in Belize. All beaches in Belize are public. **Mar de Tumbo,** 1½ mi (3 km) south of town near Tropica Hotel, is the best beach on the south end of the island. **North Ambergris,** accessible by water taxi from San Pedro or via a hand-pulled ferry across a river channel, has miles of narrow beaches and few people. **Ramon's Village's beach,** right across from the airstrip, is the best in the town area.

The beaches on Caulker are not as good as those on Ambergris. Along the front side of the island is a narrow strip of sand, but the water is shallow and swimming conditions poor. **The Split,** on the north end of the village (turn to your right from the main public pier), is the best place on Caye Caulker for swimming.

WHERE TO EAT

$$ ✕ **JamBel Jerk Pit.** The spicy jerk-style dishes here are the way to go at this eatery, which combines the cuisines of Jamaica and Belize (hence the name). This casual spot is in the middle of town next door to Big Daddy's disco. You can relax in the first-floor dining room, where reggae is always playing, or upstairs on the roof, which is often so windy you'll have to hang on to your napkin. The sea views make it worth the trouble. ✉ *Barrier Reef Dr., next to Central Park and Big Daddy's, Ambergris Caye,* ☎ *501/226–3303. AE, MC, V.*

$$ ✕ **Rasta Pasta.** This restaurant started life in San Pedro, migrated to Placencia, and somehow ended up on Caulker, where it's now serving some of the best food on the islands, in a charmingly casual setting, with sand on the floor. The conch fritters are memorable. ✉ *Front St., Caye Caulker,* ☎ *501/206–0356. MC, V. Closed Wed.*

$$ ✕ **The Sandbox.** The names of regulars are carved on the backs of the chairs at this popular eatery. Whether outside under the palms or indoors under the lazily turning ceiling fans, you'll always have your feet in the sand here. Open daily from 7 AM to 9 PM, the Sandbox serves a lobster omelet for breakfast, a roast beef sandwich for lunch, and red snapper in a mango sauce for dinner. Prices are reasonable, and the portions are enormous. ✉ *Front St. at public pier, Caye Caulker,* ☎ *501/ 226–0200. AE, MC, V.*

$–$$ ✕ **Papi's Diner.** Atmosphere is in short supply at Papi's, as are views of the sea. Hardly more than a screened porch with a few wooden tables, Papi's is an unpretentious place tucked away at the north end of town. But the seafood and other dishes are expertly prepared and served at reasonable prices. The grilled fish, served with the usual side dishes, goes for $8. ✉ *Pescador Dr. at north end of town behind Seven Seas Resort, Ambergris Caye,* ☎ *501/226–2047. No credit cards.*

British Virgin Islands

The British Virgin Islands (BVI) consist of about 50 mostly volcanic islands, islets, and cays; most are remarkably hilly. The BVI are serene, seductive, spectacularly beautiful, and still remarkably laid-back. Their pleasures are mostly understated, and overall, there is a sense of a Caribbean you don't see much anymore. Several factors have enabled the BVI to retain these qualities: no building can rise higher than the surrounding palms, and there are no direct flights from the mainland United States, so the tourism tide is held back. In fact, things only get crowded when a big cruise ship docks off Road Town, Tortola.

Sailing has always been a popular activity in the BVI. The first arrivals here were a seafaring tribe, the Ciboney Indians. They were followed (circa AD 900) by the Arawaks, who sailed from South America, established settlements, and farmed and fished. Still later came the mighty Caribs.

In 1493 Christopher Columbus was the first European visitor. Impressed by the number of islands dotting the horizon, he named them *Las Once Mil Virgines*—the 11,000 Virgins—in honor of the 11,000 virgin companions of St. Ursula, martyred in the 4th century. In the ensuing years, the Spaniards passed through, fruitlessly seeking gold. Then came pirates and buccaneers, who found the islands' hidden coves and treacherous reefs ideal bases from which to prey on passing galleons crammed with gold, silver, and spices. It was the British who established a plantation economy and for 150 years developed the sugar industry. When slavery was abolished in 1838 the plantation economy faltered, and the majority of the white population left for Europe.

The islands are still politically tied to Britain. The governor, appointed by the queen of England, has limited powers, and these are concentrated on external affairs and local security. Although tourism is the number one industry, there's little doubt that BVIers—who so love their unspoiled tropical home—will maintain their islands' easygoing charms for both themselves and their guests.

Larger cruise ships may call on Tortola, but smaller ships might call on Virgin Gorda or sometimes even Jost Van Dyke.

CURRENCY
You won't have to worry about exchanging money here, since the official currency is the U.S. dollar. Some places accept cash only, but major credit cards are widely accepted.

TELEPHONES
For credit-card or collect long-distance calls to the United States, use a phone-card telephone or look for special USADirect phones, which are linked directly to an AT&T operator. Or dial 111 from a pay phone to charge a call to your MasterCard or Visa. USADirect and pay phones can be found at most hotels and in towns.

SHORE EXCURSIONS
The following are good choices in the British Virgin Islands. They may not be offered by all cruise lines. Times and prices are approximate.

The Baths. Take a shuttle to visit Virgin Gorda's most renowned beach. ☺ *3–4 hrs,* 🚌 *$35 (often less if the ship docks in Spanish Town).*

Sage Mountain and Beach. Start with a hike up Sage Mountain, the highest peak in the British Virgin Islands. After admiring the view, head back down and take a bus to Cane Garden Beach for swimming. ☺ *4 hrs,* 🚌 *$45.*

Sailing Excursion. Climb aboard a sailing yacht in Road Town, Tortola, harbor for a half-day sail to some of the smaller surrounding islands, with stops for swimming and snorkeling. Full-day trips include lunch. ☉ 4–7 hrs, ☎ $50–$90.

Virgin Gorda Highlights Tour. After a tour of Spanish Town, climb aboard a safari bus to see the highlights of the island, including Gorda Peak and The Baths. ☉ 4 hrs, ☎ $45.

Coming Ashore

Large cruise ships usually anchor in Road Town Harbor and bring passengers ashore by tender. Small ships can sometimes tie up at Wickham's Cay dock. Either way, it's a short stroll to Road Town. If your ship isn't going to Virgin Gorda, you can make the 12-mi trip by ferry from the dock in Road Town in about 30 minutes for about $25 round-trip.

There are taxi stands at Wickham's Cay and in Road Town. Taxis are unmetered, and there are minimums for travel throughout the island, so it's usually cheaper to travel in groups. Negotiate to get the best fares, as there is no set fee schedule. If you are in the islands for just a day, it's usually cost-effective to share a taxi with a small group, since you'd have to pay an agency at Wickham's Cay or in Road Town $10 for a temporary license and car-rental charges of at least $60 a day.

On Virgin Gorda, ships often dock off Spanish Town or Leverick Bay and tender passengers to the ferry dock.

A few taxis will be available at Leverick Bay—you can set up an island tour for about $40—but Leverick Bay is far away from The Baths, the island's must-see beach, so a shore excursion is often the best choice. If you are tendered to Spanish Town, then it's possible to take a shuttle taxi to The Baths for as little as $5 per person.

If your ship calls on Jost Van Dyke, you'll probably be tendered ashore at Great Harbour, where you can easily walk from one informal bar to another.

Exploring Tortola

Tortola doesn't have many historic sights, but it does have abundant natural beauty. Beware of the roads, which are extraordinarily steep and twisting, making driving demanding. The best beaches are on the north shore.

Numbers in the margin correspond to points of interest on the British Virgin Islands map.

② Fort Burt. The most intact historic ruin on Tortola was built by the Dutch in the early 17th century to safeguard Road Harbour. It sits on a hill at the western edge of Road Town and is now the site of a small hotel and restaurant. The foundations and magazine remain, and the structure offers a commanding view of the harbor. ⊠ *Waterfront Dr., Road Town*, ☏ *no phone.* ☎ *Free.* ☉ *Daily dawn–dusk.*

④ Fort Recovery. The unrestored ruins of a 17th-century Dutch fort, 30 ft in diameter, sit amid a profusion of tropical greenery on the Villas of Fort Recovery Estates grounds. There's not much to see here, and there are no guided tours, but you're welcome to stop by and poke around. ⊠ *Waterfront Dr., Road Town*, ☏ *284/485–4467.* ☎ *Free.*

③ J. R. O'Neal Botanic Gardens. Take a walk through this 4-acre showcase of lush plant life. There are sections devoted to prickly cacti and succulents, hothouses for ferns and orchids, gardens of medicinal herbs, and plants and trees indigenous to the seashore. From the

Tourist Board office in Road Town, cross Waterfront Drive and walk one block to Main Street and turn right. Keep walking until you see the high school. The gardens are on your left. ⊠ *Botanic Station, Road Town,* ☎ *no phone.* ☑ *Free.* ⊙ *Mon.–Sat. 9–4:30.*

❺ North Shore Shell Museum. On Tortola's north shore, this casual museum has a very informal exhibit of shells, unusually shaped driftwood, fish traps, and traditional wooden boats. ⊠ *North Shore Rd., Carrot Bay,* ☎ *284/495–4714.* ☑ *Free.* ⊙ *Daily dawn–dusk.*

❶ Road Town. The laid-back capital of the BVI looks out over Road Harbour. It takes only an hour or so to stroll down Main Street and along the waterfront, checking out the traditional West Indian buildings, painted in pastel colors and sporting high-pitched, corrugated-tin roofs; bright shutters; and delicate fretwork trim. For hotel and sightseeing brochures and the latest information on everything from taxi rates to ferry-boat schedules, visit the BVI Tourist Board office. Or just choose a seat on one of the benches in Sir Olva Georges Square, on Waterfront Drive, and watch the people come and go from the ferry dock and customs office across the street.

❻ Sage Mountain National Park. At 1,716 ft (525 m), Sage Mountain is the highest peak in the BVI. From the parking area a trail leads you in a loop not only to the peak itself (and extraordinary views) but also to a small rain forest, sometimes shrouded in mist. Most of the forest was cut down over the centuries to clear land for sugarcane, cotton, and other crops; to create pastureland; or to simply utilize the stands of timber. In 1964 this park was established to preserve what rain forest remained. Up here you can see mahogany trees, white cedars, mountain guavas, elephant-ear vines, mamey trees, and giant bullet woods, to say nothing of such birds as mountain doves and thrushes. Take a taxi from Road Town or drive up Joe's Hill Road and make a left onto Ridge Road toward Chalwell and Doty villages. The road dead-ends at the park. ⊠ *Ridge Rd., Sage Mountain,* ☎ *no phone.* ☑ *Free.* ⊙ *Daily dawn–dusk.*

❼ Skyworld. Drive up here and climb the observation tower for a stunning, 360° view of numerous islands and cays. On a clear day you can even see St. Croix (40 mi [64½ km] away) and Anegada (20 mi [32 km] away). ⊠ *Ridge Rd., Joe's Hill,* ☎ *no phone.* ☑ *Free.*

Exploring Virgin Gorda

There are few roads on Virgin Gorda, and most byways don't follow the scalloped shoreline. The main route sticks resolutely to the center of the island, linking The Baths at the tip of the southern extremity with Gun Creek and Leverick Bay at North Sound and providing exhilarating views. The craggy coast, scissored with grottoes and fringed by palms and boulders, has a primitive beauty. If you drive, you can hit all the sights in one day. Stop to climb Gorda Peak, in the island's center.

Numbers in the margin correspond to points of interest on the British Virgin Islands map.

❿ The Baths. At Virgin Gorda's most celebrated sight, giant boulders are scattered about the beach and in the water. Some are almost as large as houses and form remarkable grottoes. Climb between these rocks to swim in the many pools. Early morning and late afternoon are the best times to visit if you want to avoid crowds. (If it's privacy you crave, follow the shore northward to quieter bays—Spring, the Crawl, Little Trunk, and Valley Trunk—or head south to Devil's Bay.) ⊠ *Lee Rd., The Baths,* ☎ *no phone.* ☑ *Free.*

❾ Little Fort National Park. This 36-acre wildlife sanctuary contains the ruins of an old Spanish fort. Giant boulders like those at The Baths

134

British Virgin Islands

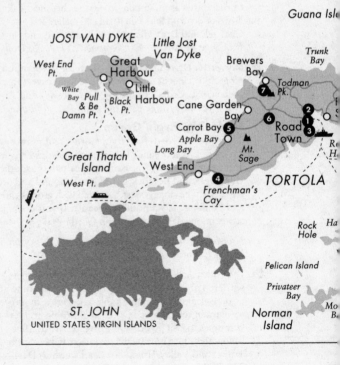

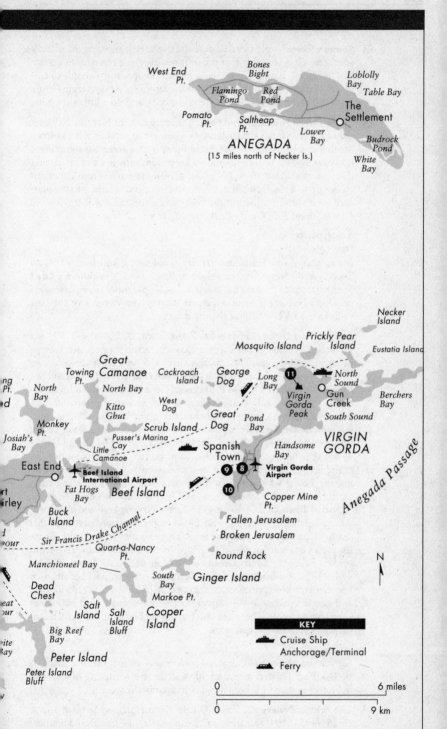

West End
Pt.

Bones
Bight

Loblolly
Bay

Flamingo
Pond

Red
Pond

Table Bay

Pomato
Pt.

Saltheap
Pt.

The
Settlement

Lower
Bay

ANEGADA
(15 miles north of Necker Is.)

Budrock
Pond

White
Bay

Necker
Island

Prickly Pear
Island

Mosquito Island

Eustatia Island

Great
Camanoe

Towing
Pt.

Cockroach
Island

George
Dog

Long
Bay

North
Sound

Gun
Creek

Berchers
Bay

North
Bay

North Bay

West
Dog

Virgin
Gorda
Peak

South Sound

Monkey
Pt.

Kitto
Ghut

Scrub Island

Great
Dog

Pond
Bay

VIRGIN
GORDA

Josiah's
Bay

Pusser's
Cay Marina

Spanish
Town

Handsome
Bay

Little
Camanoe

9 8

Virgin Gorda
Airport

Anegada Passage

East End

Beef Island
International Airport

10

Fat Hogs
Bay

Beef Island

Copper Mine
Pt.

Buck
Island

Fallen Jerusalem

Sir Francis Drake Channel

Broken Jerusalem

Quart-a-Nancy
Pt.

Round Rock

N

Manchioneel Bay

South
Bay

Ginger Island

Dead
Chest

Markoe Pt.

Salt
Island

Salt
Island
Bluff

Cooper
Island

KEY

Big Reef
Bay

Cruise Ship
Anchorage/Terminal

Peter Island

Ferry

Peter Island
Bluff

0   6 miles

0   9 km

are scattered throughout the park. ⊠ *Spanish Town Rd.,* ☎ *no phone.* 🎫 *Free.*

⑧ Spanish Town. Virgin Gorda's peaceful main settlement, on the island's southern wing, is so tiny that it barely qualifies as a town. Also known as The Valley, Spanish Town has a marina, shops, and a couple of car-rental agencies. Just north of town is the ferry slip. At the Virgin Gorda Yacht Harbour you can stroll along the dock and do a little shopping.

⑪ Virgin Gorda Peak National Park. There are two trails at this 265-acre park, which contains the island's highest point, at 1,359 ft (414 m). Small signs on North Sound Road mark both entrances; sometimes, however, the signs are missing, so keep watch for a set of stairs that disappears into the trees. It's about a 15-minute hike from either entrance up to a small clearing, where you can climb a ladder to the platform of a wooden observation tower and a spectacular 360° view. ⊠ *North Sound Rd., Gorda Peak,* ☎ *no phone.* 🎫 *Free.*

Shopping

TORTOLA

Many shops and boutiques are clustered along and just off Road Town's **Main Street.** You can shop in Road Town's **Wickham's Cay I** area adjacent to the marina, where cruise ships tender their passengers in. Don't be put off by an informal shop entrance; some of the best finds in the BVI lie behind shabby doors.

The **BVI Post Office** (⊠ Main St., Road Town, ☎ 284/494–3701) is a philatelist's dream. It has a worldwide reputation for exquisite stamps in all sorts of designs. The stamps carry U.S. monetary designations but can be used only in the BVI. **Caribbean Fine Arts Ltd.** (⊠ Main St., Road Town, ☎ 284/494–4240) carries Caribbean art, including original watercolors, oils, and acrylics, as well as signed prints, limited-edition serigraphs, and turn-of-the-20th-century sepia photographs. **Pusser's Company Store** (⊠ Main St. at Waterfront Rd., Road Town, ☎ 284/494–2467; ⊠ Soper's Hole Marina, West End, ☎ 284/495–4603) sells nautical memorabilia, ship models, marine paintings, an entire line of clothes (for both men and women), and gift items bearing the Pusser's logo, handsome decorator bottles of Pusser's rum, Caribbean books, Cuban cigars, and luggage. **Samarkand** (⊠ Main St., Road Town, ☎ 284/494–6415) crafts charming gold and silver pendants, earrings, bracelets, and pins—many with an island theme: seashells, lizards, pelicans, palm trees. There are also reproduction Spanish pieces of eight (coins—old Spanish pesos worth eight reals—from sunken galleons). **Sunny Caribbee** (⊠ Main St., Road Town, ☎ 284/494–2178), in a brightly painted West Indian house, packages its own herbs, teas, coffees, vinegars, hot sauces, soaps, skin and suntan lotions, and exotic concoctions—Arawak Love Potion and Island Hangover Cure, for example. There are also Caribbean books and art and hand-painted decorative accessories.

VIRGIN GORDA

Most boutiques are within hotel complexes—one of the best is at Little Dix Bay. There is a respectable and diverse scattering of shops in the bustling yacht harbor complex in Spanish Town.

The **Artistic Gallery** (⊠ Virgin Gorda Yacht Harbour, Spanish Town, ☎ 284/495–5104) features Caribbean jewelry, 14-karat-gold nautical jewelry, maps, collectible coins, and crystal. **Next Wave** (⊠ Virgin Gorda Yacht Harbour, Spanish Town, ☎ 284/495–5623) offers bathing suits, T-shirts, canvas tote bags, and locally made jewelry. **Pavilion Gift Shop** (⊠ Little Dix Bay Hotel, Little Dix Bay, ☎ 284/495–5555) has the latest in resort wear for men and women, as well as jewelry, books, housewares, and expensive T-shirts. **Pelican's Pouch Boutique** (⊠ Virgin Gorda Yacht Harbour, Spanish Town, ☎ 284/495–5599) carries a large selection of name-brand swimsuits plus cover-ups, T-shirts, and accessories. **Scoops** (⊠ Virgin Gorda Yacht Harbour, Spanish Town, ☎ 284/495–5722) has unusual gifts like photo frames made from Virgin Gorda beach sand and whimsical tiles hand-painted by a St. Thomas artist. **Virgin Gorda Craft Shop** (⊠ Virgin Gorda Yacht Harbour, Spanish Town, ☎ 284/495–5137) sells the work of island artisans, and carries West Indian jewelry and crafts styled from straw, shells, and other local materials. It also stocks clothing and paintings by Caribbean artists.

Outdoor Activities & Sports

TORTOLA

➤ FISHING: The deep-sea fishing here is so good that tournaments draw competitors from around the world for the largest bluefish, wahoo, swordfish, and shark. You can bring a catch back to your hotel's restaurant, and the staff will prepare it for you for dinner. A half day of deep-sea fishing runs about $425, a full day around $800. If bonefishing is your cup of tea, call **Caribbean Fly Fishing** (⊠ Nanny Cay, Tortola, ☎ 284/499–4797). For a few hours of reel fun, try **Persistence** (⊠ Sopers Hole, West End, Tortola, ☎ 284/495–4122).

➤ SAILING: The BVI are among the world's most popular sailing destinations. They're close together and surrounded by calm waters, so it's fairly easy to sail from one anchorage to the next. **Aristocat Charters** (⊠ West End, Tortola, ☎ 284/495–4087, 🖾 www.aristocatcharters. com) sets sail to the Indians and Peter Island aboard a 48-ft catamaran on a day sail for $85 per person, including lunch. **White Squall II** (⊠ Village Cay Marina, Road Town, Tortola, ☎ 284/495–2564) takes you to The Baths at Virgin Gorda or The Caves at Norman Island on an 80-ft schooner.

➤ SCUBA DIVING & SNORKELING: Clear waters and numerous reefs afford some wonderful opportunities for underwater exploration. In 1867 the RMS *Rhone,* a 310-ft-long royal mail steamer, split in two when it sank in a devastating hurricane. It's so well preserved that it was used in the movie *The Deep*. You can see the crow's nest and bowsprit, the cargo hold in the bow, and the engine and enormous propeller shaft in the stern. Every dive outfit in the BVI runs superlative scuba and snorkel tours here. Rates start at around $50 for a one-tank dive and $80 for a two-tank dive. **Baskin' in the Sun** (⊠ Prospect Reef, Tortola, ☎ 284/494–2858) offers beginner and advanced diving courses and daily trips. **Blue Waters Divers** (⊠ Nanny Cay, Tortola, ☎ 284/494–2847) teaches resort, open-water, and advanced diving courses and also makes daily trips. **Underwater Safaris** (⊠ The Moorings, Wickham's Cay II, Road Town, Tortola, ☎ 284/494–3235) has resort and advanced diving courses, including rescue and open-water, and schedules day and night dives if your ship moors overnight.

VIRGIN GORDA

➤ FISHING: Anglers come from all over the world to fish in these waters. **Virgin Gorda Charter Services** (⊠ Leverick Bay, North Sound, Virgin Gorda, ☎ 284/495–6666, 🖾 www.fishbvi.com) offers a choice of three boats for trips ranging from full-day marlin hunting to half-day inshore light-tackle angling for species like mackerel and snapper. Plan to spend $250–$1,200.

➤ SAILING: The BVI waters are calm, and terrific places to learn to sail. The **Bitter End Sailing & Windsurfing School** (⊠ Bitter End Yacht Club, North Sound, Virgin Gorda, ☎ 284/494–2746, 🖾 www.beyc.com) offers classroom, dockside, and on-the-water lessons for sailors of all levels. Private lessons are $60 per hour. If you just want to sit back, relax, and let the captain take the helm, try *Spice* (⊠ Leverick Bay Marina,

North Sound, Virgin Gorda, ☎ 284/495–7044, WEB www.spicebvi.
com), a 51-ft sloop that makes half- and full-day voyages to Anegada,
The Baths, and Cooper Island for sunning, swimming, and snorkeling.
➤ SCUBA DIVING & SNORKELING: There are some terrific snorkel and
dive sites off Virgin Gorda, including areas around The Baths, North
Sound, and The Dogs. The **Bitter End Yacht Club** (⊠ North Sound, Virgin Gorda, ☎ 284/494–2746, WEB www.beyc.com) offers day and night
snorkeling trips. Costs range from $15 per person to $90 per person
depending on the length and type of the trip. Contact **Dive BVI** (⊠ Virgin Gorda Yacht Harbour, Spanish Town, Virgin Gorda, ☎ 284/495–
5513, WEB www.divebvi.com) for expert instruction, certification, and
day trips. It costs $100 for a resort course, $85 for a two-tank dive,
and $65 for a one-tank dive; equipment rental is an additional $15.
Sunchaser Scuba (⊠ Bitter End Yacht Harbor, North Sound, Virgin
Gorda, ☎ 284/495–9638, WEB www.come.to/bvi), formerly Kilbride's,
offers resort, advanced, and rescue courses. The fee for a resort course
is $95. One-tank dives run $60, two-tank dives $85. Equipment rental
is an additional $15.

Beaches

TORTOLA

Tortola's north side has several perfect palm-fringed white-sand beaches
that curl around turquoise bays and coves. Nearly all are accessible by
car (preferably one with four-wheel-drive), albeit down bumpy roads
that corkscrew precipitously. Facilities run the gamut from absolutely
none to a number of beachside bars and restaurants as well as places
to rent water-sports equipment. The water at **Brewers Bay** (⊠ Brewers Bay Rd. W or Brewers Bay Rd. E) is good for snorkeling, and there
is a campground and beach bar here. The beach and its old sugar-mill
and rum-distillery ruins are north of Cane Garden Bay, just past Luck
Hill. There's another entrance just east of the Skyworld restaurant. En-
ticing **Cane Garden Bay** (⊠ Cane Garden Bay Rd.) has exceptionally
calm, crystalline waters and a silky stretch of sand. It's the closest beach
to Road Town—one steep uphill and downhill drive—and one of the
BVI's best-known anchorages, and it's where cruise ships send their passengers for beach excursions. You can rent sailboards and such, stargaze
from the bow of a boat, and nosh or sip at several beachside restaurants, including Quito's Gazebo. Have your camera ready for snapping
the breathtaking approach to the 1-mi (2-km) stretch of white sand at
Long Bay West (⊠ Long Bay Rd.). Although Long Bay Resort sprawls
along part of it, the entire beach is open to the public. The water isn't
as calm here as at Cane Garden or Brewers Bay, but it's still swimmable.

VIRGIN GORDA

The best beaches are easily reached by water, although they're also accessible on foot, usually after a moderately strenuous 10- to 15-minute
hike. Anybody going to Virgin Gorda should experience swimming or
snorkeling among its unique boulder formations, which can be visited
at several beaches along Lee Road. The most popular of these spots is
The Baths, but there are several others nearby that are easily reached.
Featuring a stunning maze of huge granite boulders that extend into the
sea, **The Baths** is usually crowded mid-day with day-trip visitors. Beach
lockers are available to keep belongings safe. **Leverick Bay** is a tiny, busy
beach-cum-marina that fronts the resort's restaurant and pool. Come
here if you want a break from the island's serenity. The view of Prickly
Pear Island is a plus. For a wonderfully private beach close to Spanish
Town, try **Savannah Bay.** It may not always be completely deserted, but
it's a lovely, long stretch of white sand. Bring your mask, fins, and
snorkel. From The Baths you can walk on Lee Road or swim north to
the less-populated **Spring Bay Beach,** where the snorkeling is excellent.

Where to Eat

TORTOLA

$$–$$$ ✕ **The Captain's Table.** Select the lobster you want from the pool here, and be careful not to fall in—it's in the floor in the middle of the dining room. The menu also includes escargots, fresh local fish, filet mignon with béarnaise sauce, duckling with berry sauce, and creative daily specials. Ceiling fans keep the dining room cool, but there are also tables on a breezy terrace overlooking the harbor. ⊠ *Wickham's Cay I,* ☎ 284/494–3885. *AE, MC, V. No lunch Sat.*

¢–$$ ✕ **Capriccio di Mare.** The owners of the well-known Brandywine Bay restaurant also run this Italian outdoor café. Stop by for an espresso, fresh pastry, toast Italiano (a grilled ham and Swiss cheese sandwich), a bowl of perfectly cooked linguine, or a crispy tomato and mozzarella pizza. Drink specialties include the Mango Bellini, an adaptation of the famous Bellini cocktail served at Harry's Bar in Venice. ⊠ *Waterfront Dr., Road Town,* ☎ 284/494–5369. *Reservations not accepted. MC, V. Closed Sun.*

¢–$$ ✕ **Pusser's Road Town Pub.** Almost everyone who visits Tortola stops here at least once to have a bite to eat and to sample the famous Pusser's Rum Painkiller (fruit juices and rum). The menu includes cheesy pizza, shepherd's pie, fish-and-chips, and hamburgers. Dine inside in air-conditioned comfort or outside on the verandah, which looks out on the harbor. Stop by on Thursdays for nickel beer night. ⊠ *Waterfront Dr., Road Town,* ☎ 284/494–3897. *AE, D, MC, V.*

VIRGIN GORDA

$$–$$$$ ✕ **Top of The Baths.** At the entrance to The Baths, this popular restaurant starts serving at 8 AM. Tables are outside on a terrace or in an open-air pavilion; all have stunning views of the Sir Francis Drake Channel. Hamburgers, sandwiches, and fish and chips are offered at lunch. Conch fritters and pumpkin soup are among the dinner appetizers. Entrées include fillet of yellowtail snapper, shrimp creole, and jerk chicken. For dessert, the mango-kiwi tart is excellent. ⊠ *The Valley,* ☎ 284/495–5497, WEB *www.thebathsbvi.com. AE, MC, V.*

$$–$$$ ✕ **The Restaurant at Leverick Bay.** This bi-level restaurant at the Leverick Bay Resort & Marina looks out over North Sound. The upstairs is slightly less casual and more expensive, with a menu that includes prime rib, pork chops, chicken dishes, and fresh fish specials. Below, the bar offers light fare all day—starting with breakfast and moving on to hamburgers, salads, and pizzas until well into the evening. ⊠ *Leverick Bay Resort & Marina, Leverick Bay,* ☎ 284/495–7154, WEB *www.therestaurantatleverickbay.com. AE, MC, V.*

$–$$ ✕ **Sip and Dip Grill.** Enjoy a pleasant, informal lunch by the pool at the Olde Yard Inn. Come for the grilled fish, pasta salads, spicy chili, chilled soups, and ice cream. Sunday evening there's a barbecue with live entertainment. ⊠ *The Olde Yard Inn, The Valley,* ☎ 284/495–5544, WEB *www.oldeyardinn.com. AE, MC, V. No dinner Mon.–Sat.*

¢–$$ ✕ **The Bath and Turtle.** You can really sit back and relax at this informal patio tavern with a friendly staff—although the TV noise can be a bit much. Burgers, well-stuffed sandwiches, homemade pizzas, pasta dishes, and daily specials like conch gumbo round out the casual menu. Live entertainers perform Saturday nights. ⊠ *Virgin Gorda Yacht Harbour, Spanish Town,* ☎ 284/495–5239, WEB *www.islandsonline.com/bathturtle. AE, MC, V.*

Cozumel, Mexico

Cozumel, with its sun-drenched ivory beaches fringed with coral reefs, fulfills the tourist's vision of a tropical Caribbean island. Smaller than Cancún, Cozumel surpasses its fancier neighbor in many ways. It has more history and ruins, superior diving and snorkeling, more authentic cuisine, and a greater diversity of handicrafts at better prices.

The island is a heady mix of the natural and the commercial. There is a mini-construction boom in Cozumel's sole city, San Miguel. However, there are still wild pockets scattered throughout the island where flora and fauna flourish. The numerous coral reefs, particularly the world-renowned Palancar Reef, attract divers from around the world. Cozumel is also the mainstay for ships sailing on western Caribbean itineraries, and as a result the island has grown very commercial. Waterfront shops and restaurants have taken on a glitzy appearance. Hole-in-the-wall crafts shops and tiny diners have been replaced by high-dollar duty-free shops, gem traders, and slick eateries—particularly the ubiquitous American fast-food chains. Shops stay open as long as a ship is in town, and most of the salespeople speak English. Wednesdays are the most hectic days, when it seems all the cruise ships land.

Cruise ships visiting for one day normally call only at Cozumel; ships staying for two days typically spend the second anchored off Playa del Carmen, across the channel on the Yucatán Peninsula. From there, excursions go to Cancún or to the Maya ruins at Tulum, Cobá, and Chichén Itzá.

CURRENCY

In Mexico the currency is the peso, designated as MX$. U.S. dollars and credit cards are eagerly accepted by everyone on the island, including taxi drivers. There is no advantage to paying in dollars, but there may be an advantage to paying in cash. To avoid having unused pesos, change just enough to cover public transportation, refreshments, phones, and tips. Most prices given below are in U.S. dollars.

TELEPHONES

A convenient but not necessarily cheaper option for phone calls is **Calling Station** (⊠ Av. Rafael Melgar 27 and Calle 3 Sur, San Miguel, ☎ FAX 9/872–1417). You can also e-mail, fax, rent cell phones, and exchange money. It's open 8 AM–11 PM.

Shore Excursions

Cozumel offers more worthwhile shore excursions than most Caribbean ports. The following are among the good choices. They may not be offered by all cruise lines. Times and prices are approximate. In general, you are better off using shore excursions from your ship if you want to see the Maya ruins. Many ships will stop briefly off Playa del Carmen to discharge passengers for Chichén Itzá and Tulum, saving a great deal of travel time.

Atlantis Submarine Trip. You can stay dry even as you plunge into the ocean's depths during a submarine cruise with Atlantis Submarines. ⏱ 2 hrs, 🎫 $88.

Chichén Itzá. This awe-inspiring ruin of a great Maya city is a 45-minute flight from Cozumel or a 12-hour round-trip bus ride from Playa del Carmen. A box lunch is included. Some excursions include a flight, which almost doubles the cost. ⏱ 12 hrs, 🎫 $127.

Glass-Bottom Boat. For those who don't dive, a tour boat with a see-through floor takes passengers to the famed Paraiso and Chankanaab sites to view schools of tropical fish. ⏱ 1½ hrs, 🎫 $47.

San Gervasio and Cozumel Island. If you want to see Maya ruins but don't want to spend a full day on a tour, this excursion to a local archaeological site is a good alternative. Time is also allotted for swimming and snorkeling at the Playa Sol beach. ⏱ 4 hrs, 🎫 $59.

Snorkeling. This region is famous for its reefs. Discovered by Jacques Cousteau, it is regularly featured in *Skin Diver* magazine as one of the world's top diving destinations. If your ship offers a snorkeling tour, take it. Equipment and lessons are included. ⏱ *3 hrs,* ✉ *$39.*

Tulum Ruins and Xel-ha Lagoon. An English-speaking guide leads a tour to this ancient Maya city, perched on the cliffs above a beautiful beach. A box lunch is usually included. A stop is made for swimming and snorkeling in the glass-clear waters of Xel-ha. The tour leaves from Playa del Carmen. ⏱ *7 hrs,* ✉ *$108.*

Coming Ashore

As many as six ships call at Cozumel on a busy day, tendering passengers to the downtown pier in the center of San Miguel or docking at the two international piers 6 km (4 mi) away. From the downtown pier you can walk into town or catch the ferry to Playa del Carmen. Taxi tours are also available. An island tour, including the ruins and other sights, costs about $50 to $70. The international pier is close to many beaches, but you'll need a taxi to get into town. There's rarely a wait for a taxi, but prices are high, and drivers are often aggressive, asking double or triple the reasonable fare. Expect to pay $10 for the ride into San Miguel from the pier.

Once in town, you can find tourist information at the State Tourism Office in the Plaza del Sol mall at the east end of the square; it's open weekdays 9–2:30. To get to Playa del Carmen from Cozumel, you can take a ferry or a jetfoil from the downtown pier. It takes 30–40 minutes each way. Ferries depart every hour or two; be sure to double-check the schedule, since schedules change frequently and you don't want to miss your ship's departure.

Exploring Cozumel

Numbers in the margin correspond to points of interest on the Cozumel map.

San Miguel is tiny—you cannot get lost—and is best explored on foot. The main attractions are the small eateries and shops that line the streets, and the activity centers at the main square, where the locals congregate in the evenings.

⑤ Castillo Real. A Maya site near the island's northern tip, the Royal Castle has a lookout tower, the base of a pyramid, and a temple with two chambers capped by a false arch. The waters here harbor several shipwrecks, and it's a fine spot for snorkeling, because there are few visitors to disturb the fish. The surf can get quite strong, so pick a time when the sea is tranquil.

③ El Cedral. The hub of Maya life on Cozumel was discovered by Spanish explorers in 1518. It went on to become the island's first official city, founded in 1847. These days it's a small farming community with modest houses and gardens. Conquistadors tore down most of the Maya structures, and the U.S. Army Corps of Engineers destroyed the rest during World War II to make way for the island's first airport. All that remains of the ruins is a small structure with an arch; inside are faint traces of paint and stucco. Alongside is a green-and-white cinder-block church, decorated inside with crosses shrouded in embroidered lace where, reportedly, the first mass in Mexico was celebrated. Every May there's a fair here, with dancing, music, bullfights, and a cattle show, honoring the area's agricultural roots. Hidden in the surrounding jungle are other small ruins, but you need a guide to find them. Check with the locals, who offer excellent tours on horseback. ✉ *Turn at Km*

142

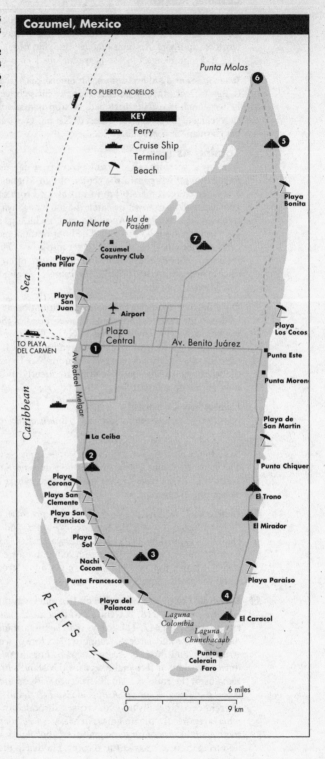

Cozumel, Mexico

TO PUERTO MORELOS

KEY

Ferry

Cruise Ship
Terminal

Beach

Punta Molas

Punta Norte

*Isla de
Pasión*

Playa
Bonita

Cozumel
Country Club

Playa
Santa Pilar

Playa
San
Juan

Airport

Plaza
Central

Av. Benito Juárez

Playa
Los Cocos

TO PLAYA
DEL CARMEN

Av. Rafael Melgar

Punta Este

Punta Moreno

Sea

Caribbean

La Ceiba

Playa de
San Martín

Playa
Corona

Playa San
Clemente

Punta Chiquer

Playa San
Francisco

El Trono

Playa
Sol

El Mirador

Nachi
Cocom

Punta Francesca

Playa Paraiso

Playa del
Palancar

*Laguna
Colombia*

El Caracol

R E E F S

*Laguna
Chunchacaab*

Punta
Celerain
Faro

0   6 miles

0   9 km

17.5 off Carretera Sur or Av. Rafael E. Melgar, then drive 3 km (2 mi) inland to the site, ☎ *no phone.* ✉ *Free.* ☉ *Daily dawn–dusk.*

Parque Chankanaab. A 15-minute drive south of San Miguel, Chankanaab (the name means "small sea") is a national park with a lovely saltwater lagoon, an archaeological park, a botanical garden, a dolphin aquarium, and a wildlife sanctuary. Chankanaab has remained in its natural state for decades; the few developments haven't destroyed its natural beauty.

Scattered throughout the archaeological park are 60 reproductions of Olmec, Toltec, Aztec, and Maya stone carvings from well-known sites in Mexico. Guides lead interesting, informative tours, explaining the history of the most significant pieces. Also on-site is a good example of a typical Maya house. The botanical garden has more than 450 species of regional plants. Enjoy a cool walk to the lagoon, inhabited by 60-odd species of marine life, including fish, coral, turtles, and various crustaceans.

Swimming isn't allowed in the lagoon; the area's ecosystem has become fragile since the collapse of underwater tunnels linking the lagoon to the sea. But you can swim and rent equipment to go scuba diving or snorkeling at the beach. There's plenty to see under the sea: a sunken ship, crusty old cannons and anchors, a Maya Chacmool (the revered rain god), and a beautiful sculpture of the Virgin del Mar (Virgin of the Sea). In addition, brilliant fish swim around the coral reef. (Note that it's forbidden to feed the fish or touch the coral.)

At the park's dolphin aquarium, you can pet, swim, or dive with the fascinating marine mammals, but if you wish to do so, make advance reservations. The price is steep, but the experience is thrilling. A small museum near the beach displays photographs illustrating the park's history as well as coral and shell exhibits and some sculptures. You can also watch sea lions perform at their daily show (for an additional fee). Come early, as the park fills up fast, particularly on the days when cruise ships dock. ✉ *Carretera Sur, Km 9,* ☎ *987/872–2940 for park; 987/872–6606 for dolphin reservations.* ✉ *$10; $119 for dolphin swim program.* ☉ *Daily 7–6.*

Parque Punta Sur. The 247-acre national preserve is on Cozumel's southernmost tip. Neither cars nor food or drink is allowed on the premises, so you must eat in the park restaurant and use park bicycles or buses. From observation towers you can spot crocodiles and birds in Laguna Colombia or Laguna Chunchacaab. Or visit the ancient Maya lighthouse, El Caracol, constructed to whistle when the wind blows in a certain direction. The Faro de Celarain (Celarain Lighthouse) is now a navigational museum outlining the history of seamanship in the area. You can climb the 134 steps to the top of the lighthouse; it's a steamy effort, but the views are incredible. The beaches here are deserted and wide, and there's great snorkeling offshore. (Equipment is available for rent, as are kayaks.) In addition to a restaurant, which is excellent, the park has an information center, a souvenir shop, and rest rooms. If you don't rent a vehicle to get here, a round-trip taxi ride from San Miguel costs close to $40. ✉ *Southernmost point in Punta Sur Park and the coastal road,* ☎ *987/872–2940 or 987/872–0914.* ✉ *$15.* ☉ *Daily 7–4.*

Punta Molas Faro. At Cozumel's northernmost point, the Molas Point Lighthouse is an excellent spot for sunbathing and birding. The jagged shoreline and the open sea offer magnificent views, making it well worth the time-consuming and somewhat difficult trip. Be prepared to walk some of the way. Car-rental companies discourage visitors from driving here. Access is easier by boat, or you can take a guided tour.

❼ **San Gervasio.** These remarkable ruins in a lovely forest make up Cozumel's largest Maya and Toltec site. San Gervasio was once the island's capital and ceremonial center, dedicated to the fertility goddess Ixchel. The Classic- and Postclassic-style buildings were continuously occupied from AD 300 to AD 1500. Typical architectural features include limestone plazas and arches atop stepped platforms, as well as stelae and bas-reliefs. Be sure to see the "hands" temple, which has red hand imprints all over its altar. Plaques clearly identify each of the ruins in Maya, Spanish, and English. At the entrance there's a snack bar and some gift shops. If you want a rugged hike, take the 15-km (9-mi) dirt road that travels north to the coast and Castillo Real. ⊠ *From San Miguel, take Av. Benito Juárez east to San Gervasio access road; turn left and follow road for 7 km (4½ mi).* ☎ *Access to road $1, ruins $3.50.* ☉ *Daily 8–5.*

❶ **San Miguel.** Although highly commercialized, Cozumel's only town has retained some of the flavor of a Mexican village. Stroll along the *malecón* (oceanfront promenade) and take in the ocean breeze. Locals hang out in the main square, which is particularly busy on Sunday night, when musical groups join the food and souvenir vendors. San Miguel is a small and normally fairly sleepy town, but it can become overwhelmed when several cruise ships anchor simultaneously offshore, so in these times expect the streets to be packed.

Shopping

San Miguel's biggest industry—even bigger than diving—is selling souvenirs to cruise-ship passengers. The primary items are ceramics, onyx, brass, wood carvings, colorful blankets and hammocks, reproductions of Maya artifacts, shells, silver, gold, sportswear, T-shirts, perfume, and liquor. Look for Mexican pewter; it's unusual, affordable, and attractive. Almost all stores take U.S. dollars. If your ship docks at International Pier, you can shop dockside for T-shirts, crafts, and more.

Before you spend any serious cash, though, keep in mind the following tips. Don't pay attention to written or verbal offers of "20% discount, today only" or "only for cruise-ship passengers"—they're nothing but bait to get you inside. Similarly, many of the larger stores advertise "duty-free" wares, but prices tend to be higher than retail prices in the United States. Avoid buying from street vendors, as the quality of their merchandise can be questionable, which may not be apparent until it's too late. Don't buy anything from the black coral "factories." The items are overpriced, and black coral is an endangered species.

The center of the shopping district is the main square off Avenida Melgar, across from the ferry terminal. The district extends north along Avenida Melgar and Calles 5 Sur and Norte. As a general rule, the newer, trendier shops line the waterfront, and the better crafts shops can be found around Avenida 5a. Other plazas include Plaza del Sol (on the east side of the main plaza), Villa Mar (on the north side of the main plaza), and the Plaza Confetti (on the south side of the main plaza). **Bugambilias** (⊠ Av. 10 Sur, between Calles Adolfo Rosado Salas and 1 Sur, ☎ 987/872–6282) sells handmade Mexican linens. **Los Cinco Soles** (⊠ Av. Rafael E. Melgar at Calle 8 Nte. ☎ 987/872–0132) is a good one-stop shop for crafts from around Mexico. The town's **crafts market** (⊠ Calle 1 Sur, behind the plaza) sells a respectable assortment of Mexican wares. **Diamond Creations** (⊠ Av. Rafael E. Melgar Sur 131, ☎ 987/872–5330) lets you custom-design pieces from its collection of loose diamonds, emeralds, rubies, sapphires, and tanzanite. **Exotica** (⊠ Av. Benito Juárez, at the plaza, ☎ 987/872–5880) has high-quality sportswear and shirts with nature-theme designs. The **Hammock House** (⊠ Av. 5 and Calle 4, ☎ no phone) has long been a local curiosity thanks to its bright blue exterior and the inventory that hangs out front.

Manuel Azueta Vivas has been selling hammocks here for more than four decades. His work isn't the finest, but the pleasant, elderly gentleman asks for fair prices. You'll find silver, gold, and coral jewelry—bracelets and earrings especially—at **Joyería Palancar** (✉ Av. Rafael E. Melgar Nte. 15, ☎ 987/872–1468). **Poco Loco** (✉ Av. Rafael E. Melgar 18 and Av. Benito Juárez 2-A, ☎ 987/872–5499) sells casual wear and beach bags. Quality gemstones and striking designs are the strong points at **Rachat & Romero** (✉ Av. Rafael E. Melgar 101, ☎ 987/872–0571). **Talavera** (✉ Av. 5 Sur 349, ☎ 987/872–0171) carries tiles from the Yucatán, masks from Guerrero, brightly painted wooden animals from Oaxaca, and carved chests from Guadalajara.

Outdoor Activities & Sports

FISHING

Regulations forbid commercial fishing, sportfishing, spear fishing, and collecting any marine life in certain areas around Cozumel. It's illegal to kill some species within marine reserves, including billfish, so be prepared to return prize catches to the sea. (Regular participants in the annual billfish tournament have seen the same fish caught over and over again.) You can charter high-speed fishing boats for $400 for a half day or $500 for a full day (maximum six people). Full-day rates at **Albatros Deep Sea Fishing** (☎ 987/872–2390 or 888/333–4643) and **Marathon Fishing & Leisure Charters** (☎ 987/872–1986) include the boat and crew, tackle and bait, and lunch with beer and soda.

SCUBA DIVING & SNORKELING

Cozumel is famous for its reefs. In addition to Chankanaab Nature Park, a great dive site is La Ceiba Reef, in the waters off La Ceiba and Sol Caribe hotels. Here lies the wreckage of a sunken airplane blown up for a Mexican disaster movie. Cozumel has plenty of dive shops to choose from. **Aqua Safari** (✉ Av. Rafael E. Melgar 429, between Calles 5 and 7 Sur, ☎ 987/872–0301) is one of the oldest and most professional shops and offers PADI certification. **Blue Bubble** (✉ Av. 5 Sur and Calle 3 Sur, ☎ 987/872–1865) offers dive trips at different times of the morning—a blessing for those who hate waking up early. **Del Mar Aquatics** (✉ Costera Sur, Km 4, ☎ 987/872–5949) offers dive instruction as well as boat and shore dives. **Dive Cozumel** (✉ Calle Adolfo Rosado Salas 72, at Av. 5 Sur, ☎ 987/872–4167) specializes in cave diving for experienced divers. **Fiesta Holidays** (✉ Calle 11 Sur 598, between Avs. 25 and 30, ☎ 987/872–0725) runs snorkeling tours from the 45-ft catamarans *El Zorro* and *Fury*. Rates begin at about $50 per day and include equipment, a guide, soft drinks and beer, and a box lunch. Sunset cruises aboard *El Zorro* are also available; they include entertainment and unlimited drinks and cost about $35.

Where to Eat

Some restaurants serving large groups may add a 10% to 15% service charge to the bill. Otherwise, a 15% to 20% tip is customary.

$–$$ ✕ **Las Tortugas.** The motto at this simple eatery is "delicious seafood at accessible prices," and Las Tortugas lives up to it. The menu consists primarily of fish, lobster, and conch caught by local fishermen, and it changes according to what's available. Fajitas and other traditional Mexican dishes are also options. ✉ *Av. 30 at Calle 19 Sur,* ☎ *987/872–1242. MC, V.*

¢–$ ✕ **Jeanie's Waffle House.** Jeanie's is a wonderful place to start the day. The tables sit on several levels of an outdoor terrace facing the sea. The waffles are fresh, light, and yummy, and they come in more variations than you can imagine. You might have to wait for a table, since lots of locals stop here before heading to work. ✉ *Av. Rafael E. Melgar 798,* ☎ *987/872–6095. No credit cards. No dinner.*

¢–$ ✕ **Plaza Leza.** You can let the hours slip away while enjoying great Mexican food and watching the action in the square. For more privacy, go indoors to the somewhat secluded, cozy inner patio for everything from *poc chuc* (grilled pork steak), enchiladas, and lime soup to chicken sandwiches and coconut ice cream. You can get breakfast here, too. ⊠ *Calle 1 Sur, south side of Plaza Central,* ☎ 987/872–1041. AE, MC, V.

Nightlife

Cozumel is not known for its nightlife, but there are a few places to party. **Cactus** (⊠ Av. Rafael E. Melgar 145, ☎ 987/872–5799) has a disco, live music, and a bar that stays open until 5 AM. For sophisticated jazz, smart cocktails, and great cigars, check out the **Havana Club** (⊠ Av. Rafael E. Melgar, between Calles 6 and 8, 2nd floor, ☎ 987/872–1268). Beware of ordering imported liquors such as vodka and scotch; drink prices are high. **Señor Frog's and Carlos 'n Charlie's** (⊠ Av. Rafael E. Melgar at Punta Langosta, ☎ 987/872–0191) attract lively crowds looking for loud rock and a liberated, anything-goes dancing scene. Sports fiends can catch all the news on ESPN at **Sports Page Video Bar and Restaurant** (⊠ Av. 5 Nte. and Calle 2, ☎ 987/872–1199).

Curaçao

Try to be on deck as your ship sails into Curaçao. The tiny Queen Emma Floating Bridge swings aside to allow ships to pass through the narrow channel. Pastel gingerbread buildings on shore look like dollhouses, especially from a large cruise ship. Although the gabled roofs and red tiles show a Dutch influence, the gleeful colors of the facades are peculiar to Curaçao. It's said that an early governor of the island suffered from migraines that were aggravated by the color white, so all the houses were painted in hues from magenta to mauve.

Fifty-six kilometers (35 mi) north of Venezuela and 67 km (42 mi) east of Aruba, Curaçao is, at 61 km (38 mi) long and 5–12 km (3–7½ mi) wide, the largest of the Netherlands Antilles. Although always sunny, it's never stiflingly hot here because of the constant trade winds. Water sports attract enthusiasts from all over the world, and the reef diving is excellent.

History books still don't agree as to whether Alonzo de Ojeda or Amerigo Vespucci discovered Curaçao, only that it happened around 1499. In 1634 the Dutch came and promptly shipped off the Spanish settlers and the few remaining Indians to Venezuela. To defend itself against French and British invasions, the city built massive ramparts, many of which now house unusual restaurants and hotels.

Curaçao's population, which comprises more than 50 nationalities, is one of the best educated in the Caribbean. The island is known for its religious tolerance, and tourists are warmly received. Although there's plenty to see and do in Willemstad, the rest of the island features rugged natural beauty in the form of rocky coves shadowed by gunmetal cliffs and a remarkable, beautifully preserved collection of *landhuisen,* or plantation land houses, many of which are open to the public.

CURRENCY

U.S. dollars are accepted everywhere except pay phones. The local currency is the Netherlands Antilles guilder or florin, indicated by "fl" or "NAf" on price tags.

TELEPHONES

The telephone system is reliable. To place a local call, dial the seven-digit number. A local call costs NAf.50 from a pay phone. If you need to place an international call, there's an overseas phone center in the cruise-ship terminal. Dialing to the United States is exactly the same as dialing long distance within the United States.

SHORE EXCURSIONS

The following are good choices in Curaçao. They may not be offered by all cruise lines. Times and prices are approximate.

Country Drive. This is a good tour if you'd like to see Westpunt and Mt. Christoffel but don't want to drive an hour there yourself. Other stops are made at a land house, Hato Caves, and the Curaçao Museum. ⊘ *3 hrs,* ⊞ *$39.*

Kayak Adventure. Paddle from Jan Sofat to Barbara Beach, where you'll enjoy a relaxing swim. ⊘ *3½ hrs,* ⊞ *$65.*

Sharks, Stingrays, and Shipwrecks. Curaçao's seaquarium, a marine park, and two sunken ships reached by a 30-minute submarine trip highlight this tour of the island's marine environment. ⊘ *3 hrs,* ⊞ *$37.*

Willemstad Trolley Train. Although there are several walking tours of the charming capital, Willemstad, they're lengthy and detailed. The trolley visits such highlights as the Floating Market, the Synagogue, Fort Amsterdam, and Waterloo Arches. ⊘ *1¼ hrs,* ⊞ *$30.*

Coming Ashore

Ships dock at the terminal just beyond the Queen Emma Bridge, which leads to the floating market and the shopping district. The walk to downtown takes less than 10 minutes. Easy-to-read maps are posted dockside and in the shopping area. The terminal has a duty-free shop, telephones, and a taxi stand. Taxis, which meet every ship, aren't metered, so confirm the fare before setting out. A taxi for up to four people will cost about $30 an hour. Car rentals are available but are not cheap (about $60 per day, plus $10 compulsory insurance).

Exploring Curaçao

Numbers in the margin correspond to points of interest on the Curaçao map.

WILLEMSTAD

❶ **Willemstad** is small and navigable on foot. You needn't spend more than two or three hours wandering around here, although the narrow alleys and various architectural styles are enchanting. English, Spanish, and Dutch are widely spoken. Narrow Santa Anna Bay divides the city into two sides: Punda, where you'll find the main shopping district, and Otrabanda (literally, the "other side"), where the cruise ships dock. Punda is crammed with shops, restaurants, monuments, and markets. Otrabanda has narrow winding streets full of colonial homes notable for their gables and Dutch-influenced designs.

You can cross from Otrabanda to Punda in one of three ways: walk over the Queen Emma Bridge; ride the free ferry, which runs when the bridge swings open to let seagoing vessels pass; or take a cab across the Juliana Bridge (about $7). On the Punda side of the city, Handelskade is where you'll find Willemstad's most famous sights—the colorful colonial buildings that line the waterfront. The original red roof tiles came from Europe on trade ships as ballast.

The **Queen Emma Bridge** is affectionately called the Swinging Old Lady by the locals. If you're standing on the Otrobanda side, take a few moments to scan Curaçao's multicolored face, on the other side of Santa Anna Bay. If you wait long enough, the bridge will swing open to let seagoing ships pass through. The original bridge, built in 1888, was the brainchild of the American consul Leonard Burlington Smith, who made a

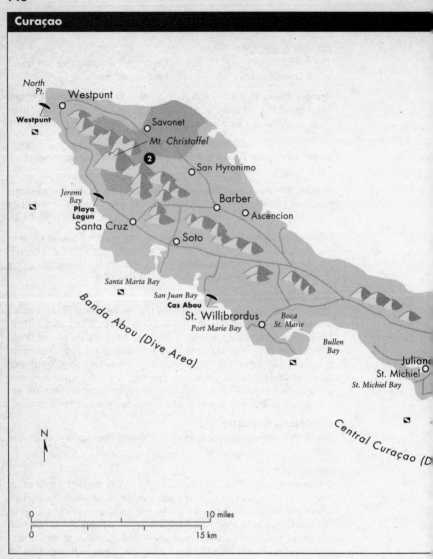

North Pt.
Westpunt
Westpunt
Savonet
Mt. Christoffel
❷
San Hyronimo
Jeremi Bay
Playa Lagun
Santa Cruz
Barber
Ascencion
Soto
Santa Marta Bay
San Juan Bay
Cas Abou
St. Willibrordus
Boca St. Marie
Port Marie Bay
Bullen Bay
Juliana
St. Michiel
St. Michiel Bay
Banda Abou (Dive Area)
Central Curaçao (D

N

0   10 miles
0   15 km

KEY

- Beaches
- Cruise Ship Terminal
- Dive Sites
- ❶ Exploring Sights

Caribbean Sea

Curaçao International Airport ✈ ❹

Brievengat

Santa Catarina

St. Joris Bay

Great St. Joris

Little St. Joris

Santa Rosa

...dorp

Brakkeput

Mt. Tafelberg

St. Anna Bay

Bottelier

Ostpunt

❶

Bapor Kibra

Spanish Water

...iscadera Bay

Willemstad

❸ Seaquarium Beach

Caracas Bay

Santa Barbara Beach

Nieuwpoort

Curaçao Underwater Marine Park

...ive Area)

(Dive Area)

mint off the tolls he charged for using it: 2¢ per person for those wearing shoes, free to those crossing barefoot. Today it's free to everyone.

At the end of Columbusstraat lies Wilhelmina Park. The statue keeping watch is of Queen Wilhelmina, the popular Dutch monarch who relinquished her throne to her daughter Juliana in 1948. At the far side of the square is the impressive Georgian facade of the McLaughlin Bank and, to its right, the courthouse with its stately balustrade.

Each morning dozens of Venezuelan schooners laden with tropical fruits and vegetables arrive at the bustling **Floating Market** (⊠ Sha Caprileskade, Punda) on the Punda side of the city. Mangoes, papayas, and exotic vegetables vie for space with freshly caught fish and herbs and spices. The buying is best at 6:30 AM—too early for many people on vacation—but there's plenty of action throughout the afternoon. Any produce bought here, however, should be thoroughly washed or peeled before being eaten.

The Wilhelmina Drawbridge connects Punda with the once-flourishing district of **Scharloo,** where the early Jewish merchants built stately homes. The end of the district closest to Kleine Werf is now a run-down red-light district, but the rest of the area is well worth a visit. The architecture along Scharlooweg (much of it from the 17th century) is intriguing, and many of the structures that had become dilapidated have been meticulously renovated.

Opened in 1999, the **Kurá Hulanda Museum** features exhibits on African history and is the largest of its kind in the Caribbean. Displays include a full-size reconstruction of a slave ship's hold and gut-wrenching first-hand accounts of the slave-trade era. ⊠ *Klipstraat 9, Otrobanda,* ☎ *5999/ 462–1400,* WEB *www.kurahulanda.com.* ⊠ *$5.* ☉ *Daily 10–5.*

The **Mikveh Israel-Emanuel Synagogue** was founded in 1651 and is the oldest temple still in use in the Western Hemisphere. It draws 20,000 visitors a year. Enter through the gates around the corner on Hanchi Di Snoa. The Jewish Cultural Museum in the back displays antiques and fine Judaica. ⊠ *Hanchi di Snoa 29, Punda,* ☎ *5999/461– 1633.* ⊠ *Small donation expected in synagogue, Jewish Cultural Museum $2.* ☉ *Weekdays 9–11:45 and 2:30–4:45.*

The 40-odd chronological exhibits at the **Maritime Museum** truly give you a sense of Curaçao's maritime history, using ship models, maps, nautical charts, navigational equipment, and audiovisual displays. Topics explored along the way include the development of Willemstad as a trading city, Curaçao's role as a contraband hub, the explosion of *De Alphen* in 1778, the slave trade, the development of steam navigation, the rise of cruise tourism, and the role of the Dutch navy on the island. The third floor hosts temporary exhibits, and the museum also offers a two-hour guided tour on its "water bus" through Curaçao's harbor—a route familiar to traders, smugglers, and pirates. When you're ready for a break, drop anchor at the Harbor Café or browse through the souvenir shop. ⊠ *Van der Brandhofstraat 7, Scharloo,* ☎ *5999/465–2327.* ⊠ *Museum only $6, museum and harbor tour $12. Tues.–Sat. 10–5.*

Step through the archway of **Fort Amsterdam** and enter another century. The entire structure dates from the 1700s, when it was the center of the city and the island's most important fort. Now it houses the governor's residence, the Fort Church, the Council of Ministers, and government offices. Outside the entrance, a series of majestic gnarled wayaka trees are fancifully carved with human forms—the work of local artist Mac Alberto. ⊠ *Foot of Queen Emma Bridge, Punda,* ☎ *5999/*

461–1139. ⌨ Fort free, church museum $1.75. ☉ Weekdays 9–noon and 2–5, Sun. service at 10.

The road that leads to the northwest tip of the island winds through landscape resembling a Georgia O'Keeffe painting—towering cacti, flamboyant dried shrubbery, aluminum-roof houses. You may see fishermen hauling in their nets, women pounding cornmeal, and donkeys blocking traffic. You can often glimpse land houses from the road.

❷ **Christoffel Park** is a good hour from Willemstad but worth a visit. This 4,450-acre garden and wildlife preserve with Mt. Christoffel at its center consists of three former plantations. As you drive through the park, watch for deer, goats, and smaller wildlife that might suddenly dart in front of your car. If you skip everything else on the island, it's possible to drive to the park and climb 1,239-ft Mt. Christoffel, which takes two to three strenuous hours. On a clear day you can then see the mountain ranges of Venezuela, Bonaire, and Aruba. ✉ *Savonet,* ☎ *5999/864-0363.* ⌨ *Park and museum $13.50. ☉ Mon.–Sat. 8–4, Sun. 6–3; last admission 1 hr before closing.*

❸ At the **Curaçao Seaquarium,** more than 400 varieties of exotic fish and vegetation are displayed. Outside is a 1,623-ft-long artificial beach of white sand, well suited to novice swimmers and children. There's also a platform overlooking the wreck of the steamship S.S. *Oranje Nassau* and an underwater observatory where you can watch divers and snorkelers swimming with stingrays and feeding sharks. ✉ *Bapor Kibra,* ☎ *5999/461–6666,* ⎁ *www.curacao-sea-aquarium.com.* ⌨ *$13.25, six-week pass $24. ☉ Daily 8–5.*

The **Dolphin Academy** is the newest attraction on the island and is attached to the Seaquarium (tell the gate staff at the Seaquarium where you are going, and they will waive the entrance fee). For $13 you can watch a dolphin show and for an additional charge you can touch them up close or even swim with them. ✉ *Bapor Kibra,* ☎ *5999/465–8900,* ⎁ *www.dolphin-academy.com.* ⌨ *$13. ☉ Daily 8–5.*

❹ Hour-long guided tours of the **Hato Caves** wind down into various chambers to the water pools, a "voodoo" chamber, a wishing well, fruit bats' sleeping quarters, and Curaçao Falls, guarded by a limestone "dragon." Hidden lights illuminate the limestone formations and gravel walkways. This is one of the better Caribbean caves open to the public, but keep in mind that there are 49 steep steps to reach the entrance, and the cave itself is dank and hot (though they've put electric fans in some areas to provide relief). To reach the caves, head northwest toward the airport, take a right onto Gosieweg, follow the loop right onto Schottegatweg, take another right onto Jan Norduynweg, a final right onto Rooseveltweg, and follow signs. ✉ *Rooseveltweg, Hato,* ☎ *5999/868-0379.* ⌨ *$6.50. ☉ Daily 10–5.*

Shopping

Curaçao has some of the best shops in the Caribbean, but in many cases the prices are no lower than in U.S. discount stores. Hours are usually Monday–Saturday 8–noon and 2–6. Most shops are within the six-block area of Willemstad described above. The main shopping streets are Heerenstraat, Breedestraat, and Madurostraat. **Bamali** (✉ Breedestraat, Punda, Willemstad, ☎ 5999/461–2258) sells Indonesian batik clothing, leather bags, and charming handicrafts. **Clog Dance** (✉ De Rouvilleweg 9B, Willemstad, ☎ 5999/462–3280) has Dutch clogs and fashions, cheeses, tulips, delftware, and chocolate. The first gift shop to open on Curaçao, **Warenhaus Van Der Ree** (✉ Breedestraat 5, Willemstad, ☎

5999/461–1645) sells stainless-steel wind chimes, dolls, frames, hammocks, Dutch cheese, hand-painted whistles, and other novelties.

Arawak Craft Factory (✉ Cruise Terminal, Otrobanda, Willemstad, ☎ 5999/462–7249) has a factory showroom of locally made crafts. You can purchase tiles, plates, pots, and tiny replicas of land houses. A walkway allows you to watch the artisans at work and ask questions.

Boolchand's (✉ Heerenstraat 4B, Willemstad, ☎ 5999/461–6233) handles an interesting combination of merchandise behind a facade of red-and-white-checkered tiles. Stock up here on electronics, jewelry, Swarovski crystal, Swiss watches, and cameras. The sweet smell of success permeates **Cigar Emporium** (✉ Gomezplein, Willemstad, ☎ 5999/ 465–3955), where you'll find the largest selection of cigars on the island, including H. Upmann, Romeo & Julietta, and Montecristo. Visit the climate-controlled cedar cigar room. However, remember that Cuban cigars cannot be taken back to the U.S. legally.

Freeport (✉ Heerenstraat 13, Willemstad, ☎ 5999/461–9500) has a fine selection of duty-free watches and jewelry (lines include David Yurman, Cristofle, Movado, and Maurice Lacroix). **Julius L. Penha & Sons** (✉ Heerenstraat 1, Willemstad, ☎ 5999/461–2266), in front of the pontoon Bridge, sells French perfumes and cosmetics. At **Little Switzerland** (✉ Breedestraat 44, Willemstad, ☎ 5999/461–2111) you can find jewelry, watches, crystal, china, and leather goods at significant savings. **New Amsterdam** (✉ Gomezplein 14, Willemstad, ☎ 5999/ 461–2437; ✉ Breedestraat 29, Willemstad, ☎ 5999/461–3239) is the place to price hand-embroidered tablecloths, napkins, and pillowcases, as well as Italian gold and Hummel figurines.

Outdoor Activities & Sports

HIKING

Christoffel Park has a number of challenging trails (☞ Exploring Curaçao).

SCUBA DIVING & SNORKELING

The **Curaçao Underwater Marine Park** is about 21 km (12½ mi) of untouched coral reef that has national park status. Mooring buoys mark the most interesting dive sites. **Curaçao Seascape** (✉ John F. Kennedy Blvd., Piscadera Bay, ☎ 5999/462–5000) offers shore dives and openwater certification programs. For detailed information on dive sites and operators, call the **Curaçao Tourism Development Board** (☎ 5999/ 461–6000 in Curaçao; 800/328–7222 in the U.S.) and ask for the brochure "Take the Plunge in Curaçao," or purchase *DIP–Curaçao's Official Dive Guide* at a nominal cost from the CTDB.

Beaches

Curaçao doesn't have long, powdery stretches of sand. Instead you'll discover the joy of inlets: tiny bays marked by craggy cliffs, exotic trees, and scads of interesting pebbles, and coral that has washed up on the beaches. To reach **Santa Barbara Beach,** a popular family beach on the eastern tip, you can drive through one of Curaçao's toniest neighborhoods, Spanish Water, where gleaming white yachts replace humble fishing fleets. The beach has changing facilities and a snack bar but charges an admission fee—usually around $2.25 per person but up to $7 per person on weekends. Around the bend, Caracas Bay is a popular dive site, with a sunken ship so close to the surface that snorkelers can view it clearly. **Cas Abou** is a white-sand gem with the brightest blue water in Curaçao. Divers and snorkelers will appreciate the on-site dive shop, and sunbathers can make use of the small snack bar. The rest rooms and showers are immaculate. You'll pay a fee ($2.25 per person) to enter **Seaquarium Beach,** but the amenities (rest rooms, showers, boutiques, water-sports center, snack bar, restaurants with beach bars, thatched shelters and palm trees for shade, security patrols) on this 1,600-ft (490-m) man-made sandy beach and the calm waters protected by a carefully placed breakwater are well worth it. On the northwest tip of the island, **Westpunt** is shady in the morning. It doesn't have much sand, but you can sit on a shaded rock ledge. The Playa Forti Bar & Restaurant offers refreshing soft drinks and beer and an exquisite fish soup. Take in the view of the boats in the marina and watch the divers jump from the high cliff. Water-sports enthusiasts, take note: the All West Dive Shop is on the beach here.

Where to Eat

Restaurants usually add a 10% to 15% service charge.

$$$ ✕ **Bistro Le Clochard.** This romantic gem is built into the 19th-century Riffort—an oasis of arched entryways, exposed brickwork, wood beams, and lace curtains. The waterside terrace has a view of the floating bridge and harbor. The Swiss chefs prepare exquisite French and Swiss meals. Their signature dish is La Potence, a swinging, red-hot metal ball covered with bits of sizzling tenderloin and sausage. Leave room for the homemade Swiss Toblerone chocolate mousse. The restaurant is wheelchair-accessible. ⊠ *Harbourside Terrace, Riffort, Otrobanda, Willemstad,* ☎ *5999/462–5666. Reservations essential. AE, DC, MC, V. No lunch Sat.*

$–$$ ✕ **Mambo Beach.** On the west end of Seaquarium Beach, this hip, open-air bar and grill, spread over the sand, serves breakfast, lunch, and dinner. Hearty sandwiches on baguette bread dominate the lunch menu; steaks, fresh seafood, and pasta fill the dinner menu. There is a fish buffet on Fridays. This is a great place to watch the sun set, but don't forget your insect repellent. ⊠ *Seaquarium Beach, Bapor Kibra,* ☎ *5999/461–8999. MC, V.*

¢–$ ✕ **Time Out Café.** Tucked into an alley in the shopping heartland of Punda, this outdoor eatery serves up light bites like tuna sandwiches and *tostis* (toasted cheese), as well as the omnipresent catch of the day. ⊠ *Keukenplein 8, Punda, Willemstad,* ☎ *5999/667–2455. No credit cards.*

Dominica

Washed by blessings of rain exploding over the peaks of her lush interior in the wee hours of the morning, this is one of the places in the Caribbean where nature is unrelenting. Everything here is giant-size and intense. Van Gogh would not have had the palette to paint her. Dominica (pronounced dom-in-*ee*-ka) is, hands down, the most unspoiled island in today's Caribbean.

In the center of the Caribbean archipelago, wedged between the two French islands of Guadeloupe, to the north, and Martinique, to the south, Dominica is a wild place. All over the island, wild orchids, anthurium lilies, ferns, heliconias, and fruit trees sprout profusely. Water chutes cascade down cliff faces at roadside. So unyielding is the terrain that colonists surrendered efforts at colonization, and the last survivors of the Caribbean's original people, the Carib Indians, have made her rugged northeast their home. From the elfin woodlands and dense, luxuriant rain forest to the therapeutic geothermal springs and world-class dive sites that mirror her terrestrial terrain, to experience Dominica is really to know the earth as it was created.

Dominica—just 29 mi long and 16 mi wide—is an independent country with a seat in the United Nations and the region's only natural World Heritage Site. Its capital is Roseau (pronounced rose-*oh*), its official language is English, and driving is on the left. Family and place names are a mélange of French, English, and Carib.

A newcomer on the tourism scene in the Caribbean, Dominica has no major hotel chains. With a population of just 70,000, and her National Forestry Division spending the last 50 years preserving and designating more national forest and marine reserves and parks per capita than almost anywhere else on earth, Dominica is the alternative Caribbean. So if you've had enough of casinos, crowds, and swim-up bars and want to take leave of everyday life—to hike, bike, trek, spot birds and butterflies in the rain forest, explore waterfalls; discover the world's largest boiling lake; kayak, dive, snorkel, or sail in marine reserves; or go out in search of the many resident whale and dolphin species—this is the place to do it.

CURRENCY
The official currency is the Eastern Caribbean dollar (EC$). Figure about EC$2.67 to the US$1. U.S. currency is readily accepted, but you will usually get change in E.C. dollars. Most major credit cards are accepted, as are traveler's checks. Prices throughout this chapter are quoted in U.S. dollars unless otherwise indicated.

TELEPHONES
To place a local call on Dominica, dial the seven-digit number that follows the 767 area code. The island has efficient direct-dial international service. All pay phones are equipped for local and overseas dialing and accept either E.C. coins or phone cards, which you can buy at many of the island's bars, restaurants, and shops. You can charge your calls to your credit card, or access the three major long-distance companies to make credit-card calls: **AT&T Direct** (☎ 800/872–2881), **MCI World Phone** (☎ 800/888–8000), **Sprint** (☎ 800/744–2250).

SHORE EXCURSIONS
The following are good choices in Dominica. They may not be offered by all cruise lines. Times and prices are approximate.

Champagne Reef Snorkel. Take a catamaran ride to the most popular snorkel site in Dominica, where the bubbly underwater geothermal vents make you feel like you're swimming in a glass of warm champagne. ☺ 3 hrs, 🎫 $55.

Dominica Favorites. From Roseau, you'll travel through the Botanic Gardens and the village of Trafalgar before starting on the trail to the double cascades of the Trafalgar Falls. Then it's on to the Emerald Pool in Dominica's Morne Trois Pitons World Heritage Site. You can swim in the refreshing but chilly pools at the base of the falls. ☺ 4½ hrs, 🎫 $45.

River Tubing. You'll travel down the beautiful Layou River by inner tube, seeing unspoiled vegetation and spectacular views of the soaring cliffs above. ☺ 3 hrs, 🎫 $59.

Whale and Dolphin Watching. Dominica is one of the best whale-watching destinations in the Caribbean. You'll have a good chance of seeing dolphins or whales in one of their favorite breeding grounds in the deep water off the southwest coast, to which you set off by catamaran. ☺ 4 hrs, 🎫 $80.

Coming Ashore
In Roseau, most ships dock along the Bayfront. Across the street from the pier, in the Old Post Office, is a visitor information center.

Taxis, minibuses, and tour operators are available at the berths. If you do decide to tour with one of them, choose one who is certified, and be explicit when discussing where you will go and how much you will pay—don't be afraid to ask questions. The drivers usually quote a fixed fare, which is regulated by the Division of Tourism and the National Taxi Association. Expect to pay about $20 per person for a four-hour island tour.

Some ships berth at the Cabrits National Park, just north of Portsmouth. Portsmouth is quieter than Roseau and in close proximity to some of Dominica's best nature sites, hikes, and river and beach bathing. The cruise-ship facility offers a cooperative crafts shop, a continuously screened film about Fort Shirley, and the occasional dance or music performance. As in Roseau, taxi and minibus drivers meet arriving cruisers near the dock. Prices are comparable to those in Roseau.

You can rent a car in Roseau for about $39, not including insurance and a mandatory EC$20 driving permit.

Exploring Dominica

Most of Dominica's roads are narrow and winding, so you'll need a few hours to take in the sights. Be adventurous, whether you prefer sightseeing or hiking—you'll be amply rewarded.

Numbers in the margin correspond to points of interest on the Dominica map.

⑥ Cabrits National Park. Along with Brimstone Hill in St. Kitts, Shirley Heights in Antigua, and Fort Charlotte in St. Vincent, the Cabrits National Park's Fort Shirley ruins are among the most significant historic sites in the Caribbean. Just north of the town of Portsmouth, this 1,300-acre park includes a marine park and herbaceous swamps, which are an important environment for several species of rare birds and plants. At the heart of the park is the Fort Shirley military complex. Built by the British between 1770 and 1815, it once comprised 50 major structures, including storehouses that were also quarters for 700 men. With the help of the Royal Navy (which sends sailors ashore to work on the site each time one of its ships is in port) and local volunteers, historian Dr. Lennox Honychurch restored the fort and its surroundings, incorporating a small museum that highlights the natural and historic aspects of the park, and an open canteen-style restaurant.

④ Carib Indian Territory. In 1903, after centuries of conflict, the Caribbean's first settlers, the Kalinago, were granted a portion of land (approximately 3,700 acres) on the island's northeast coast, on which to establish a reservation. Today it's known as Carib Territory, clinging to the northeasterly corner of Dominica, where a group of just over 3,000 Caribs, who resemble native South Americans, live like most other people in rural Caribbean communities. Many are farmers and fishermen; others are entrepreneurs who have opened restaurants, guest houses, and little shops where you can buy Carib baskets and other handcrafted items.

The Caribs' long, elegant canoes are created from the trunk of a single *gommier* tree. If you're lucky, you may catch canoe builders at work. The Catholic church in Salybia has a canoe as its altar, which was designed by Dr. Lennox Honychurch, a local historian, author, and artist.

L'Escalier Tête Chien (literally "Snake's Staircase," it's the name of a snake whose head resembles that of a dog), is a hardened lava formation that runs down to the Atlantic. The ocean here is particularly fierce, and the shore is full of coves and inlets. According to Carib legend, at night the nearby Londonderry Islets metamorphose into grand canoes to take the spirits of the dead out to sea.

Though there's not much to see that demonstrates the Caribs' ancient culture and customs, there are plans for a museum showing early Carib

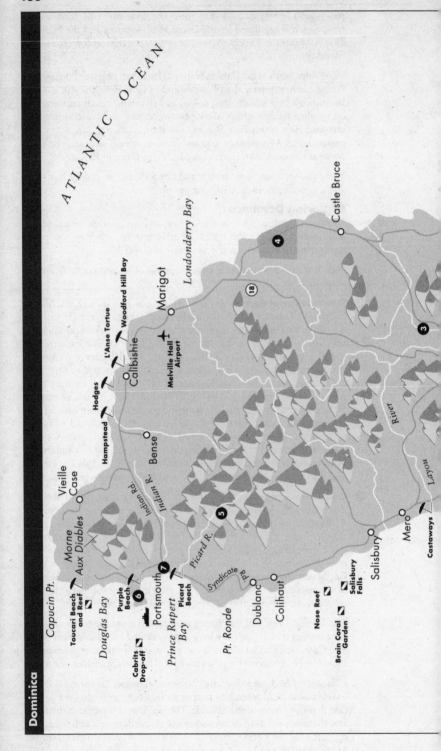

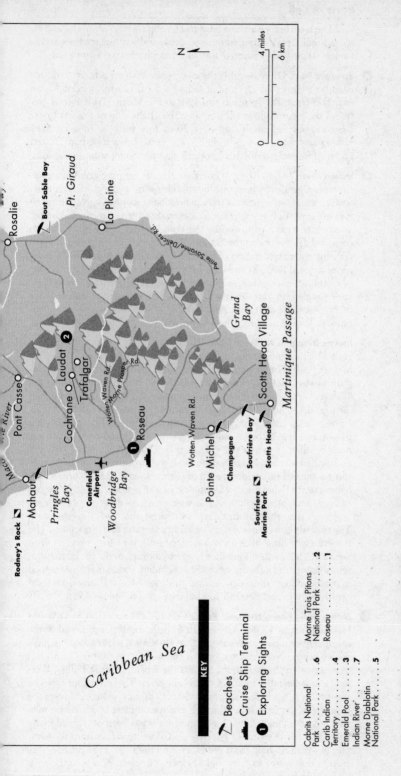

life. The territory's Karifuna Cultural Group travels nationally and internationally, performing traditional dance and wearing traditional costumes—their bodies painted and adorned with feathers and beads.

3 **Emerald Pool.** Quite possibly the most-visited nature attraction on the island, this emerald-green pool fed by a 50-ft (15-m) waterfall is an easy trip to make. To reach this spot in the Morne Trois Pitons National Park you follow a trail that starts at the side of the road near the reception center (it's an easy 20-minute walk). Along the way you'll pass lookout points with views of the windward (Atlantic) coast and the forested interior. It's a popular destination for shore excursions.

7 **Indian River.** Indian River, in Portsmouth, was once a Carib Indian settlement. A gentle rowboat ride for wildlife spotting along this river lined with *terra carpus officinalis* trees, whose buttress roots spread up to 20 ft (6 m), is not only relaxing but educational and most times entertaining. To arrange such a trip, stop by the visitor center at the mouth of the river and ask for one of the "Indian River boys." These young, knowledgeable men are members of the Portsmouth Indian River Tour Guides Association (PIRTGA) and have for years protected and promoted one of Dominica's special areas. Most boat trips take you up as far as Rahjah's Jungle Bar. You can usually do an optional guided walking tour of the swamplands and the remnants of one of Dominica's oldest plantations. Tours last one to three hours and cost $15 to $30 per person.

5 **Morne Diablotin National Park.** The park is named after one of the region's highest mountains, which at 4,747 ft (1,424 m) is Dominica's highest peak. The mountain takes its name from a bird, known in English as the black-capped petrel, which was prized by hunters in the 18th century. Though the mountain's namesake bird is now extinct on the island, Dominica is still a major birding destination. Of the island's many exotic—and endangered—species, the green-and-purple Sisserou parrot and the Jaco, or red-neck, parrot are found here in greater numbers than anywhere else in Dominica. Before the national park was established, the **Syndicate Nature Trail** was protected with the help of some 6,000 schoolchildren, each of whom donated 25¢ to protect the habitat of the flying pride of Dominica, as well as countless other species of birds and other wildlife. The west-coast road (at the bend near Dublanc) runs through three types of forest and leads into the park. The trail offers a casual walk; just bring a sweater and binoculars. The five- to eight-hour hike up Morne Diablotin isn't for everyone. You need a guide, sturdy hiking shoes, warm clothing, and a backpack with refreshments and a change of clothes (including socks) that are wrapped in plastic to keep them dry. A good guide for Morne Diablotin is local ornithology expert Betrand Jno Baptiste (☎ 767/446–6358).

2 **Morne Trois Pitons National Park.** This 17,000-acre UNESCO World Heritage Site, a 17,000-acre swath of lush, mountainous land in the south-central interior (covering 9% of Dominica), is the nature island's crown jewel. Named after one of the highest (4,600-ft [1,380-m]) mountains on the island, it contains the world's largest boiling lake, majestic waterfalls, and cool mountain lakes. There are four types of vegetation zones here. Ferns grow 30 ft (9 m) tall, wild orchids sprout from trees, sunlight leaks through green canopies, and a gentle mist rises over the jungle floor. A system of trails has been developed in the park, and the Division of Forestry and Wildlife works hard to maintain it—with no help from the excessive rainfall and the profuse vegetation that seems to grow right before your eyes. Access to the park is possible from most points of the compass, though the easiest approaches are via the small mountaintop villages of Laudat (pronounced low-*dah*) and Cochrane.

The undisputed highlight of the park is **Boiling Lake.** The world's largest such lake, it is a cauldron of gurgling gray-blue water, 70 yards wide and of unknown depth, with water temperatures from 180°F to 197°F. Although generally believed to be a volcanic crater, the lake is actually a flooded fumarole—a crack through which gases escape from the molten lava below. The two- to four-hour (one-way) hike up to the lake is challenging (on a very rainy day, be prepared to slip and slide the whole way up and back). You'll need attire appropriate for a strenuous hike, and a guide is a must. Most guided trips start early (no later than 8:30 AM) for this all-day, 7-mi (11-km) round-trip trek, so if you want to do this on your own, you will need to plan ahead. On your way to Boiling Lake you'll pass through the **Valley of Desolation,** a sight that lives up to its name. Harsh sulfuric fumes have destroyed virtually all the vegetation in what must once have been a lush forested area. Small hot and cold streams with water of various colors—black, purple, red, orange—web the valley. Stay on the trail to avoid breaking through the crust that covers the hot lava. During this hike you'll pass rivers where you can refresh yourself with a dip (a particular treat is a soak in a hot-water stream on the way back).

Just beyond the village of Trafalgar and up a short hill, there's the reception facility, where you can purchase passes to the national park and find guides to take you on a rain-forest trek to the twin **Trafalgar Falls.** En route, you will witness some of Dominica's most beautiful vistas. If you like a little challenge, let your guide take you up the riverbed to the cool pools at the base of the falls. The trek will take about 20 minutes each way and costs $10–$20 per person.

❶ Roseau. Although it is one of the smallest capitals in the Caribbean, Roseau has the highest concentration of inhabitants of any town in the Eastern Caribbean. Caribbean vernacular architecture and a bustling marketplace transport visitors back in time. Although you can walk the entire town in about an hour, you'll get a much better feel for the place on a leisurely stroll.

The 40-acre **Botanical Gardens,** founded in 1891 as an annex of London's Kew Gardens, is a great place to relax, stroll, or watch a cricket match. In addition to the extensive collection of tropical plants and trees, there's a parrot aviary. At the Forestry Division office—also on the garden grounds—you'll find publications on the island's flora, fauna, and national parks. The forestry officers know a lot about these subjects and can also recommend hiking guides. ⊠ *Between Bath Rd. and Valley Rd.* ☎ *767/448–2401 Ext. 3417.* ☯ *Mon. 8–1 and 2–5, Tues.–Fri. 8–1 and 2–4.*

Developments at bayfront on the Dame M. E. Charles Boulevard have brightened up the waterfront. The old post office now houses the **Dominica Museum.** This labor of love by local writer and historian Dr. Lennox Honychurch contains antique furnishings, documents, prints, and maps; you'll also find an entire Carib hut as well as Carib canoes, baskets, and other artifacts. ⊠ *Dame M. E. Charles Blvd., opposite cruise-ship berth,* ☎ *767/448–8923.* ▱ *$2.* ☯ *Weekdays 9–4, Sat. 9–noon.*

Shopping

Dominicans produce distinctive handicrafts, with communities specializing in materials-at-hand: *vertivert* straw rugs, screwpine tableware, *larouma* basketware, and wood carvings are just some. Also notable are local herbs, spices, condiments, and herb teas. Café Dominique, the local equivalent of Jamaican Blue Mountain coffee, is an excellent buy, as are the Dominican rums Macoucherie and Soca. Proof that the old ways live on in Dominica can be found in the number of herbal remedies available. One stimulating memento of your visit is rum steeped with *bois bandé* (bark of a tree), which is reputed to have aphrodisiac properties. These drinks are sold at shops, vendors' stalls, and supermarkets all over the island. There are a few options for duty-free shopping in Roseau.

Stores are generally open from 8 until 4 or 5 on weekdays and from 8 to 1 on Saturdays. Most are closed on Sundays. Vendors are almost always out when a ship's in port.

One of the easiest places to pick up a souvenir is the Old Market Plaza. Slaves were once sold here, but today it's the scene of happier trading: key rings, magnets, dolls, baskets, handcrafted jewelry, T-shirts, spices, souvenirs, and batiks are available from a select group of entrepreneurs in open-air booths set up on the cobblestones.

Ashbury's and Colombian Emeralds (⊠ Fort Young Hotel, Victoria St., Roseau) carries perfumes; crystals; gold and silver jewelry alone or with emeralds, diamonds, and other gems; liquor; and other gift items. Hilroy Fingol, a young artist specializing in airbrush painting, has his little studio-cum-gallery **Balisier** (⊠ 35 Great George St., Roseau, ☎ no phone) in the heart of Roseau; it's a real treasure. The **Crazy Banana** (⊠ 17 Castle St., Roseau, ☎ 767/449–8091) purveys everything from earthenware to doorstops, as well as other Caribbean-made crafts, rums, cigars, jewelry, and local art. **Island Stuff** (⊠ 25 Hanover St., Roseau, ☎ 767/449–9969), just a couple of blocks east of the ferry terminal, is a tiny shop jammed with fine art, souvenirs, and hand-carved furniture. **Rare Earth Treasures** (⊠ Fort Lane, Roseau) sells uniquely fashioned fine jewelry. Its collection of gemstones and crystals is worth seeing even if you can't afford to buy. **Tropicrafts** (⊠ corner of Queen Mary St. and Turkey La., Roseau, ☎ 767/448–2747) has a back room where you can watch women weave grass mats. You'll also find arts and crafts from around the Caribbean, local wood carvings, rum, hot sauces, perfumes, and traditional Carib baskets, hats, and woven mats.

Outdoor Activities & Sports

HIKING

Dominica's majestic mountains, clear rivers, and lush vegetation conspire to create adventurous hiking trails. The island is crisscrossed by ancient footpaths of the Arawak and Carib Indians and the Nègres Maroons, escaped slaves who established camps in the mountains. Existing trails range from easygoing to arduous. To make the most of your excursion, you'll need sturdy hiking boots, insect repellent, a change of clothes (kept dry), and a guide. Hikes and tours run $25 to $50 per person, depending on destinations and duration. Passes are required to visit some of the natural attractions within the island's national parks. These are sold for varying numbers of visits. A site pass costs $2, a day pass $5. Hiking guides can be arranged through the **Dominican Tourist Office** (⊠ Valley Rd., Roseau, ☎ 767/448–2045). The **Forestry Division** (⊠ Dominica Botanical Gardens, between Bath Rd. and Valley Rd., Roseau, ☎ 767/448–2401) is responsible for the management of forests and wildlife and has publications on Dominica as well as a wealth of information on reputable guides.

SCUBA DIVING & SNORKELING

Dominica's dive sites are awesome. There are numerous highlights all along the west coast of the island, but the best are those in the southwest—within and around **Soufrière/Scotts Head Marine Reserve**. This bay is the site of a submerged volcanic crater. Within a ½ mi (1 km) of the shore, there are vertical drops of 800 ft (240 m) to more than 1,500 ft (450 m), with visibility frequently extending to 100 ft (30 m). Shoals of boga fish, creole wrasse, and blue cromis are common, and you might even see a spotted moray eel or a honeycomb cowfish. Crinoids (rare elsewhere) are also abundant here, as are giant barrel sponges. Other noteworthy dive sites outside this reserve are **Salisbury Falls, Nose Reef, Brain Coral Garden,** and—even farther north—**Cabrits Drop-Off** and **Toucari Reef.** The conditions for underwater photography, particularly macrophotography, are unparalleled. The going rate is between $65 and $75 for a two-tank dive or $100 for a resort course with an open-water dive. All scuba-diving operators also offer snorkeling; equipment rents for $10–$20 a day.

Anchorage Dive & Whale Watch Center (⊠ Anchorage Hotel, Castle Comfort, ☎ 767/448–2639) has two dive boats that can take you out day or night. It also offers snorkeling and whale-watching trips and shore diving. **Dive Dominica** (⊠ Castle Comfort Lodge, Castle Comfort, ☎ 767/448–2188, WEB www.divedominica.com), with four boats, offers diving, snorkeling, and whale-watching trips. **Fort Young Dive Centre** (⊠ Fort Young Hotel, Victoria St., Roseau, ☎ 767/448–5000 Ext. 333, WEB www.divefortyoung.com) conducts snorkeling, diving, and whale-watching trips, which depart from the hotel's dock. **Nature Island Dive** (⊠ Soufrière, ☎ 767/449–8181) is run by an enthusiastic crew. Some of the island's best dive sites are right outside their door, and they offer diving, snorkeling, kayaking, and mountain biking.

Beaches

On Dominica you'll find mostly black-sand beaches, evidence of the island's volcanic origins, or secluded white- or brown-sand beaches along the northeast coast. The best sandy beaches are around Portsmouth, but swimming off the rocky shores has its pleasures, too: the water is deeper and bluer, and the snorkeling is far more interesting. The beaches of the southwest coast are mostly rocks and black sand. On the west coast, just south of the village of Pointe Michel, **Champagne,** a stony beach, is hailed as one of the best spots for swimming, snorkeling, and diving. It gets its name from volcanic vents that constantly puff steam into the sea, which makes you feel as if you are swimming in warm champagne. **Picard Beach,** a golden stretch of sand, is the longest and best beach on the island and a favorite of both locals and visitors. You'll find many restaurants and hotels along this part of the coast.

Where to Eat

There is a 5% sales tax added to all bills. Some restaurants include a 10% service charge in the final tab; otherwise tip 10% for good service.

$$–$$$ ✕ **Guiyave.** This popular lunchtime restaurant in a quaint Caribbean town house also has a shop downstairs serving a scrumptious selection of sweet and savory pastries, tarts, and cakes. These can also be ordered upstairs, along with more elaborate fare such as fish court bouillon or chicken in a sweet-and-sour sauce. Choose to dine either in the airy dining room or on the sunny balcony perched above Roseau's colorful streets—the perfect spot to indulge in one of the fresh-squeezed tropical juices. ⊠ *15 Cork St., Roseau,* ☎ *767/448–2930. AE, MC, V. Closed Sun. No dinner.*

$$–$$$ ✕ **La Robe Creole.** A cut-stone building steps away from the Old Market Plaza houses one of Dominica's best restaurants. In a cozy dining room with wood rafters, ladder-back chairs, and colorful madras tablecloths, you can dine on a meal selected from an eclectic à la carte menu. Callaloo soup is one specialty; lobster crepes and salads are others. The downstairs takeout annex, Mouse Hole, is an inexpensive and tasty place to snack when you're on the run. The restaurant makes delicious mango chutney and plantain chips, which you can also buy in local shops. ⊠ *3 Victoria St., Roseau,* ☎ *767/448–2896. D, MC, V. Closed Sun.*

$–$$$ ✕ **Pearl's Cuisine.** From her base in a creole town house in central Roseau, chef Pearl, with her robust and infectious character, prepares some of the island's best local cuisine. She offers everything—including *sousse* (pickled pigs' feet), blood pudding, and rotis—in typical Dominican style. When sitting down to lunch or dinner, ask for a table on the open-air gallery that overlooks Roseau and prepare for an abundant portion, but make sure you leave space for dessert. If you're on the go, enjoy a quick meal from the ground-floor snack bar. You're spoiled for choice when it comes to the fresh fruit juices. ✉ *50 King George V St., Roseau,* ☎ *767/448–8707. AE, D, MC, V.*

¢–$$ ✕ **Cornerhouse Café.** Just off the Old Market Plaza in a historic three-story stone-and-wood town house is Dominica's only true Internet café; the sign on the lattice verandah reads DOMINICA'S INFORMATION CAFÉ. Here an eclectic menu of meals and other treats is on offer: bagels with an assortment of toppings, delicious soups, sandwiches, salads, cakes, and coffee. Computers are rented by the half hour: relax on soft chairs and flip through books and magazines while you wait. Quiz night is Wednesday, and every night is game night—but arrive early, as there's always a full house. ✉ *Corner of Old and King George V Sts., Roseau,* ☎ *767/449–9000. No credit cards. Closed Sun.*

Freeport-Lucaya, Bahamas

Grand Bahama Island, the fourth-largest island in the Bahamas, lies only 52 mi off Palm Beach, Florida. In 1492, when Columbus first set foot in the Bahamas, Grand Bahama was already populated. Skulls found in caves attest to the existence of the peaceable Lucayans, who were constantly fleeing the more bellicose Caribs. But it was not until the 1950s, when the harvesting of Caribbean yellow pine trees (now protected by Bahamian environmental law) was the island's major industry, that American financier Wallace Groves envisioned Grand Bahama's grandiose future as a tax-free port for the shipment of goods to the United States.

On August 5, 1955, largely due to Groves's efforts, the government signed an agreement to develop a planned city and administer a 200-square-mi tax-free area near the island's center. Developers built a port, an airport, a power plant, roads, waterways, and utilities. They also promoted tourism and industrial development.

From that agreement, the city of Freeport and later Lucaya evolved. They are separated by a 4-mi stretch of East Sunrise Highway, although few can tell you where one community ends and the other begins. Most of Grand Bahama's commercial activity is concentrated in Freeport, the Bahamas's second-largest city. Lucaya, with its sprawling shopping complex and water-sports reputation, stepped up to the role of island tourism capital. Resorts, beaches, casinos, and golf courses make both cities popular with visitors.

CURRENCY

The Bahamian dollar is the official currency of the Bahamas. But since the U.S. dollar is universally accepted, there's no need to acquire any Bahamian currency. Prices quoted throughout this chapter are in U.S. dollars unless otherwise indicated.

TELEPHONES

Calling locally or internationally is easy in the Bahamas. To place a local call, dial the seven-digit phone number. To call the United States, dial 1 plus the area code. Pay phones cost 25¢ per call; Bahamian and U.S. quarters are accepted, as are BATELCO phone cards. To place a call using a calling card, use your long-distance carrier's access code or dial 0 for the operator.

Dolphin Encounter. You travel by ferry to Sanctuary Bay, where there are 14 bottle-nosed dolphins. After an education session, you climb into the water and interact with the cetaceans. ☉ *3 hrs,* ⌨ *$80.*

Snorkeling Tour. You board a 72-ft catamaran and anchor off Lucaya Beach, where you will snorkel among the colorful tropical fish. After a rum punch, it's a sail back to the dock. ☉ *3 hrs,* ⌨ *$35.*

Coming Ashore

Cruise-ship passengers arrive at Lucayan Harbour, which recently underwent a $10.5 million renovation and expansion that includes a clever Bahamian-style look, expanded cruise-passenger terminal facilities, and an entertainment-shopping village. The harbor lies about 10 minutes west of Freeport.

Taxis and limos meet all cruise ships. Two passengers are charged $16 and $24 for trips to Freeport and Lucaya, respectively. Fare to Xanadu Beach is $17; it's $24 to Taino Beach. The price per person drops with larger groups. It's customary to tip taxi drivers 15%. A three-hour sightseeing tour of the Freeport-Lucaya area costs $25–$35. Four-hour West End trips cost about $40.

Grand Bahama's flat terrain and straight, well-paved roads make for good scooter riding. Rentals run $35–$50 a day (about $15 an hour). Helmets are required and provided. Look for small rental stands in parking lots and along the road in Freeport and Lucaya and at the larger resorts. It's cheaper to rent a car than to hire a taxi. Automobiles, jeeps, and vans can be rented at the Grand Bahama International Airport. Some agencies provide free pickup and delivery service to the cruise-ship port and Freeport and Lucaya, but prices are still not cheap cars run $50–$100 per day.

Exploring Freeport-Lucaya

Numbers in the text correspond to numbers in the margin on the Freeport-Lucaya map.

Grand Bahama is the only planned island in the Bahamas. Its towns, villages, and sights are well laid out but far apart. Downtown Freeport and Lucaya are both best appreciated on foot. Buses and taxis can transport you the 4-mi distance between the two. In Freeport, shopping, golfing, and gambling are the main attractions. Bolstered by the recent completion of the three-hotel Our Lucaya resort complex, Lucaya has its beautiful beach and water-sports scene, plus more shopping and a casino that is expected to open soon.

Outside of town, isolated fishing villages, beaches, natural attractions, and the once-rowdy town of West End make it worthwhile to hire a tour or rent a car. The island stretches 96 mi from one end to the other.

Freeport is an attractive, planned city of modern shopping centers, resorts, and other convenient tourist facilities.

❹ **Bahamas National Trust Rand Nature Centre.** On 100 acres just minutes from downtown Freeport, ½ mi of trails show off 130 types of native plants, including many orchid species. The center is the island's birding hot spot, where you might spy a red-tailed hawk or a Cuban emerald hummingbird sipping hibiscus nectar. Don't miss the Flamingo Pond. From its observation deck you'll spot graceful pink flamingos. The reserve is named for philanthropist James H. Rand, the former president of Remington Rand, who donated a hospital and library to the island. ⌂ *E. Settlers Way, Freeport,* ☎ *242/352–5438.* ⌨ *$5.* ☉ *Weekdays 9–4.*

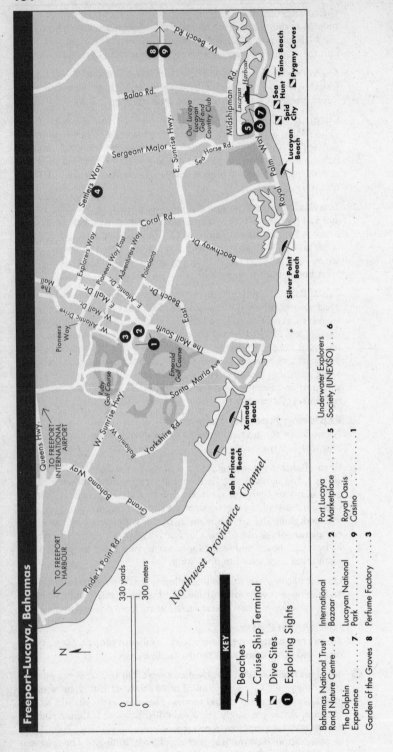

❷ **International Bazaar.** If the cobbled lanes and jumble of shops and restaurants in this 10-acre complex look like something from a Hollywood soundstage, that's not surprising: the bazaar was designed by special-effects artist Charles Perrin in 1967. These days, the shopping scene has a faded-glory air about it, as though it's waiting for someone to come rescue it from demise. The straw market at Port Lucaya is bigger and better, but International Bazaar still sells the widest selection of duty-free goods—jewelry, china, and perfume—along with clothing, T-shirts, and tacky souvenirs. ✉ *W. Sunrise Hwy. and Mall Dr., Freeport,* ☎ *no phone.* 🎟 *Free.* ✆ *Mon.–Sat. 10–6.*

❸ **Perfume Factory.** The quiet and elegant Perfume Factory is in a replica 19th-century Bahamian mansion. The interior resembles a tasteful drawing room. This is the home of Fragrance of the Bahamas, a company that produces perfumes, colognes, and lotions using the scents of jasmine, cinnamon, gardenia, spice, and ginger. Take a free five-minute tour of the mixology laboratory. For $30 an ounce, you can blend your own creations using any of the 35 scents. Sniff mixtures until they hit the right combination, then bottle, name, and take home the personalized perfume. ✉ *Behind International Bazaar, on an access road, Freeport,* ☎ *242/352–9391.* 🎟 *Free.* ✆ *Weekdays 9:30–5:30, Sat. 10–4.*

❶ **Royal Oasis Casino.** Completely renovated with new games and contemporary entertainment, this Freeport landmark (formerly the Princess Casino) now has a Mediterranean look and feel. Gamblers come in droves to try their hand at about 700 slot machines, blackjack, and other gambling temptations. Place a bet on your favorite NFL, NBA, NHL, and NCAA contenders at the digitized Sports Book, surrounded by 18 sports-tuned TVs. The casino is part of the Royal Oasis Golf Resort and adjacent to the International Bazaar. ✉ *W. Sunrise Hwy., Freeport,* ☎ *242/350–7000; 800/422–2294 in the U.S.* ✆ *Daily 8:30 AM–3 AM.*

EXPLORING LUCAYA

Lucaya, on Grand Bahama's southern coast and just east of Freeport, was developed as the island's resort center. These days, it's booming with the megaresort complex called Our Lucaya, a fine sandy beach, championship golf courses, a first-class dive operation, and Port Lucaya's marina facilities.

❼ **The Dolphin Experience.** Encounter Atlantic bottle-nosed dolphins in Sanctuary Bay at one of the world's first and largest dolphin facilities, about 2 mi east of Port Lucaya. A ferry takes you from Port Lucaya to the bay to observe and photograph the animals. If you don't mind getting wet, you can sit on a partially submerged dock or stand waist-deep in the water, and one of these friendly creatures will swim up and touch you. Within the sheltered waters of Sanctuary Bay, you can also engage in a swim-with-the-dolphins program. A two-hour dive program is available. If you really get hooked on these affectionate animals, you can enroll in an all-day program and work with the trainers. Buy tickets for the Dolphin Experience and the dive program at the Underwater Explorers Society (UNEXSO) in Port Lucaya. Make reservations as early as possible. ✉ *The Dolphin Experience, Port Lucaya,* ☎ *242/373–1250 or 888/365–3483,* 𝐅𝐀𝐗 *242/373–3948,* 𝐖𝐄𝐁 *www.dolphinexperience.com.* 🎟 *2-hr interaction program $59, 2-hr swim program $149, full-day assistant trainer program $219.* ✆ *Daily 9–5.*

❺ **Port Lucaya Marketplace.** Lucaya's capacious and lively shopping complex—a dozen low-rise, pastel-painted colonial buildings whose style was influenced by traditional island homes—is on the waterfront 4 mi east of Freeport and across the street from a massive resort compound. The shopping center, whose walkways are lined with hibiscus, bougainvillea, and croton, has about 100 well-kept establishments, among them waterfront restaurants and bars, and shops that sell clothes, crystal and china, watches, jewelry, and perfumes. Vendors display crafts in small, brightly painted wooden stalls. A straw market embraces the complex at both ends. ⊠ *Sea Horse Rd., Port Lucaya,* ☎ *242/373–8446* WEB *www.portlucaya.com* ⊙ *Mon.–Sat. 10–6.*

❻ Underwater Explorers Society (UNEXSO). One of the world's most respected diving facilities, UNEXSO welcomes more than 50,000 individuals each year and trains hundreds of them in scuba diving. UNEXSO's facilities include an 18-ft-deep training pool with windows that look out on the harbor, changing rooms and showers, docks, equipment rental, and an air-tank filling station. ⊠ *On the wharf at Port Lucaya Marketplace, Port Lucaya,* ☎ *242/373–1244 or 800/992–3483,* WEB *www.unexso.com.* ⊠ *Dives from $35, shark dives $89, dolphin dives $169.* ⊙ *Daily 8–5.*

BEYOND FREEPORT-LUCAYA

Grand Bahama Island narrows at picturesque West End, once Grand Bahama's capital and still home to descendants of the island's first settlers.

Seaside villages, with concrete block houses painted in bright blue and pastel yellow, fill in the landscape between Freeport and West End. The East End is Grand Bahama's "back-to-nature" side. The road east from Lucaya is long, flat, and mostly straight. It cuts through vast pine forest to reach McLean's Town, the end of the road.

❽ Garden of the Groves. Some 10,000 varieties of tropical flora, including fruit trees, ferns, bougainvillea, oleander, and chenille plant, flourish at this 12-acre botanical paradise. Birds, alligators, and a petting zoo add family appeal. Follow the Main Waterfall Trail to a picture-perfect church on a hill, a full-size replica of the chapel at Pine Ridge, one of Grand Bahama's earliest settlements. A small café serves breakfast and dinner daily. Guided tours are available with reservation. ⊠ *Midshipman Rd. and Magellan Dr.,* ☎ *242/373–5668,* WEB *www.gardenofthegroves.com.* ⊠ *$9.95 adults, $6.95 children.* ⊙ *Daily 9–4.*

❾ Lucayan National Park. In this 40-acre seaside land preserve, trails and elevated walkways wind through a natural forest of wild tamarind and gumbo-limbo trees, past an observation platform, a mangrove swamp, sheltered pools containing rare marine species, and what is believed to be the largest explored underwater cave system in the world (7 mi long). You can enter the caves at two access points. One is closed during bat nursing season (June and July). Just 20 mi east of Lucaya, the park contains examples of the island's five ecosystems: beach, sandy or whiteland coppice (hardwood forest), mangroves, rocky coppice, and pine forest. Across the road, trails lead through pine forest and mangrove swamp to Gold Rock Beach, a beautiful, lightly populated strand of white sand, aquamarine sea, and coral reef. Signs along the trail detail the park's distinctive features. ⊠ *Grand Bahama Hwy.,* ☎ *242/353–4149.* ⊠ *Free.* ⊙ *Daily 9–4.*

Shopping

Best known for duty-free bargains in perfume and jewelry, the shopping centers of Freeport and Lucaya also harbor straw markets, a Bahamian folk tradition where visitors will find not only the baskets that give them their name but jewelry, clothing, carvings, and other souvenir trinkets. Shops in Freeport and Lucaya are open Monday–Saturday from 9 or 10 to 6. Stores may stay open later in Port Lucaya. Most accept major credit cards. The two main shopping centers are the International Bazaar in Freeport and Port Lucaya Marketplace in Port Lucaya.

Outdoor Activities & Sports

FISHING

Fishing charters for up to four people cost $250–$460 (or $80 per person) for a half day and $350 and up for all day. In deep waters, anglers pull up dolphinfish, kingfish, or wahoo. Along the flats, the elusive bonefish is the catch of fishing aficionados. **Reef Tours Ltd.** (⊠ Port Lucaya Marketplace, ☎ 242/373–5880) offers sportfishing for four to six people on custom boats. Equipment and bait are provided free. **Running Mon Marina** (⊠ Kelly Ct., Freeport, ☎ 242/352–6834) has daily half- and full-day deep-sea fishing charters and can arrange bonefishing excursions.

GOLF

Because Grand Bahama is such a large island, it can afford long fairways puddled with lots of water and fraught with challenge. Four championship golf courses (two at the Royal Oasis Golf Resort, two at Our Lucaya) and one 9-hole course constitute a major island attraction. The Butch Harmon School of Golf at Our Lucaya is one of three in the world. **Fortune Hills Golf & Country Club** (⊠ E. Sunrise Hwy., Lucaya, ☎ 242/373–2222), a 3,453-yard, 9-hole, par-36 course, was designed by Dick Wilson and Joe Lee. **Our Lucaya Lucayan Course** (⊠ Our Lucaya, Lucaya, ☎ 242/373–1066; 242/373–1333; 877/687–2474 for Butch Harmon golf school)—6,824-yards, par-72—is a dramatic 18-hole course. The 18th hole has a double lake and a dramatic Balancing Boulders feature. Home to Butch Harmon School of Golf, it also has the Arawak Dining Room, a cocktail lounge, and a pro shop. **Our Lucaya Reef Course** (⊠ Our Lucaya Resort, Lucaya, ☎ 242/373–2002), a 6,920-yard, par-72 course, was designed by Robert Trent Jones, Jr. It has lots of water and a tricky dog-leg left on the 18th hole. **Royal Oasis Golf Resort** (⊠ W. Sunrise Hwy., Freeport, ☎ 242/350–7000) has two 18-hole, par-72 championship courses refashioned by the Fazio Design Group: the 7,000-yard Ruby and the 6,679-yard Emerald.

HORSEBACK RIDING

Pinetree Stables (⊠ Beachway Dr., Freeport, ☎ 242/373–3600) runs trail and beach rides twice a day; it's closed on Monday. All two-hour trail rides are accompanied by an experienced guide. Rides for expert equestrians are also available. Reservations are essential.

Beaches

Some 60 mi of magnificent, pristine stretches of sand extend between Freeport-Lucaya and the island's eastern end. Most are used only by people who live in adjacent settlements. The beaches have no public facilities, so beachgoers often headquarter at one of the local beach bars, which often provide free transportation. **Lucayan Beach** is readily accessible from the town's main drag and is always lively and lovely. **Taino Beach,** near Freeport, is fun for families, water-sports enthusiasts, and partyers. Near Freeport, **Xanadu Beach** provides a mile of white sand.

Where to Eat

$$–$$$ ✕ **Club Caribe.** Small and casual, this beachside haunt is an ideal place to headquarter your day at the beach. Unwind with a Bahama Mama, or try the local fare, such as conch fritters, grilled grouper, or barbecued ribs. You can also get American burgers and sandwiches. Dinner selections on Wednesday, Thursday, and Friday night change according to the chef's creative whims. Free transportation is provided from anywhere in town other than the port or airport with advance reservations. Saturday night brings a fish fry, pig roast, bonfire, and dining at picnic tables on the beach. ⊠ *Mather Town, off Doubloon Rd. on Spanish Main Dr.* ☎ *242/373–6866. AE, D, MC, V. No dinner Sun.–Tues.*

$$-$$$ × **Pier One.** Observe Lucayan Harbour's cruise-ship activity over lunch, sunset over cocktails, or the frenzied feeding of sharks over dinner. Shark—prepared blackened, curried with bananas, pan-fried, and in spicy fritters—is the specialty of the house. Steak, grouper, and lobster also star on the extensive menu. In season, call ahead to reserve an outdoor table, or dine inside, surrounded by aquariums and nautical paraphernalia. Swarms of fish and sharks frenzy for handouts at 7, 8, and 9 PM. ⊠ *Lucayan Harbour,* ☎ *242/352–6674. AE, MC, V. No lunch weekends*

¢–$$$ × **Becky's Restaurant & Lounge.** This popular eatery opens at 7 AM and may be the best place in town to fuel up before a full day of gambling or shopping. Its diner-style booths provide a comfortable backdrop for the inexpensive menu of Bahamian and American food, from conch salad and steamed mutton to steak or a BLT. Pancakes, eggs, and Bahamian breakfasts—"boil" fish, "stew" fish, or chicken souse (lime-marinated), with johnnycake or grits—are served all day. ⊠ *E. Beach Dr. and E. Sunrise Hwy.,* ☎ *242/352–5247. MC, V.*

Nightlife

If your ship doesn't depart until late at night, look to the big resorts—Our Lucaya in Lucaya and Royal Oasis in Freeport—for shows and lively nightclubs. The Royal Oasis also has a huge casino. **Bahama Mama Cruises** (⊠ Superior Watersports, ☎ 242/373–7863) offers some of the best nightlife in Grand Bahama. In addition to sunset "booze cruises," Bahama Mama serves a surf-and-turf dinner and has a colorful native show. Reservations are essential. The dinner cruise and sunset cruise with show are offered Monday, Wednesday, and Friday. **Holiday Inn Sunspree at Royal Oasis Golf Resort** (⊠ Royal Oasis Golf Resort & Casino, ☎ 242/350–7000) has the John B. outdoor lounge, with live music Wednesday through Monday. Lounge and disco open nightly 9–2; doors open for Goombaya show and dinner (optional) Tuesday and Saturday at 6:30; show time is 7:30. **Port Lucaya Marketplace** (⊠ Sea Horse Rd. ☎ 242/373–8446) has a stage that becomes lively after dark, with calypso music and other performers at Count Basie Square (ringed by three popular hangouts: the Corner Bar, Pusser's Daiquiri Bar, and the Pub at Port Lucaya). **Royal Oasis Casino** (⊠ Royal Oasis Golf Resort & Casino, W. Sunrise Hwy., ☎ 242/350–7000) packs its newly renovated 20,000 square ft with around 700 slot machines, 27 blackjack tables, 5 craps tables, 4 roulette wheels, 4 Caribbean poker games, and a table each for baccarat and mini-baccarat. In the 360° Tonic bar, 18 sports TVs and a digital sports book for betting on games charge the atmosphere. The bar also hosts tournaments and live music. An adjacent restaurant offers a view of the gambling. Slots are open daily 8:30 AM–3:30 AM, tables 10 AM–3:30 AM.

Grand Cayman, Cayman Islands

The largest and most populous of the Cayman Islands, Grand Cayman is also one of the most popular cruise destinations in the Western Caribbean, largely because it doesn't suffer from the ailments afflicting many larger ports: panhandlers, hasslers, and crime. Instead, the Cayman economy is a study in stability, and residents are renowned for their courteous behavior. Though cacti and scrub fill the dusty landscape, Grand Cayman is a diver's paradise, with pristine waters and a colorful variety of marine life.

Compared with in other Caribbean ports, there are few things to see on land here; instead, the island's most impressive sights are underwater. Snorkeling, diving, and glass-bottom boat and submarine rides top every ship's shore-excursion list and can also be arranged at major aquatic shops. Grand Cayman is also famous for the 554 offshore banks in George Town; not surprisingly, the standard of living is high, and nothing is cheap.

CURRENCY
The Cayman Island dollar (CI$) is worth about US$1.20. The U.S. dollar is accepted everywhere and ATMs often dispense cash in both currencies, though you may receive change in Cayman dollars. Prices are often quoted in Cayman dollars, so make sure you know which currency you're dealing with. Prices given below are in U.S. dollars unless otherwise indicated.

TELEPHONES
To call the United States, dial 01 followed by the area code and telephone number. To place a credit-card call, dial 110; credit-card and calling-card calls can be made from any public phone.

SHORE EXCURSIONS
The following are good choices in Grand Cayman. They may not be offered by all cruise lines. Times and prices are approximate.

Atlantis Submarine. A real submarine offers an exciting view of Grand Cayman's abundant marine life. ☉ *2 hrs,* ☒ *$85.*

Island Tour. A tour around the island usually includes the turtle farm, "Hell" (a one-note tourist stop that is little more than a post office and a gift shop), the blowholes, Seven Mile Beach, Pedro St. James Castle, and the rum-cake factory. ☉ *2 hrs,* ☒ *$32.*

Seaworld Explorer Cruise. A glass-bottom boat takes you on an air-conditioned, narrated voyage where you sit 5 ft below the water's surface and see sunken ships, tropical fish, and coral reefs in the George Town Harbour. ☉ *1 hr,* ☒ *$39.*

Sting Ray City Snorkel Tour. These boat trips go to shallow Sting Ray Sandbar, inside the North Sound reef. Eager stingrays approach as soon as your boat stops; then you jump into 3-ft-deep water and play among them, even feeding them. This is by far the best excursion on Grand Cayman for nondivers. ☉ *3 hrs.,* ☒ *$45.*

Coming Ashore

Ships anchor in George Town Harbour and tender passengers onto Harbour Drive, the center of the shopping district. A tourist information booth is on the pier, and taxis cue for disembarking passengers. Taxi fares are determined by an elaborate structure set by the government, and although rates may seem high, cabbies rarely try to rip off tourists. Ask to see the chart if you want to check a quoted fare. Sightseeing companies organize tours here, so it's not likely you will be able to take a guided taxi tour with a small group. Car rentals start at $35 a day (plus a $7.50 driving permit).

Exploring Grand Cayman

Numbers in the margin correspond to points of interest on the Grand Cayman map.

❽ Blow Holes. These make the ultimate photo opportunity as crashing waves force water into caverns and send geysers shooting up through the ironshore. ✉ *Frank Sound Rd., near East End.*

❺ Bodden Town. In the island's original south-shore capital you'll find an old cemetery on the shore side of the road. Graves with A-frame structures are said to contain the remains of pirates. There are also the ruins of a fort and a wall erected by slaves in the 19th century. A curio shop serves as the entrance to what's called the Pirate's Caves, par-

Grand Cayman, Cayman Islands

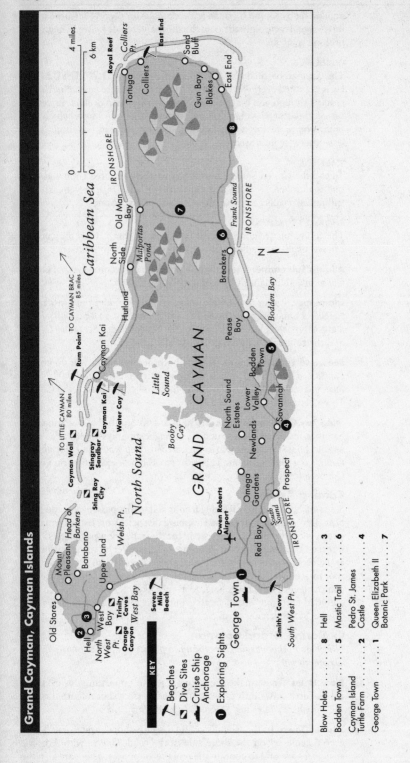

KEY

- Beaches
- Dive Sites
- Cruise Ship Anchorage
- 1 Exploring Sights

Blow Holes 8	Hell 3
Bodden Town 5	Mastic Trail 6
Cayman Island Turtle Farm 2	Pedro St. James Castle 4
George Town 1	Queen Elizabeth II Botanic Park ... 7

tially underground natural formations that are more hokey (decked out with fake treasure chests and mannequins in pirate garb) than spooky.

🐢 ❷ **Cayman Island Turtle Farm.** The farm has reopened after a hurricane seriously damaged it in 2001, though thousands of turtles are in holding tanks across the street from the original location. You can see turtles in various stages of growth, and some can be picked up from the tanks—a real treat for children and adults. Rebuilding of tanks and replenishment of lost turtles continue. The gift shop has been rebuilt and is filled with educational and fun turtle- and ocean-themed merchandise. ⊠ *West Bay Rd.* ☎ *345/949–3893,* WEB *www.turtle.ky.* ⊡ *$6.* ☉ *Mon.–Sat. 8:30–5.*

❶ **George Town.** Begin exploring the capital by strolling along the Harbour Drive waterfront. The circular gazebo is where passengers from cruise ships disembark. Diagonally across the street from the cruise-ship dock is the **Elmslie Memorial United Church,** named after Scotsman James Elmslie, the first Presbyterian missionary to serve in the Caymans. The church was the first concrete-block building built in the Cayman Islands. Its vaulted ceiling, wooden arches, and sedate nave reflect the quietly religious nature of island residents. At **Fort Street,** a main shopping street, is a small clock tower dedicated to Britain's King George V, and a huge fig tree manicured into an umbrella shape. Here, too, is a statue of national hero James Bodden, the father of Cayman tourism. Across the street is the Cayman Islands Legislative Assembly Building, next door to the 1919 Peace Memorial Building. That the Caymanians built a memorial to peace rather than war speaks of their character.

On **Edward Street** you'll find the charming library, built in 1939; it has English novels, current U.S. newspapers, and a small reference section. It's worth a visit just for its old-fashioned charm and a look at the shields with insignias of Britain's prominent institutions of learning; they decorate the ceiling beams. Across the street is the courthouse. Down the next block is the financial district, where banks from all over the world have offices.

Down from the financial district is the **General Post Office,** also built in 1939, with its strands of decorative colored lights and some 2,000 private mailboxes on the outside (mail is not delivered on the island). Behind the post office is **Elizabethan Square,** a shopping and office complex on Shedden Road with food, clothing, and souvenir establishments. The courtyard has benches placed around a garden and a fountain; it's a pleasant place to rest your feet.

Built in 1833, the home of the **Cayman Islands National Museum** has had several incarnations, including that of courthouse, jail (now the gift shop), post office, and dance hall. It's small but fascinating, with excellent displays and videos that illustrate local geology, flora, and fauna, and island history. Pick up a walking-tour map of George Town at the museum gift shop before leaving. ⊠ *Harbour Dr., George Town,* ☎ *345/949–8368.* ⊡ *$5.* ☉ *Weekdays 9–5, Sat. 10–2.*

❸ **Hell.** This tiny village is little more than a patch of incredibly jagged rock formations called ironshore. The big attractions here are the small post office and a nearby gift shop, where you can get cards and letters postmarked from Hell (a postcard of bikini-clad beauties emblazoned with WHEN HELL FREEZES OVER gives you a picture of what this place is like).

❻ **Mastic Trail.** In the 1800s this woodland trail was used as a shortcut to and from the North Side. The low-lying area was full of hardwood trees, including mahogany, West Indian cedar, and the mastic that early settlers used in building their homes. Along the trail you'll see trees, birds, and plants unique to this old-growth forest. Walk it on your own (about two hours round-trip) or call the National Trust to book a guide. ⊠ *Frank Sound Rd., entrance by the fire station and across from the Botanic Park,* ☎ *345/949–0121 for guide reservations.*

④ Pedro St. James Castle. Built in 1780, the great house is Cayman's oldest stone structure and the only remaining late-18th-century residence on the island. The buildings are surrounded by 8 acres of parks and woodlands. You can stroll through landscaping of native Caymanian flora and experience one of the most spectacular views on the island from atop the Great Pedro Bluff. The multimedia theater show has smoking pots, misting rains, and two film screens where the story of Pedro's Castle is presented. The show plays on the hour; see it before you tour the site. On Sundays there is a brunch serving all local cuisine. ⊠ *S. Sound Rd., Savannah,* ☎ *345/947–3329.* 🎫 *$8.*

❼ Queen Elizabeth II Botanic Park. This 65-acre wilderness preserve showcases indigenous and nonindigenous tropical vegetation. Interpretive signs identify the flora along the walking trail. Rare blue iguanas are bred and released in the gardens; there's usually one named Charlie hanging around the entrance gate. You can also see native orchids and, if you're lucky, the brilliant green Cayman parrot. ⊠ *Frank Sound Rd., Frank Sound,* ☎ *345/947–9462; 345/947–3558 for information.* 🎫 *$3.* ⊙ *Daily 9–6:30 (last admission at 5:30).*

Shopping

Fort Street and Cardinal Avenue are the main shopping streets in George Town. On Cardinal Avenue is Kirk Freeport Plaza, with lots of jewelry shops. The **Heritage Crafts Shop** (⊠ George Town, ☎ 345/945–6041), near the harbor, sells crafts and gifts. **Cathy Church's Underwater Photo Centre and Gallery** (⊠ S. Church St., George Town, ☎ 345/949–7415) has a collection of underwater photos by the famed photographer Cathy Church. Debbie van der Bol runs the arts-and-crafts shop **Pure Art** (⊠ S. Church St., George Town, ☎ 345/949–9133; ⊠ Hyatt Regency, West Bay Rd., Seven Mile Beach, ☎ 345/945–5633), which sells watercolors, wood carvings, and lacework by local artists, as well as her own sketches and cards. The **Tortuga Rum Company** (⊠ N. Sound Rd., George Town, ☎ 345/949–7701 or 345/949–7867) has scrumptious rum cake (sealed fresh) that's sweet and moist and makes a great souvenir.

Outdoor Activities & Sports

FISHING

Cayman waters are abundant with blue and white marlin, yellowfin tuna, sailfish, dolphinfish, bonefish, and wahoo. Two dozen boats are available for charter. **Bayside Watersports** (☎ 345/949–3200) offers half-day snorkeling trips, North Sound Beach lunch excursions, and full-day deep-sea fishing and dinner cruises.

SCUBA DIVING & SNORKELING

Pristine water (visibility often exceeding 100 ft [30 m]), breathtaking coral formations, and plentiful and exotic marine life mark the **Great Wall**—a world-renowned dive site just off the north side of Grand Cayman. A must-see for adventurous souls is **Stingray City** in the North Sound, noted as the best 12-ft (3½-m) dive in the world, where dozens of stingrays congregate, tame enough to suction squid from your outstretched palm. Nondivers gravitate to **Stingray Sandbar,** a shallower part of the North Sound, which has become a popular snorkeling spot; it is also a popular spot for the stingrays. **Bob Soto's Reef Divers** (☎ 345/949–2020 or 800/262–7686) was the first dive operation in

Cayman and now has several locations; it has film-processing facilities and underwater photo courses, as does **Don Foster's** (☎ 345/949–5679 or 800/833–4837) in George Town. **Eden Rock** (☎ 345/949–7243) provides easy access to excellent George Town shore diving at Eden Rock and Devil's Grotto; both reefs are a short swim from shore. **Red Sail Sports** (☎ 345/949–8745 or 800/255–6425) offers daily trips to Stingray City and has branches at many Grand Cayman hotels along Seven Mile Beach.

Beaches

The west coast, the island's most developed area, is where you'll find the famous **Seven Mile Beach.** This white, powdery, 5½-mi-long strand is Grand Cayman's busiest vacation center, and most of the island's resorts, restaurants, and shopping centers are along this strip. The Holiday Inn rents Aqua Trikes, Paddle Cats, and Banana Rides.

Where to Eat

Many restaurants add a 10% to 15% service charge. If a service charge is not added, tip 15% of the total bill.

$$–$$$$ ✕ **Rackam's Pub.** North of George Town, jutting out onto a jetty, is this low-key bar and grill popular for drinks and terrific sunset views. The young, friendly staff serves good jerk burgers (basted with Jamaican jerk sauce), grouper fish-and-chips, and tasty chiles rellenos. ⊠ *N. Church St., George Town,* ☎ *345/945–3860. AE, MC, V.*

$$$ ✕ **Cracked Conch by the Sea.** Nautical memorabilia and artifacts—many of which were collected by famed scuba professional Bob Soto, co-owner of the establishment—are scattered throughout the dining room and bar. The restaurant is next door to the Turtle Farm, and turtle steak is a signature dish. It's tender, succulent, and served with sautéed onions and mushrooms in a coconut-rum sauce. Entrée portions are huge. Bring a hearty appetite or spilt an entrée and a few appetizers. The conch fritters and conch salad are good, the lobster bisque outstanding. ⊠ *N. West Point Rd., West Bay,* ☎ *345/945–5217. AE, MC, V.*

$$ ✕ **Breadfruit Tree Garden Cafe.** Favored by locals, the jerk chicken rivals any on the island. Also on the menu are curry chicken and stewed pork, oxtail, rice and beans, and homemade soups. Drinks include breadfruit, mango, passion-fruit, and carrot juices. The interior is kitschy, with silk roses, white porch swings, straw hats, empty birdcages, and fake ivy crawling along the ceiling. It's open until the wee hours, which makes it a good midnight munchie stop. ⊠ *58 Eastern Ave., George Town,* ☎ *345/945–2124. No credit cards.*

$$ ✕ **Crow's Nest.** This local favorite serves island dishes such as conch burgers, Jamaican curry chicken, turtle steak, and Cayman-style fish. The fiery deep-fried coconut is among the best on the island, as is the Caesar salad with marinated conch. The key lime mousse pie is a must. Dine on the screened patio overlooking the sea. ⊠ *S. Sound Rd., George Town,* ☎ *345/949–9366. AE, MC, V.*

Grenada and Carriacou

Nutmeg, cinnamon, cloves, cocoa . . . those heady aromas fill the air in Grenada (pronounced gruh-*nay*-da). Only 33½ km (21 mi) long and 19½ km (12 mi) wide, the Isle of Spice is a tropical gem of lush rain forests, white-sand beaches, secluded coves, exotic flowers, and enough locally grown spices to fill anyone's kitchen cabinet.

Until 1983, when the U.S. Eastern Caribbean intervention catapulted this little nation into the headlines, Grenada was a relatively obscure island hideaway for lovers of fishing, snorkeling, or simply lazing in the sun. Grenada has been back to normal for years. It's a safe and secure vacation spot with friendly, hospitable people and enough good shopping, restaurants, historic sites, and natural wonders to make it a popular port of call. About one-third of Grenada's visitors arrive by cruise ship, and that number continues to grow each year. Nevertheless, the expansion of tourist facilities is carefully controlled. New construction on the beaches must be at least 165 ft back from the highwater mark, for instance, and no building can stand taller than a coconut palm. Happily, this means Grenadians have no plans to compromise the appearance of their island or their distinctive West Indian culture and lifestyle.

Nearby Carriacou (pronounced carry-a-*coo*) is visited mostly by smaller sailing ships since its port is simply not prepared for the infusion of thousands of passengers from a large liner. Part of the three-island nation of Grenada, which also includes tiny Petite Martinique (pronounced pitty mar-ti-*neek*) 3 km (2 mi) north of Carriacou, the 21-square-km (13-square-mi) island is 37 km (23 mi) north of the island of Grenada. Carriacou is the largest and southernmost island of the Grenadines, an archipelago of 32 small islands and cays that stretch northward from Grenada to St. Vincent.

The colonial history of Carriacou parallels Grenada's, but the island's small size has restricted its role in the nation's political history. Carriacou is hilly and not lush like Grenada. In fact, it's quite arid in some areas. A chain of hills cuts a wide swath through the center, from Gun Point in the north to Tyrrel Bay in the south. The island's greatest attractions for cruise passengers are diving and snorkeling.

CURRENCY

Grenada uses the Eastern Caribbean dollar (EC$). The exchange rate is EC$2.70 to US$1, although taxi drivers, stores, and vendors will frequently calculate at a rate of EC$2.50. U.S. dollars, major credit cards, and traveler's checks are readily accepted, but always ask which currency is being referenced when asking prices. Prices given below are in U.S. dollars unless otherwise indicated.

TELEPHONES

International telephone numbers can be dialed directly. Pay phones and phone cards are available at the welcome center, on The Carenage in St. George's, where cruise-ship passengers come ashore. To place an international call using a major credit card, dial 111; there's no surcharge. To place a collect call or use a calling card, dial 800/225–5872 from any phone.

SHORE EXCURSIONS

The following are good choices in Grenada. They may not be offered by all cruise lines. Times and prices are approximate.

Island Drive and Annandale Falls. Ride north along the west coast, through small villages and past lush greenery, to the Gouyave Nutmeg Cooperative in Grenville for a fascinating look at how Grenada's most famous export is processed. From Grenville, drive to the National Park Nature Center and climb to Annandale Falls before returning to the ship. ⊙ *3 hrs,* ▭ *$50.*

Island Jeep Tour. After driving through St. George Parish, travel north, stopping at a sulphur spring and pond, then through Grenada's central mountain range to the rain forest, Crater Lake, and Grand Étang National Park. ⊙ *4 hrs,* ▭ *$75.*

Nature Walk. You travel to an undisturbed rain forest, which is an important island watershed. There, you'll climb to the summit of the hill (1,420 ft) and get a panoramic view of Port Salines in the south, all the way to Grand Étang forest. Then it's back to St. George. ☉ *2 hrs,* 🎫 *$32.*

Coming Ashore

Large ships anchor outside St. George's Harbour and deliver passengers by launch to the south side of The Carenage, a thoroughfare that surrounds the horseshoe-shape harbor. Smaller ships dock at the pier beside the welcome center. You can easily tour the capital on foot, but be prepared to climb up and down steep hills. At the welcome center, you can hire a walking-tour guide ($5 an hour), a taxi to take you around The Carenage to Market Square ($3 each way), or a water taxi across the harbor (50¢ each way).

To explore areas outside St. George's, hiring a taxi or arranging a guided tour is more sensible than renting a car. Taxis are plentiful, and fixed rates to popular island destinations are posted at the welcome center. Taxi drivers charge $20 per hour; island tours generally cost $25 to $55 per person, depending on the destination and whether lunch is included.

A taxi ride from the welcome center to the beach will cost $10, but water taxis are a less expensive and more picturesque way to get there; the one-way fare is $4 to Grand Anse and $8 to Morne Rouge. Minibuses are the least expensive (and most crowded) way to travel between St. George's and Grand Anse; pay EC$1.50 (55¢), but hold on to your hat. Taxis, water taxis, and minibuses are all available at the pier.

If you want to rent a car and explore on your own, be prepared to pay $12 for a temporary driving permit and about $55 for a day's car rental.

Exploring Grenada and Carriacou

Numbers in the margin correspond to points of interest on the Grenada and Carriacou map.

GRENADA

❸ Annandale Falls. A mountain stream cascades 40 ft into a pool surrounded by exotic vines, such as liana and elephant ears. This is a lovely cool spot for swimming and picnicking. *Main interior road, 15 mins northeast of St. George's* ☎ *473/440–2452* 🎫 *$1* ☉ *Daily 9–5*

❺ Concord Falls. About 8 mi (13 km) north of St. George's, a turnoff from the West Coast Road leads to Concord Falls, which is actually three separate waterfalls. The first is at the end of the road; during the dry months (January–May), when the currents aren't too strong, you can take a dip under the cascade. Reaching the other waterfalls requires an hour's hike into the forest reserve. The most spectacular waterfall, at Fountainbleu, thunders 65 ft over huge boulders and creates a small pool where you can cool off before hiking back down the trail. It's smart to hire a guide. The path is clear, but slippery boulders toward the end can be treacherous without assistance. ⊠ *West Coast Rd.* 🎫 *Changing room $2.*

🌿 ❻ Dougaldston Spice Estate. Just south of Gouyave, this plantation, now primarily a living museum, grows and processes spices the old-fashioned way. You can see cocoa, nutmeg, mace, cloves, and other spices laid out on giant racks to dry in the sun. A worker will be glad to explain the process (and will appreciate a small donation). You can buy spices for about $2 a bag. ⊠ *Gouyave.* ☎ *No phone.* 🎫 *Free.* ☉ *Weekdays 9–4.*

🌿 ❼ Gouyave Nutmeg Processing Cooperative. In the center of the west-coast fishing village of Gouyave (pronounced *gwahve*), this is a fragrant, fascinating place to spend a half hour. Workers in the three-story

176

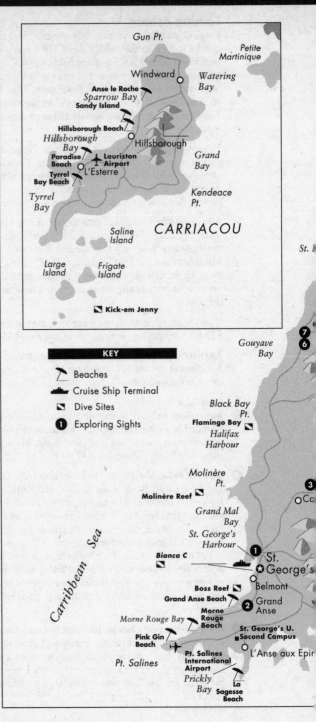

Grenada and Carriacou

Gun Pt.

Petite Martinique

Windward

Watering Bay

Anse le Roche
Sparrow Bay
Sandy Island

Hillsborough Beach

Hillsborough
Bay

Hillsborough

Grand Bay

Paradise Beach
Lauriston Airport
L'Esterre

Tyrrel Bay Beach

Tyrrel Bay

Kendeace Pt.

Saline Island

CARRIACOU

St.

Large Island

Frigate Island

Kick-em Jenny

KEY

Beaches

Cruise Ship Terminal

Dive Sites

1 Exploring Sights

Gouyave Bay

7
6

Black Bay Pt.
Flamingo Bay
Halifax Harbour

Molinère Pt.

Molinère Reef

Grand Mal Bay

St. George's Harbour

Bianca C

3
Co

Boss Reef

Grand Anse Beach

Belmont

1 St. George's

2 Grand Anse

Morne Rouge Beach

Morne Rouge Bay

Pink Gin Beach

St. George's U. Second Campus

L'Anse aux Epir

Pt. Salines

Pt. Salines International Airport

Prickly Bay

La Sagesse Beach

Carribbean Sea

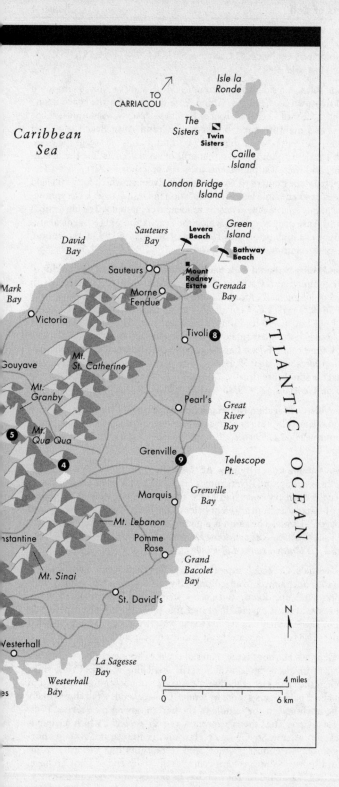

plant, which turns out 3 million pounds of Grenada's most famous export each year, sort nutmegs by hand and pack them in burlap bags for shipping worldwide. ⊠ *Gouyave,* ☎ *473/444–8337.* 🎫 *$1.* ☉ *Weekdays 10–1 and 2–4.*

🐾 ❷ **Grand Anse.** A residential and commercial area about 5 mi (8 km) south of downtown St. George's, Grand Anse is named for the beach it surrounds. Most of Grenada's tourist facilities—resorts, restaurants, shopping, and nightlife—are in this area. **Grand Anse Beach** is a 2-mi (3-km) crescent of sand shaded by coconut palms and seagrape trees, with gentle turquoise surf. A handful of resort hotels line the beachfront, and there's a public entrance at Camerhogne Park, just a few steps from the main road. **St. George's University,** which for years held classes at its enviable beachfront location in Grand Anse, has a sprawling campus in True Blue, a nearby residential community. The university's Grand Anse property, from which the evacuation of U.S. medical students was a high priority of U.S. forces during the 1983 intervention, is used for administrative purposes.

🐾 ❹ **Grand Étang National Park and Forest Reserve.** Deep in the interior of lush, mountainous Grenada is a bird sanctuary and forest reserve with miles of hiking trails, lookouts, and fishing streams. **Grand Étang Lake** is a 36-acre expanse of cobalt-blue water that fills the crater of an extinct volcano 1,740 ft (530 m) above sea level. Although legend has it the lake is bottomless, maximum soundings are recorded at 18 ft (5½ m). **Grand Étang Forest Center** has displays about wildlife and vegetation. A forest manager is on hand to answer questions. A snack bar and souvenir stands are nearby. ⊠ *Main interior road, between Grenville and St. George's,* ☎ *473/440–6160.* 🎫 *$1.* ☉ *Daily 8:30–4.*

🐾 ❾ **Grenville Cooperative Nutmeg Association** has guided tours. You can see and learn about the process of receiving, drying, sorting, and packing nutmegs. ⊠ *Grenville,* ☎ *473/442–7241.* 🎫 *$1.* ☉ *Weekdays 10–1 and 2–4.*

❽ **River Antoine Rum Distillery.** At this rustic operation, kept open primarily as a museum, Rivers rum is produced by the same methods used since the distillery opened in 1785. The process begins with the crushing of sugarcane from adjacent fields in the River Antoine (pronounced an-*twine*) Estate. The result is a potent overproof rum that will knock your socks off. ⊠ *River Antoine Estate, St. Patrick's,* ☎ *473/442–7109.* 🎫 *$2.* ☉ *Guided tours daily 9–4.*

❶ **St. George's.** Grenada's capital is a busy West Indian city, most of which remains unchanged from colonial days. Narrow streets lined with shops wind up, down, and across steep hills. Pastel-painted warehouses with roofs covered in orange tiles (brought from Europe as ballast in 18th-century ships) cling to the waterfront. Small rainbow-hued houses rise from the waterfront and disappear into steep green hills.

St. George's Harbour is the center of town. Schooners, ferries, and tour boats tie up along the seawall or at the small dinghy dock. Cruise ships dock at the large pier at the harbor entrance or anchor just outside and transport passengers ashore by tender. On weekends a tall ship is likely to be anchored in the middle of the harbor, giving the scene a 19th-century flavor. **The Carenage** (pronounced car-a-*nahzh*), which surrounds horseshoe-shape St. George's Harbour, is the capital's main thoroughfare. Warehouses, shops, and restaurants line the waterfront. Near the cruise-ship welcome center, at the south end of The Carenage, the Grenada Board of Tourism has its offices, and you can buy inexpensive spices and crafts at vendor stalls nearby. At the center of The Carenage, on the pedestrian plaza, sits the *Christ of the Deep* statue.

It was presented to Grenada by Costa Cruise Line in remembrance of its ship *Bianca C,* which burned and sank in the harbor in 1961 and is now a favorite dive site. The **Grenada National Museum,** a block from The Carenage, is set in the foundation of a French army barracks and prison that was built in 1704. The small museum exhibits news items, photos, and proclamations relating to the 1983 intervention, along with Empress Joséphine's childhood bathtub and other memorabilia from earlier periods. ✉ *Young and Monckton Sts.,* ☎ *473/440–3725.* 💳 *$1.* ☺ *Weekdays 9–4:30, Sat. 10–1.* An engineering feat for its time, the 340-ft-long (103-m-long) **Sendall Tunnel** was built in 1895 and named for an early governor. It separates the harborside of St. George's from the Esplanade on the bay side of town, where you'll find the open-air meat, fish, and produce markets. The Esplanade is also the terminus of the minibus route. **Market Square** (✉ Granby St.), a block from the Esplanade, is open every weekday morning but really comes alive on Saturday from 8 to noon. Vendors sell baskets, spices, brooms, clothing, knickknacks, coconut water, and heaps of fresh produce. Market Square is where parades and political rallies take place—and the beginning of minibus routes to all areas of the island. **St. Andrew's Presbyterian Church,** built in 1830, is at the intersection of Halifax and Church streets. Also known as Scots' Kirk, it was constructed with the help of the Freemasons. Built in 1825, the beautiful stone-and-pink-stucco **St. George's Anglican Church,** on Church Street, is filled with statues and plaques depicting Grenada in the 18th and 19th centuries. **St. George's Methodist Church,** on Green Street near Herbert Blaize Street, was built in 1820 and is the oldest original church in the city. The Gothic tower of **St. George's Roman Catholic Church** dates from 1818, but the current structure was built in 1884; the tower is the city's most visible landmark. On Church Street, **York House** (1801) is home to Grenada's Houses of Parliament and Supreme Court. It, the neighboring Registry Building (1780), and Government House (1802) are fine examples of early Georgian architecture.

Fort George (✉ Church St.) is high on the hill at the southern tip of Church Street. The fort, which rises above the entrance to St. George's Harbour, is Grenada's oldest—built by the French in 1705 to protect the harbor. No shots were fired here until October 1983, when Prime Minister Maurice Bishop and some of his followers were assassinated in the courtyard. The fort now houses police headquarters but is open to the public daily; admission is free. The 360° view of the capital city, St. George's Harbour, and the open sea is spectacular.

On Richmond Hill, high above the city of St. George's and the inland side of the harbor, **Fort Frederick** commands a panoramic view of two-thirds of Grenada. The fort was completed in 1791; it was the headquarters of the People's Revolutionary Government during the 1983 coup. You can get a bird's-eye view of the prison, on top of an adjacent hill, where the rebels remain incarcerated—and have, by all accounts, one of the best views in all of Grenada.

In St. Paul's, five minutes outside St. George's, **de la Grenade Industries** produces syrups, jams, jellies, and liqueurs made from nutmeg and other homegrown fruits and spices. It began in 1960 as a cottage industry. You're welcome to watch the process and purchase gifts from the retail operation on-site. ☎ *473/440–3241.* 💳 *Free.* ☺ *Weekdays 8–5, Sat. 9–12:30.*

CARRIACOU

"The land of many reefs" is a hilly island and (unlike its lush sister island, Grenada) has neither lakes nor rivers—only rainwater, caught in cisterns and purified with bleach. It gets arid during the dry season (January–May). Nevertheless, plenty of fruit is grown here, and the climate seems to suit the mahogany trees used for furniture-making and the white cedar critical to the boatbuilding that has made Carriacou famous.

Hillsborough is Carriacou's main town. Just offshore, Sandy Island is one of the nicest beaches around; almost anyone with a boat can give you a ride out, and you can leave your cares on the dock. Rolling hills cut a wide swath through the island's center, from Gun Point in the north to Tyrrel Bay in the south. The small town of Windward, on the northeast coast, is a boatbuilding community. You'll likely encounter half-finished hulls on the roadside. Originally constructed for inter-island commerce, the boats are now built for fishing and pleasure sailing.

Tiny Carriacou has several distinct cultures. Hillsborough is decidedly English; the southern region, around L'Esterre, reflects French roots; and the northern town of Windward has Scottish ties. African culture, of course, is the overarching influence. Passenger ferries and cargo schooners (that also take passengers) to Grenada's other islands, including Carriacou, depart from The Carenage. The fare for the 90-minute trip by ferry is $19; the slower freighters and mail boats cost about $10.

Shopping

Spices are a best buy. All kinds are grown and processed in Grenada and cost a fraction of what they command in an American supermarket. They're available at vendor stalls just outside the welcome center and at the market.

Stores are generally open weekdays from 8 until 4 or 4:30 and Saturdays from 8 to 1. If ships are in port on a Sunday, some shops and vendors do business. Grenada is not a major duty-free shopping port, although some stores along The Carenage sell duty-free items.

In Grand Anse, Grand Anse Shopping Center, Le Marquis Complex, and the new Spiceland Mall are within walking distance of each other and of Grand Anse Beach. You'll find gift shops and art galleries here, as well as supermarkets, pharmacies, and banks.

Art Fabrik (⊠ 9 Young St., St. George's, ☎ 473/440–0568) is a studio where you can watch artisans create batik before turning it into clothing or accessories. In the shop you'll find fabric by the yard or fashioned into dresses, shirts, shorts, hats, and scarves. The **Grand Anse Craft & Spice Market** (⊠ Grand Anse, ☎ 473/444–3780), managed by the Grenada Board of Tourism, is between the main road and the beach. The facility has 82 booths for vendors who sell arts, crafts, spices, music tapes, clothing, produce, and refreshments. It's open daily 7–7. **Tikal** (⊠ Young St., St. George's, ☎ 473/440–2310) is known for its exquisite baskets, artwork, jewelry, batik items, and fashions, both locally made and imported from Africa and Latin America. **Yellow Poui Art Gallery** (⊠ 9 Young St., St. George's, ☎ 473/440–3001) displays and sells paintings, sculpture, photography, lithographs, and antique engravings by artists from Grenada and elsewhere in the Caribbean.

Outdoor Activities & Sports

FISHING

Deep-sea fishing around Grenada is excellent, with marlin, sailfish, yellowfin tuna, and dolphinfish topping the list of good catches. You can arrange half- or full-day sportfishing trips for $250–$500, depending on the type of boat, number of people, and length of trip. **Bezo Charters** (☎ 473/443–5477 or 473/443–5021) has a tournament-equipped Bertram 31 Flybridge Sport Fisherman, called *Bezo,* with air-conditioned cabin, fighting chair, and an experienced crew waiting to take you deep-sea fishing. Charters can be customized; equipment and beverages are included. **Evans Fishing Charters** (☎ 473/444–4422 or 473/444–4217) has a Bertram 35 Sport Fisherman, *Xiphias Seeker,* with an air-conditioned cabin; equipment includes Penn International and Shimano reels. **True Blue Sportfishing** (☎ 473/444–2048) offers big-game charters on its "purpose-built" 31-ft Sport Fisherman, *Yes Aye.* It has an enclosed cabin, fighting chair, and professional tackle. Refreshments and courtesy transport are included.

WATER SPORTS

Hotels on Grand Anse Beach have water-sports centers where you can rent small sailboats, Windsurfers, and Sunfish (as well as beach chairs). At **Aquanauts Grenada** (⊠ Rendezvous Beach Resort, L'Anse aux Épines, ☎ 473/444–1126; ⊠ Spice Island Beach Resort, Grand Anse, ☎ 473/439–2500), instruction is available in English, German, Dutch, French, and Spanish. Two-tank dive trips, accommodating no more than eight divers, are offered each morning on both the Caribbean and Atlantic sides of Grenada. **Dive Grenada** (⊠ Flamboyant Hotel, Morne Rouge, ☎ 473/444–1092) offers dive trips at 10 AM and 2 PM, specializing in diving the *Bianca C.* **EcoDive** (⊠ Coyaba Beach Resort, Grand Anse, ☎ 473/444–7777) offers two dive trips daily, both drift and wreck dives, as well as weekly day trips to dive Isle de Rhonde. The company also runs Grenada's marine conservation and education center, which conducts coral-reef monitoring and turtle projects. **Sanvics Scuba** (⊠ Grenada Grand Beach Resort, Grand Anse, ☎ 473/444–4753) offers daily one- and two-tank dive trips to coral reefs, walls, and wreck sites.

Arawak Divers (⊠ Tyrrel Bay, Carriacou, ☎ 473/443–6906) has its own jetty at Tyrrel Bay; it takes small groups on daily dive trips and night dives and offers courses in German and English. **Carriacou Silver Diving** (⊠ Main St., Hillsborough, Carriacou, ☎ 473/443–7882) accommodates up to 12 divers on one of its dive boats and up to 6 on another. The center operates two guided single-tank dives daily, as well as individually scheduled excursions. **Tanki's Watersport Paradise Ltd.** (⊠ Paradise Beach, Carriacou, ☎ 473/443–8406) offers dive trips to nearby reefs and snorkeling trips to Sandy Island.

Beaches

Grenada has 45 white-sand beaches along its 80 mi (128 km) of coastline. All beaches are open to cruise passengers, and some great stretches of sand are just 10 minutes from the dock in St. George's. **Grand Anse Beach,** in the southwest, about 3 mi (5 km) south of St. George's, is Grenada's loveliest and most popular beach. It's a gleaming 2-mi (3-km) semicircle of white sand lapped by clear, gentle surf. Seagrape trees and coconut palms provide shady escapes from the sun. Brilliant rainbows frequently spill into the sea from the high green mountains that frame St. George's Harbour to the north. The Grand Anse Craft & Spice Market is at the midpoint of the beach. Just 1 mi (1½ km) south of Grand Anse Bay, ½-mi-long (1-km-long) **Morne Rouge Beach** has a gentle surf that is excellent for swimming. Light meals are available nearby.

Sandy Island, just off the shore of Carriacou, is a deserted island off Hillsborough—there's just a strip of white sand with a few palm trees, surrounded by a reef and crystal-clear waters. Anyone hanging around the jetty with a motorboat will provide transportation for a few dollars. Bring your snorkeling gear and, if you want, a picnic. Don't forget to arrange for your ride back to Carriacou.

Where to Eat

Restaurants add an 8% government tax to your bill and usually add a 10% service charge; if not, tip 10% to 15% for a job well done.

GRENADA

$–$$$ ✕ **Tout Bagay Restaurant & Bar.** Its name means "everything is possible," and the eclectic menu proves the point. At lunch, for example, you might select a salad (lobster, shrimp, Caesar) or try a local specialty, such as a roti, flying-fish sandwich, or creole-style fish. At dinner, the menu is equally broad—lobster thermidor, cappellini with red-pepper pesto and shrimp, curry goat, or sweet-and-sour lambi. On the water at the northern end of The Carenage, the view (day or night) is spectacular. It's a popular lunch choice for businesspeople, as well as those touring the capital or shopping on adjacent streets. ⊠ *The Carenage, St. George's,* ☎ *473/440–1500. MC, V.*

$$ ✕ **Coconut Beach Restaurant.** Take local seafood; add butter, wine, and Grenadian spices; and you have excellent French creole cuisine. Throw in a beautiful location at the northern end of Grand Anse Beach, and this West Indian cottage becomes an even more delightful spot. Lobster is a specialty; it might come wrapped in a crepe, dipped in garlic butter, or added to pasta. There are also the seafood platter, lambi Calypso, and T-bone steak. Homemade coconut pie is a winner. In season there's a beach barbecue with live music Wednesday and Sunday nights. ⊠ *Grand Anse,* ☎ *473/444–4644. AE, D, MC, V. Closed Tues.*

¢–$ ✕ **The Nutmeg.** Fresh seafood, homemade West Indian dishes, great hamburgers, and the waterfront view make this a favorite with locals and visitors. It's upstairs on The Carenage (above Sea Change bookstore), with large, open windows from which you can watch the harbor activity as you eat. Try the callaloo soup, curried lambi, lobster thermidor, grilled filet mignon—or just stop by for a rum punch and a roti, a fish sandwich and a Carib beer, or a hamburger and a Coke. ⊠ *The Carenage, St. George's,* ☎ *473/440–2539. AE, MC, V.*

CARRIACOU

¢–$$ ✕ **Callaloo by the Sea Restaurant & Bar.** On the main road, south of town, diners enjoy extraordinary views of Sandy Island and Hillsborough Bay. The emphasis is on West Indian dishes and seafood, including lobster thermidor. The callaloo soup, of course, is outstanding. ⊠ *Hillsborough,* ☎ *473/443–8004. AE, MC, V. Closed Sept.*

Jamaica

The third-largest island in the Caribbean, the English-speaking nation of Jamaica enjoys considerable self-sufficiency thanks to tourism, agriculture, and mining. Its physical attractions include jungle-covered mountains, clear waterfalls, and unforgettable beaches, yet the country's greatest resource may be its people. Although 95% of Jamaicans trace their bloodlines to Africa, their national origins also lie in Great Britain, the Middle East, India, China, Germany, Portugal, and South America, as well as in many other islands in the Caribbean. Their cultural life is a rich one—the music, art, and cuisine of Jamaica are vibrant with a spirit easy to sense but as hard to describe as the rhythms of reggae or the streetwise patois.

Don't let Jamaica's beauty cause you to relax the good sense you would use at home. Resist the promise of adventure should any odd character offer to show you the "real" Jamaica. Jamaica on the beaten track is wonderful enough, so don't take chances by wandering too far off it.

CURRENCY

Currency-exchange booths are set up on the docks at Montego Bay and Ocho Rios whenever a ship is in port. The U.S. dollar is accepted virtually everywhere, but change is made in Jamaican dollars (J$). At this writing the exchange rate was J$49.85 to US$1. Prices given below are in U.S. dollars unless otherwise indicated.

Direct telephone services are available in communication stations at the ports. Because of recent fraud problems, some U.S. phone companies (such as MCI) will not accept credit card calls placed from Jamaica. Phones take only Jamaican phone cards, available from kiosks or variety shops.

The following are good choices in Jamaica. They may not be offered by all cruise lines. Times and prices are approximate.

Appleton Estate Rum Tour. Travel to the Appleton Estate and tour the rum distillery there before enjoying a Jamaica buffet lunch. Usually offered on Montego Bay stops. ⊗ *7 hrs*, ▭ *$65*.

Croydon Estate Trip. Travel to Croydon Estate, a working plantation in Jamaica's rural interior. After a tour, enjoy a barbecue lunch and stop in Montego Bay for shopping on the way back to the ship. Usually offered on Montego Bay stops. ⊗ *6 hrs*, ▭ *$65*.

Prospect Plantation and Dunn's River Falls. Visit the beautiful gardens of Prospect Plantation; then stop at Dunn's River Falls to climb through the cool water. This is one of the most popular shore excursions in Jamaica for ships stopping in Ocho Rios. ⊗ *4 hrs*, ▭ *$46*.

Rafting on the Martha Brae River. Glide down this pristine river in a 30-ft, two-seat bamboo raft, admiring the verdant plant life along the river's banks. Usually offered for ships stopping in Ocho Rios or Montego Bay. ⊗ *5 hrs*, ▭ *$50*.

Coming Ashore
IN MONTEGO BAY
Some ships use Montego Bay, 108 km (67 mi) west of Ocho Rios, as their Jamaican port of call. The cruise port in Montego Bay is a $10 taxi ride from town; however, there's one shopping center within walking distance of the docks. The Jamaica Tourist Board office is about 3½ mi (5½ km) away on Gloucester Avenue on Doctor's Cave Beach.

IN OCHO RIOS
Most cruise ships dock at this port on Jamaica's north coast, near Dunn's River Falls. Less than 1 mi (2 km) from the Ocho Rios pier are the Taj Mahal Duty-Free Shopping Center and the Ocean Village Shopping Center, where the Jamaica Tourist Board maintains an office. Getting anywhere else in Ocho Rios will require a taxi.

Some of Jamaica's taxis are metered; rates are per car, not per passenger. You can flag cabs on the street. All licensed and properly insured taxis display red Public Passenger Vehicle (PPV) plates. Licensed minivans also bear the red PPV plates. If you hire a taxi driver as a tour guide, be sure to agree on a price before the vehicle is put into gear. Because of the cost of insurance, which you must buy since most credit cards offering coverage exclude Jamaica, it's expensive to rent a car; you may also find it difficult to arrange a rental on-island. It's far easier to arrange a taxi.

Exploring Jamaica
Numbers in the margin correspond to points of interest on the Jamaica map.

MONTEGO BAY
❶ **Greenwood Great House.** Although this historic home has no spooky legend to titillate, it's much better than Rose Hall at evoking life on a

Jamaica

Mahoe Bay

Cornwall Beach
Doctor's Cave Beach
Walter Fletcher Beach
Airport Reef

3 **1**

Falmouth

Discovery Bay

Runaw
Bay

Puerta Seco
Beach

Duncans

Donald Sangster
International
Airport

Pedro Pt.

Lucea

A1

Barnett Estates

Montego Bay

Clark's
Town

Brown'
Town

B1

Green
Island

Sandy
Bay

2

Alexandria

Glasgow

B8

Montpelier

Albert
Town

B3

Long Bay

B6

Balaclava

Christiana

Negril
Beach

Negril

Savanna-
la-Mar

A2

*Southwest
Pt.*

Bluefields
Beach

Bluefields

B6

Santa
Cruz

Mandeville

Middle
Quarters

Black R.

A2

Black River

Crane Beach

Alligator
Pond

*Treasure
Beach*

A

Treasure Beach

*Great Pedro
Bluff*

*Old
Woman's
Pt.*

Long Bay

N

0   10 miles
0   15 km

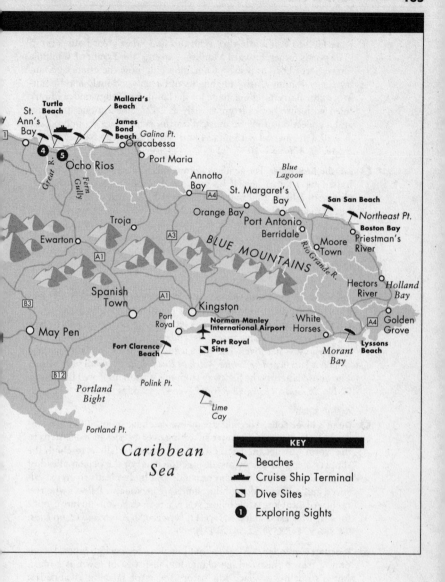

St. Ann's Bay

Turtle Beach

Mallard's Beach

James Bond Beach

Galina Pt.

4 5

Oracabessa

Ocho Rios

Port Maria

Annotto Bay

A4

St. Margaret's Bay

Blue Lagoon

San San Beach

Orange Bay

Northeast Pt.

A3

Port Antonio

Berridale

Boston Bay

Priestman's River

Troja

BLUE MOUNTAINS

Moore Town

Rio Grande R.

Ewarton

A1

Hectors River

Holland Bay

Spanish Town

A1

Kingston

Port Royal

Norman Manley International Airport

White Horses

Golden Grove

A4

B3

May Pen

Port Royal Sites

Fort Clarence Beach

Morant Bay

Lyssons Beach

B12

Portland Bight

Polink Pt.

Lime Cay

Portland Pt.

Caribbean Sea

KEY	
Beaches	
Cruise Ship Terminal	
Dive Sites	
❶	Exploring Sights

sugar plantation. The Barrett family, from whom the English poet Elizabeth Barrett Browning descended, once owned all the land from Rose Hall to Falmouth; they built this and other great houses on it. (The poet's father, Edward Moulton Barrett, "the Tyrant of Wimpole Street," was born at nearby Cinnamon Hill, now the estate of country singer Johnny Cash.) Highlights of Greenwood include oil paintings of the Barretts, china made for the family by Wedgwood, a library filled with rare books from as early as 1697, fine antique furniture, and a collection of exotic musical instruments. There's a pub on-site as well. Greenwood is 15 mi (24 km) east of Montego Bay. ⊠ *Greenwood,* ☎ *876/953–1077.* ☒ *$12.* ☉ *Daily 9–6.*

❷ **Martha Brae River.** The gentle waterway takes its name from an Arawak Indian who killed herself because she refused to reveal the whereabouts of a local gold mine to the Spanish. According to legend, she agreed to take them there and, on reaching the river, used magic to change its course, drowning herself and the greedy Spaniards with her. Her *duppy* (ghost) is said to guard the mine's entrance. Rafting on this river is a popular activity. Martha Brae River Rafting arranges trips downriver. Near the rafting company ticket office you'll find gift shops, a bar and restaurant, and a swimming pool.

❸ **Rose Hall.** In the 1700s, Rose Hall may have been the greatest of great houses in the West Indies. Today it's popular less for its architecture than for the legend surrounding its second mistress: Annie Palmer was credited with murdering three husbands and a *busha* (plantation overseer) who was her lover. The story is told in a novel that's sold everywhere in Jamaica: *The White Witch of Rose Hall.* There's a pub on-site. The house is across the highway from the Wyndham Rose Hall resort. ⊠ *North Coast Hwy.,* ☎ *876/953–2341.* ☒ *$15.* ☉ *Daily 9–6.*

OCHO RIOS

❹ **Dunn's River Falls.** The falls are an eye-catching sight: 600 ft (184 m) of cold, clear mountain water splashing over a series of stone steps to the warm Caribbean. The best way to enjoy the falls is to climb the slippery steps: don a swimsuit, take the hand of the person ahead of you, and trust that the chain of hands and bodies leads to an experienced guide. The leaders of the climbs are personable fellows who reel off bits of local lore while telling you where to step; you can hire a guide for a tip of a few dollars. ⊠ *Off A1, between St. Ann's and Ocho Rios,* ☎ *876/974–2857.* ☒ *$6.* ☉ *Daily 9–5.*

❺ **Prospect Plantation.** To learn about Jamaica's former agricultural economy, a trip to this working plantation, just west of town, is a must. But it's not just a place for history lovers or farming aficionados; everyone seems to enjoy the views over the White River Gorge and the tour by jitney (a canopied open-air cart pulled by a tractor). The grounds are full of exotic fruits and tropical trees, some planted by such celebrities as Winston Churchill and Charlie Chaplin. You can also go horseback riding on the plantation's 900 acres or play miniature golf, grab a drink in the bar, or buy souvenirs in the gift shop. ⊠ *Hwy. A1,* ☎ *876/994–1058.* ☒ *$12.* ☉ *Daily 8–5; tours Mon.–Sat. at 10:30, 2, and 3:30, Sun. at 11, 1:30, and 3.*

Shopping

Jamaican artisans express themselves in silk-screening, wood carvings, resort wear, hand-loomed fabrics, and paintings. Jamaican rum makes a great gift, as do Tia Maria (the famous coffee liqueur) and Blue Mountain coffee.

Before visiting the crafts markets in Montego Bay and Ocho Rios, consider how much tolerance you have for pandemonium and price haggling. If you're looking to spend money, head for City Centre Plaza, Half Moon Village, Holiday Inn Shopping Centre, Montego Bay Shopping Center, St. James's Place, or Westgate Plaza in Montego Bay; in Ocho Rios, go to Pineapple Place, Ocean Village, the Taj Mahal, Coconut Grove, and Island Plaza. Some cruise lines run shore excursions that focus on shopping.

Gallery of West Indian Art (✉ 11 Fairfield Rd., Montego Bay, ☎ 876/ 952–4547) is the place to find Jamaican and Haitian paintings. A corner of the gallery is devoted to hand-turned pottery (some painted) and beautifully carved and painted birds and animals. **Harmony Hall** (✉ Hwy. A1, Ocho Rios, ☎ 876/975–4222), an 8-minute drive east of the main part of town, is a restored great house where Annabella Proudlock sells her unique wooden boxes (their covers are decorated with reproductions of Jamaican paintings). Also on sale—and magnificently displayed—are larger reproductions of paintings, lithographs, and signed prints of Jamaican scenes, and hand-carved wooden combs. Harmony Hall is also known for its shows of local artists' work.

Outdoor Activities & Sports

GOLF

Montego Bay has more good options for golf than Ocho Rios, but there are a couple of courses in Ocho Rios that are easily accessible and worth the effort. The 18-hole course at **Breezes Runaway Bay** (✉ North Coast Hwy., Runaway Bay, ☎ 876/973–7319) has hosted many championship events (greens fees are $80 for nonguests; guests play for free). **Half Moon Golf, Tennis, and Beach Club** (✉ Montego Bay, ☎ 876/953–3105), a Robert Trent Jones–designed 18-hole course 7 mi (11 km) east of town, is the home of the Red Stripe Pro Am (greens fees are $130 for nonguests). **Ironshore** (✉ Montego Bay, ☎ 876/953–2800), 3 mi (5 km) east of the airport, is an 18-hole links-style course (the greens fees are $50). The golf course at **Sandals Golf and Country Club** (✉ Ocho Rios, ☎ 876/ 975–0119) is 700 ft (214 m) above sea level (greens fees for 18 holes are $100, or $70 for 9 holes for nonguests). **Tryall Golf, Tennis, and Beach Club** (✉ North Coast Hwy., Sandy Bay, ☎ 876/956–5681), 15 mi (24 km) west of Montego Bay, has an 18-hole championship course on the site of a 19th-century sugar plantation (greens fees are $115 for nonguests).

HORSEBACK RIDING

Jamaica is fortunate to have an outstanding equestrian facility in **Chukka Cove** (✉ Ocho Rios, ☎ 876/972–2506, WEB www.chukkablue. com). This resort offers riding, polo, and jumping (starting at $50), as well as hour-long trail rides ($30) and three-hour beach rides ($55). During in-season weekends this is the place for polo (and social) action. **Prospect Plantation** (✉ Ocho Rios, ☎ 876/974–2058) offers horseback riding for $20 per hour, but reservations are required. You can saddle up for $30–$50 at the **Rocky Point Riding Stables at Half Moon** (✉ Montego Bay, ☎ 876/953–2286), which is east of the Half Moon Club.

Beaches

There are several good beaches near Montego Bay. A lively beach with lots of places that sell food and drink, **Cornwall Beach** also has a water-sports concession. **Doctor's Cave Beach** has been spotlighted in so many travel articles and brochures that it often resembles Florida during spring break. On the bright side, the 5-mi (8-km) strand has much to offer beyond sugary sand, including changing rooms, water sports, colorful if overly insistent vendors, and plenty of places to grab a snack. Near the center of town, there's protection from the surf on a windy day and therefore unusually fine swimming at **Walter Fletcher Beach;** the calm waters make it a good bet for children.

East of Ocho Rios in the village of Oracabessa is **James Bond Beach,** which is popular because of the reggae performances that take place on its bandstand. **Turtle Beach,** stretching behind the Renaissance Jamaica Grande, is the busiest beach in Ocho Rios (where the islanders come to swim).

Where to Eat

Many restaurants add a 10% service charge to the bill. Otherwise, a tip of 10% to 20% is customary.

$$–$$$ ✕ **Sugar Mill.** Seafood is served with flair at this terrace restaurant at the Half Moon Golf, Tennis, and Beach Club. Caribbean specialties, steak, and lobster are usually offered in a pungent sauce that blends Dijon mustard with Jamaica's own Pickapeppa sauce. Otherwise, the best choices are the daily à la carte specials and anything flame-grilled. Live music and a well-stocked wine cellar round out the experience. ⊠ *Half Moon Golf, Tennis, and Beach Club, North Coast Rd., Montego Bay, 7 mi (11 km) east of town,* ☎ *876/953–2228. Reservations essential. AE, MC, V.*

$–$$$ ✕ **Almond Tree.** One of the most popular restaurants in Ocho Rios, the Almond Tree has a menu of Jamaican and Continental favorites: pumpkin soup, pepper pot, and wonderful preparations of fresh fish, veal *piccata,* and fondue. The swinging rope chairs of the terrace bar and the tables perched above a Caribbean cove are great fun. ⊠ *83 Main St., Ocho Rios,* ☎ *876/974–2813. Reservations essential. AE, DC, MC, V.*

$–$$$ ✕ **Evita's Italian Restaurant.** The large windows of this hilltop 1860s gingerbread house open to cooling mountain breezes and stunning views of city and sea. More than 30 kinds of pasta range from lasagna Rastafari (vegetarian) and fiery jerk spaghetti to *rotelle colombo* (crabmeat with white sauce and noodles). Other excellent choices include sautéed fillet of red snapper with orange sauce, scampi and lobster in basil-cream sauce, red snapper stuffed with crabmeat, and tasty grilled sirloin with mushroom sauce. Kids under 12 eat for half price, and light eaters will appreciate half-portion orders. The restaurant offers free transportation from area hotels. ⊠ *Mantalent Inn, Eden Bower Rd., Ocho Rios* ☎ *876/974–2333. AE, MC, V.*

¢–$$ ✕ **The Native.** Shaded by a large poinciana tree and overlooking Gloucester Avenue, this open-air stone terrace serves Jamaican and international dishes. To go native, start with smoked marlin, move on to the *boonoonoonoos* platter (a sampler of local dishes), and finish with coconut pie or *duckanoo* (a sweet dumpling of cornmeal, coconut, and banana wrapped in a banana leaf and steamed). Entertainers and candlelit tables make this a romantic choice for dinner on weekends. The popular afternoon buffets on Friday and Sunday are family affairs. ⊠ *29 Gloucester Ave., Montego Bay,* ☎ *876/979–2769. Reservations essential. AE, MC, V.*

¢–$ ✕ **Ocho Rios Village Jerk Centre.** This blue-canopied, open-air eatery is a good place to park yourself for frosty Red Stripe beer and fiery jerk pork, chicken, or seafood. Milder barbecued meats, also sold by weight (typically, ¼ or ½ pound makes a good serving), turn up on the fresh daily chalkboard menu posted on the wall. It's lively at lunch and popular with cruise-ship passengers. ⊠ *DaCosta Dr., Ocho Rios,* ☎ *876/974–2549. MC, V.*

Key West, Florida

The southernmost city in the continental United States was originally a Spanish possession. Along with the rest of Florida, Key West became part of American territory in 1821. In the late 19th century, Key West was Florida's wealthiest city per capita. The locals made their fortunes from "wrecking."—rescuing people and salvaging cargo from ships that foundered on nearby reefs. Cigar making, fishing, shrimping, and sponge gathering also became important industries.

Capital of the self-proclaimed "Conch Republic," Key West today makes for a unique port of call for the 10 or so ships that visit each week. A genuinely American town, it nevertheless exudes the relaxed atmosphere and pace of a typical Caribbean island. Major attractions for cruise passengers are the home of the Conch Republic's most famous citizen, Ernest Hemingway; the imposing Key West Museum of Art & History, a former U.S. Customs House and site of the military inquest of the USS *Maine*; and, if your cruise ship stays in port late enough, the island's renowned sunset celebrations.

CURRENCY

The U.S. dollar is the only currency accepted in Key West.

TELEPHONES

Public phones are found at the pier and on street corners. Local calls from most public phones cost 35¢.

SHORE EXCURSIONS

The following are good choices in Key West. They may not be offered by all cruise lines. Times and prices are approximate.

Historic Key West Walking Tour. You'll see the Harry S. Truman Little White House, the Hemingway House, and the Audubon House and Gardens on a short guided stroll through the historic district. ⊙ 1½ hrs, ▣ $19.

Reef Snorkeling. The last living coral reefs in Continental America are your destination on a catamaran. Changing facilities, snorkeling gear, and beverages are included. ⊙ 3 hrs, ▣ $44.

Coming Ashore

Cruise ships dock at Mallory Square or near the Truman Annex. Both are within walking distance of Duval and Whitehead streets, the two main tourist thoroughfares. Because Key West is so easily explored on foot, there is rarely a need to hire a cab. If you plan to venture beyond the main tourist district, a fun way to get around is by bicycle or scooter. Key West is a cycling town. In fact, there are so many bikes around that cyclists must watch out for one another as much as for cars. **Keys Moped & Scooter** (⊠ 523 Truman Ave., ☎ 305/294–0399) rents beach cruisers with large baskets as well as scooters. Rates start at $15 for three hours. Look for the huge American flag on the roof. **Moped Hospital** (⊠ 601 Truman Ave., ☎ 305/296–3344) supplies balloon-tire bikes with yellow safety baskets for adults and kids, as well as mopeds and double-seater scooters for adults.

For maps and other tourist information, drop by the **Greater Key West Chamber of Commerce** (⊠ 402 Wall St., Key West 33040, ☎ 305/294–2587 or 800/527–8539), which is just off Mallory Square.

The **Conch Tour Train** (☎ 305/294–5161) is a 90-minute narrated tour of Key West, traveling 14 mi through Old Town and around the island. Board at Mallory Square and Flagler Station (901 Caroline St.) every half hour (9–4:30 from Mallory Square, later at other stops). The cost is $20. **Old Town Trolley** (⊠ 6631 Maloney Ave., Key West, ☎ 305/296–6688) operates trackless trolley-style buses, departing from the Mallory Square and Roosevelt Boulevard depots every 30 minutes (9:15–4:30 from Mallory Square, later at other stops), for 90-minute narrated tours of Key West. The smaller trolleys go places the train won't fit. You may disembark at any of nine stops and reboard a later trolley. The cost is $20.

Exploring Key West

Numbers in the margin correspond to points of interest on the Key West map.

⑥ Audubon House and Gardens. If you've ever seen an engraving by ornithologist John James Audubon, you'll understand why his name is synonymous with birds. See his work in this three-story house, which was built in the 1840s for Captain John Geiger but now commemorates Audubon's 1832 stop in Key West while he was traveling through Florida to study birds. Several rooms of period antiques and a children's room are also of interest. Admission includes an audiotape (in English, French, German, or Spanish) for a self-guided tour of the house and tropical gardens, complemented by an informational booklet and signs that identify the rare indigenous plants and trees. ⊠ *205 Whitehead St.,* ☎ *305/294–2116,* WEB *www.audubonhouse.com.* ⌑ *$9.* ☾ *Daily 9:30–5.*

⑦ Duval Street Wreckers Museum. Most of Key West's early wealthy residents made their fortunes from the sea. Among them was Francis Watlington, a sea captain and wrecker, who in 1829 built this house, alleged to be the oldest house in South Florida. Six rooms are open, furnished with 18th- and 19th-century antiques and providing exhibits on the island's wrecking industry of the 1800s, which made Key West one of the most affluent towns in the country. ⊠ *322 Duval St.,* ☎ *305/294–9502.* ⌑ *$5.* ☾ *Daily 10–4.*

⑤ Harry S Truman Little White House Museum. In a letter to his wife during one of his visits, President Harry S. Truman wrote, "Dear Bess, you should see the house. The place is all redecorated, new furniture and everything." If he visited today, he'd write something similar. There is a photographic review of visiting dignitaries and permanent audiovisual and artifact exhibits on the Florida Keys as a presidential retreat, starting with Ulysses Grant in 1880 and ending with George Bush in the 1990s. Tours lasting 45 minutes begin every 15 minutes. On the grounds of **Truman Annex,** a 103-acre former military parade grounds and barracks, the home served as a winter White House for Presidents Truman, Eisenhower, and Kennedy. The two-bedroom Presidential Suite with a verandah and sundeck is available for a novelty overnight stay. ⊠ *111 Front St.,* ☎ *305/ 294–9911,* WEB *www.trumanlittlewhitehouse.com.* ⌑ *$10.* ☾ *Daily 9–5, grounds 8–sunset.*

⑧ Hemingway Home and Museum. Guided tours of Ernest Hemingway's home are full of anecdotes about the author's life in the community and his household quarrels with wife Pauline. While residing here between 1931 and 1942, Hemingway wrote about 70% of his life's work, including *For Whom the Bell Tolls.* Few of the family's belongings remain, but photographs help illustrate his life, and scores of descendants of Hemingway's cats have free reign of the property. Literary buffs should be aware that there are no curated exhibits from which to gain much insight into Hemingway's writing career. Tours begin every 10 minutes and take 25–30 minutes; then you're free to explore on your own. ⊠ *907 Whitehead St.,* ☎ *305/294–1136,* WEB *www. hemingwayhome.com.* ⌑ *$10.* ☾ *Daily 9–5.*

⑩ Historic Seaport at the Key West Bight. What used to be a funky—in some places even seedy—part of town is now an 8½-acre restoration project of 100 businesses, including waterfront restaurants, open-air people- and dog-friendly bars, museums, clothing stores, bait shops,

Key West, Florida

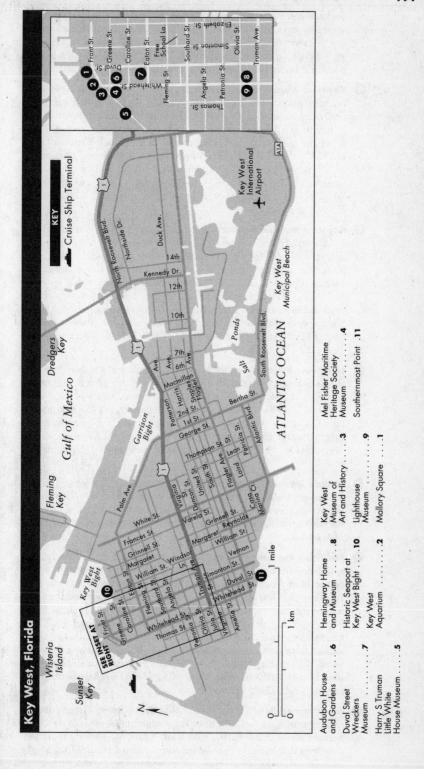

KEY

🚢 Cruise Ship Terminal

Gulf of Mexico

ATLANTIC OCEAN

Key West Municipal Beach

Key West International Airport

Audubon House
and Gardens 6

Duval Street
Wreckers
Museum 7

Harry S Truman
Little White
House Museum 5

Hemingway Home
and Museum 8

Historic Seaport at
Key West Bight ...10

Key West
Aquarium 2

Key West
Museum of
Art and History 3

Lighthouse
Museum 9

Mallory Square ...1

Mel Fisher Maritime
Heritage Society
Museum 4

Southernmost Point .11

SEE INSET AT RIGHT

docks, a marina, a wedding chapel, the Waterfront Market, the Key West Rowing Club, and dive shops. It's all linked by the 2-mi waterfront **Harborwalk**, which runs between Front and Grinnell streets, passing big ships, schooners, sunset cruises, fishing charters, and glass-bottom boats. Additional construction continues on outlying projects.

2 Key West Aquarium. Explore the underwater realm of the Keys without getting wet at this kid-friendly aquarium. Hundreds of brightly colored tropical fish and sea creatures live here. A touch tank enables you to handle starfish, sea cucumbers, horseshoe and hermit crabs, even horse and queen conchs—living totems of the Conch Republic. Built in 1934 by the Works Progress Administration as the world's first open-air aquarium, most of the building has been enclosed for all-weather viewing. Guided tours include shark feedings. ⊠ *1 Whitehead St.,* ☎ *305/296–2051,* WEB *www.keywestaquarium.com.* ☞ *$9.* ☉ *Daily 9–6; tours at 11, 1, 3, and 4:30.*

3 Key West Museum of Art and History. When Key West was designated a U.S. port of entry in the early 1820s, a customs house was established. Salvaged cargoes from ships wrecked on the reefs could legally enter here, thus setting the stage for Key West to become the richest city in Florida. Following a $9 million restoration, the imposing redbrick and terra-cotta Richardsonian Romanesque–style U.S. Customs House reopened as a museum. Its main gallery displays major rotating exhibits. Smaller galleries have long-term and changing exhibits about the history of Key West. ⊠ *281 Front St.,* ☎ *305/295–6616,* WEB *www.kwahs. com.* ☞ *$6.* ☉ *Daily 9–5.*

9 Lighthouse Museum. For the best view in town and a history lesson at the same time, climb the 88 steps to the top of this 92-ft lighthouse. It was built in 1847. About 15 years later, a Fresnel lens was installed at a cost of $1 million. The keeper lived in the adjacent 1887 clapboard house, which now exhibits vintage photographs, ship models, nautical charts, and lighthouse artifacts from all along the Key reefs. ⊠ *938 Whitehead St.,* ☎ *305/294–0012.* ☞ *$8.* ☉ *Daily 9:30–5 (last admission at 4:30).*

1 Mallory Square. The central meeting point in old Key West is named for Stephen Mallory, secretary of the Confederate Navy, who later owned the Mallory Steamship Line. On nearby Mallory Dock, a nightly sunset celebration draws street performers, food vendors, and thousands of onlookers.

4 Mel Fisher Maritime Heritage Society Museum. In 1622, two Spanish galleons loaded with riches from South America foundered in a hurricane 40 mi west of the Keys. In 1985, Mel Fisher recovered the treasures from the lost ships, the *Nuestra Señora de Atocha* and the *Santa Margarita.* In this museum, see, touch, and learn about some of the artifacts, including a gold bar weighing 6.3 troy pounds and a 77.76-carat natural emerald crystal worth almost $250,000. Exhibits on the second floor rotate and might cover slave ships, including the excavated 17th-century *Henrietta Marie,* or the evolution of Florida maritime history. ⊠ *200 Greene St.,* ☎ *305/294–2633,* WEB *www.melfisher. org.* ☞ *$9.* ☉ *Daily 9:30–5.*

11 Southernmost Point. At the foot of Whitehead Street, a huge concrete marker proclaims this spot to be the southernmost point in the continental United States. Turn left on South Street. To your right are two dwellings that both claim to be the Southernmost House. Take a right onto Duval Street, which ends at the Atlantic Ocean, and you will be at the Southernmost Beach.

Shopping

Passengers looking for T-shirts, trinkets, and other souvenirs will find them along Duval Street and around the cruise-ship piers. **Fast Buck Freddie's** (⊠ 500 Duval St., ☎ 305/294–2007) sells a classy, hip selection of crystal, furniture, tropical clothing, and every flamingo item imaginable. It also carries such imaginative items as a noise-activated rat in a trap and a raccoon tail in a bag. **Key West Aloe** (⊠ 524 Front St., ☎ 305/294–5592 or 800/445–2563; factory store: ⊠ Greene and Simonton Sts.) was founded in a garage in 1971; today it produces some 300 perfume, sunscreen, and skin-care products for men and women. Also visit the factory store. They expanded the **Key West Island Bookstore** (⊠ 513 Fleming St., ☎ 305/294–2904), the literary bookstore of the large Key West community writers' group. It carries new, used, and rare titles and specializes in Hemingway, Tennessee Williams, and South Florida mystery writers. **Lucky Street Gallery** (⊠ 1120 White St., ☎ 305/294–3973) sells high-end contemporary paintings, watercolors, and jewelry by internationally recognized, Key West–based artists.

Outdoor Activities & Sports

BOAT TOURS

M/V *Discovery* (⊠ Land's End Marina, 251 Margaret St., ☎ 305/293–0099) offers glass-bottom boat rides for $30. *Pride of Key West* (⊠ 2 Duval St., ☎ 305/296–6293) is a 65-ft glass-bottom boat, offering rides for $30.

FISHING

Key West Bait and Tackle (⊠ 241 Margaret St., ☎ 305/292–1961) carries live bait, frozen rigged and unrigged bait, and fishing and rigging equipment. It also has the Live Bait Lounge; unwind and sip ice-cold beer while telling tall tales after fishing. Be sure to ask why the marlin on the roof is red. Captain Steven Impallomeni works as a flats-fishing guide, specializing in ultralight and fly-fishing for tarpon, permit, and bonefish, as well as near-shore and light-tackle fishing. Charters on the *Gallopin' Ghost* leave from **Murray's Marina** (⊠ MM 5, Stock Island, ☎ 305/292–9837).

GOLF

Key West Resort Golf Course (⊠ 6450 E. College Rd., ☎ 305/294–5232) is an 18-hole course on the bay side of Stock Island. Nonresident fees are $140 for 18 holes (cart included) in season, $80 off-season.

SCUBA DIVING & SNORKELING

Adventure Charters & Tours (⊠ 6810 Front St., ☎ 305/296–0362 or 888/817–0841) has sail-and-snorkel coral reef adventure tours ($30) aboard the 42-ft trimaran sailboat *Fantasea,* with a maximum of 16 people. There are two daily departures and sometimes one at sunset. **Captain's Corner** (⊠ 125 Ann St., 33040, ☎ 305/296–8865), a PADI five star–rated shop, has dive classes in several languages and twice-daily snorkel and dive trips to reefs and wrecks aboard the 60-ft dive boat *Sea Eagle.*

Beaches

Key West doesn't have any great swimming beaches, but there are a few that might be worth a visit. **Fort Zachary Taylor State Historic Site** (⊠ end of Southard St., through Truman Annex) has an uncrowded beach, which is the best in Key West. There is an adjoining picnic area with barbecue grills and shade trees. Small **Simonton Street Beach** (⊠ north end of Simonton St.), facing the gulf, is a great place to watch boat traffic in the harbor. Parking, however, is difficult. There are rest rooms and a boat ramp. **Smathers Beach** (⊠ S. Roosevelt Blvd.) has nearly 2 mi of sand, rest rooms, picnic areas, and volleyball courts, all of which make it popular with the spring-break crowd. Trucks along the road rent rafts, Windsurfers, and other beach "toys." **South Beach** (✉ foot of Duval St.), on the Atlantic, is also known as City Beach. It's popular with travelers staying at nearby motels but has limited parking.

Where to Eat

$$–$$$$ ✕ **Louie's Backyard.** Feast your eyes on a steal-your-breath-away view and beautifully presented dishes prepared by executive chef Doug Shook. The winter menu might include grilled catch of the day with ginger butter, tomato chutney, and five-spice fried onions. Louie's key lime pie has a pistachio crust and is served with a raspberry coulis. Come for lunch if you're on a budget; the menu is less expensive and the view is just as fantastic. For night owls, the Afterdeck Bar serves cocktails on the water until the wee hours. ✉ *700 Waddell Ave.,* ☎ *305/294– 1061. AE, DC, MC, V.*

$–$$$ ✕ **Alice's at LaTeDa.** Chef-owner Alice Weingarten serves breakfast, brunch, lunch, and dinner poolside with live evening entertainment. It's right in the middle of LaTeDa Hotel, an in-vogue, gay-friendly hotel-bar complex. Her talent shows in her exemplary selection of wines that complement the creative mix of seafood, game, beef, pork, and poultry dishes. She's as confident serving Aunt Alice's magic meat loaf as she is whipping up an aromatic pan-roasted Mediterranean chicken served over baby wild greens, kalamata olives, and feta cheese. The bar is as popular as the dining room. ✉ *1125 Duval St.,* ☎ *305/296– 6706. AE, D, MC, V. No lunch Mon.*

$–$$$ ✕ **Rick's Blue Heaven.** There's much to like about this historic restaurant where Hemingway once refereed boxing matches and customers watched cockfights. Fresh eats are served in the house and the big leafy yard. Specials include blackened grouper or lobster with citrus beurre blanc; there are vegetarian options and Caribbean dishes. Desserts and breads are baked on-site. There's a shop and bar, the latter named after the water tower hauled here in the 1920s. Expect a line—everybody knows how good this is. ✉ *305 Petronia St.,* ☎ *305/296–8666. Reservations not accepted. D, MC, V.*

Nightlife

Three spots stand out for first-timers among the saloons frequented by Key West denizens. All are within easy walking distance of the cruise-ship piers. In its earliest incarnation, in 1851, **Capt. Tony's Saloon** (✉ 428 Greene St., ☎ 305/294–1838) was a morgue and icehouse. After housing Key West's first telegraph station, it became, in the mid-1930s, the original Sloppy Joe's. Later, a young Jimmy Buffett sang here. Bands play nightly. There's more history and good times at **Sloppy Joe's** (✉ 201 Duval St., ☎ 305/294–5717), the successor to the famous speakeasy named for its founder, Captain Joe Russell. Ernest Hemingway came here to gamble and tell stories. Decorated with Hemingway memorabilia and marine flags, the bar is popular with travelers and is full and noisy all the time. Musicians perform daily, noon–2 AM. The **Schooner Wharf Bar** (✉ 202 William St., ☎ 305/292–9520), an open-air waterfront bar and grill in the historic seaport district, retains its funky Key West charm, and it doesn't sell T-shirts. There's live music all day, plus happy hour and special events.

Martinique

Martinique is lush with wild orchids, frangipani, anthurium, jade vines, flamingo flowers, and hundreds of hibiscus varieties. Trees bend under the weight of tropical fruits such as mangoes, papayas, lemons, limes, and bright-red West Indian cherries. Acres of banana plantations, pineapple fields, and waving sugarcane stretch to the horizon.

The towering mountains and verdant rain forest in the north lure hikers, while underwater sights and sunken treasures attract snorkelers and scuba divers. Martinique is also wonderful if your idea of exercise is turning over every 10 minutes to get an even tan and your taste in adventure runs to duty-free shopping.

The largest of the Windward Islands, Martinique is 4,261 mi (6,817 km) from Paris, but its spirit and language are decidedly French, with more than a soupçon of West Indian spice. Tangible, edible evidence of the fact is the island's cuisine, a superb blend of French and creole.

Fort-de-France is the capital, but at the turn of the 20th century, St-Pierre, farther up the coast, was Martinique's premier city. In 1902, volcanic Mont Pelée blanketed the city in ash, killing all its residents except a condemned prisoner. Today, the ruins are a popular excursion for cruise passengers.

CURRENCY

The French franc is no longer. It has been replaced by the euro (€). U.S. dollars are accepted in some hotels, but it's better to convert money. Banks give a more favorable rate than hotels. A currency exchange service that also offers a favorable rate is Change Caraïbes. If you are cashing less than $100, it is usually better to go to the exchange or to use your ATM card. Prices given below are in U.S. dollars unless otherwise indicated.

TELEPHONES

There are no coin-operated phone booths. Public phones now use a *télécarte,* which you can buy at post offices, café-tabacs, hotels, and at *bureaux de change.* To call the United States, dial 00 + 1, the area code, and the local number. You can make collect calls to Canada through the Bell operator; you can get the AT&T or MCI operator from special-service phones at the cruise ports and in town. These phones are blue; there's one at the Super Sumo snack bar, on rue de la Liberté, near the library. **AT&T** (☎ 800/99–00–11). **Bell** (☎ 800/99–00–16). **MCI** (☎ 800/99–00–19).

Shore Excursions

The following are good choices but may not be offered by all cruise lines. Times and prices are approximate.

Bat Caves and Snorkel. A catamaran trip to the bat caves, followed by an opportunity to snorkel near a colorful reef. ☉ *3 hrs,* 🖃 *$45.*

Canyoning Adventure. A popular soft-adventure option is a trip to a canyon in Martinique's rain forest, where you will rappel down a cliff face and hike through the thick vegetation. ☉ *4½ hrs,* 🖃 *$79.*

Four-by-Four Adventure. You'll travel in a four-wheel-drive vehicle to explore the rain forest on the slopes of Mont Pelée. Includes a stop at a rum distillery and usually a beach. ☉ *5 hrs,* 🖃 *$68.*

Island Tour including St-Pierre. By bus or taxi, drive through the lush green mountains, past picturesque villages, to St-Pierre, stopping at the museum there. This is one of the best island tours in the Caribbean. ☉ *4 hrs,* 🖃 *$65.*

Coming Ashore

Cruise ships call at the Maritime Terminal east of Fort-de-France. The only practical way to get into town is by cab ($15 round-trip). To reach the Maritime Terminal tourist information office, turn right and walk along the waterfront. Large ships that anchor in the Baie des Flamands tender passengers to the Fort-de-France waterfront. It is always advisable to check in with the tourist office, which is staffed with friendly,

helpful, English-speaking personnel and is just across the street from
the landing pier, in the Air France building. Ask about the guided walking tours that can be arranged at the nearby open-air market.

Before hiring a taxi driver, especially for an island tour, see if his or
her English is up to par, especially if your French isn't. Taxis are metered, and there's no extra charge for extra passengers. The minimum
charge is about $1.50, but a journey of any distance can cost $25 or
more, and traffic in Fort-de-France can be nightmarish. The alternative costs just $6 round-trip, takes only 25 minutes each way, and is
most pleasant. It is the ferry, or *vedette,* leaving the city from quai d'Esnambuc and docking at the marina of Le Hotel Méridien. It runs as
frequently as every half hour. Also, ferries from the quai run between
Anse-Mitan and Anse-à-l'Ane.)

Renting a car in Fort-de-France is possible, but the heavy traffic can
be forbidding. Rates start at $60 per day for a car with manual trans-
mission; those with automatic transmissions are substantially more expensive and rarely available.

There's a 40% surcharge on taxis in effect between 8 PM and 6 AM and
on Sunday. Drivers of **M. Marital Mercedes taxis** (☎ 0596/64–20–24;
0696/45–69–07 mobile) speak English and Spanish as well as French,
but using a radio taxi is going to cost more than hailing one on the street.

Exploring Martinique

*Numbers in the margin correspond to points of interest on the Mar-
tinique map.*

A nice way to see the lush island interior and St-Pierre is to take the
N3, which snakes through dense rain forests, north through the mountains to Le Morne Rouge, then take the coastal N2 back to Fort-de-
France via St-Pierre. You can do the 40-mi (64-km) round-trip in an
afternoon—that is if you don't get lost, can comprehend the road signs,
avoid collisions in the roundabouts, drive as fast as the flow of frenetic
traffic, and can ask directions in French (probably of someone on the
street who only speaks a creole patois). In other words, hire a driver.
Tell him which of these routes you'd like while pointing to a map.

❹ Ajoupa-Bouillon. This flower-filled 17th-century village amid pineapple fields is the jumping-off point for several sights. The Saut Babin is
a 40-ft-high (12-m-high) waterfall, half an hour's walk from Ajoupa-
Bouillon. The Gorges de la Falaise is a river gorge where you can swim.
Les Ombrages botanical gardens has marked trails that traverse the
rain forest. ⊠ *Ajoupa-Bouillon.* 🎟 €3.36. ☉ *Daily 9–5:30.*

❷ Balata. This quiet town has two sights worth visiting. Built in 1923 to
commemorate those who died in World War I, **Balata Church** is an exact
replica of Paris's Sacré-Coeur Basilica. The **Jardin de Balata** (Balata Gardens), created in the 19702 by landscaper and horticulturist Jean-
Philippe Thoze, has thousands of varieties of tropical flowers and
plants. There are shaded benches from which to take in the mountain
view. You can order anthurium and other flowers to be delivered to the
airport. ⊠ *Rte. de Balata,* 🎟 0596/64–48–73. 🎟 €7. ☉ *Daily 9–5.*

❶ Fort-de-France. With its historic fort and superb location beneath the
towering Pitons du Carbet on the Baie des Flamands, Martinique's
capital—home to about one-third of the island's 360,000 inhabitants—
should be a grand place. It isn't. The most pleasant districts, such as
Didier, Bellevue, and Schoelcher, are on the hillside, and you need a car
to reach them. But don't come through town if you rent a car; you may
find yourself trapped in gridlock in the warren of narrow streets in the
center of town, which is especially bad on cruise-ship days. Parking is

difficult, and it's best to try for one of the parking garages or—as a second choice—outside public parking areas. A taxi is a good alternative.

There are some good shops with Parisian wares (at Parisian prices) and lively street markets that sell, among other things, human hair for wigs (starting price: €40). Near the harbor is a marketplace where local crafts and souvenirs are sold. Going to town can be fun, but the heat, exhaust fumes, and litter tend to make exploring here a chore rather than a pleasure. At night the city feels dark and gloomy, with little street life except for the extravagantly dressed prostitutes who openly parade the streets after 10 PM. If you plan to go out, it's best to go with a group.

The heart of Fort-de-France is **La Savane,** a 12½-acre park filled with trees, fountains, and benches. It's a popular gathering place and the scene of promenades, parades, and impromptu soccer matches. Along the east side are snack wagons. Alas, it is no longer a desirable oasis, what with a lot of litter and other problems often found in urban parks. A statue of Pierre Belain d'Esnambuc, leader of the island's first settlers, is unintentionally upstaged by Vital Dubray's vandalized—now headless—white Carrara marble statue of the empress Joséphine, Napoléon's first wife. The most imposing historic site is **Fort St-Louis,** which runs along the east side of La Savane. It's open Monday–Saturday 9–3, and admission is €4. Across from La Savane, you can catch the ferry *La Vedette* for the beaches at Anse-Mitan and Anse-à-l'Ane and for the 20-minute run across the bay to Pointe du Bout. It costs just €6 and is stress-free—much safer, more pleasant, and faster than by car.

The **Bibliothèque Schoelcher** is the wildly elaborate Romanesque public library. It's named after Victor Schoelcher, who led the fight to free the slaves in the French West Indies. The eye-popping structure was built for the 1889 Paris Exposition, after which it was dismantled, shipped to Martinique, and reassembled piece by ornate piece. ⊠ *Corner of rue de la Liberté (runs along west side of La Savane) and rue Perrinon,* ☎ *0596/70–26–67.* ⊡ *Free.* ☉ *Mon. 1–5:30, Tues.–Fri. 8:30–5:30, Sat. 8:30–noon.*

Le Musée Régional d'Histoire et d'Ethnographie is housed in an elaborate former residence (circa 1888) with balconies and fretwork. It has everything from displays of the garish gold jewelry that prostitutes wore after emancipation to reconstructed rooms of a home of proper, middle-class Martinicans. There is even a display of madras creole headdresses with details of how they were tied to indicate if a woman was single, married, or otherwise occupied. ⊠ *10 bd. General de Gaulle,* ☎ *0596/72–81–87.* ⊡ *€4.* ☉ *Mon. and Wed.–Fri. 2–5, Tues. 8–5, Sat. 8–noon.*

Rue Victor Schoelcher runs through the center of the capital's primary shopping district, a six-block area bounded by rue de la République, rue de la Liberté, rue de Victor Severe, and rue Victor Hugo. Stores sell Paris fashions and French perfume, china, crystal, liqueurs, and local handicrafts. The Romanesque **St-Louis Cathedral** (⊠ rue Victor Schoelcher), with its lovely stained-glass windows, was built in 1878, the sixth church on this site (the others were destroyed by fire, hurricane, and earthquake). The Galerie de Biologie et de Géologie at the **Parc Floral et Culturel,** in the northeastern corner of the city center, will acquaint you with the island's exotic flora. There's also an aquarium. The park contains the island's official cultural center, where there are sometimes free evening concerts. ⊠ *Pl. José-Marti, Sermac,* ☎ *0596/ 71–66–25.* ⊡ *Grounds free; aquarium €5.60; botanical and geological gallery €1.12.* ☉ *Park daily dawn–10 PM; aquarium daily 9–7; gallery Tues.–Fri. 9:30–12:30 and 3:30–5:30, Sat. 9–1 and 3–5.*

198

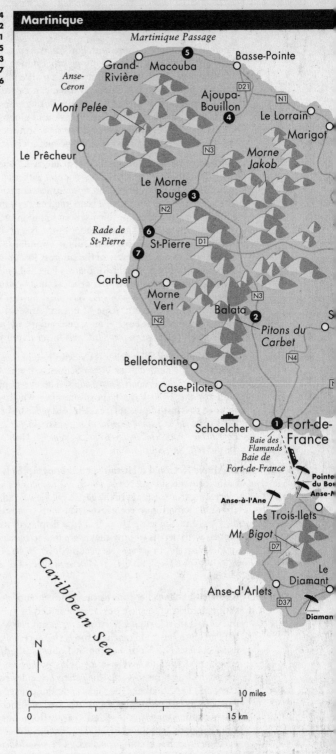

Martinique

Martinique Passage

Grand-Rivière

Macouba **5**

Basse-Pointe

Anse-Ceron

Ajoupa-Bouillon **4**

D21

N1

Le Lorrain

Mont Pelée

Marigot

Le Prêcheur

Morne Jakob

N3

Le Morne Rouge **3**

N2

St-Pierre **6** D1

Rade de St-Pierre **7**

Carbet

Morne Vert

N2

Balata **2**

N3

Pitons du Carbet

N4

Bellefontaine

Case-Pilote

S

Schoelcher

1 Fort-de-France

Baie des Flamands

Baie de Fort-de-France

Pointe du Bo

Anse-M

Anse-à-l'Ane

Les Trois-Ilets

Mt. Bigot

D7

Caribbean Sea

Le Diamant

Anse-d'Arlets

D37

Diaman

N

0   10 miles

0   15 km

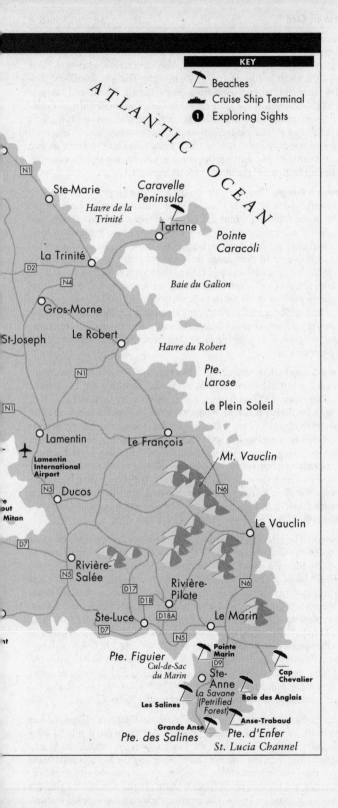

KEY

Beaches

Cruise Ship Terminal

1 Exploring Sights

ATLANTIC OCEAN

N1

Ste-Marie

Havre de la Trinité

Caravelle Peninsula

Tartane

Pointe Caracoli

La Trinité

D2

N4

Baie du Galion

Gros-Morne

Le Robert

St-Joseph

Havre du Robert

Pte. Larose

N1

Le Plein Soleil

N1

Lamentin

Lamentin International Airport

Le François

Mt. Vauclin

N6

N5

Ducos

re out

Mitan

Le Vauclin

D7

Rivière-Salée

N5

D17

Rivière-Pilote

N6

D18

Ste-Luce

D18A

Le Marin

D7

N5

nt

Pte. Figuier

Cul-de-Sac du Marin

Pointe Marin

D9

Ste-Anne

Cap Chevalier

Baie des Anglais

Les Salines

La Savane (Petrified Forest)

Grande Anse

Anse-Trabaud

Pte. des Salines

Pte. d'Enfer

St. Lucia Channel

❺ Macouba. Named after the Carib word for "fish," this village was a prosperous tobacco town in the 17th century. Its clifftop location affords magnificent views of the sea, the mountains, and—on clear days—the neighboring island of Dominica. The **JM Distillery** produces some of the best *vieux rhum* on the island. A tour and samples are free. Macouba is the starting point for a spectacular drive, the 6-mi (9½-km) **route to Grand' Rivière** on the northernmost point. This is Martinique at its greenest: groves of giant bamboo, cliffs hung with curtains of vines, and 7-ft (2-m) tree ferns that seem to grow as you watch them. At the end of the road is Grand' Rivière, a colorful, sprawling fishing village at the foot of high cliffs.

❸ Le Morne Rouge. This town sits on the southern slopes of the volcano that destroyed it in 1902. Today it's a popular resort spot and offers hikers some fantastic mountain scenery. From Le Morne Rouge you can start the climb up the 4,600-ft (1,406-m) **Mont Pelée.** But don't try it without a guide unless you want to get buried under pumice stones. Instead, drive up to the Refuge de l'Aileron. From the parking lot it's a mile (2 km) up a well-marked trail to the summit. Bring a sweatshirt, because there's often a mist that makes the air damp and chilly. From the summit follow the route de la Trace (Route N3), which winds south of Le Morne Rouge to St-Pierre. It's steep and winding, but that didn't stop the *porteuses* of old: balancing a tray, these women would carry up to 100 pounds of provisions on their heads for the 15-hour trek to the Atlantic coast.

❼ Musée Gauguin. Martinique was a brief station in Paul Gauguin's wanderings but a decisive moment in the evolution of his art. He arrived from Panama in 1887 with friend and fellow painter Charles Laval and, having pawned his watch at the docks, rented a wooden shack on a hill above the village of Carbet. Dazzled by the tropical colors and vegetation, Gauguin developed a style that directly anticipated his Tahitian paintings. Disappointingly, this modest museum has only reproductions, and an exhibit of letters and documents relating to the painter. Also remembered here is the writer Lafcadio Hearn. In his endearing book *Two Years in the West Indies* he provides the most extensive description of the island before St-Pierre was buried in ash and lava. ⊠ *Anse-Turin, Carbet,* ☎ *0596/78–22–66.* ▱ *€4.* ⊙ *Daily 9–5:30.*

❻ St-Pierre. The rise and fall of St-Pierre is one of the most remarkable stories in the Caribbean. Martinique's modern history began here in 1635. By the turn of the 20th century St-Pierre was a flourishing city of 30,000, known as the Paris of the West Indies. As many as 30 ships at a time stood at anchor. It was the most modern town in the Caribbean, with electricity, phones, and a tram. On May 8, 1902, two thunderous explosions rent the air. As the nearby volcano erupted, Mont Pelée split in half, belching forth a cloud of burning ash, poisonous gas, and lava that raced down the mountain at 250 mph. At 3,600°F, it instantly vaporized everything in its path; 30,000 people were killed in two minutes. One man survived. His name was Cyparis, and he was a prisoner in an underground cell in the town's jail. He was pardoned and became a sideshow attraction in the Barnum & Bailey Circus.

Today St-Pierre is trying to reinvent itself. An Office du Tourisme has been built, as well as a seafront promenade. There are plenty of sidewalk cafés, and you can stroll the main streets and check the blackboards before deciding where to lunch, or go up the hill to a restaurant where the view is spectacular. At night some places have live music. Like stage sets for a dramatic opera, there are the ruins of the island's first church (built in 1640), the imposing theater, the toppled statues. This city, situated on its naturally beautiful harbor and with its narrow, winding streets, has the feel of a European seaside hill town. Although a lot of the oldest buildings need work, stark modernism has not invaded this burg. As much potential as it has, this is one town in Martinique where real estate is cheap—for obvious reasons.

Musée Vulcanologique Frank Perret, established 30 years after the eruption, houses photographs of the old town, documents, and relics—some gruesome—excavated from the ruins, including molten glass, melted iron, and contorted clocks stopped at 8 AM. ⊠ *Rue de Victor Hugo,* ☎ *0596/78–15–16.* ⌑ *€3.* ☉ *Daily 9–5.*

The *Cyparis Express* is a small tourist train that runs through the city, hitting the important sights with a running narrative (in French). ⊠ *Pl. des Ruines du Figuier,* ☎ *0596/55–50–92.* ⌑ *€9.* ☉ *Departs hourly, weekdays 9:30–1 and 2:30–5:30.*

An excursion to **Depaz Distillery** is one of the island's nicest treats. For four centuries it has been at the foot of the volcano. The great house was destroyed in the 1902 eruption, but soon after it was rebuilt and the fields were replanted. A self-guided tour includes the workers' gingerbread cottages, and an exhibit of art and sculpture made from wooden casks and parts of distillery machinery. Products sold in the tasting room include golden and aged rum (notably Rhum Dore) and distinctive liqueurs made from ginger and basil. ⊠ *Mont Pelée Plantation,* ☎ *0596/78–13–14.*

Shopping
French products, such as perfume, wines, liquors, designer scarves (Hermès, for example), leather goods, and crystal, are good buys in Fort-de-France. Luxury goods are discounted 20% when paid for with traveler's checks or major credit cards. Look for creole gold jewelry; white, dark, flavored, and aged rums; and handcrafted straw goods, pottery, madras fabric, and tapestries. Shops that sell luxury items are abundant around the cathedral in Fort-de-France, particularly on rue Victor Hugo, rue Moreau de Jones, rue Antoine Siger, and rue Lamartine. **Cadet Daniel** (⊠ 72 rue Antoine Siger, Fort-de-France, ☎ 0596/71–41–48) sells Lalique, Limoges, and Baccarat. **Centre des Métiers d'Art** (⊠ Rue Ernest Deproge, Fort-de-France, ☎ 0596/70–25–01) exhibits local arts and crafts. **Galerie Arti-Bijoux** (⊠ 89 rue Victor Hugo, Fort-de-France, ☎ 0596/63–10–62) has unusual and excellent Haitian art—paintings, sculptures, ceramics, and intricate jewelry cases. **Roger Albert** (⊠ 7 rue Victor Hugo, Fort-de-France, ☎ 0596/71–71–71) carries designer crystal and perfumes.

Outdoor Activities & Sports
FISHING
Fish cruising these waters include tuna, barracuda, dolphinfish, kingfish, bonito, and the big game—white and blue marlins. **Bleu Marine Evasion** (⊠ Le Diamant, ☎ 0596/76–46–00) offers fishing excursions and day sails. The owner of the **Limited Edition** (⊠ Marina du Marin, Le Marin, ☎ 0596/76–24–20 or 0696/98–48–68), a fully loaded Davis 47-ft fishing boat, goes out with five anglers for $150 per person for a half day, or a $260 for a full day.

GOLF
The **Golf Country Club de la Martinique** (⊠ Les Trois-Ilets, ☎ 0596/68–32–81) has a par-71, 18-hole Robert Trent Jones–designed course with an English-speaking pro, a pro shop, bar, and restaurant. The club offers special greens fees to cruise-ship passengers. Normal greens fees are $46; an electric cart costs another $46. For those who don't mind walking while admiring the Caribbean view between the palm trees, club trolleys are $6. There are no caddies.

HIKING

The island has 31 marked hiking trails. At the beginning of each, a notice is posted advising on the level of difficulty, the duration of a hike, and any interesting points to note. The **Parc Naturel Régional de la Martinique** (⌧ 9 bd. Général de Gaulle, Fort-de-France, ☎ 0596/73–19–30) organizes inexpensive guided excursions year-round.

HORSEBACK RIDING

At **Black Horse Ranch** (⌧ Les Trois-Ilets, ☎ 0596/68–37–80), 1-hour trail rides ($22) go into the countryside and across waving cane fields; two hours on the trail ($32) brings riders near the beach. Only western saddles are used. Semi-private lessons ($32 per person) are in French or English. **Ranch Jack** (⌧ Anse-d'Arlets, ☎ 0596/68–37–69) has trail rides (English saddle) across the countryside for $22 an hour; for $43 (which includes beverages), half-day excursions go through the country and forest to the beach. Little English is spoken at **Ranch de Trois Caps** (⌧ Ste-Anne, ☎ 0596/74–70–65), but for $36 you can ride (western) for two hours on the wild southern beaches and across the countryside. Rides go out in the morning and afternoon every day but Monday. Reservations are recommended.

Beaches

All of Martinique's beaches are open to the public, but hotels charge a fee for nonguests to use changing rooms and facilities. Topless bathing is prevalent at the large resort hotels. Unless you're an expert swimmer, steer clear of the Atlantic waters, except in the area of Cap Chevalier and the Caravelle Peninsula—an incredibly beautiful area, with cliffs that stagger down to the sea. **Anse-à-l'Ane** has picnic tables and a nearby shell museum. Cool off in the bar of Le Calalou hotel. You'll find golden sand and excellent snorkeling at **Anse-Mitan.** Family-owned bistros are half hidden among palm trees nearby. **Pointe du Bout** has small, manmade beaches that are lined with luxury resorts, including the Sofitel Bakoua. **Les Salines,** a 1½-mi (2½-km) cove of soft white sand lined with coconut palms, is a short drive south of Ste-Anne, which is about an hour from Fort-de-France. Les Salines is awash with families and children during holidays and on weekends, but quiet and uncrowded during the week—even at the height of the winter season. This beach, especially the far end, is most appealing.

Where to Eat

All restaurants include a 15% service charge in their prices. Leaving a little extra gives Americans a good name.

$$ ✕ **Le Grange Inn.** Nearly every item is cooked over the open grill: top-quality meats, fish, and fresh jumbo crayfish, and with five sauces, from *chien* to beurre blanc, available. A fun starter is the chicken wings in a Bacardi and brown sugar sauce. The prix-fixe menus, at several price levels, represent a good value. A kids' menu offers crispy fried fish or chicken tenders rub-a-dub style (with peanut sauce). You'll find a large and good selection of French wines. The circular redbrick bar has promoted many friendships. ⌧ *Village Créole, Pointe du Bout, Les Trois-Ilets,* ☎ *0596/66–01–66. AE, MC, V.*

$$ ✕ **Mille Et Une Brindilles.** At this trendy salon, aromatic pots of tea come in flavors like vanilla and black currant, as well as Darjeeling and other favorites. These complement some of the best-ever desserts, like the cocoa-dusted *marquise au chocolat*. Several *fraicheurs* offer a litany of tapenades, olive cakes, flans, and so on for lunch. Fred, the cute, bubbly Parisian who is both chef and proprietress, is the queen of terrines and can make a delicious pâté out of anything—vegetable, fish, or meat. For non-teetotalers, there are cocktails, beer, and wine. With red walls, the decor is Moroccan à la Paris flea market. ⌧ *27 rue du*

Prof. R. Garcin, Rte. de Didier, Didier, Fort-de-France, ☎ *596/71–75–61. No credit cards. No dinner except on the last Fri. of each month.*

¢–$$　✕ **Le Fromager.** To reach this restaurant from the port, take a left at Font St-Denis and ask your car to climb the steep hill. Once you park and walk down a long set of stairs, you will be rewarded with a superb, 360° harbor view and cooling breezes. Tables in the open-air dining room are covered in white lace, in contrast to the big bamboo wall adornments. Chef Nancy's avocado stuffed with saltfish and farina rests on banana leaves and is *the* best. The *écrevisses Columbo* (curried crayfish) are remarkable. Her husband René happily dispenses pastis, punch coco, or that perfect half-bottle of Sancerre. ✉ *Quartier St-James, St-Pierre,* ☎ *0596/78–19–07. MC, V.*

Nassau, Bahamas

Nassau, the capital of the Bahamas, has witnessed Spanish invasions and hosted pirates, who made it their headquarters for raids along the Spanish Main. The American navy seized Fort Montagu here in 1776, when it won a victory without firing a shot. The heritage of old Nassau blends the Southern charm of British loyalists from the Carolinas, the African tribal traditions of freed slaves, and a bawdy history of blockade-running during the Civil War and rum-running in the Roaring '20s. Over it all is a subtle layer of civility and sophistication, derived from three centuries of British rule.

Reminders of the island's British heritage are everywhere in Nassau. Court justices sport wigs and scarlet robes. The police wear colonial garb: starched white jackets, red-striped navy trousers, and tropical pith helmets. Traffic keeps to the left, and the spoken language has a British-colonial lilt, softened by a slight drawl. Nassau's charm, however, is often lost in its commercialism. There's excellent shopping, but if you look past the duty-free shops, you'll also find sights of historical significance that are worth seeing.

CURRENCY

The Bahamian dollar ($ or B$) is the official currency. Since the U.S. dollar is universally accepted, however, there's no need to acquire Bahamian money. Prices quoted throughout this chapter are in U.S. dollars unless otherwise indicated.

TELEPHONES

Calling locally or internationally is easy in the Bahamas. To place a local call, dial the seven-digit phone number. To call the United States, dial 1 plus the area code. Pay phones cost 25¢ per call; Bahamian and U.S. quarters are accepted, as are BATELCO phone cards. To place a call using a calling card, use your long-distance carrier's access code or dial 0 for the operator.

Shore Excursions

The following are good choices in Nassau. Times and prices are approximate.

Day at Atlantis Beach. After a 30-minute harbor tour, you will be taken to the Atlantis Resort on Paradise Island and given a day pass, which entitles you to a beach chair and towel, admission to the aquarium, and lunch at a beachside restaurant. ⊙ *6 hrs,* 🎫 *$68.*

Dolphin Encounter. Close Encounter excursions are offered on Blue Lagoon Island (Salt Cay), just east of Paradise Island. Sit on a platform with your feet in the water while dolphins play around you, or wade in the waist-deep water to get up close and personal with them. Trainers are available to answer questions. Swim-with-the-Dolphins offers a half hour for you to interact with these friendly creatures. ◷ *3 hrs,* 🚌 *$93.*

Nassau and Ardastra Gardens. Take a tour of historic Nassau and then stop at Ardastra Gardens and Conservation Center, a tropical zoo. ◷ *2½ hrs,* 🚌 *$33.*

Sailing and Snorkeling. This snorkeling trip takes you offshore to Spruce Cay or Ahtoll Island, where you will see a maze of boulders and corals inhabited by colorful angelfish and sponges. After snorkeling, you'll be served a rum punch. ◷ *3½ hrs,* 🚌 *$41.*

Coming Ashore

Cruise ships dock at one of three piers on Prince George's Wharf. Taxi drivers who meet the ships may offer you a $2 ride into town, but the historic government buildings and duty-free shops lie just steps from the dock area. As you leave the pier, look for a tall pink tower—diagonally across from here is the tourist information office. Stop in for maps of the island and downtown Nassau. On most days you can join a one-hour walking tour ($10 per person) conducted by a well-trained guide. Tours generally start every hour on the hour from 10 AM to 4 PM; confirm the day's schedule in the office. Just outside, an ATM dispenses U.S. dollars.

As you disembark from your ship, you will find a row of taxis and air-conditioned limousines. Fares are fixed by the government by zones. The fare is $6 for trips within downtown Nassau and around Paradise Island; $9 from downtown Nassau to Paradise Island (which includes the bridge toll); $8 from Paradise Island to downtown Nassau; and $18 from Cable Beach to Paradise Island, including toll ($17 for the return trip). Fares cover two passengers; each additional passenger is $3, regardless of destination. It is customary to tip taxi drivers 15%. You can also hire a car or small van for sightseeing for $45 to $60 per hour or about $13 per person.

Beautifully painted horse-drawn carriages will take as many as four people around Nassau at a rate of $10 per person for a 20-minute ride; don't hesitate to bargain. Most drivers give a comprehensive tour of the Bay Street area while delivering an extensive history lesson. You'll find the surreys on Woodes Rogers Walk, in the center of Rawson Square.

Two people can ride around the island on a motor scooter for about $40 for a half day, $50 for a full day. Helmets for both driver and passenger and insurance are mandatory and are included in the rental price. Many hotels have scooters on the premises. There are stands in Rawson Square.

To get to Paradise Island on your own, take the ferry from the dock area ($3 each way).

Exploring Nassau
Numbers in the margins correspond to points of interest on the Nassau map.

Nassau's sheltered harbor bustles with cruise-ship hubbub, while a block away, broad, palm-lined Bay Street is alive with commercial activity. Shops angle for tourist dollars with fine imported goods at duty-free prices, yet you will find a handful of stores overflowing with authentic Bahamian crafts, foods, and other delights. Most of Nassau's historic sites are centered around downtown.

With its thoroughly revitalized downtown—the revamped British Colonial Hilton lead the way—Nassau is recapturing some of its glamour. Nevertheless, modern influence is apparent: fancy restaurants, suave

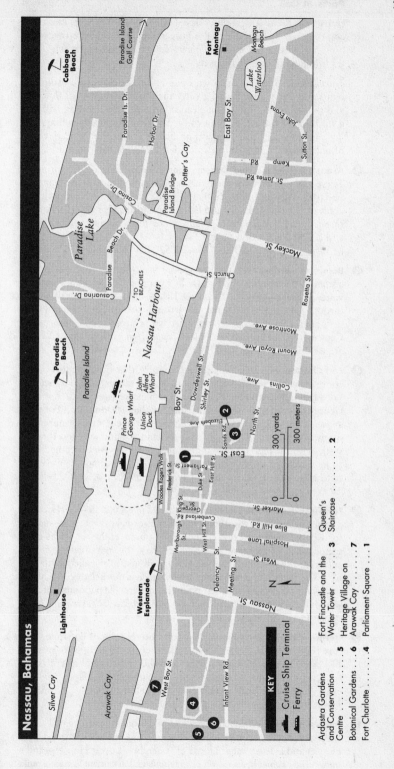

Nassau, Bahamas

Silver Cay

Lighthouse

Arawak Cay

Cabbage Beach

Paradise Island Golf Course

Fort Montagu

Montagu Beach

Paradise Island Bridge

Paradise Is. Dr.

Harbor Dr.

Paradise Island

Potter's Cay

Lake Waterloo

East Bay St.

Casino Dr.

Beach Dr.

Paradise Lake

Paradise Dr.

Casuarina Dr.

TO BEACHES

Nassau Harbour

Mackey St.

Church St.

St. James Rd.

Kemp Rd.

Sutton St.

John Evans

Paradise Beach

Rosetta St.

Montrose Ave.

Mount Royal Ave.

Collins Ave.

North St.

Prince George Wharf

John Alfred Wharf

Union Dock

Bay St.

Dowdeswell St.

Shirley St.

Elizabeth Ave.

Sands Rd.

East St.

Woodes Rogers Walk

Parliament St.

Frederick St.

Duke St.

East Hill St.

Market St.

①
②
③

0   300 yards
0   300 meters

King St.

George St.

Cumberland Rd.

Hospital Lane

Blue Hill Rd.

Marlborough St.

West Hill St.

West St.

Delancy St.

Meeting St.

Nassau St.

N

Western Esplanade

West Bay St.

Infant View Rd.

⑦

④

⑤ **⑥**

KEY

⚓ Cruise Ship Terminal

⛴ Ferry

Ardastra Gardens
and Conservation
Centre **5**

Botanical Gardens . . . **6**

Fort Charlotte **7**

Fort Fincastle and the
Water Tower **3**

Heritage Village on
Arawak Cay **6**

Parliament Square . . . **4**

Queen's
Staircase **2**

clubs, and trendy coffeehouses have popped up everywhere. This trend comes partly in response to the burgeoning upper-crust crowds that now supplement the spring-breakers and cruise passengers who have traditionally flocked to Nassau.

Today the seedy air of the town's not-so-distant past is almost unrecognizable. Petty crime is no greater than in other towns of this size, and the streets not only look cleaner but feel safer. You can still find a wild club or a rowdy bar, but you can also sip cappuccino while viewing contemporary Bahamian art or dine by candlelight beneath prints of old Nassau, serenaded by soft, island-inspired calypso music.

❺ Ardastra Gardens and Conservation Centre. Marching flamingos? These national birds of the Bahamas give a parading performance at Ardastra daily at 10:30, 2:10, and 4:10. The zoo, with more than 5 acres of tropical greenery and flowering shrubs, also has an aviary of rare tropical birds, native Bahamian creatures such as rock iguanas, and a global collection of small animals. ⊠ *Chippingham Rd., south of W. Bay St.,* ☏ *242/323–5806.* 🎫 *$12.* ⊙ *Daily 9–5.*

❻ Botanical Gardens. Six hundred species of flowering trees and shrubs, a small cactus garden, and two fresh-water ponds filled with with lilies, water plants, and tropical fish cover 18 acres. The many trails that wind through the gardens are perfect for leisurely strolls. The Botanical Gardens are across the street from the Ardastra Gardens and Conservation Centre, home of Nassau's zoo. ⊠ *Chippingham Rd., south of W. Bay St.,* ☏ *242/323–5975.* 🎫 *$1.* ⊙ *Weekdays 8–4, weekends 9–4.*

❹ Fort Charlotte. Built in the late 18th century, this imposing fort comes complete with a waterless moat, drawbridge, ramparts, and dungeons. Lord Dunmore, who built it, named the massive structure in honor of George III's wife. Some contemporaries called it Dunmore's Folly because of the staggering cost of its construction; eight times more than originally planned. (Dunmore's superiors in London were less than ecstatic with the high costs, but he managed to survive unscathed.) No shots were ever fired in battle from the fort. It is about 1 mi west of central Nassau. ⊠ *W. Bay St. at Chippingham Rd.,* ☏ *242/325–9186.* 🎫 *Free.* ⊙ *Tours daily 8–4.*

❸ Fort Fincastle and the Water Tower. Shaped like a paddle-wheel steamer and perched near the top of the Queen's Staircase, Fort Fincastle—named for Royal Governor Lord Dunmore (Viscount Fincastle)—was completed in 1793 to serve as a lookout post for marauders trying to sneak into the harbor. It served as a lighthouse in the early 19th century. The fort's 126-ft-tall water tower, which is more than 200 ft above sea level, is the island's highest point. From here, the panorama of Nassau and its harbor is spectacular. ⊠ *Top of Elizabeth Ave. hill, south of Shirley St.* 🎫 *Water tower $1.* ⊙ *Daily 8–5.*

❼ Heritage Village on Arawak Cay. For a literal taste of Bahamian culture throughout the island chain, take the slightly long walk west on Bay Street to this cluster of eateries and shops. You can buy crafts and food, especially squeaky-fresh conch salad, often made before your very eyes. An ice-cold Kalik beer makes the perfect foil. ⊠ *W. Bay St.* 🎫 *Free.* ⊙ *Daily.*

❶ Parliament Square. Nassau is the seat of national government. The Bahamian Parliament comprises two houses—a 16-member Senate (Upper House) and a 40-member House of Assembly (Lower House)—and a ministerial cabinet headed by a prime minister. Parliament Square's pink, colonnaded government buildings were constructed in the early 1800s by loyalists who came to the Bahamas from North Carolina. The square is dominated by a statue of a slim young Queen Victoria that was erected on her birthday, May 24, in 1905. In the immediate area are a half dozen magistrates' courts (open to the public; obtain a pass at the door to view a session). Behind the House of Assembly is the **Supreme Court.** Its four-times-a-year opening ceremonies (held the first weeks of January, April, July, and October) recall the wigs and mace-bearing pageantry of the British Houses of Parliament. The Royal Bahamas Police Force Band is usually on hand for the event. ⊠ *Bay St.* ☎ *242/322–3315 for information on Supreme Court ceremonies,* ▨ *Free.* ⊙ *Weekdays 10–5:30.*

② **Queen's Staircase.** These 66 steps are thought to have been carved out of the solid limestone cliff by slaves in the 1790s. The staircase was later named to honor Queen Victoria's 65-year reign. Recent innovations include a waterfall cascading from the top and an ad hoc straw market along the narrow road that leads to the site. ⊠ *Top of Elizabeth Ave. hill, south of Shirley St.*

Shopping

Forbes magazine once claimed that the cities with the best buys on wristwatches were Hong Kong and Nassau. Most of the stores selling these and other duty-free items are clustered along an eight-block stretch of Bay Street in Old Nassau and on a few downtown side streets. Most stores are open Monday–Saturday 9–5 and accept credit cards.

On Bay Street at Market Street, the **Straw Market** has convened for hundreds of years. After a disastrous fire in 2001, it relocated to a nearby concrete structure. Its counterpart on Paradise Island, **BahamaCraft Centre,** is set up in a collection of colorful kiosks. The straw markets carry inexpensive straw and carved items, plus T-shirts and other souvenir apparel and jewelry.

Doongalik Studios Gallery (⊠ Village Rd., ☎ 242/394–1886) showcases Bahamian fine art, crafts, and culture in an old-Bahamian setting with a focus on the islands' annual Junkanoo festival.

Outdoor Activities & Sports

FISHING

The waters here are generally smooth and alive with many species of game fish, which is one of the reasons why the Bahamas has more than 20 fishing tournaments open to visitors every year. A favorite spot just west of Nassau is the Tongue of the Ocean, so called because it looks like that part of the body when viewed from the air. The channel stretches for 100 mi. For boat rental, parties of two to six will pay $300 or so for a half day, $600 for a full day.

Born Free Charters (☎ 242/393–4144) has three boats and guarantees a catch on full-day charters—if you don't get a fish, you don't pay. **Brown's Charters** (☎ 242/324–1215) specializes in shark fishing trips, as well as reef and deep-sea fishing. The **Charter Boat Association** (☎ 242/393–3739) has 15 boats available for fishing charters. **Chubasco Charters** (☎ 242/324–3474, ᵂᴱᴮ www.chubascocharters.com) has two boats for sportfishing and shark-fishing charters. **Nassau Yacht Haven Marina** (☎ 242/393–8173, ᵂᴱᴮ www.nassauyachthaven.com) runs fishing charters out of its 150-slip marina.

GOLF

Cable Beach Golf Club (⊠ Cable Beach), at 7,040 yards and with a par of 72, is the oldest golf course in the Bahamas. It recently underwent a major renovation to improved playability. The links are owned by the Radisson Cable Beach Casino & Golf Resort. **Ocean Club Golf Course** (⊠ Paradise Island Dr., Paradise Island, ☎ 242/363–6682 800/321–

3000 in the U.S.), formerly the Paradise Island Golf Club, has undergone a major redesign by Tom Weiskopf. The 6,805-yard, par-72 championship course is surrounded by the ocean on three sides, which means that winds can get stiff. Call to check on current availability and up-to-date prices (those not staying at Atlantis or the Ocean Club may find themselves shut out completely). Fairways are narrow at the **South Ocean Golf Club** (☎ 242/362–4391 Ext. 23) on New Providence's secluded southern coast. The course (6,707 yards, par 72) was designed by Joe Lee and built in 1969.

PARASAILING

Premier Watersports (☎ 242/324–1475; 242/427–0939 cellular) lifts you off a platform and into the skies for five to eight minutes. Ask for Captain Tim or his crew on Cabbage Beach in front of the large hotels.

Beaches

New Providence is blessed with stretches of white sand studded with palm and sea-grape trees. Some of the beaches are small and crescent-shaped; others stretch for miles. On the north side of the island lies Paradise Island's showpiece, **Cabbage Beach,** which is popular with locals and tourists and is the home of most of the island's resorts. The beach rims the north coast from the Atlantis lagoon to Snorkeler's Cove. At the north end you can rent Jet Skis and nonmotorized pedal boats and go parasailing. **Cable Beach** is on New Providence's north shore, about 3 mi west of downtown Nassau. Resorts line much of this beautiful, broad swath of white sand, but there is public access. Jet-skiers and beach vendors abound, so don't expect quiet isolation. Just west of Cable Beach is a rambling pink house on the Rock Point promontory, where much of the 1965 James Bond movie *Thunderball* was filmed.

Downtown, the **Western Esplanade** sweeps westward from the British Colonial Hotel on Bay Street (a 10-minute walk from the cruise-ship pier). It's just across the street from shops and restaurants, and it has rest rooms, a snack bar, and changing facilities. **Paradise Beach** stretches for more than 1½ km (1 mi) on the western end of Paradise Island.

Where to Eat

$$$$ ✕ **Graycliff.** A meal at Graycliff—an experience that lingers in the memory—begins in the elegant parlor, where, over live piano music, drinks are served and orders taken; when your appetizer is ready, you're escorted into one of several dining rooms. Signature dishes here include lamb medallions and the thermidor-style Lobster Graycliff. The clientele includes presidents and celebrities, but the prices are, surprisingly, no higher than those at other top-notch Nassau restaurants, except for wine: the cellar contains more than 175,000 bottles, some running into the tens of thousands of dollars, handpicked by owner Enrico Garzaroli, a connoisseur par excellence. Finish with a hand-rolled cigar produced in Graycliff's own factory. ⊠ *W. Hill St. at Cumberland Rd., across from Government House,* ☎ *242/322–2796 or 800/688–0076,* WEB *www.graycliff.com. AE, MC, V. No lunch weekends.*

$$–$$$ ✕ **The Poop Deck.** Just east of the bridge from Paradise Island and a quick cab ride from the center of town is this favorite haunt of locals. Breezy tables on the large waterfront deck scan the vista of the Bahamas's largest marina. The restaurant's popularity has resulted in a second Poop Deck on Cable Beach's west end, but for residents, this is still the place. Expect spicy dishes with such names as Mama Mary's Steamed Fish and Rosie's Chicken; there's also an extensive wine list. Save room for guava duff and a calypso coffee spiked with secret ingredients. ⊠ *E. Bay St., at Nassau Yacht Haven Marina, east of bridge from Paradise Island,* ☎ *242/393–8175,* WEB *www.thepoopdeck.com. AE, D, MC, V.*

$–$$ ✗ **Crocodiles Waterfront Bar & Grill.** The informal outdoor grill, with deck tables shaded by palms and adorned with signs from a plethora of Nassau establishments, is a good place to linger under thatched umbrellas and take in harbor views. You can opt for a light bite—conch salad, burgers (standard and conch varieties), calamari, nachos, and sandwiches—or try one of the heartier choices, such as the 16-ounce T-bone steak. The sea breezes, relaxing music, and friendly staff make happy hour at Crocodiles (daily 5 to 7:30) a Nassau classic. ⊠ *E. Bay St., west of bridge to Paradise Island,* ☎ *242/323–3341. MC, V.*

$–$$$ ✗ **Conch Fritters Bar & Grill.** A favorite in downtown Nassau, this lively, tropically themed restaurant is best known for its namesake specialty, served here in chowders, salads, and, of course, fritters. That said, conch-phobes need not worry: they'll find a diverse menu brimming with burgers, sandwiches, pasta, and a selection of steaks and ribs. Breakfast is also served. Bands play 7 to 11 nightly except Monday and there's a festive Junkanoo celebration on Saturday from 8 to 11 PM. ⊠ *Marlborough St., across from the British Colonial Hilton,* ☎ *242/323–8778. AE, MC, V.*

Nightlife

Some ships stay late into the night or until the next day so that passengers can enjoy Nassau's nightlife. You'll find nonstop entertainment nightly along Cable Beach and on Paradise Island. All the larger hotels offer lounges with island combos for listening or dancing and restaurants with soft guitar or piano music.

CASINOS

At 50,000 square ft (100,000 if you include the dining and drinking areas), the **Atlantis Casino** (⊠ Atlantis Resort, Paradise Island, ☎ 242/363–3000, WEB www.atlantis.com) is the Caribbean's largest gambling hall. Ringed with restaurants, it offers more than 1,000 slot machines, baccarat, blackjack, roulette, craps tables, and such local specialties as Caribbean stud poker. There's a high-limit table area, additional games available at most of the eateries within its walls, and a spectacularly open and airy design. Tables are open from 10 AM to 4 AM daily; slots, 24 hours daily. At the **Crystal Palace Casino** (⊠ Wyndham Nassau Resort, Cable Beach, ☎ 242/327–6200), slots, craps, baccarat, blackjack, roulette, Big Six, and face-up 21 are among the games in the 35,000-square-ft space. There's a Sports Book facility for sports betting, equipped with big-screen TVs, which air ongoing sporting events. Both VIPs and low-limit bettors have their own areas. Casino gaming lessons are available for beginners. Tables and slots are open 24 hours daily.

NIGHTCLUBS

Club Waterloo (⊠ E. Bay St. ☎ 242/393–7324) claims to be Nassau's largest indoor-outdoor nightclub, with five bars and nonstop dancing Monday through Saturday until 4 AM (with bands on weekends). Try the spring-break-special Waterloo Hurricane, a mixture of rums and punches. Nassau's largest indoor nightclub, **Zoo Nightclub** (⊠ W. Bay St., across from Saunders Beach, ☎ 242/322–7195), has five regular bars, a sports bar, and a VIP lounge where the drinks keep coming while party animals dance the night away to top chart hits. Its café is open from noon until the wee hours. There is a cover charge.

THEATER

Plays and musicals by local and visiting artists are staged throughout the year at **Dundas Centre for the Performing Arts** (⊠ Mackey St., ☎ 242/393–3728). The **Rainforest Theatre** (⊠ Wyndham Nassau Resort, Cable Beach, ☎ 242/702–4200 Ext. 6758) has an atmosphere true to its name and presents lavish shows.

Panama Canal

Transit of the Panama Canal takes only one day. The rest of your cruise will be spent on islands in the Caribbean or at ports along the Mexican Riviera. Increasingly, Panama Canal itineraries include stops in Central America; some may also call along the northern coast of South America. Most Panama Canal cruises are one-way trips, part of a 10- to 14-day cruise between the Atlantic and Pacific oceans. Shorter loop cruises enter the canal from the Caribbean, sail around Gatún Lake for a few hours, and return to the Caribbean.

The Panama Canal is best described as a water bridge that raises ships up and over Central America and then lets them down, using a series of locks or water steps. Artificially created Gatún Lake, 85 ft above sea level, is the canal's highest point. The route is approximately 50 mi (80 km) long, and the crossing takes from 8 to 10 hours. Cruise ships pay more than $100,000 for each transit, which is less than half of what it would cost them to sail around Cape Horn, at the southern tip of South America.

Just before dawn, your ship will line up with dozens of other vessels to await its turn to enter the canal. Before it can proceed, two pilots and a narrator will come on board. The sight of a massive cruise ship being raised dozens of feet into the air by water is so fascinating that passengers will crowd all the forward decks at the first lock. If you can't see, go to the rear decks, where there is usually more room and the view is just as intriguing. Later in the day you won't find as many people up front.

On and off throughout the day, commentary is broadcast over the ship's loudspeakers, imparting facts and figures as well as anecdotes about the history of the canal. The canal stands where it does not because it's the best route but because the railroad was built there first, making access to the area relatively easy. The railway had followed an old Spanish mule trail that had been there for more than 300 years.

St. Barthélemy

Hilly St. Barthélemy, popularly known as St. Barths or St. Barts, is just 8 square mi (21 square km), but the island has at least 20 good beaches, one reason it is a favorite with well-to-do travelers. The island was always a free port, building its wealth on trading commercial goods rather than on agricultural. What has drawn visitors is its sophisticated but unstudied approach to relaxation: the finest food, excellent wine, high-end shopping, and lack of large-scale commercial development.

A favorite among upscale cruise-ship passengers, who appreciate the shopping opportunities, fine dining, and beautiful beaches, St. Barths isn't really equipped for large-scale cruise-ship visits, which is why most ships calling here are smaller premium lines. This is one place where you don't need to take the ship's shore excursions to have a good time. Just hail a cab or rent a car and go to one of the many wonderful beaches, or linger in Gustavia, shopping and eating. It's the best way to relax on this most relaxing of islands.

CURRENCY

The official currency in St. Barths is the euro (€). However, U.S. dollars are accepted in almost all shops and in many restaurants, though you will probably receive euros in change. All credit-card transactions are charged in euros.

TELEPHONES

MCI and AT&T services are available. Public telephones do not accept coins; they accept *télécartes,* prepaid calling cards that you can buy at post offices in Lorient, St-Jean, and Gustavia. Making an international call using a télécarte is the best way to go. To call the United States from St. Barths, dial 001 + the area code + the local seven-digit number.

SHORE EXCURSIONS

The following are good choices in St. Barths. They may not be offered by all cruise lines. Times and prices are approximate.

Catamaran Cruise. A short sail from Gustavia Harbor takes you to Rockefeller Beach for snorkeling and swimming. ⊙ *2 hrs,* ⊠ *$52.*

Horseback Riding. This popular excursion takes you into the ruggedest northwest part of the island, where you ride along narrow trails, enjoying dramatic views from the cliffs to the ocean below. ⊙ *2 hrs,* ⊠ *$76.*

Coming Ashore

Even medium-size ships must anchor in Gustavia Harbor and bring passengers ashore on tenders. The tiny harbor area is right in Gustavia, which is best explored on foot at your leisure. Taxis, which meet all cruise ships, can be expensive. Technically, there's a flat rate for rides up to five minutes long, which a charge for each additional three minutes. In reality, however, cabbies usually name a fixed rate and will not budge. Fares are 50% higher from 8 PM to 6 AM and on Sunday and holidays. St. Barths is one port where it's really worth it to arrange a car rental, since this will give you the freedom to explore some of the island's out-of-the-way beaches. But be aware that during high season there is often a three-day minimum, so this may not be possible. **Smart of St. Barth** (☎ 0590/29–71–31) rents the tiny, colorful two-seaters called Smart Cars.

Exploring St. Barths

With a little practice, negotiating St. Barths' narrow, steep roads soon becomes fun. Free maps are everywhere, roads are well marked, and painted signs will point you where you want to be. Take along a towel, sandals, and a bottle of water, and you will surely find a beach upon which to linger.

Numbers in the margin correspond to points of interest on the St. Barthélemy map.

❶ **Anse des Flamands.** From this wide, white-sand, hotel-lined beach you can take a brisk hike to the top of the now-extinct volcano believed to have given birth to St. Barths.

❺ **Anse du Gouverneur.** Legend has it that pirates' treasure is buried at this beautiful beach. The road from Gustavia offers spectacular vistas. If the weather is clear you'll be able to see the islands of Saba, St. Eustatius, and St. Kitts from the beach.

❷ **Corossol.** The island's French-provincial origins are most evident in this two-street fishing village with a little rocky beach. Older women weave lantana straw into handbags, baskets, hats, and delicate strings of birds. Ingenu Magras's **Inter Oceans Museum** has more than 9,000 seashells and an intriguing collection of sand samples from around the world. You can buy souvenir shells. ⊠ *Corossol,* ☎ *0590/27–62–97.* ⊠ *€3.* ⊙ *Tues.–Sun. 9–12:30 and 2–5.*

❻ **Grande Saline.** The big salt ponds of Grande Saline are no longer in use, and the place looks a little desolate. Still, you should climb the short hillock behind the ponds for a surprise—the long arc of Anse de Grande Saline.

❹ **Gustavia.** You can easily explore all of Gustavia during a two-hour stroll. Street signs in both French and Swedish illustrate the island's history.

212

St. Barthélemy

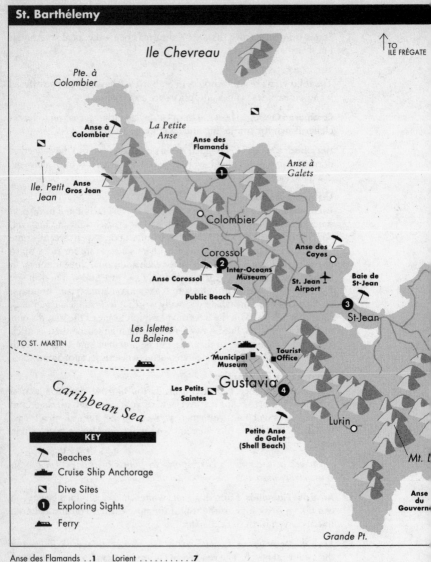

Ile Chevreau

TO
ILE FRÉGATE

Pte. à Colombier

Anse à Colombier

La Petite Anse

Anse des Flamands ❶

Anse à Galets

Ile. Petit Jean **Anse Gros Jean**

○ Colombier

Corossol **❷**

Anse Corossol

Inter-Oceans Museum

Public Beach

Anse des Cayes ○

St. Jean Airport ✈

Baie de St-Jean

❸ St-Jean

Les Islettes La Baleine

TO ST. MARTIN

Municipal Museum

Tourist Office

Gustavia ❹

Les Petits Saintes

Caribbean Sea

Petite Anse de Galet (Shell Beach)

Lurin ○

Mt.

Anse du Gouverne

KEY

- Beaches
- Cruise Ship Anchorage
- Dive Sites
- ❶ Exploring Sights
- Ferry

Grande Pt.

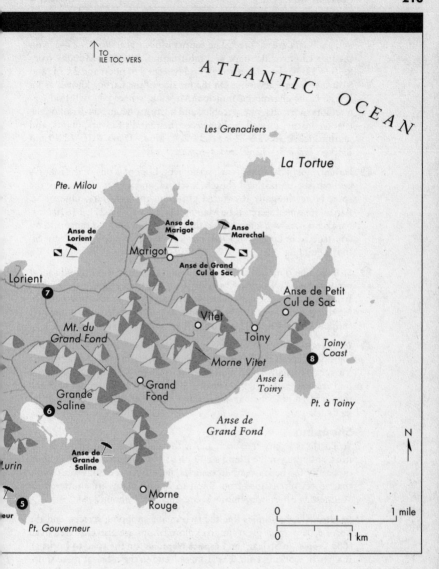

TO
ILE TOC VERS

ATLANTIC OCEAN

Les Grenadiers

La Tortue

Pte. Milou

Anse de
Lorient

Anse de
Marigot

Anse
Marechal

Marigot

Anse de Grand
Cul de Sac

Lorient

7

Anse de Petit
Cul de Sac

Vitet

Toiny

Mt. du
Grand Fond

Morne Vitet

Toiny
Coast

8

Anse à
Toiny

Pt. à Toiny

Grand
Fond

Grande
Saline

6

Anse de
Grand Fond

Lurin

Anse de
Grande
Saline

N

5

Morne
Rouge

eur

Pt. Gouverneur

0   1 mile

0   1 km

Shops close from noon to 2, so plan lunch accordingly. A good spot to park your car is Rue de la République, where catamarans, yachts, and sailboats are moored. The **tourist office** (☎ 0590/27–87–27) on the pier can provide maps and information. It's open Monday from 8:30 to 12:30, Tuesday through Friday from 8 to noon and 2 to 5, and Saturday from 9 to noon. On the far side of the harbor known as La Pointe is the charming **Municipal Museum,** where you will find watercolors, portraits, photographs, and historic documents detailing the island's history as well as displays of the island's flowers, plants, and marine life. ☎ 599/29–71–55. ☒ €2. ☽ Mon.–Thurs. 8:30–12:30 and 2:30–6, Fri. 8:30–12:30 and 3–6, Sat. 9–11.

❼ Lorient. Site of the first French settlement, Lorient is one of the island's two parishes; a restored church, a school, and a post office mark the spot. Note the gaily decorated graves in the cemetery. One of St. Barths' treasured secrets is **Le Manoir** (☎ 0590/27–79–27), a 1610 Norman manor, now a guest house, that was shipped from France and reconstructed in Lorient in 1984. Look for the entrance by the Ligne St. Barth building.

❸ St-Jean. The ½-mi (1-km) crescent of sand at St-Jean is the island's most popular beach. Windsurfers skim along the water here, catching the strong trade winds. A popular activity is watching and photographing the hair-raising airplane landings. You'll also find some of the best shopping on the island here, as well as several restaurants.

❽ Toiny coast. Over the hills beyond Grand Cul de Sac is this much-photographed coastline. Stone fences crisscross the steep slopes of Morne Vitet, one of many small mountains on St. Barths, along a rocky shore that resembles the rugged coast of Normandy. It is one island beach that is often described as a "washing machine" because of its turbulent surf.

Shopping

St. Barths is a duty-free port, and with its sophisticated crowd of visitors, shopping in the island's 200-plus boutiques is a definite delight, especially for beachwear, accessories, jewelry, and casual wear. Note that stores often close from noon to 2, and many are shuttered all Wednesday afternoon, but most are open until about 7 PM.

In Gustavia, boutiques line the two major shopping streets, and the **Carré d'Or** plaza is great fun to explore. Shops are also clustered in **La Villa Créole** (in St-Jean) and **Espace Neptune** (on the road to Lorient). It's worth working your way from one end to the other at these shopping complexes—just to see or, perhaps, be seen. Boutiques in all areas carry the latest in French and Italian sportswear and some haute couture. Prices, although on the high side, are often well below those for comparable merchandise in France or the United States.

Look for Fabienne Miot's unusual gold jewelry at **L'Atelier de Fabienne** (☒ Rue de la République, Gustavia, ☎ 0590/27–63–31). **Black Swan** (☒ Le Carré d'Or, Gustavia, ☎ 0590/27–65–16; ☒ La Villa Créole, St-Jean) has an unparalleled selection of bathing suits. **Le Comptoir du Cigare** (☒ Rue Général-de-Gaulle, Gustavia, ☎ 0590/27–50–62), run by Jannick and Patrick Gerthofer, is a top purveyor of cigars. The walk-in humidor has an extraordinary selection. Try the Cubans while you are on the island, and take home the Davidoffs. They will ship refills stateside. Be sure to try on the Panama hats. A good selection of watches, including Patek Phillippe and Chanel, can be found at **Diamond Genesis** (☒ Rue Général-de-Gaulle, Gustavia). Fans of Longchamp handbags and leather goods will find a good selection at about 20% off stateside prices at **Elysée Caraïbes** (☒ Le Carré d'Or,

Gustavia, ☎ 0590/52–00–94). The **Hermès** (✉ Rue de la République, Gustavia) store in St. Barths is an independently owned franchise, and prices are about 20% below those in the States. Don't miss the superb skin-care products made on-site from local tropical plants by **Ligne de St. Barths** (✉ Rte. de Saline, Lorient, ☎ 0590/27–82–63). **Lolita Jaca** (✉ Le Carré d'Or, Gustavia, ☎ 0590/27–59–98) has trendy, tailored sportswear by Paul and Joe and other fresh names. Locally produced artworks, including paintings, are sold in the bright **Made in St-Barth La Boutique** (✉ La Villa Créole, St-Jean, ☎ 0590/27–56–57). **Pati de Saint Barth** (✉ Passage de la Crémaillière, Gustavia, ☎ 0590/29–78–04) is the largest of the three shops that stock the chic, locally made T-shirts that have practically become the "logo" of St. Barths. The newest styles have hand-rendered graffiti-like lettering. **Stéphane & Bernard** (✉ Rue de la République, Gustavia, ☎ 0590/27–69–13) stocks fashions by French designers, including Rykiel, Tarlazzi, Kenzo, Feraud, and Mugler. **SUD SUD.ETC** (✉ Galerie du Commerce, St-Jean, ☎ 0590/27–98–75) stocks hippie-chic styles from Betty Boom and shell and mother-of-pearl jewelry. Cute sandals and raffia accessories complete the look.

Outdoor Activities & Sports

BOATING

St. Barths is a popular yachting and sailing center, thanks to its location midway between Antigua and St. Thomas. Gustavia's harbor, 13 to 16 ft deep, has mooring and docking facilities for 40 yachts. There are also good anchorages available at Public, Corossol, and Colombier. **Marine Service** (✉ Gustavia, ☎ 0590/27–70–34) offers full-day outings on a 40-ft catamaran to the uninhabited Ile Fourchue for swimming, snorkeling, cocktails, and lunch; the cost is $100 per person. Marine Service can also arrange an hour's cruise ($32) on the glass-bottom boat *L'Aquascope*.

HORSEBACK RIDING

Two-hour horseback trail-ride excursions in the morning or the afternoon led by Coralie Fournier are about $40 per person at St. Barth Equitation, headquartered at **Ranch des Flamands** (✉ Anse des Flamands, ☎ 0690/62–99–30).

WINDSURFING

You can rent boards for about $20 an hour at water-sports centers along Baie de St-Jean and Grand Cul de Sac beaches. Lessons are offered for about $40 an hour at **Eden Rock Sea Sport Club** (✉ Eden Rock Hotel, Baie de St-Jean, ☎ 0590/29–79–93), which also rents boards. **Mat Nautic** (✉ Quai du Yacht Club, Gustavia, ☎ 0690/49–54–72) can help you arrange to tour the island on a Jet Ski or Waverunner. On an hour's notice you can have a lesson, then rent by the hour or the half day. **Wind Wave Power** (✉ St. Barth Beach Hotel, Grand Cul de Sac, ☎ 0590/27–82–57) offers an extensive, six-hour training course.

Beaches

There are many *anses* (coves) and nearly 20 *plages* (beaches) scattered around the island, each with a distinctive personality and each open to the general public. Even in season you can find a nearly empty beach. Topless sunbathing is common, but nudism is technically forbidden—although both Saline and Gouverneur are de facto nude beaches. Because **Anse du Gouverneur** is so secluded, nude sunbathing is popular here; the beach is truly beautiful, with blissful swimming and views of St. Kitts, Saba, and St. Eustatius. Tiny **Anse Marechal,** next to the Guanahani Hotel, offers some of the island's best snorkeling. Like a mini Côte d'Azur—beachside bistros, bungalow hotels, bronzed bodies, windsurfing, and lots of day-trippers—the reef-protected strip along

Baie de St-Jean is divided by Eden Rock promontory, and there's good snorkeling west of the rock. **Flamands** is the most beautiful of the hotel beaches—a roomy strip of silken sand. The shallow, reef-protected beach at **Grand Cul de Sac** is especially nice for small children, fly fishermen, and windsurfers; it has excellent lunch spots and lots of pelicans. Secluded, with a sandy ocean bottom, **Grande Saline** is just about everyone's favorite beach and a great place for swimmers. In spite of the prohibition, young and old alike go nude. It can get windy here, so go on a calm day. **Lorient** beach is popular with St. Barths families and surfers, who like its rolling waves. Be aware of the level of the tide, which can come in very fast. Hikers and avid surfers like the walk over the hill to Point Milou in the late afternoon sun when the waves roll in. A five-minute walk from Gustavia, **Petite Anse de Galet** is named for the tiny shells on its shore.

Where to Eat

Check restaurant bills carefully. A service charge is always added by law, but you should leave the server 5% to 10% extra. It is generally advisable to charge restaurant meals on a credit card, as the issuer will offer a better exchange rate than the restaurant.

$$$–$$$$ ✕ **Do Brazil.** At this cozy restaurant nestled at the cliff side of Gustavia's Shell Beach, you'll be able to sample more of restaurateur Boubou's delicious fusion creations. The not-exactly-Brazilian cuisine is served in a vaguely jungle-chic decor—romantic at night, lively at lunch. Choose between varied salads, ceviche, hand-chopped steak and fish tartares, grilled fresh-caught fish, and barbecue specialties; many are served with great fries. ⊠ *Shell Beach, Gustavia,* ☎ *0590/29–06–66. Reservations essential. AE, MC, V.*

$$–$$$ ✕ **Le Tamarin.** A leisurely lunch here en route to Grand Saline beach is a St. Barths *must*. Delicious French and creole cuisine is served at this sophisticated open-air restaurant. Get to know the parrot, or relax in a hammock after the house-special carpaccios of salmon, tuna, and beef. The lemon tart deserves its excellent reputation. ⊠ *Salines,* ☎ *0590/27–72–12. AE, MC, V. Open erratically May–Nov. Call to confirm.*

$$ ✕ **La Marine.** In-the-know islanders settle at the popular dockside picnic tables for mussels that arrive from France every Wednesday. The menu also includes fish, oysters, hamburgers, steaks, and omelets. Many think that meals here are the best buys on the island. ⊠ *Rue Jeanne d'Arc, Gustavia,* ☎ *0590/27–68–91. AE, MC, V.*

$–$$ ✕ **Le Rivage.** This popular, affordable restaurant serves wonderful gazpacho and huge salads, like warm chèvre (goat cheese) with bacon, cold mixed seafood, and classic *salade niçoise* (with tuna, olives, green beans, and hard-boiled eggs). There are grilled fresh seafood and steaks for heartier appetites—but save room for the warm apple pastry or warm chocolate cake with vanilla sauce. Come for lunch and spend the rest of the afternoon sunning or windsurfing on the beautiful beach. ⊠ *St. Barths Beach Hôtel, Grand Cul de Sac,* ☎ *0590/27–82–42. AE, MC, V.*

St. Croix, U.S. Virgin Islands

St. Croix is the largest of the three U.S. Virgin Islands (USVI) that form the northern hook of the Lesser Antilles; it's 40 mi (64 km) south of its sister islands, St. Thomas and St. John. Christopher Columbus landed here in 1493, skirmishing briefly with the native Carib Indians. Since then, the USVI have played a colorful, if painful, role as pawns in the game of European colonialism. Theirs is a history of pirates and privateers, sugar plantations, slave trading, and slave revolt and liberation. Through it all, Denmark had staying power. From the 17th to the 19th century, Danes oversaw a plantation slave economy that produced molasses, rum, cotton, and tobacco. Many of the stones you tread on in the streets were once used as ballast on sailing ships, and the yellow fort of Christiansted is a reminder of the value once placed on this island treasure. Never a major cruise destination, it is still a stop for several ships each year.

CURRENCY

The U.S. dollar is the official currency of St. Croix.

TELEPHONES

Calling the United States from St. Croix works the same way as calling within the U.S. Local calls from a public phone cost up to 35¢ for every five minutes. You can use your regular toll-free connections for long-distance services.

SHORE EXCURSIONS

The following are good choices on St. Croix. They may not be offered by all cruise lines. Times and prices are approximate.

Buck Island. The most popular trip on St. Croix involves a catamaran or other boat trip to Buck Island Reef National Monument to see the reef and enjoy the sandy beach. ☉ *4 hrs,* ✉ *$55.*

Island Tour. See St. Croix's top historical sights on a daylong island tour, which might include Whim Planation, the Cruzan Rum Factory, and the rain forest. The tour ends with lunch in Frederiksted. ☉ *6 hrs,* ✉ *$51.*

Salt River Kayaking. This trip takes you through Salt River National Historic Park and Ecological Preserve, one of the island's most pristine areas. ☉ *4 hrs,* ✉ *$53.*

Coming Ashore

Larger cruise ships dock in Frederiksted; smaller ships dock at Gallows Bay, outside Christiansted. You'll find information centers at both piers, and both towns are easy to explore on foot. Beaches are nearby.

Taxis of all shapes and sizes are available at the cruise-ship piers and at various shopping and resort areas. Remember, too, that you can hail a taxi that's already occupied. Drivers take multiple fares and sometimes even trade passengers at midpoints. Taxis don't have meters, so you should check the list of official rates (available at the visitor centers or from drivers) and agree on a fare before you start, but there are standard rates for most trips. A taxi to Christiansted will cost about $20.

If you want to explore on your own, it's easy to rent a car in either Frederiksted or Christiansted. If you make a reservation with a major agency, they will usually pick you up at the pier, and a car costs less than $40 a day. St. Croix also has some of the lowest gas prices in the Caribbean. **Olympic** (☎ 340/773–8000 or 888/878–4227), a local company, has offices in both Frederiksted and Christiansted and will pick you up.

Exploring St. Croix

Numbers in the margin correspond to points of interest on the St. Croix map.

Frederiksted speaks to history buffs with its quaint Victorian architecture and historic fort. There's very little traffic, so this is the perfect place for strolling and shopping. Christiansted is a historic Danish-style town that served as St. Croix's commercial center. Your best bet is to see the historic sights in the morning, when it's still cool. This two-hour endeavor won't tax your walking shoes and will leave you with energy to poke around the town's eclectic shops.

② **Carl and Marie Lawaetz Museum.** For a trip back in time, tour this circa-1750 farm. Owned by the prominent Lawaetz family since 1899, just

St. Croix

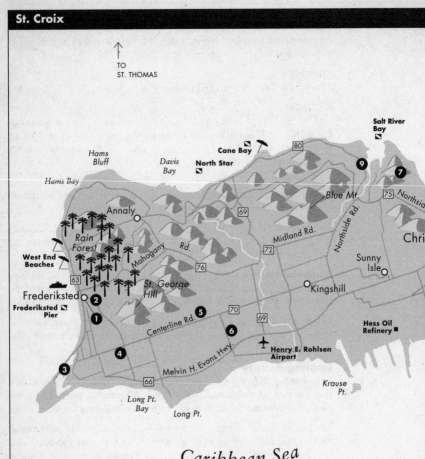

TO
ST. THOMAS

Salt River
Bay

Hams
Bluff

Davis
Bay

Cane Bay

North Star

Hams Bay

80

9

7

Blue Mt.

75

Northside

Annaly

Rain
Forest

Mahogany

Rd.

69

Midland Rd.

72

Northside Rd.

Chris

West End
Beaches

63

St. George
Hill

76

Sunny
Isle

Frederiksted

Frederiksted
Pier

2

Kingshill

1

Centerline Rd.

5

70

69

Hess Oil
Refinery

6

4

Henry E. Rohlsen
Airport

3

Melvin H. Evans Hwy.

66

Krause
Pt.

Long Pt.
Bay

Long Pt.

Caribbean Sea

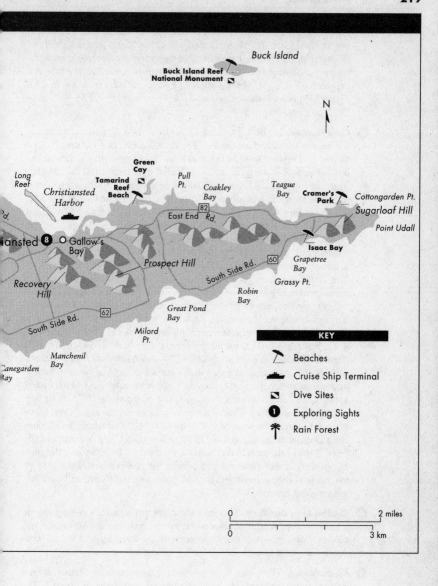

Buck Island

Buck Island Reef
National Monument

N

Long
Reef

Christiansted
Harbor

Green
Cay

Tamarind
Reef
Beach

Pull
Pt.

Coakley
Bay

Teague
Bay

Cramer's
Park

Cottongarden Pt.

Sugarloaf Hill

East End Rd.

82

Point Udall

...ansted

8   O Gallow's
Bay

Prospect Hill

South Side Rd.

Isaac Bay

60

Grapetree
Bay

Recovery
Hill

Robin
Bay

Grassy Pt.

62

South Side Rd.

Great Pond
Bay

Milord
Pt.

Canegarden
Bay

Manchenil
Bay

KEY	
⟍	Beaches
⛴	Cruise Ship Terminal
◩	Dive Sites
❶	Exploring Sights
🌴	Rain Forest

0 ——————————————— 2 miles

0 ——————————————— 3 km

after Carl arrived from Denmark, the two-story house is in a valley at La Grange. A Lawaetz family member shows you the four-poster mahogany bed Carl and Marie shared, the china Marie painted, the family portraits, and the fruit trees that fed the family for several generations. Initially a sugar plantation, it was subsequently used to raise cattle and produce. ⊠ *Rte. 76, Mahogany Rd., Estate Little La Grange*, ☎ *340/ 772–1539,* WEB *www.stcroixlandmarks.com/lawaetz.* ⊆ *$6.* ⊙ *Tues.– Wed. and Fri.–Sun. 10–4.*

8 **Christiansted.** In the 1700s and 1800s this town was a trading center for sugar, rum, and molasses. Today there are law offices, tourist shops, and restaurants, but many of the buildings, which start at the harbor and go up into the gentle hillsides, date from the 18th century. You can't get lost. All streets lead gently downhill to the water. Still, if you want some friendly advice, stop by the **Visitor Center** (⊠ 53A Company St., ☎ 340/773–0495) weekdays between 8 and 5 for maps and brochures. Large, yellow **Fort Christiansvaern** (⊠ Hospital St., ☎ 340/773–1460, WEB www.nps.gov/chrii) dominates the waterfront. Because it's so easy to spot, it makes a good place from which to begin a walking tour. In 1749 the Danish built the fort to protect the harbor, but the structure was repeatedly damaged by hurricane-force winds and was partially rebuilt in 1771. It's now a national historic site, the best preserved of the few remaining Danish-built forts in the Virgin Islands, and houses the park's visitor center. The $3 admission fee includes entry to the Steeple Building. Hours are daily from 8 to 4:45. Built in 1830 on foundations that date from 1734, the **Danish Customs House** (⊠ King St., ☎ 340/773–1460, WEB www.nps.gov/chrii) near Fort Christiansvaern originally served as both a customs house and a post office (second floor). In 1926 it became the Christiansted Library, and it has been a national-park office since 1972. It's open weekdays from 8 to 5. One of the town's most elegant structures, **Government House** (⊠ King St., ☎ 340/773–1404) was built as a home for a Danish merchant in 1747. Today it houses USVI government offices. If the building is open (hours are weekdays from 8 to 5), slip into the peaceful inner courtyard to admire the still pools and gardens. A sweeping staircase leads you to a second-story ballroom, still used for government functions.

6 **Cruzan Rum Distillery.** A tour of the company's factory culminates in a tasting of its products, all sold here at bargain prices. Admission includes a tour and rum drinks afterward. ⊠ *West Airport Rd., Estate Diamond,* ☎ *340/692–2280.* ⊆ *$4.* ⊙ *Daily 9–4.*

1 **Frederiksted.** The town is noted less for its remaining Danish structures than for the Victorian buildings erected after the great fire of 1878. The **Visitor Center** (⊠ Waterfront, ☎ 340/772–0357), right on the pier, has brochures from St. Croix businesses. Stop in weekdays from 8 to 5 to view the exhibits on St. Croix. On July 3, 1848, 8,000 slaves marched on the redbrick **Fort Frederik** (⊠ Waterfront, ☎ 340/772–2021) to demand their freedom. Danish governor Peter von Scholten, fearing they would burn the town to the ground, stood up in his carriage, parked in front of the fort, and granted their wish. The fort, completed in 1760, houses historical exhibits and an art gallery and a display of police memorabilia. The fort is within earshot of the Visitor Center. Admission is free; hours are weekdays from 8 to 5. **St. Patrick's** Roman Catholic church (⊠ Prince St.), complete with three turrets, was built of coral in 1843. Wander inside, and you'll see woodwork handcrafted by Frederiksted artisans. The churchyard is filled with 18th-century gravestones. **St. Paul's Anglican Church** (⊠ Prince St.), built circa 1812, is a mix of Georgian and Gothic Revival architecture. The bell tower of exposed sandstone was added later. The simple interior has gleaming woodwork and a tray ceiling (it looks like an upside-down tray) popular in Caribbean architecture. Built in 1839, **Apothecary Hall** (✉ King Cross St.) is a good example of polyglot 19th-century architecture; its facade has Gothic and Greek Revival elements. Stop at the Queen Street **market** for fresh fruits and vegetables (be sure to wash or peel this produce before eating it) sold each morning, just as they have been for more than 200 years.

7 **Judith's Fancy.** In this upscale neighborhood are the ruins of an old great house and tower of the same name, both remnants of a circa-1750 Danish sugar plantation. It's named after a woman buried on the property. From the guard house at the neighborhood entrance, follow Hamilton Drive past some of St. Croix's loveliest homes. At the end of Hamilton Drive the road overlooks Salt River Bay, where Christopher Columbus anchored in 1493. On the way back, make a detour left off Hamilton Drive onto Caribe Road for a close look at the ruins. ✉ *Turn north onto Rte. 751, off Rte. 75.*

5 **St. George Village Botanical Gardens.** At this 17-acre estate, lush, fragrant flora grows amid the ruins of a 19th-century sugarcane plantation village. There are miniature versions of each ecosystem on St. Croix, from a semiarid cactus grove to a verdant rain forest. ✉ *Rte. 70, turn north at the sign, St. George,* ☎ *340/692–2874,* WEB *www.sgvbg.com.* 💲 *$6.* ☉ *Tues.–Sat. 9–4.*

9 **Salt River Bay National Historical Park and Ecological Preserve.** This joint national and local park commemorates the area where Christopher Columbus's men skirmished with the Carib Indians in 1493 on his second visit to the New World. The peninsula on the bay's east side is named for the event: Cabo de las Flechas (Cape of the Arrows). Although the park isn't developed, it has several sights with cultural significance. A ball court, used by the Caribs in religious ceremonies, was discovered at the spot where the taxis park. Take a short hike up the dirt road to the ruins of an old earthen fort for great views of Salt River Bay and the surrounding countryside. The area also encompasses a biodiverse coastal estuary with the largest remaining mangrove forest in the USVI, a submarine canyon, and several endangered species, including the hawksbill turtle and the roseate tern. ✉ *Rte. 75 to Rte. 80, Salt River,* ☎ *340/773–1460,* WEB *www.nps.gov/sari.*

3 **West End Salt Pond.** A bird-watcher's delight, this salt pond attracts large numbers of winged creatures, including flamingos. Because of the remote location, it's best to visit in a group. ✉ *Veteran's Shore Dr., Hesselberg.*

4 **Whim Plantation Museum.** The lovingly restored estate, with a windmill, cook house, and other buildings, will give you a sense of what life was like on St. Croix's sugar plantations in the 1800s. The oval-shaped great house has high ceilings and antique furniture and utensils. Notice its fresh, airy atmosphere—the waterless stone moat around the great house was used not for defense but for gathering cooling air. If you have kids, the grounds are the perfect place for them to stretch their legs, perhaps while you browse in the museum gift shop. It's just outside of Frederiksted. ✉ *Rte. 70, Estate Whim,* ☎ *340/772–0598,* WEB *www.stcroixlandmarks.com.* 💲 *$6.* ☉ *Wed.–Mon. 10–4.*

Shopping

The selection of duty-free goods on St. Croix is fairly good. The best shopping is in Christiansted, where most stores are in the historic district near the harbor. King Street, Strand Street, and the arcades that lead off them compose the main shopping district. The longest arcade

is Caravelle Arcade, adjacent to the hotel of the same name. Gallows
Bay, just east of Christiansted, has an attractive boutique area that features unusual island-made silver jewelry and gift items. In Frederiksted, a handful of shops face the cruise-ship pier. The coffees, jams, and
spices—produced locally or elsewhere in the Caribbean—available at
Island Webe (⊠ 210 Strand St., Frederiksted, ☎ 340/772–2555) will
tempt your taste buds. Small *mocko jumbie* dolls depict an African tradition transported to the islands (they represent the souls of the an-
cestors of African slaves). The fabric dolls wearing Caribbean costumes
delight kids of all ages. Turn the double dolls upside down to see a white
face on one side and a black one on the other. Sonya Hough, owner
of **Sonya's** (⊠ 1 Company St., Christiansted, ☎ 340/778–8605), in-
vented the hook bracelet, popular among locals as well as visitors. With
hurricanes hitting the island so frequently, she has added an interesting decoration to these bracelets: the swirling symbol used in weather
forecasts to indicate these storms.

Outdoor Activities & Sports

GOLF
The **Buccaneer** (⊠ Rte. 82, Shoys, ☎ 340/773–2100) has an 18-hole
course that is conveniently close to Christiansted. The spectacular 18-
hole course at **Carambola Golf Club** (⊠ Rte. 80, Davis Bay, ☎ 340/778–
5638), in the northwest valley, was designed by Robert Trent Jones, Sr.

HORSEBACK RIDING
Well-kept roads and expert guides make horseback riding on St. Croix
pleasurable. At Sprat Hall, just north of Frederiksted, Jill Hurd runs
Paul and Jill's Equestrian Stables (⊠ Rte. 58, Frederiksted, ☎ 340/
772–2880 or 340/772–2627) and will take you clip-clopping through
the rain forest, across pastures, and to hilltops (explaining the flora,
fauna, and ruins on the way). A 1½-hour ride costs $50.

SNORKELING TRIPS
Day sail to Buck Island aboard a charter boat. Most leave from the
Christiansted waterfront or from Green Cay Marina. They stop for a
snorkel at the island's eastern end before dropping anchor off a gorgeous sandy beach for a swim, a hike, and lunch. A full-day sail runs
about $65, with lunch included on most trips. A half-day sail costs about
$50. **Big Beard's Adventure Tours** (☎ 340/773–4482) takes you on a
catamaran, the *Renegade* or the *Flyer*, from the Christiansted waterfront to Buck Island for snorkeling before dropping anchor at a private beach for a barbecue lunch. **Mile Mark Charters** (☎ 340/773–2628)
departs from the Christiansted waterfront for half- and full-day trips
on various boats. The **Teroro Charters** (☎ 340/773–3161) trimaran
Teroro II leaves Green Cay Marina for full- or half-day sails. Bring your
own lunch.

Beaches

A visit to **Buck Island,** part of Buck Island Reef National Monument,
is a must. The beach is beautiful, but its finest treasures are those you
can see when you plop off the boat and adjust your mask, snorkel, and
flippers. To get here, you'll have to charter a boat or go on an organized trip. The waters aren't always gentle at **Cane Bay,** a breezy north
shore beach, but there are seldom many people around, and the scuba
diving and snorkeling are wondrous. You'll see elkhorn and brain
corals, and less than 200 yards out is the drop-off called Cane Bay Wall.
Small but attractive **Tamarind Reef Beach** is east of Christiansted. Both
Green Cay and Buck Island seem smack in front of you. The view is
arresting, and the snorkeling is good. There are several unnamed **West
End Beaches** along the coast road north of Frederiksted. Just pull over

at whatever piece of powdery sand catches your fancy. The beach at the Rainbow Beach Club, a five-minute drive outside Frederiksted on Route 63, has a bar, a casual restaurant, water sports, and volleyball.

Where to Eat

$$–$$$$ ✕ **Le St. Tropez.** A ceramic-tile bar and soft lighting set the mood at this pleasant Mediterranean bistro tucked into a courtyard off Frederiksted's main thoroughfare. Seated either inside or on the adjoining patio, you can enjoy such items as grilled meats in delicate French sauces. The menu changes daily, often taking advantage of local seafood. The fresh basil, tomato, and mozzarella salad is heavenly. ✉ *227 King St., Frederiksted,* ☎ *340/772–3000. AE, MC, V. Closed Sun. No lunch Sat.*

$$–$$$ ✕ **Blue Moon.** This terrific little bistro has a changing menu that draws on Asian, Cajun, and local flavors. Try the spicy gumbo with andouille or crab cakes with a spicy aioli as an appetizer; shrimp scampi, loaded with garlic and served over pasta as an entrée; and the Almond Joy sundae for dessert. ✉ *17 Strand St.,* ☎ *340/772–2222. AE, MC, V. Closed Mon.*

$$–$$$ ✕ **Indies.** Tables covered with handmade floral-print cloths are scattered through the historic courtyard of this wonderful restaurant. The menu of island-inspired dishes changes each day to take advantage of St. Croix's freshest bounties. Indulge in the mango-basil crab cakes with curry onion to start, then the wahoo with ginger-coconut dasheen and roasted-pineapple vinaigrette. Finish with a yam and pecan custard tart. Enjoy live jazz Thursday through Saturday evenings and Sunday afternoons. ✉ *55–56 Company St.,* ☎ *340/692–9440. AE, D, MC, V. Closed Mon.*

St. Kitts and Nevis

Mountainous St. Kitts, the first English settlement in the Leeward Islands, crams some stunning scenery into its 65 square mi (168 square km). Vast, brilliant green fields of sugarcane run to the shore. The fertile, lush island has some fascinating natural and historical attractions: a rain forest replete with waterfalls, thick vines, and secret trails; a central mountain range, dominated by the 3,792-ft Mt. Liamuiga, whose crater has long been dormant; and Brimstone Hill, known in the 17th century as the Gibraltar of the West Indies.

In 1493, when Columbus spied a cloud-crowned volcanic isle during his second voyage to the New World, he named it Nieves—the Spanish word for "snows"—because it reminded him of the peaks of the Pyrenees. Nevis rises from the water in an almost perfect cone, the tip of its 3,232-ft central mountain hidden by clouds. Even less developed than St. Kitts, Nevis is known for its long beaches with white and black sand, its lush greenery, and its restored sugar plantations that now house charming inns.

St. Kitts and Nevis, along with Anguilla, achieved self-government as an Associated State of Great Britain in 1967. In 1983, St. Kitts and Nevis became an independent nation. English with a strong West Indian lilt is spoken here. People are friendly but shy; always ask before you take photographs. Also, be sure to wear wraps or shorts over beach attire when you're in public places.

CURRENCY

Legal tender is the Eastern Caribbean (E.C.) dollar. At this writing, the rate of exchange was EC$2.70 to US$1. U.S. dollars are accepted practically everywhere, but you'll usually get change in E.C. currency. Prices quoted throughout this chapter are in U.S. dollars unless otherwise noted.

To make a local call, dial the seven-digit number. Phone cards, which you can buy in denominations of $5, $10, and $20, are handy for making local calls, calling other islands, and accessing U.S. direct lines. A warning for both islands: many private lines and hotels charge access rates if you use your AT&T, Sprint, or MCI calling card; there's no regularity, so phoning can be frustrating. Pay phones, usually found in major town squares, take E.C. coins or phone cards.

The following are good choices in St. Kitts and Nevis. They may not be offered by all cruise lines. Times and prices are approximate.

Brimstone Hill Fortress and Gardens. You visit Brimstone Hill, a 300-year-old fortress and World Heritage Site, before going to Romney Gardens, where you'll be able to browse through the wares of Caribelle Batik Studios. Finally, take a jaunt through Basseterre. ⊙ *3 hrs,* ⊠ *$39–$48.*

Catamaran Fan-ta-sea. This day sail goes to the neighboring island of Nevis, with a stop at Smitten's Bay for snorkeling and a beach barbecue on a Nevis beach. ⊙ *7 hrs,* ⊠ *$100.*

Catamaran Sail and Snorkeling Adventure. Take a catamaran to Ballast Bay, where you'll view the area's myriad fish and coral. ⊙ *3 hrs,* ⊠ *$54–$68.*

Kayaking Tour. Board an ocean kayak in White House Bay and tour the secluded coves along the shore, making stops for snorkeling. ⊙ *3 hrs,* ⊠ *$62.*

Coming Ashore

Cruise ships calling at St. Kitts and Nevis dock at Port Zante in Basseterre, the capital of St. Kitts. At this writing, Port Zante was expected to be under construction through 2003; when completed, it will comprise a welcome center, hotel and casino, shops, and restaurants.

On both St. Kitts the cruise-ship terminal is located downtown, two minutes' walk from sights and shops. Taxis on the islands are unmetered, but fixed rates, in E.C. dollars, are posted at the jetty. A one-way ride from Basseterre, St. Kitts, to Brimstone Hill costs $32 (for one to four passengers), a ride to Romney Manor costs $26, and a trip to Turtle Beach costs $40. A three-hour driving tour of Nevis costs about $50; a four-hour tour of St. Kitts about $60. On both islands, several restored great-house plantations are known for their lunches; your driver can provide information and arrange drop-off and pickup. Before setting off in a cab, be sure to clarify whether the rate quoted is in E.C. or U.S. dollars.

Exploring St. Kitts

Numbers in the margin correspond to points of interest on the St. Kitts map.

❶ Basseterre. On the south coast, St. Kitts's walkable capital is graced with tall palms, and although many of the buildings appear run-down, there are interesting shops, excellent art galleries, and some beautifully maintained houses.

The octagonal Circus, built in the style of London's famous Piccadilly Circus, has duty-free shops along the contiguous streets and courtyards. There are lovely gardens on the site of a former slave market at **Independence Square** (⊠ off Bank St.). The square is surrounded on three sides by 18th-century Georgian buildings. **St. George's Anglican Church** (⊠ Cayon St.) is a handsome stone building with a crenellated tower built by the French in 1670 and called Nôtre-Dame. The British burned it in 1706 and rebuilt it four years later, naming it after the patron saint of England. Since then it has suffered a fire, an earthquake, and hurricanes and was once again rebuilt, in 1869. **Port Zante** (⊠ Waterfront, behind The Circus) is an ambitious, much-delayed, 27-acre cruise-ship pier-marina reclaimed from the sea. The domed welcome center features an imposing neoclassical design, with columns and stone arches; when completed (construction will continue through 2003), it will have walkways, fountains, and West Indian–style buildings housing luxury shops, galleries, and restaurants.

National Museum. In the restored former Treasury Building, the museum, which opened in 2002, presents an eclectic collection reflecting the history and culture of the island. ⊠ *Bay Rd., Basseterre,* ☎ *869/ 465–5584.* ▣ *EC$1 residents, US$1 nonresidents.* ☉ *Mon and Sat. 9:30 –2, Tues.–Fri. 9–1 and 2–5.*

❹ **Brimstone Hill.** The well-restored 38-acre fortress, a UNESCO World Heritage Site, is part of a national park dedicated by Queen Elizabeth in 1985. The steep walk up the hill from the parking lot is well worth it if military history or spectacular views interest you. After routing the French in 1690, the English erected a battery here, and by 1736 the fortress held 49 guns. In 1782, 8,000 French troops laid siege to the stronghold, which was defended by 350 militia and 600 regular troops of the Royal Scots and East Yorkshires. When the English finally surrendered, the French allowed them to march from the fort in full formation out of respect for their bravery (the English afforded the French the same honor when they surrendered the fort a mere year later). A hurricane severely damaged the fortress in 1834, and in 1852 it was evacuated and dismantled. The beautiful stones were carted away to build houses.

The citadel has been partially reconstructed and its guns remounted. A seven-minute orientation film recounts the fort's history and restoration. You can see what remains of the officers' quarters, the redoubts, the barracks, the ordnance store, and the cemetery. Its museum collections were depleted by hurricanes, but some pre-Columbian artifacts, objects pertaining to the African heritage of the island's slaves (masks, ceremonial tools, etc.), weaponry, uniforms, photographs, and old newspapers remain. The view from here includes Montserrat and Nevis to the southeast; Saba and St. Eustatius to the northwest; and St. Barths and St. Maarten to the north. Nature trails snake through the tangle of surrounding hardwood forest and savanna; it's a fine spot from which to view the green vervet monkeys skittering about. ⊠ *Main Rd., Brimstone Hill,* ☎ *869/465–2609.* ▣ *$5.* ☉ *Daily 9:30–5:30.*

❷ **Old Road Town.** This site marks the first permanent English settlement in the West Indies, founded in 1624 by Thomas Warner. Take the side road toward the interior to find some Carib petroglyphs, testimony of even earlier habitation. The largest depicts a female figure on black volcanic rock, presumably a fertility goddess. Less than a mile east of Old Road along Main Road is **Bloody Point,** where French and British soldiers joined forces in 1629 to repel a mass Carib attack; reputedly so many Caribs were killed that the stream ran red for three days. ⊠ *Main Rd., west of Challengers.*

❸ **Romney Manor.** The ruins of this partially restored house and surrounding cottages that duplicate the old chattel-house style are set in 6 acres of gardens, with exotic flowers, an old bell tower, and an enormous, gnarled, 350-year-old *samaan* tree (sometimes called a rain tree). Inside, at **Caribelle Batik,** you can watch artisans hand-printing fabrics. Look for signs indicating a turnoff for Romney Manor near Old Road.

226

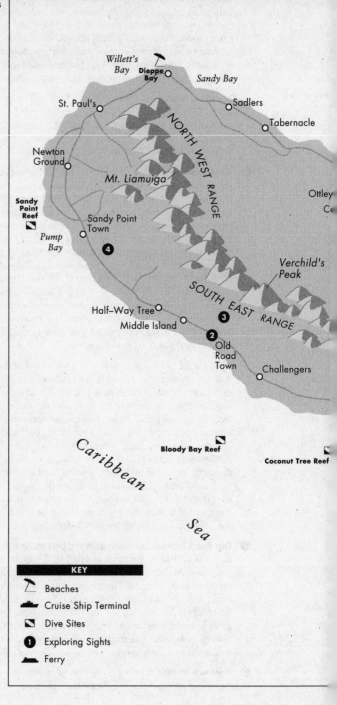

St. Kitts

Willett's Bay

Dieppe Bay

Sandy Bay

St. Paul's

Sadlers

Tabernacle

NORTH WEST RANGE

Newton Ground

Mt. Liamuiga

Ottley C

Sandy Point Reef

Sandy Point Town

4

Pump Bay

Verchild's Peak

SOUTH EAST RANGE

Half–Way Tree

Middle Island

3

2 Old Road Town

Challengers

Caribbean

Bloody Bay Reef

Coconut Tree Reef

Sea

KEY

Beaches

Cruise Ship Terminal

Dive Sites

1 Exploring Sights

Ferry

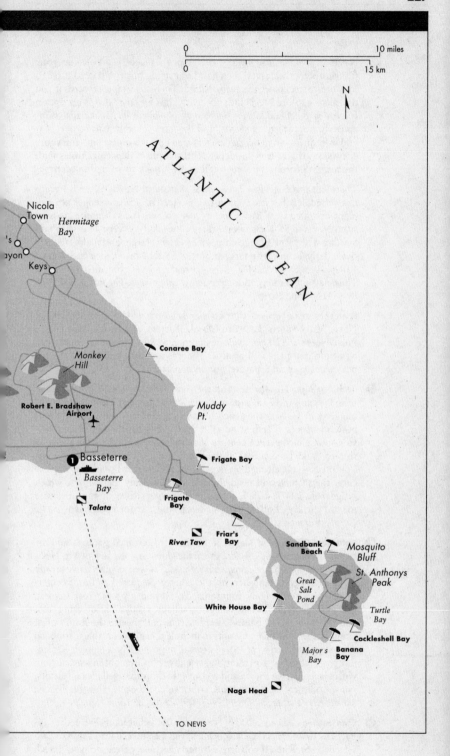

N

0   10 miles
0   15 km

ATLANTIC OCEAN

Nicola
Town

Hermitage
Bay

's

ayon

Keys

Monkey
Hill

Robert E. Bradshaw
Airport

Conaree Bay

Muddy
Pt.

Basseterre

Basseterre
Bay

Frigate Bay

Talata

Frigate
Bay

River Taw

Friar's
Bay

Sandbank
Beach

Mosquito
Bluff

St. Anthonys
Peak

Great
Salt
Pond

Turtle
Bay

White House Bay

Cockleshell Bay

Major s
Bay

Banana
Bay

Nags Head

TO NEVIS

Exploring Nevis

Numbers in the margin correspond to points of interest on the Nevis map.

Nevis is a 45-minute ferry ride from Basseterre. You can tour Charlestown, the capital, in a half hour or so, but you'll need three to four hours to explore the entire island. There are ample rewards if you decide to explore Nevis independently, but whether this is an option for you will depend largely on your ship's schedule. Most cruise ships arrive in port at around 8 AM, and the ferry schedule can be irregular and infrequent, so many passengers sign up for a cruise line–run shore excursion. If you travel independently, confirm departure times with the tourist office to be sure you'll make it back to your ship on time.

There are three services between St. Kitts and Nevis, all with byzantine schedules that are subject to change. The 150-passenger government-operated ferry M/V *Caribe Queen* makes the 45-minute crossing from Nevis to St. Kitts two to three times daily, except Thursday and Sunday. The former cargo ship *Sea Hustler* is larger and makes the trip twice daily. Round-trip fare for both is $8. The faster, air-conditioned, 110-passenger ferry M/V *Caribe Breeze* makes the run twice daily Thursday and Sunday, more frequently other days. The fare is $12 ($15 first class) round-trip.

Sea-taxi service between the two islands is operated by Kenneth Samuel, Nevis Water Sports, Leeward Island Charters, and Austin Macleod of Pro-Divers for $20 one-way in summer, $25 in winter; discounts can be negotiated for small groups. There is an additional EC$1 tax for port security, paid separately upon departure.

❷ **Bath Springs.** The springs and the Bath Hotel, built by businessman John Huggins in 1778, sustained hurricane and most likely some earthquake damage over the years, but the government is using parts of it now for offices. The first hotel in the Caribbean, the Bath Hotel was so popular in the 19th century that visitors traveled two months by ship to "take the waters" in the hot thermal springs on the property. Volunteers have cleaned up the spring, built a stone pool and steps to enter the waters, and residents and visitors enjoy the springs, which range from 104°F–108°F. This is a fascinating site, with much promise for the future. Follow Main Street south from Charlestown. ⊠ *Charlestown outskirts.*

❹ **Botanical Gardens of Nevis.** In addition to terraced gardens and arbors, this remarkable 7.8-acre site in the glowering shadow of Mt. Nevis has natural lagoons, streams, and waterfalls, as well as superlative bronze mermaids, egrets, and herons, old copper pots used as floral centerpieces, and extravagant fountains. You'll find a proper rose garden, sections devoted to orchids and bromeliads, cacti, and flowering trees and shrubs—even a bamboo garden. The entrance to the Rain Forest Conservatory—which attempts to include every conceivable Caribbean ecosystem and then some—duplicates an imposing Maya temple. A splendid re–creation of a plantation-style great house contains a tearoom with sweeping sea views and a souvenir shop that sells teas, teapots, jams, botanical oils, candles, Caribbean cookbooks, and the like. ⊠ *Montpelier Estate,* ☎ 869/469–3509. ⊟ *$9.* ⊙ *Mon.–Sat. 9–4:30.*

❶ **Charlestown.** About 1,200 of Nevis's 10,000 inhabitants live in the capital. The town faces the Caribbean, about 12½ mi (20 km) south of Basseterre on St. Kitts. If you arrive by ferry, as most people do, you'll walk smack onto Main Street from the pier. It's easy to imagine how tiny Charlestown, founded in 1660, must have looked in its heyday. The weathered buildings still have their fanciful galleries, elaborate gingerbread fretwork, wooden shutters, and hanging plants. The stonework building with the clock tower (1825) houses the courthouse and the second-floor **library** (a cool respite on sultry days). A fire in 1873 damaged the building and destroyed valuable records; much of the present structure dates from the turn of the 20th century. The little park next to the library is Memorial Square, dedicated to the fallen of World Wars I and II. Down the street from the square, archaeologists have discovered the remains of a Jewish cemetery and synagogue (Nevis reputedly had the Caribbean's second-oldest congregation), but there's little to see. The **Alexander Hamilton Birthplace,** which contains the Museum of Nevis History, is on the waterfront, covered in bougainvillea and hibiscus. This Georgian-style house is a reconstruction of what is believed to have been the American patriot's original home, built in 1680 and thought to have been destroyed during an earthquake in the mid-19th century. Hamilton was born here in 1755 and moved to St. Croix when he was about 12. A few years later, at 17, he moved to the American colonies to continue his education; he became Secretary of the Treasury to George Washington and died in a duel with political rival Aaron Burr. The Nevis House of Assembly occupies the second floor of this building, and the museum downstairs contains Hamilton memorabilia, documents pertaining to the island's history, and displays about island geology, politics, architecture, culture, and cuisine. ⊠ *Low St.* ☎ *869/469–5786,* WEB *www. nevis-nhcs.com.* ☎ *$3; $2 if admission already paid to affiliated Nelson Museum.* ☉ *Weekdays 9–4, Sat. 9–noon.*

③ Nelson Museum. This collection merits a visit for its memorabilia of Lord Nelson, including letters, documents, paintings, and even furniture from his flagship. Historical archives of the Nevis Historical and Conservation Society are housed here and are available for public viewing. Nelson was based in Antigua but on military patrol came to Nevis, where he met and eventually married Frances Nisbet, who lived on a plantation here. ⊠ *Bath Rd., outside Charlestown,* ☎ *869/469–0408.* ☎ *$3; $2 if admission already paid to affiliated Museum of Nevis History.* ☉ *Weekdays 9–4, Sat. 9–noon.*

Shopping

Shops used to close for lunch from noon to 1, but more and more establishments are remaining open Monday–Saturday 8–4. Some shops close earlier on Thursday.

ST. KITTS

St. Kitts has limited shopping, but there are a few duty-free shops with good deals on jewelry, perfume, china, and crystal. Don't forget to pick up some CSR, a "new cane spirit drink" that's distilled from fresh sugarcane right on St. Kitts.

Most shopping plazas are in downtown Basseterre—try the **Palms Arcade,** on Fort Street near the Circus; the **Pelican Mall,** across the street from Port Zante (which has a tourism office); and **Port Zante,** the cruiseship pier, where construction of a shopping-dining complex is under way.

The work of **Caribelle Batik** (⊠ Romney Manor, Old Road, ☎ 869/465–6253) is well known; the studio sells batik wraps, T-shirts, dresses, wall hangings, and the like. **Kate Design** (⊠ Bank St., Basseterre, ☎ 869/465–5265) showcases the highly individual style of Kate Spencer, whose paintings, serigraphs, note cards, and other pieces are also available from her studio outside the Rawlins Plantation. **Spencer Cameron Art Gallery** (⊠ 10 N. Independence Sq., Basseterre, ☎ 869/465–1617) has historical reproductions of Caribbean charts and prints, in addition to owner Rosey Cameron's popular Carnevale clown prints and a selection of exceptional work by Caribbean artists. It will mail anywhere.

Nevis

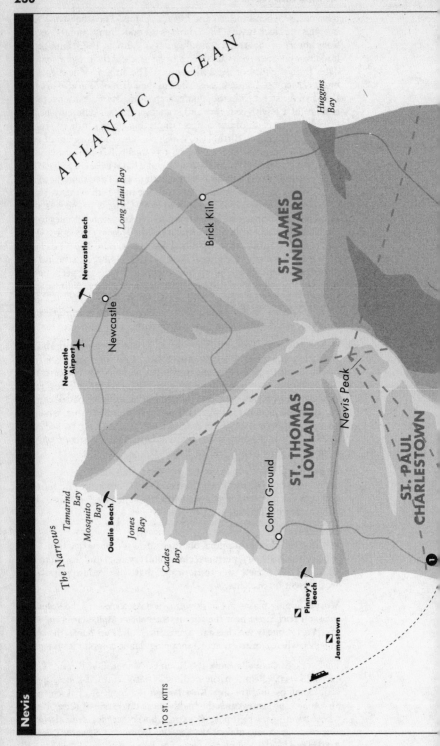

ATLANTIC OCEAN

Huggins
Bay

Long Haul Bay

Brick Kiln

ST. JAMES
WINDWARD

Newcastle Beach

Newcastle

Newcastle
Airport

Nevis Peak

ST. THOMAS
LOWLAND

Cotton Ground

ST. PAUL
CHARLESTOWN

The Narrows

Tamarind
Bay

Mosquito Bay

Oualie Beach

Jones
Bay

Cades
Bay

Pinney's
Beach

Jamestown

TO ST. KITTS

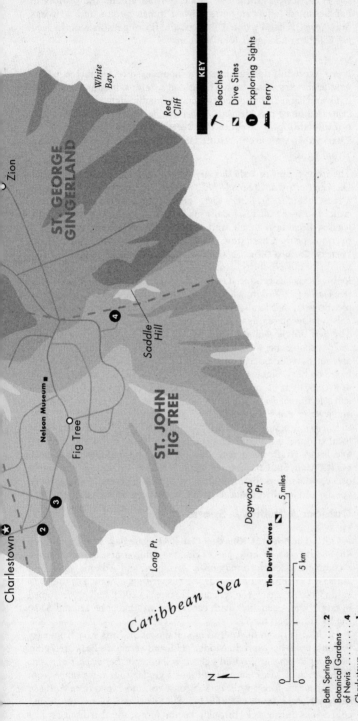

KEY

↗ Beaches

◨ Dive Sites

① Exploring Sights

⛴ Ferry

ST. GEORGE
GINGERLAND

White
Bay

Red
Cliff

Zion

④ Saddle
Hill

Nelson Museum ■

○ Fig Tree

ST. JOHN
FIG TREE

Charlestown ✪

③

②

Long Pt.

Dogwood
Pt.

The Devil's Caves ◨

Caribbean Sea

N

0
0

5 km

5 miles

Bath Springs **2**
Botanical Gardens
of Nevis **4**
Charlestown **1**
Nelson Museum **3**

Stonewall's Tropical Boutique (✉ 7 Princes St., Basseterre, ☎ 869/466–9124) carries top-of-the-line products from around the Caribbean: hand-painted Jamaican pottery, West Indian photos and artworks, brass jewelry, hand-painted T-shirts, and flowing resort wear by leading Caribbean designer John Warden.

NEVIS

Nevis is certainly not the place for a shopping spree, but there are some wonderful surprises, notably the island's stamps, fragrant honey, and batik and hand-embroidered clothing. Virtually all the shopping is concentrated on or just off Main Street in Charlestown, but there is one notable shopping arcade: the **Cotton Ginnery Complex** on the Charlestown waterfront, restored in 1997, which houses stalls of local artisans.

The front rooms of **Café des Arts** (✉ Main St. and Samuel Hunkins Dr., Charlestown, ☎ 869/469–7098) show the works of 15 Caribbean artists, including St. Kitts's Kate Spencer, plus teak furnishings, hand-crafted straw handbags, locally made linen clothing, and gourmet delicacies. Breakfast, lunch, and espresso are served in the backyard, overlooking the Charlestown harbor, adjacent to the Museum of Nevis History. **Caribco Gifts** (✉ Main St., Charlestown, ☎ 869/469–1432) sells affordable T-shirts, candles, and pottery emblazoned with Nevis logos. Nevis has produced one artist of some international repute, the late Dame Eva Wilkin, who for more than 50 years painted island people, flowers, and landscapes in an evocative art naïf style. Her originals are now quite valuable, but prints are available in some local shops. The **Eva Wilkin Gallery** (✉ Clay Ghaut, Gingerland, ☎ 869/469–2673) occupies her former atelier. If the paintings, drawings, and prints are out of your price range, consider buying the lovely note cards based on her designs. **Island Fever** (✉ Main St., Charlestown, ☎ 869/469–0867) has become the island's classiest boutique, with an excellent selection of everything from bathing suits and dresses to straw bags and jewelry. **Knick Knacks** (✉ between Waterfront and Main Sts., next to Unella's Restaurant, Charlestown, ☎ 869/469–5784) showcases top local artisans, including Marvin Chapman (stone and wood carvings) and Jeannie Rigby (exquisite dolls). The **Nevis Handicraft Co-op Society** (✉ Main St., Charlestown, ☎ 869/469–1746), next to the tourist office, offers work by local artisans (clothing, ceramic ware, woven goods) and locally produced honey, hot sauces, and jellies.

Outdoor Activities & Sports

ST. KITTS

➤ GOLF: The **Royal St. Kitts Golf Club** (✉ Frigate Bay, St. Kitts, ☎ 869/465–8339) is an 18-hole, par-72 championship course that underwent a complete redesign to maximize Caribbean and Atlantic views and increase the number of hazards. At this writing, a branch of the Nick Faldo Gold Academy was scheduled to open in 2003. Full play resumed in late 2003; greens fees with cart rental will likely be around $120 for 18 holes, $80 for 9.

➤ HIKING: Trails in the central mountains of St. Kitts vary from easy to don't-try-it-by-yourself. Monkey Hill and Verchild's Peak aren't difficult, although the Verchild's climb will take the better part of a day. Don't attempt Mt. Liamuiga without a guide. Tour rates range from $35 for a rain-forest walk to $65 for a volcano expedition. Addy of **Addy's Nature Tours** (☎ 869/465–8069) offers a picnic lunch and cold drinks during treks through the rain forest; she also discusses history and folklore relating to native plants. Greg Pereira of **Greg's Safaris** (☎ 869/465–4121), whose family has lived on St. Kitts for well over a century, takes groups on half-day trips into the rain forest and on full-day hikes up the volcano and through the grounds of a privately owned 250-year-old great house, followed by excursions down canyons and past petroglyphs. He and his staff relate fascinating historical, folkloric, and botanical information. **Kriss Tours** (☎ 869/465–4042) takes small groups up to the crater, through the rain forest, and to Dos d'Anse Pond, on Verchild's Mountain, heading off-road for trips in a customized Jeep truck.

➤ HORSEBACK RIDING: On St. Kitts, wild North Frigate Bay and desolate Conaree Beach are great for riding. Guides from **Trinity Stables** (☎ 869/465–3226) offers beach rides ($35) and trips into the rain forest ($45).

➤ SCUBA DIVING & SNORKELING: St. Kitts has more than a dozen excellent dive sites. Kenneth Samuel of **Kenneth's Dive Centre** (☎ 869/465–2670) is a PADI-certified dive master who takes small groups of divers with C cards to nearby reefs. Rates average $50 for single-tank dives and $80 for double-tank dives; add $10 for equipment. Night dives, including lights, are $50, and snorkeling trips (four-person minimum) are $35, drinks included. Austin Macleod, a PADI-certified dive master and instructor and owner of **Pro-Divers** (☎ 869/466–3483), offers resort and certification courses. His prices are the lowest on the island: $50 less than anyone else for an open-water certification course. **St. Kitts Scuba** (✉ Frigate Bay, 2 mi [3 km] east of Basseterre, St. Kitts, ☎ 869/465–1189) offers competitive prices, friendly dive masters, and a more international clientele.

NEVIS

➤ GOLF: Duffers doff their hats to the beautiful, impeccably maintained Robert Trent Jones, Jr.–designed 18-hole, par-72, 6,766-yard championship course at the **Four Seasons Resort Nevis** (✉ Pinney's Beach, Nevis, ☎ 869/469–1111). The signature hole is the 15th, a 660-yard monster that encompasses a deep ravine; other holes include bridges, steep drops, rolling pitches, and fierce doglegs. The virtual botanical gardens surrounding the fairways almost qualify as a hazard themselves. Greens fees are $100 per person for 9 holes, $150 for 18.

➤ HIKING: **Eco-Tours Nevis** (☎ 869/469–2091), headed by David Rollinson, rambles through 18th-century estates and explores what remains of Nevis's last working sugar factory as well as archaeological evidence of pre-Columbian settlements. David also offers treks up Mountravers, a spectacular great-house ruin, and historical walks through Charlestown. The fee is $20 per person, $10 for the Charlestown walk. **Michael Herbert** (☎ 869/469–2856) leads four-hour nature hikes up to Herbert Heights, where you can enjoy fresh fruit juice as you drink in the views of Montserrat; the view through a powerful telescope makes you feel as if you're staring right into that island's simmering volcano. The price is $20; for $25 you can ride one of Herbert's donkeys. Michael also brings people up by appointment to Saddle Hill Battery and Nelson's Lookout, where he has constructed a thatched hut. The festive activities include crab races, refreshments, rock climbing, and whale-watching in season, through a telescope donated by Greenpeace. **Sunrise Tours** (☎ 869/469–3512), run by Lynell and Earla Liburd, offers a range of hiking tours, but their most popular is the trip to Devil's Copper, a rock configuration full of ghostly legends. Local people gave it its name because at one time the water was hot—a volcanic thermal stream. They also do a Nevis village walk, a Hamilton Estate Walk, and trips to the rain forest and Nevis Peak. Hikes range from $20 to $40 per person. **Top to Bottom** (☎ 869/469–9080), run by Jim and Nikki Johnston, offers ecorambles (slower tours) and hikes that emphasize Nevis's volcanic and horticultural heritage (including pointing out medicinal herbs). The Johnstons are also keen star- and bird-watchers. Three-hour rambles or hikes are $20 per person (snacks and juice included); it's $30 for a more strenuous climb up Mt. Nevis.

➤ HORSEBACK RIDING: On Nevis you can arrange for leisurely beach rides, more demanding trail rides through the lush hills ($50 per person), and lessons ($20 per hour) through **Nevis Equestrian Centre** (⊠ Clifton Estate, Pinney's Beach, Nevis, ☎ 869/469–8118). Kids love the petting zoo, which has donkeys, goats, peacocks, and tortoises.

➤ SCUBA DIVING & SNORKELING: On Nevis, **Scuba Safaris** (⊠ Oualie Beach, Nevis, ☎ 869/469–9518) is a PADI five-star facility, NAUI Dream Resort, and NASDS Examining Station. It also provides a snorkeling-learning experience that enables you to not only see but listen to sealife, including whales and dolphins.

Beaches

ST. KITTS

The powdery white-sand beaches of St. Kitts, free and open to the public (even those occupied by hotels), are in the Frigate Bay area or on the lower peninsula. **Banana Bay,** one of the island's loveliest beaches, stretches over a mile (1½ km) at the southeastern tip of the island. Several large hotels were abandoned in the early stages of development; their skeletal structures mar an otherwise idyllic scene. **Cockleshell Bay,** Banana Bay's twin beach, is another eyebrow of glittering sand backed by lush vegetation and reachable on foot. Locals consider the Caribbean (southern) side of **Friar's Bay** the island's finest beach. It has two hopping beach bars, Monkey and Sunset, which serve excellent inexpensive grilled and barbecued food. You can haggle with fishermen here to take you snorkeling off the eastern point. The waters on the Atlantic (northern) side are rougher, but the beach has a wild, desolate beauty. On the Caribbean side of **Frigate Bay** you'll find talcum powder–fine sand, while on the Atlantic side, the 4-mi-wide (6½-km-wide) stretch is a favorite with horseback riders.

NEVIS

On Nevis all the beaches are free to the public, but there are no changing facilities, so wear a swimsuit under your clothes. **Oualie Beach,** south of Mosquito Bay and north of Cades and Jones bays, is a beige-sand beach where the folks at Oualie Beach Hotel can mix you a drink and fix you up with water-sports equipment. **Pinney's Beach,** the island's showpiece, has almost 4 mi (6½ km) of soft, golden sand on the calm Caribbean, lined with a magnificent grove of palm trees. The Four Seasons Resort is here, as are the private cabanas and pavilions of several mountain inns and casual beach bars.

Where to Eat

Restaurants occasionally add a 10% service charge to your bill; if this information isn't printed on the menu, ask about it. When there's no service charge, a tip of 15% is appropriate.

ST. KITTS

$$$$ ✕ **Rawlins Plantation.** The refined dining room at the Rawlins Plantation Inn has fieldstone walls, lovely family antiques and period furnishings, and high-vaulted ceilings. Owner Claire Rawson is one of the island's most sophisticated chefs. The bountiful lunch buffet offers such classic West Indian items as breadfruit salad, shrimp fritters with mango salsa, and lobster and spinach crepes. ⊠ *Rawlins Plantation Inn, St. Paul's,* ☎ 869/465–6221. *Reservations essential. AE, MC, V.*

$$–$$$ ✕ **Ballahoo.** This second-floor terrace restaurant draws a crowd for breakfast, lunch, and dinner. Lilting calypso and reggae on the sound system, whirring ceiling fans, potted palms, and colorful island prints are appropriately tropical. Specialties include chili shrimp, conch simmered in garlic butter, Madras-style beef curry, lobster stir-fry, and a

toasted rum-and-banana sandwich. Go at lunchtime, when you can watch the bustle of the Circus and the prices for many dishes are slashed nearly in half. ⊠ *Fort St., Basseterre,* ☎ *869/465–4197. AE, MC, V. Closed Sun.*

$–$$ ✕ **Turtle Beach Bar and Grill.** Treats at this popular daytime watering hole include honey-mustard ribs, coconut-shrimp salad, grilled lobster, and the freshest fish in town. Business cards and pennants from around the world plaster the bar; the room is decorated with nautical accoutrements. You can snorkel here, spot hawksbill turtles, feed the tame monkeys that boldly belly up to the bar, laze in a palm-shaded hammock, or rent a kayak or snorkel gear. On Sunday afternoon, locals come for volleyball and dancing to bands. It's at the south end of S.E. Peninsula Road, but it's open only until 6 PM. ⊠ *S.E. Peninsula Rd., Turtle Beach,* ☎ *869/469–9086. AE, MC, V. No dinner.*

NEVIS

$$$$ ✕ **Golden Rock Plantation Inn.** The romantic, dimly lit room has fieldstone walls dating from the Golden Rock Inn's plantation days. Enchanting Eva Wilkin originals grace the walls, copper sugar-boiling pots are used as planters, and straw mats and unglazed local pottery provide island interest; distressed French highback chairs, maroon linens, and gold napery contribute colonial accents. The prix-fixe menu might include velvety pumpkin soup, raisin curry chicken, and grilled local snapper with *tania* (a type of tuber) fritters. Don't miss the homemade juices, like passion fruit, soursop, and ginger beer. ⊠ *Gingerland,* ☎ *869/469–3346. Reservations essential. AE, MC, V. Closed Sun.*

$–$$$ ✕ **Unella's.** It's nothing fancy here—just tables on a second-floor porch overlooking Charlestown's waterfront. Stop for exceptional lobster (more expensive than the rest of the menu), curried lamb, island-style spareribs, and steamed conch, all served with local vegetables, rice, and peas. Unella's opens around 9 AM, when locals and boaters appear, eager for breakfast, and stays open all day. ⊠ *Waterfront, Charlestown,* ☎ *869/469–5574. No credit cards.*

¢–$$ ✕ **Sunshine's.** Everything about this beach shack is larger than life, including the proprietor, Rasta man Llewelyn "Sunshine" Caines. Flags from around the world drape the lean-to and complement the international patrons (including an occasional movie star), who wander over from the adjacent Four Seasons. Picnic tables are splashed with bright sunrise-to-sunset colors; even the palm trees are painted. Fishermen cruise up with their catches—you might savor lobster rolls or snapper creole. Don't miss the lethal house specialty, Killer Bee rum punch. As Sunshine boasts, "One and you're stung, two you're stunned, three it's a knockout." ⊠ *Pinney's Beach,* ☎ *869/469–1089. No credit cards.*

St. Lucia

Magnificent St. Lucia—with towering mountains, dense rain forest, fertile green valleys, and acres of banana plantations—lies in the middle of the Windward Islands. Nicknamed "the Helen of the West Indies" because of its natural beauty, St. Lucia is distinguished from its neighbors by its distinctive geological landmarks, the Pitons, twin peaks on the southwest coast that have become a symbol of this island, soar nearly 1 km (½ mi) above the ocean floor. Nearby, outside the French colonial town of Soufrière, is a "drive-in" volcano, with neighboring sulfur springs that have rejuvenated bathers for nearly three centuries.

A century and a half of battles between the French and English resulted in St. Lucia's changing hands 14 times before 1814, when England established possession. In 1979 the island became an independent state within the British Commonwealth of Nations. The official language is English, although most people also speak a French-creole patois.

CURRENCY

St. Lucia uses the Eastern Caribbean (E.C.) dollar. The exchange rate is EC$2.70 to US$1. Although U.S. dollars are readily accepted, you'll often get change in E.C. currency. Credit cards and traveler's checks are widely accepted. Prices given below are in U.S. dollars unless otherwise indicated.

TELEPHONES

You can dial international numbers from St. Lucia's pay phones and card phones. Telephone services are available at Pointe Seraphine, the cruise-ship port of entry. To charge an overseas call to a major credit card, dial 811; there's no surcharge.

SHORE EXCURSIONS

The following are good choices in St. Lucia. They may not be offered by all cruise lines. Times and prices are approximate.

La Soufrière and the Pitons. "If you haven't been to Soufrière, you haven't been to St. Lucia," the local people say. Travel the mountainous and winding West Coast Road for a spectacular view of the Pitons on the way to La Soufrière volcano, the sulfur springs, nearby Diamond Falls and Mineral Baths, and the Botanical Gardens. Lunch will be a creole buffet. ⊙ *6 hrs,* ⊠ *$68.*

Northern Highlights. You tour the lush, tropical northern part of the island, going to Morne Fortune, Rodney Bay, Pigeon Island, and Reduit Beach, where you'll have time to swim and snorkel. ⊙ *4 hrs,* ⊠ *$38.*

Pitons by Land and Sea. This trip to St. Lucia's popular attractions—La Soufrière volcano, Diamond Botanical Gardens, and Soufrière Estate—catamarans up and down the coast, with a stop for snorkeling. ⊙ *7 hrs,* ⊠ *$82.*

Rain-forest Biking Adventure. After traveling into the island's rain forest, you'll get on a mountain bike and travel along a fairly level path through a private banana plantation to Errard Falls, where you will have a chance to swim in the cool water. ⊙ *4 hrs,* ⊠ *$64.*

Coming Ashore

Most cruise ships call at the capital city of Castries, on the island's northwest coast. Either of two docking areas is used: Pointe Seraphine, a port of entry and duty-free shopping complex, or Port Castries, a commercial dock across the harbor. Ferry service connects the two piers.

Smaller vessels can call at Soufrière, on the island's southwest coast. Ships calling at Soufrière usually anchor offshore and transport passengers to the wharf via launch.

Tourist information offices are at Pointe Seraphine in Castries and along the waterfront on Bay Street in Soufrière. Downtown Castries is within walking distance of the pier, and the produce market and adjacent crafts and vendors' markets are the main attractions. Soufrière is a sleepy West Indian town, but it's worth a short walk around the central square to view the French colonial architecture. Most of St. Lucia's sightseeing attractions are in or near Soufrière.

Taxis are available at the docks. Although they are unmetered, the government has issued a list of standard fares that are posted at the entrance to Pointe Seraphine. Taxi drivers are well informed and can give you a full tour—often an excellent one, thanks to government-sponsored training programs. From the Castries area, full-day island tours cost $140 for up to four people; sightseeing trips to Soufrière, $120. If you plan your own day, expect to pay the driver $20 per hour plus tip. Whatever your destination, negotiate the price with the driver before you depart—and be sure that you both understand whether the rate is in E.C. or U.S. dollars. Drivers appreciate a 10% tip.

Exploring St. Lucia

Numbers in the margin correspond to points of interest on the St. Lucia map.

CASTRIES AREA

① Castries. The capital, a busy commercial city of about 65,000 people, wraps around a sheltered bay. Morne Fortune rises sharply to the south of town, creating a dramatic green backdrop. The charm of Castries lies almost entirely in its liveliness, since most of the colonial buildings were destroyed by four fires that occurred between 1796 and 1948. Freighters (exporting bananas, coconut, cocoa, mace, nutmeg, and citrus fruits) and cruise ships come and go daily, making Castries Harbour one of the Caribbean's busiest ports. **Pointe Seraphine** is a duty-free shopping complex on the north side of the harbor, about a 20-minute walk or 2-minute cab ride from the city center; a launch ferries passengers across the harbor when ships are in port. Pointe Seraphine's attractive Spanish-style architecture houses more than 20 upscale duty-free shops, a tourist information kiosk, a taxi stand, and car-rental agencies. **Derek Walcott Square** is a green oasis bordered by Brazil, Laborie, Micoud, and Bourbon streets. Formerly Columbus Square, it was renamed to honor the hometown poet who won the 1992 Nobel prize for literature—one of two Nobel laureates from St. Lucia (the late Sir W. Arthur Lewis won the 1979 prize in economics). Some of the 19th-century buildings that have survived fire, wind, and rain can be seen on Brazil Street, the square's southern border. On the Laborie Street side, there's a huge, 400-year-old *samaan* tree with leafy branches that shade a good portion of the square. Directly across Laborie Street from Derek Walcott Square is the Roman Catholic **Cathedral of the Immaculate Conception,** which was built in 1897. Though it is rather somber on the outside, its interior walls are decorated with colorful murals reworked by St. Lucian artist Dunstan St. Omer in 1985, just prior to the pope's visit. This church has an active parish and is open daily for both public viewing and religious services. At the corner of Jeremie and Peynier streets, spreading beyond its brilliant orange roof, is the **Castries Market.** Full of excitement and bustle, the market is open every day except Sunday. It is liveliest on Saturday morning, when farmers bring their fresh produce and spices to town, as they have for more than a century. Next door to the produce market is the **Craft Market,** where you can buy pottery, wood carvings, and hand-woven straw articles. Across Peynier Street from the Craft Market, at the **Vendor's Arcade,** there are still more handicrafts and souvenirs.

⑤ Fort Charlotte. Begun in 1764 by the French as the Citadelle du Morne Fortune, Fort Charlotte was completed after 20 years of battling and changing hands. Its old barracks and batteries are now government buildings and educational facilities, but you can drive around and look at the remains, including redoubts, a guardroom, stables, and cells. You can also walk up to the Inniskilling Monument, a tribute to the 1796 battle in which the 27th Foot Royal Inniskilling Fusiliers wrested the Morne from the French. At the military cemetery, first used in 1782, faint inscriptions on the tombstones tell the tales of French and English soldiers who died here. Six governors of the island are buried here as well. From this point atop Morne Fortune you can view Martinique to the north and the twin peaks of the Pitons to the south.

④ Morne Fortune. Morne Fortune forms a striking backdrop for the capital. This "Hill of Good Luck" has overlooked more than its share of bad luck over the years—including devastating hurricanes and four fires

238

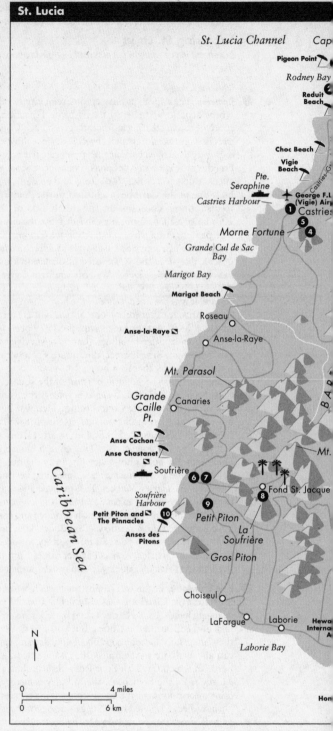

St. Lucia

St. Lucia Channel   Cap

Pigeon Point

Rodney Bay

Reduit
Beach

Choc Beach

Vigie
Beach

Pte.
Seraphine

Castries Harbour   George F.L.
                                (Vigie) Airp

Castries

Morne Fortune

Grande Cul de Sac
Bay

Marigot Bay

Marigot Beach

Roseau

Anse-la-Raye

Anse-la-Raye

Mt. Parasol

Grande
Caille
Pt.   Canaries

Anse Cochon
Anse Chastanet

Soufrière

Caribbean Sea

Soufrière
Harbour

Petit Piton and
The Pinnacles

Anses des
Pitons

Petit Piton

La
Soufrière

Gros Piton

Fond St. Jacque

Choiseul

LaFargue   Laborie   Hewa
                             Interna
                                 A

Laborie Bay

N

0   4 miles
0   6 km

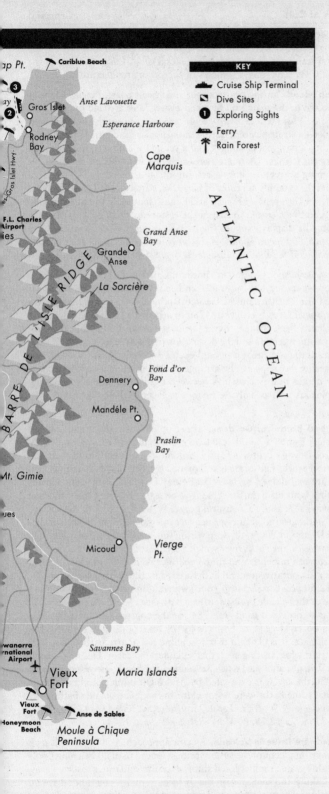

ap Pt.   🛩 Cariblue Beach

③
ay
②   Gros Islet   *Anse Lavouette*

🏊 Rodney   *Esperance Harbour*
    Bay
                              Cape
                            Marquis

F.L. Charles
Airport
ies   *Grand Anse
                            Bay*
                  Grande○
                  Anse
              La Sorcière

KEY
🚢 Cruise Ship Terminal
◣ Dive Sites
① Exploring Sights
⚓ Ferry
🌴 Rain Forest

ATLANTIC OCEAN

*Fond d'or
Bay*
          Dennery○

      Mandéle Pt.○

                *Praslin
                Bay*

Mt. Gimie

ues

          Micoud○   *Vierge
                        Pt.*

wanorra
rnational
Airport   *Savannes Bay*
   ✈ Vieux   *Maria Islands*
     Fort
🏊 ○

Vieux
Fort   ⚓ Anse de Sables
Honeymoon
Beach   *Moule à Chique
            Peninsula*

that leveled Castries. The drive to Morne Fortune from Castries will take you past **Government House**, on Government House Road, the official residence of the governor-general of St. Lucia and one of the island's few remaining examples of Victorian architecture.

🖐 ❸ **Pigeon Island.** Jutting out from the northwest coast, Pigeon Island is connected to the mainland by a causeway. Tales are told of the pirate Jambe de Bois (Wooden Leg), who once hid out on this 44-acre hilltop islet—a strategic point during the struggles for control of St. Lucia. Now, it's a national landmark and a venue for concerts, festivals, and family gatherings. There are two small beaches with calm waters for swimming and snorkeling, a restaurant, and picnic areas. Scattered around the grounds are ruins of barracks, batteries, and garrisons that date from 18th-century French and English battles. In the Museum and Interpretative Centre, housed in the restored British officers' mess, a multimedia display explains the island's ecological and historical significance. ✉ *Pigeon Island, St. Lucia National Trust, Rodney Bay,* ☎ *758/452–5005,* WEB *www.slunatrust.org.* 🎫 *$4.* ☉ *Daily 9–5.*

❷ **Rodney Bay.** About 15 minutes north of Castries, the 80-acre man-made lagoon—surrounded by hotels and many popular restaurants—is named for British admiral George Rodney, who sailed the English Navy out of Gros Islet Bay in 1780 to attack and ultimately decimate the French fleet. Rodney Bay Marina is one of the Caribbean's premier yachting centers and the destination of the Atlantic Rally for Cruisers (transatlantic yacht crossing) each December. Yacht charters and sightseeing day trips can be arranged at the marina. The Rodney Bay Ferry makes hourly crossings between the marina and the shopping complex, as well as daily excursions to Pigeon Island.

SOUFRIÈRE AREA

🖐 ❼ **Diamond Botanical Gardens.** These splendid gardens are part of Soufrière Estate, a 2,000-acre land grant made in 1713 by Louis XIV to three Devaux brothers from Normandy in recognition of their services to France. The estate is still owned by their descendants; the gardens are maintained by Joan Du Boulay Devaux. Bushes and shrubs bursting with brilliant flowers grow beneath towering trees and line pathways that lead to a natural gorge. Water bubbling to the surface from underground sulfur springs streams downhill in rivulets to become Diamond Waterfall, deep within the botanical gardens. Through the centuries, the rocks over which the cascade spills have become encrusted with minerals and tinted yellow, green, and purple. Adjacent to the falls, curative mineral baths are fed by the underground springs. For $2.50 you can slip into your swimsuit and bathe for 30 minutes in one of the outside pools; a private bath costs $3.75. King Louis XVI of France provided funds in 1784 for the construction of a building with a dozen large stone baths to fortify his troops against the St. Lucian climate. It is claimed that Joséphine Bonaparte bathed here as a young girl while visiting her father's plantation nearby. During the Brigand's War, just after the French Revolution, the bathhouse was destroyed. In 1930 the site was excavated by André Du Boulay, and two of the original stone baths were restored for his use. The outside baths were added later. ✉ *Soufrière Estate, Soufrière,* ☎ *758/452–4759 or 758/454–7565.* 🎫 *$2.75.* ☉ *Mon.–Sat. 10–5, Sun. 10–3.*

🖐 ❽ **La Soufrière Drive-In Volcano.** As you approach, your nose will pick up the strong scent of the sulfur springs—more than 20 belching pools of muddy water, multicolored sulfur deposits, and other assorted minerals baking and steaming on the surface. Actually, you don't drive in. You drive up within a few hundred feet of the gurgling, steaming mass, then walk behind your guide—whose service is included in the admission price—around a fault in the substratum rock. It's a fascinating, educational half hour that can also be pretty stinky on a hot day. ⊠ *Bay St., Soufrière, ☎ 758/459–5500. 🖃 $1.25. ⊙ Daily 9–5.*

Morne Coubaril Estate. This 250-acre coconut and cocoa plantation in Soufrière, the first major estate established on St. Lucia, has a rich French history that dates from 1713, when Crown land was granted by King Louis XIV to three St. Lucian brothers. Authentic 18th-century plantation life is explained as a guide escorts you along an original mule-carriage pathway and through reconstructed slave quarters. On the 90-minute tour you see how cocoa, copra, and manioc were processed in the days before mechanization. The foliage is thick and green, and the tropical flowers are beautiful. The plantation house has been renovated and furnished according to original plans. You can purchase freshly made cocoa, straw goods, and hand-carved wooden pieces. A delicious creole buffet lunch is available by reservation for about $10 per person. ⊠ *Soufrière, ☎ 758/459–7340. 🖃 $6. ⊙ Daily 9–5.*

The Pitons. These incredible mountains have become the symbol of St. Lucia. The road south from Soufrière offers a magnificent view of the twin peaks, which rise precipitously from the cobalt blue Caribbean. The pyramidal cones, covered with thick tropical vegetation, were formed by lava from a volcanic eruption 30 to 40 million years ago. They are not identical twins since—confusingly—2,619-ft (801-m) Petit Piton is taller than 2,461-ft (753-m) Gros Piton, though Gros Piton is, as the word translates, broader. Gros Piton is currently the only one where climbing is permitted, though the trail up even this shorter Piton is one very tough trek and requires the permission of the **Forest and Lands Department** (☎ 758/450–2231 or 758/450–2078) and a knowledgeable guide—whose services cost about $45.

Soufrière. It's a 1½-hour drive on the winding West Coast Road (or a 45-minute boat ride) from Castries to Soufrière, the oldest town in St. Lucia and the former French colonial capital. The town was founded in 1746 and named for its proximity to the volcano. The wharf is the center of activity in this sleepy town (which has a population of about 9,000), particularly when a cruise ship is moored in pretty Soufrière Bay. French-colonial influences can be noticed in the architecture of the wooden buildings, with second-story verandahs and gingerbread trim, that surround the market square. The market building is decorated with colorful murals. The **Soufrière Tourist Information Centre** (⊠ Bay St., Soufrière, ☎ 758/459–7200) provides information about area attractions.

Shopping

Soufrière is not much of a shopping port, although a small arts-and-crafts center is adjacent to the wharf. Local products include silk-screened or batik fabric and clothing, pottery, wood carvings, cocoa and spices, and baskets. The only duty-free shopping is at **Pointe Seraphine** or **La Place Carenage,** on opposite sides of the harbor. You must show your cabin key to get duty-free prices. You'll want to experience the **Castries Market** and scour the adjacent **Vendor's Arcade** and **Craft Market** for handicrafts and souvenirs at bargain prices.

Artsibit Gallery (⊠ Brazil and Mongiraud Sts., Castries, ☎ 758/452–7865) exhibits and sells moderately priced pieces by St. Lucian painters and sculptors. **Bagshaw Studios** (⊠ La Toc Rd., La Toc Bay, Castries, ☎ 758/452–2139 or 758/451–9249) sells clothing and table linens in colorful tropical patterns using Stanley Bagshaw's original designs. The fabrics are silk-screened by hand in the adjacent workroom. You can also find Bagshaw boutiques at Pointe Seraphine, La Place Carenage, and Rodney Bay, and a selection of items in gift shops at Hewanorra Airport. Stop by this workshop to see how Stanley Bagshaw's original tropical designs are turned into colorful silk-screened fabrics, which are fashioned into clothing and household articles that are created and sold on-site. Admission is free; it's open weekdays 8:30–5, Saturday 8:30–4, and Sunday 10–1. Weekend hours may be extended if a cruise ship is in port. At **Caribelle Batik** (⊠ Howelton House, Morne Fortune, Castries, ☎ 758/452–3785), craftsmen demonstrate the art of batik and silk-screen printing. Meanwhile, seamstresses create clothing and wall hangings, which you can purchase in the shop. The studio is in an old Victorian mansion, high atop the Morne overlooking Castries. There's a terrace where you can have a cool drink, and there's a garden full of tropical orchids and lilies. Caribelle Batik creations are featured in many gift shops throughout St. Lucia.

Eudovic Art Studio (⊠ Morne Fortune, Castries, ☎ 758/452–2747) is a workshop and studio where you can buy trays, masks, and figures sculpted from local mahogany, red cedar, and eucalyptus wood. **Noah's Arkade** (⊠ Jeremie St., Castries, ☎ 758/452–2523; ⊠ Pointe Seraphine, Castries, ☎ 758/452–7488) has hammocks, wood carvings, straw mats, T-shirts, books, and other regional goods. At **Zaka** (⊠ Rodney Bay, ☎ 758/452–0946), next to Shamrock's Pub, you can find contemporary Caribbean masks and totems carved from local driftwood and painted in brilliant colors. All pieces are created in a home studio, just down the road, by London-born woodcarver Simon Gajadhar and his wife, St. Lucian artist Sophie Barnard.

Outdoor Activities & Sports

FISHING

Among the deep-sea creatures you can find in St. Lucia's waters are dolphinfish (dorado), barracuda, mackerel, wahoo, kingfish, sailfish, and white or blue marlin. Sportfishing is generally done on a catch-and-release basis, but the captain may permit you to take a fish back to your hotel to be prepared for your dinner. Neither spearfishing nor collecting live fish in coastal waters is permitted. Half- or full-day deep-sea fishing excursions can be arranged at either Vigie Cove or Rodney Bay Marina. A half-day of fishing on a scheduled trip runs about $80 per person. **Captain Mike's** (⊠ Vigie Cove, ☎ 758/452–1216 or 758/452–7044) has a fleet of Bertram fishing boats (up to 38 ft long) that accommodate as many as eight passengers; equipment and cold drinks are supplied. **Mako Watersports** (⊠ Rodney Bay Marina, Rodney Bay, ☎ 758/452–0412) takes fishing enthusiasts out on the well-equipped six-passenger *Annie Baby*.

GOLF

Courses on St. Lucia are scenic and enjoyable, but they're not championship quality. **St. Lucia Golf and Country Club** (⊠ Cap Estate, ☎ 758/452–8523), the island's only public course, is at the island's northern tip and offers panoramic views of both the Atlantic and Caribbean. It's an 18-hole course (6,829 yards, par 72). The clubhouse has a bar and a pro shop where you can rent clubs and shoes and arrange lessons. Greens fees are $70 for 9 holes or $95 for 18 holes; carts are included. Reservations are essential.

HIKING

The island is laced with trails, but you shouldn't attempt the challenging peaks on your own. The **St. Lucia Forestry Department** (☎ 758/450–2231) manages trails throughout the rain forest and provides guides who explain the plants and trees you'll encounter and keep you on the right track for a small fee—about $10 per person. The **St. Lucia National Trust** (☎ 758/452–5005) maintains two trails: one is at Anse La

Liberté, near Canaries on the Caribbean coast; the other is on the Atlantic coast, from Mandélé Point to the Fregate Islands Nature Reserve. Full-day excursions with lunch cost about $55 per person and can be arranged through hotels or tour operators.

HORSEBACK RIDING

Creole horses, an indigenous breed, are fairly small, fast, sturdy, and even-tempered animals suitable for beginners. Established stables can accommodate all skill levels and offer countryside trail rides, beach rides with picnic lunches, plantation tours, carriage rides, and lengthy treks. Prices run about $40 for one hour, $50 for two hours, and $70 for a three-hour beach ride and barbecue. Transportation is usually provided between the stables and nearby hotels. People sometimes appear on beaches with their steeds and offer 30-minute rides for $10; ride at your own risk. **International Riding Stables** (⊠ Beauséjour Estate, Gros Islet, ☏ 758/452–8139 or 758/450–8665) offers either English- or Western-style riding. Its beach-picnic ride includes time for a swim—with or without your horse. **Trim's National Riding Stable** (⊠ Cas-en-Bas, Gros Islet, ☏ 758/452–8273 or 758/450–9971), the island's oldest equine establishment, offers four riding sessions per day, plus beach tours, trail rides, and carriage tours to Pigeon Island.

SCUBA DIVING

The coral reefs at Anse Cochon and Anse Chastanet, on the southwest coast, are popular beach-entry dive sites. In the north, Pigeon Island is the most convenient site. **Buddies** (⊠ Rodney Bay Marina, Rodney Bay, ☏ 758/452–9086) offers wall, wreck, reef, and deep dives; resort courses and open-water certification with advanced and specialty courses are taught by PADI-certified instructors. **Frogs** (⊠ Windjammer Landing Villa Beach Resort, Labrelotte Bay, ☏ 758/452–0913; ⊠ Jalousie Hilton, Anse des Pitons, ☏ 758/452–0913 or 758/459–7666 Ext. 4024) provides resort courses and open-water certification. Two-tank and night dives are also offered, and rental equipment is available. **Scuba St. Lucia** (⊠ Anse Chastanet, Soufrière, ☏ 758/459–7755; ⊠ Rex St. Lucian Hotel, Rodney Bay, ☏ 758/452–8009) is a PADI five-star training facility. Daily beach and boat dives and resort and certification courses are offered; underwater photography and snorkeling equipment are available. Day trips from the north of the island include round-trip speedboat transportation.

Beaches

All of St. Lucia's beaches are open to the public, but resorts are sometimes less than welcoming to large groups of cruise-ship passengers. **Anse Chastanet,** in front of the resort of the same name, is just north of Soufrière. This palm-studded dark-sand beach has a backdrop of green hills, brightly painted fishing skiffs bobbing at anchor, and the island's best reefs for snorkeling and diving. The resort's wooden gazebos are nestled among the palms; its dive shop, restaurant, and bar are on the beach and open to the public, but unless you are with a group, a taxi ride may be prohibitively expensive. At **Pigeon Point,** a small beach within Pigeon Island National Historic Park, a restaurant serves snacks and drinks, but this is also a perfect spot for picnicking. It's about a 30-minute taxi ride ($20) from Pointe Seraphine. **Reduit Beach,** a long stretch of golden sand, is next to Rodney Bay. The Rex St. Lucian Hotel, which faces the beach, has a water-sports center. Many feel that Reduit (pronounced red-*wee*) is the island's finest beach.

Where to Eat

An 8% government tax is applicable to your bill, and most restaurants add a 10% service charge in lieu of tip.

$$ ✕ **The Coal Pot.** Popular since the early 1960s, this tiny waterfront restaurant (only 10 tables) is managed by Michelle Elliott, daughter of the original owner, and her French husband, chef Xavier. For a light lunch opt for Greek or shrimp salad, or broiled fresh fish with creole sauce. Dinner might start with divine pumpkin soup, followed by fresh seafood accompanied by one (or more) of the chef's fabulous sauces—ginger, coconut-curry, lemon–garlic butter, or wild mushroom. Hearty eaters may prefer duck, lamb, beef, or chicken laced with peppercorns, red wine, and onion or Roquefort sauce. ⊠ *Vigie Marina, Castries,* ☎ *758/452–5566. Reservations essential. AE, D, MC, V. Closed Sun. No lunch Sat.*

$–$$ ✕ **The Hummingbird.** The chef at this cheerful restaurant-bar in the Hummingbird Beach Resort specializes in French creole cuisine, starting with fresh seafood or chicken seasoned with local herbs and accompanied by a medley of vegetables just picked from the Hummingbird's garden. Sandwiches and salads are also available. If you stop for lunch, be sure to visit the batik studio and art gallery of proprietor Joan Alexander and her son, adjacent to the dining room. ⊠ *Hummingbird Beach Resort, Anse Chastanet Rd., Soufrière,* ☎ *758/459–7232. AE, D, MC, V.*

$–$$ ✕ **The Still.** If you're visiting Diamond Waterfall, this is a good lunch spot. The two dining rooms of the Still Plantation & Beach Resort seat up to 400 people, so it's a popular stop for tour groups and cruise passengers. The emphasis is on creole cuisine using local vegetables—christophenes, breadfruits, yams, callaloo—and seafood, but there are also pork and beef dishes. All fruits and vegetables used in the restaurant are organically grown on the estate. ⊠ *Still Plantation & Beach Resort, Bay St., Soufrière,* ☎ *758/459–7232. MC, V.*

¢–$$ ✕ **The Lime.** A casual bistro with lime-green gingham curtains, straw hats decorating the ceiling, and hanging plants, the Lime specializes in char-grilled steaks and fresh-caught fish, along with spicy jerk chicken or pork. The meals are well prepared, the portions are plentiful, and the prices are reasonable, which is perhaps why you often see St. Lucians and visitors alike "liming" at this popular all-day (and most of the night) restaurant. The Late Lime, a club where the crowd gathers as night turns to morning, is next door. ⊠ *Rodney Bay,* ☎ *758/452–0761. MC, V.*

St. Maarten/St. Martin

St. Martin/St. Maarten: one tiny island, just 37 square mi (59 square km), with two different accents, and ruled by two sovereign nations. Here French and Dutch have lived side by side for hundreds of years, and when you cross from one country to the next there are no border patrols, no customs. In fact, the only indication that you have crossed a border at all is a small sign and a change in road surface.

St. Martin/St. Maarten epitomizes tourist islands in the sun, where services are well developed but there's still some Caribbean flavor. The Dutch side is ideal for people who like plenty to do. The French side has a more genteel ambience, more fashionable shopping, and a Continental flair. The combination makes an almost ideal port. On the negative side, the island has been completely developed. There's gambling, but table limits are so low that high rollers will have a better time gamboling on the beach. It can be fun to shop, and you'll find an occasional bargain, but many goods are cheaper in the United States.

Though Dutch is the official language of St. Maarten, and French of St. Martin, almost everyone speaks English. If you hear a language you can't quite place, it's most likely Papiamento, a Spanish-based Creole.

Legal tender on the Dutch side is the Netherlands Antilles florin (guilder), written NAf; on the French side, the official currency is the euro (€). There's little need to exchange money. On the Dutch side, prices are usually given in both NAf and U.S. dollars, and dollars are accepted all over the island.

TELEPHONES

To call the Dutch side from the U.S., dial 011–599/54 plus the local number; for the French side, 011–590–590 plus the six-digit local number. Remember that a call from one side to the other is an international call.

At the Landsradio in Philipsburg, there are facilities for overseas calls and an AT&T USADirect phone, where you are directly in touch with an AT&T operator who will accept collect or credit-card calls. On the French side, you can't make collect calls to the U.S., and there are no coin phones. If you need to use public phones, go to the special desk at Marigot's post office and buy a *télécarte*. There's a public phone at the tourist office in Marigot where you can make credit-card calls: the operator takes your card number (any major card) and assigns you a PIN (Personal Identification Number), which you then use to charge calls to your card.

SHORE EXCURSIONS

The following are good choices in St. Martin/St. Maarten. They may not be offered by all cruise lines. Times and prices are approximate.

Beach Sojourn. Take a short bus ride to beautiful Baie Orientale (Orient Bay) on the French side of the island. The 1½-mi (3 km) beach is often referred to as the French Riviera of the Caribbean, with its trendy, chic beachside restaurants and bars and colorful chaises longues and umbrellas. Lunch and drinks are included. ☉ *4½ hrs,* ▨ *$49.*

Butterfly Farm. You start by touring the island's butterfly farm, followed by a stop at Marigot for shopping and strolling. ☉ *3½ hrs,* ▨ *$38.*

Ile Fourche Snorkel Trip. Sail to the best snorkel spot on the island and enjoy a party with drinks and music on the way back. ☉ *4 hrs* ▨ *$59.*

Under Two Flags. This bus tour takes you around the island, from the Dutch capital of Philipsburg. You'll also stop at Hope Hill to take in the view and a drink. ☉ *3½ hrs,* ▨ *$27.*

Coming Ashore

Most cruise ships drop anchor off the Dutch capital of Philipsburg or dock in the marina at the southern tip of the Philipsburg harbor. If your ship anchors, tenders will ferry you to the town pier in the middle of town, where taxis await passengers. If your ship docks at the marina, downtown is a 15-minute taxi ride away. The walk is not recommended. To get to major sights outside of Philipsburg or Marigot, your best bet is a tour via taxi; negotiate the rate before you get in. A 2½-hour to 3-hour tour of the island for two people should be about $30, plus $10 per additional person. No place on the island is more than a 30-minute drive from Marigot or Philipsburg. Car-rental rates are moderate, starting at as little as $25 a day during the low season, and you do not need a temporary driving permit.

Taxis are government-regulated and fairly costly. Authorized taxis display stickers of the St. Maarten Taxi Association. Taxis are also available at Marigot.

Exploring St. Maarten/St. Martin

Numbers in the margin correspond to points of interest on the St. Martin/St. Maarten map.

4 Butterfly Farm. Visitors enter a serene, tropical environment when they walk through the terrarium-like Butterfly Sphere. At any given time, as many as 600 butterflies, representing some 40 species, flutter inside the garden under a tented net. Butterfly art and memorabilia are for sale in the gift shop. ✉ *Rte. de Le Galion, Quartier d'Orléans,* ☎ *590/87–31–21,* WEB *www.thebutterflyfarm.com.* 🎟 *$12.* ۞ *Daily 9–3:30.*

6 French Cul de Sac. North of Orient Bay Beach, the French-colonial mansion of St. Martin's mayor is nestled in the hills. Little red-roof houses look like open umbrellas tumbling down the green hillside. The area is peaceful and good for hiking. There's a lot of construction, however, as the surroundings are slowly being developed. From the beach here, shuttle boats make the five-minute trip to **Ilet Pinel,** an uninhabited island that's fine for picnicking, sunning, and swimming.

7 Grand Case. The island's most picturesque town is set in the heart of the French side on a beach at the foot of green hills and pastures. Though it has only a 1-mi-long (1½-km-long) main street, it's known as the "restaurant capital of the Caribbean." More than 27 restaurants serve French, Italian, Indonesian, and Vietnamese fare here. The budget-minded love the half-dozen *lolos*—kiosks at the far end of town that sell savory barbecue and seafood. Grand Case Beach Club is at the end of this road and has two beaches where you can take a dip.

2 Guana Bay Point. On the rugged, windswept east coast about 10 minutes north of Philipsburg, Guana Bay Point offers isolated, untended beaches and a spectacular view of St. Barths.

8 Le Fort Louis. Though not much remains of the structure itself, the fort, completed by the French in 1789, commands a sweeping view of Marigot, its harbor, and the English island of Anguilla, which alone makes it worth the climb. There are few signs to show the way, so the best way to find the fort is to go to Marigot and look up. ✉ *Marigot.*

9 Marigot. This town's southern European flavor is most in evidence at its beautiful harborfront, with its shopping stalls, open-air cafés, and fresh-food vendors. It is well worth a few hours to explore if you are a shopper, a gourmand, or just a Francophile. Marina Royale is the shopping complex at the port, but rue de la République and rue de la Liberté, which border the bay, are also filled with duty-free shops, boutiques, and bistros. The West Indies Mall offers a deluxe shopping experience. There is less bustle here than in Philipsburg, and the open-air cafés are tempting places to sit and people-watch. Marigot doesn't die at night, so you might wish to stay here into the evening—particularly on Wednesdays, when the market opens its art, crafts, and souvenir stalls, and on Thursdays, when the shops of Marina Royale remain open until 10 and shoppers enjoy live music. From the harborfront you can catch the ferry for Anguilla or St. Barths. Overlooking the town is Le Fort Louis, from which you get a breathtaking, panoramic view of Marigot and the surrounding area. The small, ambitious **Musée de Saint-Martin** (St. Martin Museum), south of town, has artifacts from the island's pre-Columbian days. Included are pottery exhibits, rock carvings, and petroglyphs, as well as displays from colonial and sugar-plantation days. Upstairs is a small art gallery, where you'll find locally produced art, including lithographs and posters. ✉ *Sandy Ground Rd.,* ☎ *590/29–22–84.* 🎟 *$5.* ۞ *Mon.–Sat. 9–1 and 3–6.*

❸ **Orléans.** North of Oyster Pond and the Étang aux Poissons (Fish Lake) is the island's oldest settlement, also known as the French Quarter. You'll find classic, vibrantly painted West Indian–style homes with elaborate gingerbread fretwork.

❶ **Philipsburg.** The capital of Dutch St. Maarten stretches about a mile (1½ km) along an isthmus between Great Bay and the Salt Pond and has five parallel streets. Most of the village's dozens of shops and restaurants are on Front Street, narrow and cobblestoned, closest to Great Bay, where you'll find a high concentration of duty-free shops as well as several casinos. This part of town is generally congested when cruise ships are in port. Little lanes called *steegjes* connect Front Street with Back Street, which has fewer shops and considerably less congestion.

Wathey Square (pronounced watty) is in the heart of the village. Directly across from the square are the town hall and the courthouse, in the striking white building with the cupola. The structure was built in 1793 and has served as the commander's home, a fire station, a jail, and a post office. The streets surrounding the square are lined with hotels, duty-free shops, fine restaurants, and cafés—most of them in West Indian cottages gussied up with gingerbread trim. Alleys lead to arcades and flower-filled courtyards where there are yet more boutiques and eateries. The **Captain Hodge Pier**, just off the square, is a good spot from which to view Great Bay and the beach that stretches alongside it. The **Sint Maarten Museum** hosts rotating cultural exhibits and a permanent historical display called Forts of St. Maarten/St. Martin. Artifacts range from Arawak pottery shards to objects salvaged from the wreck of the HMS *Proselyte*. ⊠ *7 Front St.,* ☎ *599/542–4917.* ⌨ *Free.* ☉ *Weekdays 10–4, Sat. 10–2.*

❺ **Pic du Paradis.** From Friar's Bay Beach, a bumpy, tree-canopied road leads inland to this peak. At 1,492 ft (490 m), it's the island's highest point. Though the vistas from it are breathtaking, the road is quite isolated, so it is best to travel in groups. Near the bottom of Pic du Paradis is **Loterie Farm,** a peaceful 150-acre private nature preserve opened to the public in 1999 by American expat B. J. Welch. Designed to preserve island habitats, Loterie Farm offers a rare glimpse of Caribbean forest and mountain land. Welch has renovated an old farmhouse and welcomes visitors for horseback riding, hiking, mountain biking, ecotours, or such non-activities as meditation and yoga. The Hidden Forest Café is open for lunch and dinner Tuesday through Sunday. ⊠ *Route de Pic du Paradis,* ☎ *590/87–86–16,* ⟨WEB⟩ *www.loteriefarm.com.* ⌨ *$5, 1½-hr tour $25, 4-hr tour $35.* ☉ *Daily sunrise–sunset.*

Shopping

Prices can be 25% to 50% below those in the United States and Canada for French perfume, liquor, cognac and fine liqueurs, leather, Swiss watches, and other luxury items. However, it pays to know the prices back home; not all goods are a bargain. Although most merchants are reputable, there are occasional reports of inferior or fake merchandise being sold as the real thing—in particular, inferior cigars are sometimes passed off as genuine Havanas. When vendors bargain excessively, their wares are often suspect.

In Philipsburg, **Front Street** is one long strip of boutiques and shops; **Old Street,** near the end of Front Street, is packed with stores, boutiques, and open-air cafés. Shops are a bit more upscale at the **Maho** shopping plaza and the **Plaza del Lago,** at the Simpson Bay Yacht Club complex, which also offers an excellent selection of restaurants.

In general, you'll find smarter fashions in Marigot than in Philipsburg. On the French side, wrought-iron balconies, colorful awnings, and gin-

248

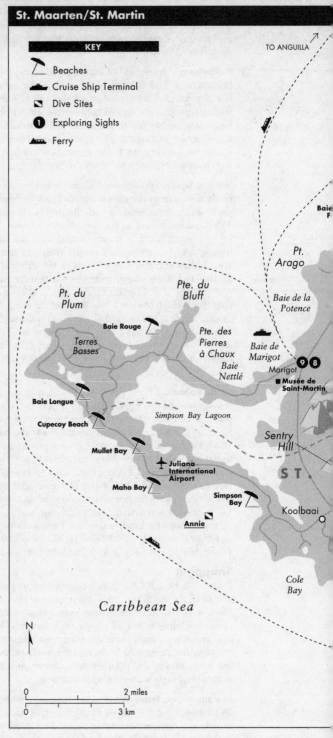

St. Maarten/St. Martin

KEY

☂ Beaches

⛴ Cruise Ship Terminal

◆ Dive Sites

❶ Exploring Sights

⛴ Ferry

TO ANGUILLA

Baie
F

Pt.
Arago

Baie de la
Potence

*Pt. du
Plum*

*Pte. du
Bluff*

Pte. des
Pierres
à Chaux

Baie de
Marigot

Baie Rouge

Terres
Basses

*Baie
Nettlé*

❾❽
Marigot

■ **Musée de
Saint-Martin**

Baie Longue

Simpson Bay Lagoon

Cupecoy Beach

Sentry
Hill

Mullet Bay

✈ **Juliana
International
Airport**

S T .

Maho Bay

**Simpson
Bay**

Koolbaai

◆
Annie

○

Cole
Bay

Caribbean Sea

N

0   2 miles

0   3 km

TO ST. BARTHÉLEMY →

Creole Rock

Pt. des Froussards

Anse Marcel

Bell Pt.

Red Rock

Grandes Cayes

Ile → Tintamarre

Baie de Grand Case

e de riar

7

Aeroport de l'Espérance

6

Ilet Pinel

Baie Orientale

Green Key

Colombier

ST.   MARTIN

5

3

Orléans

4

Galion Beach

Etang aux Poissons

Baie de l'Embouchure

Mt. Flagstaf

Babit Pt.

Beneden Prinsen

Dutch Cul-de-Sac

Boven Prinsen

MAARTEN

Sucker Garden Road

Dawn Beach

Salt Pond

2

Philipsburg

Great Bay

1

Geneve Bay

Little Bay

Pelican Key

ATLANTIC OCEAN

Pt. Blanche

Proselyte Reef

TO ST. BARTHÉLEMY →

gerbread trim decorate Marigot's smart shops, tiny boutiques, and bistros in the **Marina Royale** complex and on the main streets, **rue de la Liberté** and **rue de la République.** Also in Marigot is the chic and pricy **West Indies Mall.**

Outdoor Activities & Sports

FISHING

You can angle for yellowtail snapper, grouper, marlin, tuna, and wahoo on deep-sea excursions. Costs (for four people) range from $400 for a half day to $700 for a full day. Prices usually include bait and tackle, instruction for novices, and refreshments. Ask about licensing and insurance. **Lee Deepsea Fishing** (⊠ 84 Welfare Rd., Simpson Bay, ☎ 599/544–4233 or 599/544–4234) organizes excursions. **Rudy's Deep Sea Fishing** (⊠ 14 Airport Rd., Simpson Bay, ☎ 599/545–2177, WEB www.rudysdeepseafishing.com) has been around for years and is one of the more experienced sport angling outfits. **Sailfish Caraïbes** (⊠ Anse Marcel, ☎ 590/87–31–94 or 590/27–40–90) is your best bet on the north side of the island.

GOLF

St. Maarten is not a golf destination. **Mullet Bay Resort** (⊠ Airport Rd., north of the airport, ☎ 599/545–3069), on the Dutch side, has the island's only 18-hole course. It's in poor condition, nonetheless offers duffers a unique experience: playing through the eerie ruins of Mullet Bay Resort, once the island's largest, but destroyed by a hurricane and never rebuilt. Greens fees, with cart, are $55 for 9 holes, $88 for 18.

SCUBA DIVING & SNORKELING

Although St. Maarten is not known as a dive destination, the water temperature here is rarely below 70°F, and visibility is usually excellent, averaging about 100 ft (30 m). For snorkelers, the area around Orient Bay, Caye Verte (Green Key), Ilet Pinel, and Flat Island is especially lovely and is officially classified, and protected, as a regional underwater nature reserve. You can take a half-day snorkeling trip for around $25. On the Dutch side, **Dive Safaris** (⊠ Bobby's Marina, Yrausquin Blvd., Philipsburg, ☎ 599/544–4056) is a full-service outfit. SSI- (Scuba Schools International) and PADI-certified dive centers include **Ocean Explorers Dive Shop** (⊠ 113 Welfare Rd., Simpson Bay, ☎ 599/544–5252).

On the French side, **Blue Ocean** (⊠ Sandy Ground Rd., Baie Nettlé, ☎ 590/87–89–73) is a PADI-certified dive center and also has regularly scheduled snorkeling trips. Arrange equipment rentals and snorkeling trips through **Kontiki Watersports** (⊠ northern beach entrance, Baie Orientale, ☎ 590/87–46–89). **Octoplus** (⊠ Bd. de Grand Case, Grand Case, ☎ 590/87–20–62) is a complete PADI-certified dive center. **O2 Limit** (⊠ Bd. de Grand Case, Grand Case, ☎ 690/50–04–00), in the Grand Case Beach Club, is PADI-certified.

Beaches

The island's 10 mi (16 km) of beaches are all open to cruise-ship passengers. On beaches owned by resorts, you might be charged a small fee (about $3) for access to changing facilities. Water-sports equipment can be rented at most hotels. Topless bathing is common on the French side. If you take a cab to a remote beach, be sure to arrange a specific time for the driver to return for you. Don't leave valuables unattended on the beach or in a rental car, even in the trunk.

The nice, well-maintained beach at **Baie de Friar** is at the end of a poorly maintained dirt road. On a small, picturesque cove between Marigot and Grand Case, it attracts a casual crowd of locals and has a small snack bar and restaurant. Getting to secluded **Baie Longue,** a mile-long curve of white sand on the island's westernmost tip, requires a bumpy, 10-minute, we-must-be-lost drive off the main road, with just one small, unmarked entry down to the water. Though the beach is gravelly in places, this is a good place for snorkeling and swimming, but beware of a strong undertow when the waters are rough. If you want privacy, visit this isolated spot. There are no facilities or vendors. By far the most beautiful beach on the island, mile-long **Baie Orientale** has something for everyone, with its clean white sand, clear blue water, and an assortment of beach bars serving Mexican, Caribbean, American, and even kosher fare. There are plenty of places to rent equipment for water activities. The north end tends to be conservative and family oriented, while the far south is almost exclusively for nudists. Near the Dutch-French border and south of Baie Longue, **Cupecoy Beach,** a small clothing-optional strip, is one of the finest beaches on the island, with soft, white sand. Though the beach is a bit secluded, vendors sell cold drinks and rent chairs and umbrellas.

Where to Eat

Restaurants on the French side often figure a service charge into the menu prices. On the Dutch side, most restaurants add 10% to 15% to the bill. You can, if so moved by exceptional service, leave a tip.

$$–$$$$ ✕ **La Vie En Rose.** This bustling curbside café on the Marigot waterfront conflates classic French cuisine with the occasional Caribbean twist, as in the fillet of red snapper in a puff pastry served with fresh herbs and lime sauce. The food is excellent and the service attentive. For lunch, start off with the cold mango soup and follow with a baked-goat-cheese salad ($11). ⊠ *On the waterfront, at rue de la République, Marigot,* ☎ *590/87–54–42. AE, D, MC, V.*

$$–$$$ ✕ **Claude Mini-Club.** This brightly decorated upstairs restaurant on Marigot Harbor has served traditional creole and French cuisine for more than 30 years. The chairs and madras tablecloths are a mélange of sun-yellow and orange, and the whole place is built (tree house–style) around the trunks of coconut trees. It's the place to be on Wednesday and Saturday nights, when the dinner buffet includes roast pig, lobster, roast beef, and all the trimmings. ⊠ *Front de Mer, Marigot,* ☎ *590/87–50–69. AE, MC, V. No lunch Sun.*

$$ ✕ **Chesterfield's.** On the Great Bay waterfront, a five-minute walk from the ship pier in Philipsburg, nautically themed "Chesty's" serves breakfast, lunch, and dinner at reasonable prices. The main fare is steak and seafood, though the dinner menu includes French onion soup, roast duckling with fresh pineapple and banana sauce, and several shrimp dishes. The Mermaid Bar is popular with yachties. ⊠ *Great Bay Marina, Philipsburg,* ☎ *599/542–3484. MC, V.*

$$ ✕ **Shiv Sagar.** This large second-floor restaurant in Philipsburg emphasizes Kashmiri and Mughal specialties. Marvelous tandoori and curry dishes are on offer, but try one of the less familiar preparations such as *madrasi machi* (red snapper with hot spices). ⊠ *20 Front St., opposite Barclay's Bank, Philipsburg,* ☎ *599/542–2299. AE, D, DC, MC, V. Closed Sun.*

St. Thomas and St. John, U.S. Virgin Islands

St. Thomas is the busiest cruise port of call in the world. Up to eight giant ships may visit in a single day. Don't expect an exotic island experience: one of the three U.S. Virgin Islands (with St. Croix and St. John), St. Thomas is as American as any place on the mainland, complete with McDonald's and HBO. The positive side of all this development is that there are more tours here than anywhere else in the Caribbean, and every year the excursions get better. Of course, shopping is the big draw in Charlotte Amalie, but experienced travelers remember the days of "real" bargains. Today, so many passengers fill the stores that it's a seller's market. One of St. Thomas's best tourist attractions is its neighboring island, St. John, with its beautiful Virgin Islands National Park and beaches.

CURRENCY

The U.S. dollar is the official currency of St. Thomas and St. John.

TELEPHONES

It's as easy to call home from St. Thomas and St. John as from any city in the United States. On St. Thomas, public phones are easily found, and AT&T has a telecommunications center across from the Havensight Mall. On St. John, public phones are in front of the post office, east of the tender landing, and at the ferry dock. **Parcel Plus** (⊠ across from Havensight Mall, Charlotte Amalie, St. Thomas, ☎ 340/776–9134) has three computers available for accessing e-mail; the cost is $5 per half hour.

SHORE EXCURSIONS

The following are good choices on St. Thomas and St. John. They may not be offered by all cruise lines. Times and prices are approximate.

Coki Beach Snorkeling. A trip to this St. Thomas beach is a good choice for novices who want to learn snorkeling (instruction and equipment usually are included) and see wildlife. ☉ *3 hrs,* ⊡ *$35.*

Helmet Dive. A unique diving opportunity for non-divers is at Coral World Marine Park, where you wear helmets that provide oxygen while you walk along the bottom of the sea. Afterwards, you can visit the aquarium. ☉ *3 hrs.,* ⊡ *$82.*

Kayaking and Snorkeling Tour. Paddle on sit-atop kayaks through a marine sanctuary while a guide narrates both the on- and undersea scenes. ☉ *3½ hrs,* ⊡ *$69.*

St. John Eco Hike. You hike approximately 1¼ mi (3 km) to Linde Point and on to Honeymoon Beach for a refreshing swim. Then it's on to Caneel Bay to visit some ruins before returning by safari van to the ferry pier. ☉ *5 hrs,* ⊡ *$53.*

St. John Island Tour. Either your ship tenders you in to St. John in the morning before docking at St. Thomas, or you take a bus from the St. Thomas docks to the St. John ferry. On St. John, an open-air safari bus winds through the national park to a beach for snorkeling, swimming, and sunbathing. (If you have the option, go to any beach but Trunk Bay.) ☉ *4½ hrs,* ⊡ *$39.*

Sailing the Virgin Islands. You sail aboard a private yacht with a small group to Turtle Cove on St. Thomas's own Buck Island, where you can look at a sunken ship and swim among sea turtles. ☉ *4 hrs,* ⊡ *$59.*

Coming Ashore

Depending on how many ships are in port, cruise ships drop anchor in the harbor at Charlotte Amalie and tender passengers directly to the waterfront duty-free shops, dock at the Havensight Mall at the eastern end of the crescent-shaped bay, or dock at Crown Bay Marina a few miles west of town. The distance from Havensight to the duty-free shops is 1½ mi (3 km), which can be walked in less than half an hour, or a taxi can be hired for $2.50 per person. Tourist information offices are at the Havensight Mall (across from Bldg. No. 1) for docking passengers and downtown near Fort Christian (at the eastern end of the waterfront shopping area) for those coming ashore by tender. Both offices distribute free maps. From Crown Bay, it's also a half-hour walk or a $2.50 per person cab ride.

In St. John, your ship may pause outside Cruz Bay Harbor to drop you off or drop anchor if it's spending the day. You'll be tendered to shore at the main town of Cruz Bay. The shopping district starts just across the street from the tender landing. You'll find an eclectic collection of shops, cozy restaurants, and places where you can just sit and take it all in. The island has few sights to see. Your best bet is to take a tour of the Virgin Islands National Park. (If your ship doesn't offer such a tour, arrange one with one of the taxi drivers who will meet your tender.) The drive takes you past luscious beaches to a restored sugar plantation.

Exploring St. Thomas

Numbers in the margin correspond to points of interest on the St. Thomas & St. John map.

❶ **Charlotte Amalie.** St. Thomas's major burg is a hilly, overdeveloped shopping town. There are plenty of interesting historic sights here, and much of the town is quite pretty—so while you're shopping, take the time to see at least a few. For a great view of the town and the harbor, begin at the Spanish-style Hotel 1829, on Government Hill (also called Kongens Gade). A few yards farther up the road to the east is the base of the 99 Steps, a staircase "street" built by the Danes in the 1700s. Go up the steps (there are more than 99) and continue to the right to Blackbeard's Castle, originally Fort Skytsborg. The massive five-story watchtower was built in 1679. It's now a dramatic perch from which to sip a drink, admire the harbor, and snap a photo of your ship.

Built to honor the freeing of slaves in 1848, **Emancipation Garden** was the site of a 150th-anniversary celebration of emancipation. A bronze bust of a freed slave blowing a symbolic conch shell commemorates this anniversary. The gazebo here is used for official ceremonies. Two other monuments show the island's Danish and American ties—a bust of Denmark's King Christian and a scaled-down model of the U.S. Liberty Bell. ⊠ *Between Tolbod Gade and Fort Christian.*

Fort Christian, St. Thomas's oldest standing structure, anchors the shopping district. It was built in 1672–80 and now has U.S. National Landmark status. The clock tower was added in the 19th century. This remarkable building has been used as a jail, governor's residence, town hall, courthouse, and church. Fort Christian now houses the **Virgin Islands Museum,** where you can see exhibits on USVI history, natural history, and turn-of-the-20th-century furnishings. Artists display their works monthly in the gallery. A gift shop sells locally produced crafts, books, and other souvenirs. This is also the site of the Chamber of Commerce's Hospitality Lounge, where there are rest rooms, brochures, and a place you can stash your luggage for some last-minute shopping on the way to the airport. ⊠ *Waterfront Hwy. just east of shopping district,* ☎ *340/776–4566.* ▱ *Free.* ☺ *Weekdays 8:30–4:30.*

Frederick Lutheran Church has a massive mahogany altar, and its pews—each with its own door—were once rented to families of the congregation. Lutheranism is the state religion of Denmark, and when the territory was without a minister the governor—who had his own elevated pew—filled in. ⊠ *Norre Gade,* ☎ *340/776–1315.* ☺ *Mon.–Sat. 9–4.*

Built in 1867, **Government House,** a neoclassical white brick-and-wood structure, houses the offices of the Virgin Islands's governor. Inside, the staircases are of native mahogany, as are the plaques hand-lettered in gold with the names of the governors appointed and, since 1970, elected. Brochures detailing the history of the building are available, but you may have to ask for them. A deputy administrator can lead you on a guided tour; call to schedule an appointment. ⊠ *Government Hill,* ☎ *340/774–0001.* ▱ *Free.* ☺ *Weekdays 8–5.*

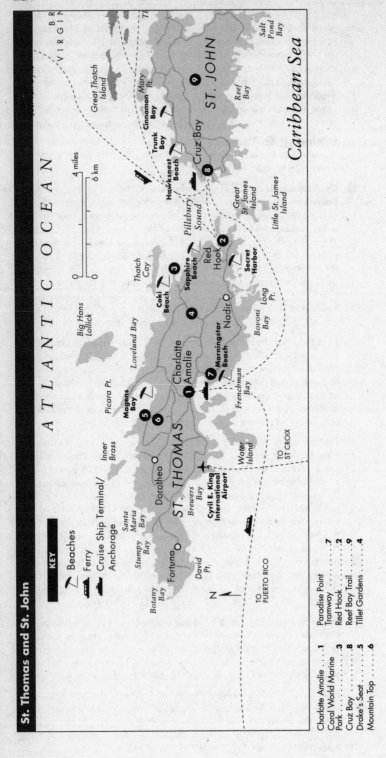

St. Thomas and St. John

ATLANTIC OCEAN

Caribbean Sea

KEY

Beaches

Ferry

Cruise Ship Terminal/
Anchorage

BR
VIRGIN

Great Thatch
Island

ST. JOHN

Salt
Pond
Bay

Mary
Pt.

Cinnamon
Bay

Trunk
Bay

Hawksnest
Beach

Cruz Bay

Reef
Bay

4 miles

6 km

Thatch
Cay

Pillsbury
Sound

Great
St. James
Island

Little St. James
Island

Big Hans
Lollick

Sapphire
Beach

Red
Hook

Secret
Harbor

Coki
Beach

Loveland Bay

Picara Pt.

Charlotte
Amalie

Nadir

Long
Pt.

Bovoni
Bay

Morningstar
Beach

Magens
Bay

Inner
Brass

Santa
Maria
Bay

Dorothea

Frenchman
Bay

ST. THOMAS

Water
Island

Cyril E. King
International
Airport

Brewers
Bay

Stumpy
Bay

Fortuna

Botany
Bay

David
Pt.

N

TO
PUERTO RICO

TO
ST CROIX

Charlotte Amalie **1**	Paradise Point
Coral World Marine	Tramway **7**
Park **3**	Red Hook **2**
Cruz Bay **8**	Reef Bay Trail . . . **9**
Drake's Seat **5**	Tillet Gardens . . . **4**
Mountain Top **6**	

The pastoral-looking lime-green exterior of the **Legislature Building** conceals the vociferous political wrangling of the Virgin Islands Senate going on inside. Constructed by the Danish as a police barracks, the building was later used to billet U.S. Marines, and much later it housed a public school. You're welcome to sit in on sessions in the upstairs chambers. ⊠ *Waterfront Hwy., across from Fort Christian,* ☎ *340/774–0880.* ☉ *Daily 8–5.*

❸ Coral World Marine Park. Coral World has an offshore underwater observatory that houses the Predator Tank, one of the world's largest coral-reef tanks, and an aquarium with more than 20 portholes providing close-ups of Caribbean sea life. *Sea Trekkin'* lets you tour the reef outside the park at a depth of 15 ft (4½ m), thanks to specialized headgear and a continuous air supply that's based on the surface. A guide leads the half-hour tour and the narration is piped through a specialized speaker inside each trekker's helmet; the cost is $50 per person. The park also has several outdoor pools where you can touch starfish, pet a baby shark, feed stingrays, and view endangered sea turtles. There's also a mangrove lagoon and a nature trail full of tropical flora. Daily feedings and talks take place at most every exhibit. ⊠ *Coki Point, turn north off Rte. 38 at sign, Estate Frydendal,* ☎ *340/775–1555,* WEB *www.coralworldvi.com.* ⊠ $18. ☉ *Daily 9–5.*

❺ Drake's Seat. Sir Francis Drake was supposed to have kept watch over his fleet and looked for enemy ships from this vantage point. The panorama is especially breathtaking (and romantic) at dusk, if your ship is staying late in port; and if you arrive late in the day you'll miss the hordes of fellow cruise-ship passengers on taxi tours who stop here to take a picture and buy a T-shirt from one of the many vendors. ⊠ *Rte. 40, Estate Zufriedenheit.*

❻ Mountain Top. Stop here for a banana daiquiri and spectacular views from the observation deck more than 1,500 ft (459 m) above sea level. There are also shops that sell everything from Caribbean art to nautical antiques, ship models, and T-shirts. Kids will like talking to the parrots—and hearing them answer back. *Head north off Rte. 33; look for signs,* WEB *www.greathouse-mountaintop.com.*

❼ Paradise Point Tramway. Fly skyward in a gondola to Paradise Point, an overlook with breathtaking views of Charlotte Amalie and the harbor. There are several shops, a bar, and a restaurant. A ¼-mi (½-km) hiking trail leads to spectacular views of St. Croix to the south. Wear sturdy shoes; the trail is steep and rocky. ⊠ *Rte. 30 across from Havensight Mall, Charlotte Amalie,* ☎ *340/774–9809,* WEB *www. paradisepointtramway.com.* ⊠ $15. ☉ *Daily 7:30–4:30.*

❷ Red Hook. In this nautical center there are fishing and sailing charter boats, dive shops, and powerboat-rental agencies at the American Yacht Harbor marina. There are also several bars and restaurants, including Molly Molone's, Duffy's Love Shack, and Off the Hook. One grocery store and two delis offer picnic fixings—from sliced meats and cheeses to rotisserie-cooked chickens, salads, and freshly baked breads.

❹ Tillett Gardens. East of Charlotte Amalie, Tillett Gardens is an oasis of artistic endeavor across from the Tutu Park Shopping Mall. The late Jim Tillett and then-wife Rhoda converted this old Danish farm into an artists' retreat in 1959. Today you can watch artisans produce silk-screen fabrics, pottery, candles, watercolors, jewelry, and other handicrafts. Something special is often happening in the gardens: there's a Classics in the Gardens music series, and the Pistarckle Theater performs here. ⊠ *Rte. 38.*

Exploring St. John

St. John's best sights are preserved in the sprawling Virgin Islands National Park, which covers most of the island. Stunning vistas and beaches can be reached by taxi tour or car. If you want to spend a relaxing day, head for Cinnamon Bay. This National Park Service campground has a beach with water-sports equipment for rent, hiking, a modest restaurant, and cool showers.

❽   **Cruz Bay.** St. John's main town may be compact (it consists of a few blocks), but it's definitely a hub: the ferries from St. Thomas and the BVI pull in here, and it's where you can get a taxi or rent a car to travel around the island. There are shops in which to browse, watering holes, restaurants, and a grassy square with benches where you can sit back and take everything in. Look for the handy, amusing "St. John Map" featuring Max the Mongoose. To pick up a handy guide to St. John's hiking trails, see large maps of the island, and find out about current park service programs, including guided walks and cultural demonstrations, stop by the **V. I. National Park Visitors Center** (✉ in an area known as the Creek, near Cruz Bay bulkhead and baseball field, Cruz Bay, ☏ 340/776–6201, WEB www.nps.gov/viis). It's open daily from 8 to 4:30.

❾   **Reef Bay Trail.** Although this is one of the most interesting hikes on St. John, unless you're a rugged individualist who wants a physical challenge (and that describes a lot of people who stay on St. John), you'll probably get the most out of the trip if you join a hike led by a park service ranger, who can identify the trees and plants on the hike down, fill you in on the history of the Reef Bay Plantation, and tell you about the petroglyphs on the rocks at the bottom of the trail. A side trail takes you to the Reef Bay Plantation great house, a gutted but mostly intact structure that maintains vestiges of its former beauty. If you're without a car, take a taxi or the Vitran bus from the Cruz Bay ferry dock to the trailhead on Route 10, where you'll meet a ranger for the hike downhill. A boat will take you to Cruz Bay, saving you the uphill return climb. ✉ *Rte. 10, Reef Bay,* ☏ *340/776–6201 Ext. 238,* WEB *www.nps.gov/viis.* ☉ *Tours at 10 AM; days change seasonally.* ✇ *Free; return boat trip to Cruz Bay $15.*

Shopping

There are more than 400 shops in Charlotte Amalie, and near the Havensight docks there are at least 60 more, clustered in converted warehouses. Even die-hard shoppers won't want to cover all the boutiques, since many peddle the same T-shirts and togs. Many visitors devote their shopping time on St. Thomas to the stores that sell handicrafts.

Although giveaway prices no longer abound, shoppers on St. Thomas can still save money. Today, a realistic appraisal puts prices on many items at about 20% off stateside prices, although liquor and perfume are often 50% to 70% less expensive. What's more, there's no sales tax in the USVI, and you can take advantage of the $1,200-per-person duty-free allowance. Remember to save receipts.

Prices on luxury goods vary from shop to shop—if you find a good deal, take it. Prices on jewelry vary the most, and it's here that you'll still run across some real finds. Bargaining is not appreciated.

The major shopping area is Charlotte Amalie, a district of centuries-old buildings that once served as merchants' warehouses. Both sides of **Main Street** are lined with shops, as are the side streets and walkways between Main Street and the waterfront. These narrow lanes and arcades have names like Drake's Passage, Royal Dane Mall, Palm Passage, Trompeter Gade, Hibiscus Alley, and Raadet's Gade. **Back Street,** also called Vimmelskaft Gade (one block north of Main Street off Nye Gade) and streets adjacent to it—Garden Street, Kongens Gade, and Norre Gade—are also very good areas for browsing. At **Havensight Mall,** near the deep-water port, you'll find branches of downtown stores, as well as specialty shops and boutiques. Next door, there are additional shops at **Port of Sale. Tillett Gardens and Craft Complex** is more than worth the cab fare to reach it. The late Jim Tillett's artwork is on display, and you can watch craftsmen and artisans produce watercolors, silk-screen fabrics, pottery, enamel work, candles, and other handicrafts.

Unless otherwise noted, the following stores have branches both downtown and in Havensight Mall and are easy to find. Shopping maps are available at the tourist offices and often from your ship's shore-excursion desk. U.S. citizens can carry back a gallon, or six "fifths," of liquor duty-free.

A. H. Riise Liquors (⊠ 37 Main St., at Riise's Alley, Charlotte Amalie, ☎ 340/776–2303; ⊠ Rte. 30 at Havensight Mall, Charlotte Amalie, ☎ 340/776–7713) offers a large selection of tobacco (including imported cigars), as well as cordials, wines, and rare vintage Armagnacs, cognacs, ports, and Madeiras. It also stocks fruits in brandy and barware from England. Enjoy rum samples at the tasting bar. The wine selection is large at warehouse-style **Al Cohen's Discount Liquor** (⊠ Rte. 30 across from Havensight Mall, Charlotte Amalie, ☎ 340/774–3690.) At **Blue Carib Gems** (⊠ 2–3 Back St., Charlotte Amalie, ☎ 340/774–8525, WEB www.bluecaribgems.com.), family-owned and -run, watch Alan O'Hara, Sr., polish Caribbean amber and larimar, agate, and other gems and mount them in gold and silver settings.

Caribbean Marketplace (⊠ Rte. 30 at Havensight Shopping Mall, Charlotte Amalie, ☎ 340/776–5400) is a great place to buy handicrafts from the Caribbean and elsewhere. Also look for Sunny Caribee spices, soaps, coffee, and teas from Tortola, and coffee from Trinidad. **Down Island Traders** (⊠ Waterfront Hwy. at Post Office Alley, Charlotte Amalie, ☎ 340/776–4641) carries hand-painted calabash bowls; finely printed Caribbean note cards; jams, jellies, spices, hot sauces, and herbs; teas made of lemongrass, passion fruit, and mango; coffee from Jamaica; and handicrafts from throughout the Caribbean. The **English Shop** (⊠ 106–108 Drake's Passage, Charlotte Amalie, ☎ 340/776–3776) offers figurines, cutlery, and china and crystal from major European and Japanese manufacturers, including Spode, Royal Doulton, Portmeirion, Noritaki, and Wedgwood. You can choose what you like from the catalogs here, and shopkeepers will order and factory-ship it for you. (Be sure to keep your receipts in case something goes awry.)

Little Switzerland (⊠ Tolbod Gade, across from Emancipation Garden, Charlotte Amalie, ☎ 340/776–2010; ⊠ 3B Main St., Charlotte Amalie, ☎ 340/776–2010; ⊠ Rte. 30 at Havensight Mall, Charlotte Amalie, located dockside, ☎ 340/776–2198, WEB www.littleswitzerland.com) carries crystal from Baccarat, Waterford, and Orrefors; china from Kosta Boda, Rosenthal, Wedgwood, and others; Swarovski cut-crystal animals; Lladró and other porcelain figurines; gemstone globes; and many other affordable collectibles. It also does a booming mail-order business; ask for a catalog. Men, women, and children will find something to choose from at **Local Color** (⊠ Royal Dane Mall, Charlotte Amalie, at the Waterfront, ☎ 340/774–2280), among brand-name wear like Jams World and Urban Safari, and St. John artist Sloop Jones's colorful, hand-painted island designs on cool dresses, T-shirts, and sweaters. There are also tropically oriented accessories like big-brimmed straw

hats, bold-color bags, and casual jewelry. More than 40 local artists—
including schoolchildren, senior citizens, and people with disabilities—create the handcrafted items for sale at **Native Arts and Crafts
Cooperative** (✉ Tolbod Gade, across from Emancipation Garden and
next to visitor center, Charlotte Amalie, ☎ 340/777–1153): African-
style jewelry, quilts, calabash bowls, dolls, carved-wood figures, woven
baskets, straw brooms, note cards, and cookbooks.

Tropical sports and travel clothing for men, women, and children all
have a nautical theme at **Pusser's Tropical & Nautical Co. Store** (✉ Waterfront Hwy. at Riise's Alley, Charlotte Amalie, ☎ 340/777–9281.)
Look for bottles of Pusser's rum at the sales counter. **Royal Caribbean**
(✉ 23 Main St., Charlotte Amalie, ☎ 340/776–5449. ✉ 33 Main St.,
Charlotte Amalie, ☎ 340/776–4110; ✉ Rte. 30 at Havensight Mall,
Charlotte Amalie, ☎ 340/776–8890 WEB www.royalcaribbean.vi),
which has no affiliation with the cruise line, has cameras, camcorders,
stereos, watches, and clocks.

ST. JOHN

In St. John, the small shopping district runs from Wharfside Village
near the ferry landing to Mongoose Junction, just up the street from
the cruise-ship dock and tender landing, with lots of shops tucked in
between. The owner of **Bamboula** (✉ Mongoose Junction, North
Shore Rd., Cruz Bay, ☎ 340/693–8699), Jo Sterling, travels the
Caribbean and beyond to find unusual housewares, art, rugs, bedspreads,
accessories, shoes, and men's and women's clothes for this multicul-
tural boutique. If you want to look like you stepped out of the pages
of the resort-wear spread in an upscale travel magazine, try **Bougainvillea Boutique** (✉ Mongoose Junction, North Shore Rd., Cruz Bay, ☎
340/693–7190.) Owner Susan Stair carries chic men's and women's
clothes, straw hats, leather handbags, and fine gifts. Owner Radha Speer
of **Caravan Gallery** (✉ Mongoose Junction, North Shore Rd., Cruz
Bay, ☎ 340/779–4566) travels the world to find much of the unusual
jewelry she sells here. And the more you look, the more you see—folk
art, tribal art, and masks cover the walls and tables, making this a great
place to browse.

The branch of **Colombian Emeralds** (✉ Mongoose Junction, North Shore
Rd., Cruz Bay, ☎ 340/776–6007) has high-quality emeralds and also
sells rubies, diamonds, and other jewels in attractive yellow- and white-
gold settings. **Pink Papaya** (✉ Lemon Tree Mall, King St., Cruz Bay,
☎ 340/693–8535) is the home of longtime Virgin Islands resident M.
L. Etre's well-known artwork, plus a huge collection of one-of-a-kind
gifts, including bright tablecloths, unusual trays, dinnerware, and
unique tropical jewelry. **St. John Editions** (✉ North Shore Rd., Cruz
Bay, ☎ 340/693–8444) has nifty cotton dresses that go from beach to
dinner with a change of shoes and accessories. Owner Ann Soper also
carries attractive straw hats and inexpensive jewelry.

Outdoor Activities & Sports

ST. THOMAS

➤ FISHING: Fishing here is synonymous with blue marlin angling. If you're
not into marlin fishing, try hooking sailfish in the winter, dolphinfish
come spring, and wahoo in the fall. To really find the trip that will best
suit you, walk down the docks at either American Yacht Harbor or
Sapphire Beach Marina in the late afternoon and chat with the captains and crews. At the **American Yacht Harbor** (✉ 6100 Red Hook
Plaza, Red Hook, ☎ 340/775–6454) you can charter two boats: the
Marlin Prince and *Prowler*. The **Charter Boat Center** (✉ 6300 Red Hook
Plaza, Red Hook, ☎ 340/775–7990 or 800/866–5714, WEB www.
charterboat.vi) is a major source for sportfishing charters.

➤ GOLF: The **Mahogany Run Golf Course** (✉ Rte. 42, Estate Loven-lund, ☎ 340/777–5000, WEB www.mahoganyrungolf.com) attracts golfers for its spectacular view of the British Virgin Islands and the challenging 3-hole Devil's Triangle on this Tom and George Fazio–designed par-70, 18-hole course. There's a fully stocked pro shop, snack bar, and open-air clubhouse. The course is open daily and there are frequently informal weekend tournaments.

➤ SCUBA DIVING & SNORKELING: **Aqua Action** (✉ 6501 Red Hook Plaza, Red Hook, ☎ 340/775–6285 or 888/775–6285, WEB www.aadivers.com) is a full-service, PADI five-star shop that offers all levels of instruction at Secret Harbour Beach Resort. **Chris Sawyer Diving Center** (☎ 340/775–7320 or 877/929–3483, WEB www.sawyerdive.vi) is a PADI five-star outfit that specializes in dives to the wreck of the 310-ft-long *Rhone*, in the British Virgin Islands. Hotel/dive packages are offered through the Renaissance Grand Beach Resort and Wyndham Sugar Bay Beach Club & Resort. **Snuba of St. Thomas** (✉ Rte. 388 at Coki Point, Estate Frydendal, ☎ 340/693–8063, WEB www.visnuba.com) offers a cross between snorkeling and scuba diving: a 20-ft (6-m) air hose connects you to the surface. The cost is $59 per person. Children must be 8 years or older.

ST. JOHN

➤ FISHING: Well-kept charter boats head out to the north and south drops or troll along the inshore reefs. The captains usually provide bait, drinks, and lunch, but you'll need to bring your own hat and sunscreen. Fishing charters run around $100 per hour per person. The **Charter Boat Center** (☎ 340/775–7990), in Red Hook on St. Thomas, also arranges fishing trips for folks on St. John. **Gone Ketchin'** (☎ 340/714–1175), in St. John, arranges trips with old salt Captain Griz. **St. John World Class Anglers** (☎ 340/779–4281) offers light-tackle shore and offshore half- and full-day trips.

➤ HIKING: Although it's fun to go hiking with a Virgin Islands National Park guide, don't be afraid to strike out on your own. To find a hike that suits your ability, stop by the park's visitor center in Cruz Bay and pick up the free trail guide; it details points of interest, dangers, trail lengths, and estimated hiking times. Although the park staff recommends pants to protect against thorns and insects, most people hike in shorts because pants are too hot. Wear sturdy shoes or hiking boots even if you're hiking to the beach. Don't forget to bring water and insect repellent. The **Virgin Islands National Park** (☎ 340/776–6201, WEB www.nps.gov/viis) maintains more than 20 trails on the north and south shores and offers guided hikes along popular routes. A full-day trip to Reef Bay is a must; it's an easy hike through lush and dry forest, past the ruins of an old plantation, and to a sugar factory adjacent to the beach. Take the public Vitran bus or a taxi to the trailhead, where you'll meet a ranger who'll serve as your guide. The park provides a boat ride back to Cruz Bay for $15 to save you the walk back up the mountain. The schedule changes from season to season; call for times and reservations, which are essential.

➤ SCUBA DIVING & SNORKELING: **Cruz Bay Watersports** (☎ 340/776–6234) has two locations: in Cruz Bay and at the Westin Resort, St. John. Owners Marcus and Patty Johnston offer regular reef, wreck, and night dives and USVI and BVI snorkel tours. **Low Key Watersports** (☎ 340/693–8999 or 800/835–7718), at Wharfside Village, offers PADI certification and resort courses, one- and two-tank dives, and specialty courses.

Beaches

ST. THOMAS

All beaches in the USVI are public, but occasionally you'll need to stroll through a resort to reach the sand. **Coki Beach,** next to Coral World (turn north off Route 38), is a popular snorkeling spot for cruise-ship excursions, though there's no reason why you can't go there on your own. Colorful beachside shops rent water-sports equipment. Some also sell snack foods, cold drinks, and even fish food (dry dog food). On Route 35, **Magens Bay** is usually lively because of its spectacular crescent of white sand, more than ½ mi (¾ km) long, and its calm waters, which are protected by two peninsulas. It's often listed among the world's most beautiful beaches. (If you arrive between 8 AM and 5 PM, you have to pay an entrance fee of $3 per person, $1 per vehicle, and 25¢ per child under age 12.) The bottom is flat and sandy, so this is a place for sunning and swimming rather than snorkeling. There's also a bar, snack bar, and bathhouses with toilets and saltwater showers. Close to Charlotte Amalie and fronting the Marriott Frenchman's Reef Hotel, pretty **Morning Star Beach** is where many young locals body-surf or play volleyball. Snorkeling is good near the rocks when the current doesn't affect visibility. There's a fine view of St. John and other islands from **Sapphire Beach.** The snorkeling is excellent at the reef to the right, or east, near Pettyklip Point. The constant breeze makes this a great spot for windsurfing. The condo resort at **Secret Harbor** doesn't detract from the attractiveness of the cove-like beach. Not only is this East End spot pretty, it also has superb snorkeling—head out to the left, near the rocks.

ST. JOHN

Long, sandy **Cinnamon Bay** faces beautiful cays and abuts the national park campground. Facilities are open to the public and include cool showers, toilets, a commissary, and a restaurant. You can rent water-sports equipment here. There's excellent snorkeling off the point to the right; look for the big angelfish and large schools of purple triggerfish. Afternoons on Cinnamon Bay can be windy, so arrive early to beat the gusts. **Hawksnest Beach** is the closet beach to Cruz Bay, so it's often crowded. Sea-grape trees line this narrow beach, and there are rest rooms, cooking grills, and a covered shed for picnicking. **Trunk Bay,** St. John's most-photographed beach, is also the preferred spot for beginning snorkelers because of its underwater trail, but if you're looking for seclusion, don't come here. Crowded or not, this stunning beach is still beautiful. There are changing rooms, a snack bar, picnic tables, a gift shop, phones, lockers, and snorkeling-equipment rentals. You have to pay an entrance fee of $4 if you don't have a National Park Pass.

Where to Eat

Some restaurants add a 10% to 15% service charge. If not, leave a 15% tip.

ST. THOMAS

$$$–$$$$ ✕ **Tavern on the Waterfront.** White linen tablecloths, silver and crystal table settings, and a rich mahogany interior set the scene for an elegant meal at this second-floor, air-conditioned restaurant, which overlooks the harbor. Tiger Woods, Michael Jordan, and Walter Cronkite have all supped here. The menu offers flavors from every corner of the globe. Try the salmon Margarita flavored with tequila and lime, or spiced marinated pork loin with a rum-soaked raisin sauce. Sunday is Latin night. ✉ *Waterfront at Royal Dane Mall, Charlotte Amalie,* ☎ *340/776–4328,* WEB *www.tavernonthewaterfront.com. AE, MC, V.*

$–$$ ✕ **Gladys' Cafe.** Even if the local specialties—conch in butter sauce, saltfish and dumplings, hearty red bean soup—didn't make this a recommended café, it would be worth coming for Gladys's smile. While you're here, pick up a $5 or $10 bottle of her hot sauce. ✉ *Waterfront at Royal Dane Mall, Charlotte Amalie,* ☎ *340/774–6604. AE. No dinner.*

$–$$ ✕ **Lillian's Caribbean Grill.** This is where the local business community fuels up for its day of selling in Main Street stores. Breakfast specialties include dumb bread and cheese, spicy oatmeal, and bush tea; everything from hamburgers to conch in butter sauce, fish and fungi, curried chicken, and stewed mutton is served at lunch. ⊠ *Grand Galleria, Charlotte Amalie,* ☎ *340/774–7900,* WEB *pws.prserv.net/lillian. AE, MC, V. No dinner. Closed Sun.*

ST. JOHN

$$–$$$ ✕ **Lime Inn.** Mainland transplants who call St. John home as well as visitors flock to this alfresco spot for the congenial hospitality and good food, including all-you-can-eat shrimp on Wednesday nights. There are shrimp and steak dishes and such specials as pistachio chicken breasts with plantains and Thai curry-cream sauce. Fresh lobster is always a dinner option here. ⊠ *Lemon Tree Mall, King St., Cruz Bay* ☎ *340/776–6425. AE, MC, V. Closed Sun. No lunch Sat.*

$–$$$ ✕ **Morgan's Mango.** A long flight of stairs leads you to this alfresco eatery, but good food makes it worth the climb. Although fish is the specialty—try the voodoo snapper topped with a many-fruit salsa—the chef also creates a vegetarian platter with black beans, fried plantains, salad, and an ear of corn. ⊠ *North Shore Rd., across from V.I. National Park Visitors Center, Cruz Bay,* ☎ *340/693–8141. AE, MC, V. No lunch.*

$–$$ ✕ **Uncle Joe's Barbecue.** Juicy ribs and tasty chicken legs dripping with the house barbecue sauce make for one of St. John's best dining deals. Corn on the cob, rice, and a generous scoop of macaroni salad or coleslaw round out the plate. This casual spot crowds the edge of a busy sidewalk in the heart of Cruz Bay. There are a few open-air tables, but the ambience is more than a tad on the pedestrian side, so take-out is a better bet. ⊠ *North Shore Rd., across from post office, Cruz Bay,* ☎ *340/693–8806. No credit cards.*

St. Vincent and Bequia

You won't find glitzy resorts or flashy discos in St. Vincent or Bequia. Rather, you'll be dazzled by picturesque villages, secluded beaches, and fine sailing waters. St. Vincent is the largest and northernmost island in the Grenadines archipelago; Kingstown, the capital city, is the government and business center and major port. Except for one barren area on the island's northeast coast—remnants of the 1979 eruption of La Soufrière, one of the last active volcanoes in the Caribbean—the countryside is mountainous, lush, and green.

The Grenadines extend in a 45-mi (73-km) arc from St. Vincent to Grenada. As similar as they may appear, each inhabited island has its own personality. Just south of St. Vincent is Bequia (pronounced *beck*-way), one of the most popular anchorages in the Caribbean for smaller cruise ships. Next is Mustique, getaway of the glitterati. Making up the southern Grenadines are sleepy Canouan (*can*-oo-wan), pastoral Mayreau (*my*-row), and busy Union, along with tiny Palm Island and Petit St. Vincent.

St. Vincent's mountains and forests thwarted European settlement for many years. As colonization advanced elsewhere in the Caribbean, in fact, the island became a refuge for Carib Indians—descendants of whom still live in northeastern St. Vincent. Eventually, British troops prevailed, overpowering the French and banishing Carib warriors to Central America. Independent since 1979, St. Vincent and the Grenadines remains a member of the British Commonwealth. The official language is English.

CURRENCY

St. Vincent and the Grenadines uses the Eastern Caribbean (E.C.) dollar. The exchange rate is EC$2.70 to US$1. U.S. dollars are generally accepted, although E.C. currency is preferred. Large U.S. bills may be difficult to change in small shops. Hotels and many restaurants and shops accept credit cards and traveler's checks. Prices given below are in U.S. dollars unless otherwise indicated.

TELEPHONES

You can dial international numbers from pay phones and card phones in St. Vincent and the Grenadines. Telephone services are available at the cruise ship terminal in Kingstown, St. Vincent, and near the jetty in Port Elizabeth, Bequia. For an international operator, dial 115; to charge your call to a credit card, call 117. To make an international call using your credit card, dial 800/877–8000.

SHORE EXCURSIONS

The following are good choices in St. Vincent and Bequia. They may not be offered by all cruise lines. Times and prices are approximate. Note that the St. Vincent shore excursions are often offered by ships that dock in Bequia but will include a ferry to St. Vincent.

Falls of Baleine. A bus takes you to Villa Beach, where you board a boat for the trip north along the coast of St. Vincent. When you arrive at the Falls of Baleine, you have to wade through shallow water to get to the beach, then trek about five minutes to the falls. Wear a bathing suit. ⊙ *6 hrs,* 🖃 *$50*

Island History and Natural Beauty Tour. A bus will first take you to Dorsetshire Hill for a panoramic view of Kingstown Harbour and the Grenadines, then to 18th-century Fort Charlotte, where murals depict the turbulent history of St. Vincent. On a tour of the Botanical Gardens, the oldest in the Western Hemisphere, you'll learn fascinating facts about the various trees and shrubs. ⊙ *4 hrs,* 🖃 *$45.*

Sailing Tour to Mustique. Sail from Bequia to Mustique, where you can have lunch at Basil's Bar and then swim and snorkel in Cotton House Bay. ⊙ *7 hrs,* 🖃 *$85.*

Coming Ashore

Some cruise ships call at Kingstown, St. Vincent's capital city. Its berth accommodates two cruise ships; additional vessels anchor outside the harbor and bring passengers to the jetty by launch. The facility has about two dozen shops that sell duty-free items and handicrafts. There's a communications center, post office, tourist information desk, restaurant, and food court. Buses and taxis are available at the wharf. Taxi drivers are well equipped to take you on an island tour; expect to pay $25 per hour for up to four passengers. The ferry to Bequia (1 hr each way) is at the adjacent pier. Renting a car for just one day isn't advisable, since car rentals are expensive (at least $55 per day) and require a $20 temporary driving permit.

Many smaller cruise ships call at Port Elizabeth, on Bequia. They anchor offshore and bring passengers ashore by launch. Shops, restaurants, and a tourist information office are all just steps from the jetty. Taxis are available for island tours and transportation to the beach; taxi drivers charge about $15 per hour for up to four passengers. Water taxis are also available for beach transport; the cost is a couple of dollars.

Exploring St. Vincent and Bequia

Numbers in the margin correspond to points of interest on the St. Vincent and Bequia map.

🐚 ❷ **Botanical Garden.** A few minutes north of downtown by taxi is the oldest botanical garden in the Western Hemisphere, founded in 1765. Captain Bligh—of *Bounty* fame—brought the first breadfruit tree to this island for landowners to propagate. The prolific bounty of the breadfruit tree was used to feed the slaves. You can see a direct descendant of this tree among the garden's 20 acres of mahogany, rubber, teak, and other tropical trees and shrubs. Two dozen rare St. Vincent parrots live in the small aviary. Guides explain the medicinal and ornamental trees and shrubs; they appreciate a tip at the end of the tour. ⊠ *Off Leeward Hwy., Montrose,* ☎ *784/457–1003.* 🖃 *$3.* ☉ *Daily 6–6.*

❺ **Falls of Baleine.** They're impossible to reach by car, so book an escorted, all-day boat trip from Villa Beach or the Lagoon Marina. The boat ride along the coast offers scenic island views. When you arrive, you have to wade through shallow water to get to the beach. Then guides help you make the easy five-minute trek to the 60-ft (18-m) falls and the rock-enclosed fresh-water pool the falls create—plan to take a dip.

🐚 ❸ **Fort Charlotte.** Started by the French in 1786 and completed by the British in 1806, the fort was named for King George III's wife. It sits on Berkshire Hill, a dramatic promontory 636 ft (195 m) above sea level, with a stunning view of Kingstown and the Grenadines. Interestingly, cannons face inward—the fear of attack by native peoples was far greater than any threat approaching from the sea, though, truth be told, the fort saw no action. The fort now serves as a signal station for ships; its ancient cells house paintings, by Lindsay Prescott, depicting early island history.

❶ **Kingstown.** The capital city of St. Vincent and the Grenadines is on the island's southwestern coast. The town of 25,000 residents—about a fourth of the nation's population—wraps around Kingstown Bay; a ring of green hills and ridges, studded with homes, forms a backdrop for the city. This is very much a working city, with a busy harbor and few concessions to tourists. Kingstown Harbour is the only deepwater port on the island.

What few gift shops there are can be found on and around **Bay Street,** near the harbor. Upper Bay Street, which stretches along the bayfront, bustles with daytime activity; workers going about their business and housewives doing their shopping. Many of Kingstown's downtown buildings are built of stone or brick brought to the island in the holds of 18th-century ships as ballast (and replaced with sugar and spices for the return trip to Europe). The Georgian-style stone arches and second-floor overhangs on former warehouses create shelter from midday sun and the brief, cooling showers common to the tropics.

Grenadines Wharf, at the south end of Bay Street, is busy with schooners loading supplies and ferries loading people bound for the Grenadines. The **Cruise Ship Terminal,** south of the commercial wharf, has a duty-free mall with 20 shops, plus restaurants, a post office, communications facilities, and a taxi/minibus stand.

An almost infinite selection of produce fills the **Kingstown Produce Market,** a three-story building that occupies an entire city block on Upper Bay, Hillsboro, and Bedford streets in the center of town. It's noisy, colorful, and open Monday through Saturday—but the busiest times (and the best times to go) are Friday and Saturday mornings. In the courtyard, vendors sell local arts and crafts. On the upper floors, merchants sell clothing, household items, gifts, and other products.

Little Tokyo, so called because funding for the project was a gift from Japan, is a waterfront shopping area with a bustling indoor fish mar-

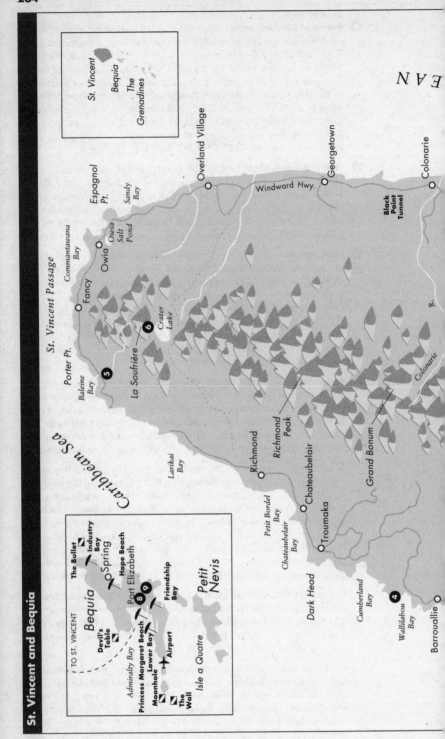

St. Vincent and Bequia

St. Vincent
Bequia
The
Grenadines

~EAN

Overland Village

Windward Hwy.

Georgetown

Colonarie

Black Point
Tunnel

Espagnol Pt.

Sandy Bay

Owia Salt Pond

Owia

Commantawana Bay

Fancy

Crater Lake

❻

❺

La Soufrière

Porter Pt.

Baleine Bay

St. Vincent Passage

Caribbean Sea

Richmond

Richmond Peak

Grand Bonum

Larikai Bay

Chateaubelair

Troumaka

Petit Bordel Bay

Chateaubelair Bay

Dark Head

Cumberland Bay

Wallilabou Bay

❹

Barroualie

Colonarie R.

Bequia

The Bullet

Industry Bay

Spring

Hope Beach

Port Elizabeth

❽ ❾

Friendship Bay

Devil's Table

TO ST. VINCENT

Admiralty Bay

Princess Margaret Beach

Moonhole

Lower Bay

The Wall

Airport

Isle a Quatre

Petit Nevis

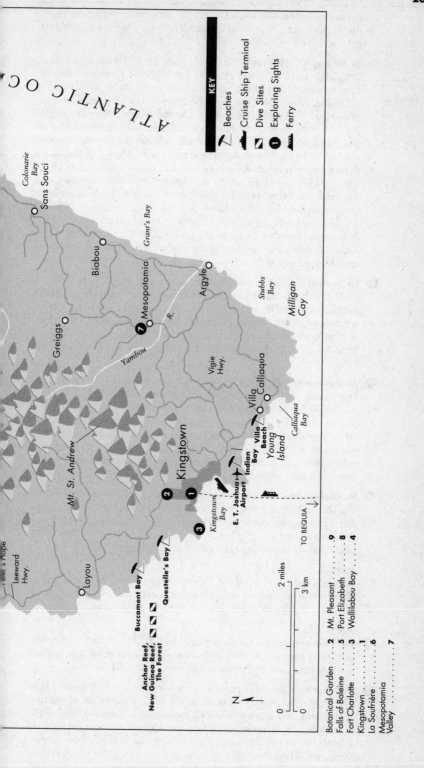

ATLANTIC OC.

Colonarie
Bay
Sans Souci

Grant's Bay

Biabou

Argyle

Stubbs
Bay

Milligan
Cay

Greiggs

Mesopotamia
7

R.

Yambou

Vigie
Hwy.

Calliaqua

Villa

Calliaqua
Bay

Mt. St. Andrew

Kingstown

Indian
Bay Villa
Beach

Young
Island

2

1

Kingstown
Bay

E. T. Joshua
Airport

Peter's Hope

Leeward
Hwy.

Layou

Buccament Bay

Questelle's Bay

3

TO BEQUIA

Anchor Reef,
New Guinea Reef,
The Forest

2 miles

3 km

N

KEY

∠ Beaches

▟ Cruise Ship Terminal

◪ Dive Sites

❶ Exploring Sights

⛴ Ferry

ket and dozens of stalls where you can buy inexpensive homemade meals, drinks, ice cream, bread and cookies, clothing, and trinkets and even get a haircut.

St. George's Cathedral, on Grenville Street, is a pristine, creamy-yellow Anglican church built in 1820. The dignified Georgian architecture includes simple wooden pews, an ornate chandelier, and beautiful stained-glass windows; one was a gift from Queen Victoria, who commissioned it for London's St. Paul's Cathedral in honor of her first grandson. When the artist created an angel with a red robe, she was horrified and sent it abroad. The markers in the cathedral's graveyard recount the history of the island. Across the street is **St. Mary's Cathedral of the Assumption** (Roman Catholic), built in stages beginning in 1823. The strangely appealing design is a blend of Moorish, Georgian, and Romanesque styles applied to black brick. Nearby, freed slaves built the **Kingstown Methodist Church** in 1841. The exterior is brick, simply decorated with quoins (solid blocks that form the corners), and the roof is held together by metal straps, bolts, and wooden pins. **Scots Kirk** (1839–80) was built by and for Scottish settlers but became a Seventh-Day Adventist church in 1952.

6 **La Soufrière.** The volcano, which last erupted in 1979, is 4,000 ft (1,219 m) high and so huge in area that it covers virtually the entire northern third of the island. The eastern trail to the rim of the crater, a two-hour ascent, begins at Rabacca Dry River. But remember, when it rains on La Soufrière, the river is no longer dry—and you can be stranded on one side or the other for an hour or two or, in rare cases, longer.

7 **Mesopotamia Valley.** The rugged, ocean-lashed scenery along St. Vincent's windward coast is the perfect counterpoint to the lush, calm west coast. The fertile Mesopotamia Valley (nicknamed "Mespo") offers a panoramic view of dense rain forests, streams, and endless banana and coconut plantations. Breadfruit, sweet corn, peanuts, and arrowroot also grow in the rich soil here. The valley is surrounded by mountain ridges, including 3,181-ft (973 m) Grand Bonhomme Mountain, which overlooks the Caribbean.

4 **Wallilabou Bay.** You can sunbathe, swim, picnic, or buy your lunch at Wallilabou (pronounced wally-la-*boo*) Anchorage, on the bay. This is a favorite stop for day-trippers returning from the Falls of Baleine and boaters anchoring for the evening. Nearby there's a river with a small waterfall where you can take a fresh-water plunge.

BEQUIA

Bequia is the Carib word for "island of the cloud." Hilly and green, with several gold-sand beaches, Bequia is just 9 mi (14½ km) south of St. Vincent's southwestern shore; with 5,000 inhabitants, it's the most populous of the Grenadines.

9 **Mt. Pleasant.** Bequia's highest point (881 ft [270 m]) is a reasonable goal for a hiking trek. Alternatively, it's a pleasant drive. The reward is a stunning view of the island and surrounding Grenadines.

8 **Port Elizabeth.** Bequia's capital is on the northeast side of Admiralty Bay. The ferry from St. Vincent docks at the jetty, in the center of the tiny town that's only a few blocks long and a couple of blocks deep. Walk north along Front Street, which faces the water, to the open-air market, where you can buy fruits and vegetables and some handicrafts; farther along, you'll find the model-boat builders' workshops for which Bequia is renowned. Walk south along Belmont Walkway, which meanders along the bay front past shops, cafés, restaurants, bars, and hotels.

Shopping

The 12 blocks that hug the waterfront in downtown Kingstown compose St. Vincent's main shopping district. Among the shops that sell goods to fulfill household needs are a few that sell local crafts, gifts, and souvenirs. Street vendors position themselves along the main shopping streets and sell items for local consumption as well as handcrafted leather goods, carvings, artwork, and handmade jewelry. Bargaining is neither expected nor appreciated.

Stores are generally open weekdays from 8 to 4 or 4:30, Saturday 8–1, and are closed on Sunday. St. Vincent is not a major duty-free shopping port, although several shops at the cruise-ship terminal and a few stores in town sell duty-free items.

ST. VINCENT

The best place for duty-free shopping is the **Cruise Ship Terminal** (⊠ Upper Bay St., Kingstown, ☎ 784/456–1830). Among its 20 shops are several that specialize in duty-free goods. At **FranPaul's Selections** (⊠ 2nd floor, Bonadie's Plaza, Bay St., Kingstown, ☎ 784/456–2662), Francelia St. John fashions dresses, pants, and shirts from colorful fabrics she selects in Trinidad. The emphasis is on African, Afro-Caribbean, and casual wear. At **Gonsalves Duty-Free Liquor** (⊠ Airport Departure Lounge, Arnos Vale, ☎ 784/456–4781), spirits and liqueurs are available at discounts of up to 40%. To bring back sounds of the islands, stop by **Music World** (⊠ Egmont St., Kingstown, ☎ 784/547–1884), where you'll find the latest reggae, soca, and calypso music on CD and tape. **Nzimbu Browne** (⊠ Bay St., in front of the Cobblestone Inn, Kingstown, ☎ 784/457–1677) creates original art from dried banana leaves, carefully selecting and snipping bits and arranging them on pieces of wood to depict local scenes. He sets up shop on Bay Street, near the Cobblestone Inn. **St. Vincent Craftsmen's Centre** (⊠ Frenches St., Kingstown, ☎ 784/457–2516), three blocks from the wharf, sells locally made grass floor mats, place mats, and other straw articles, as well as batik cloth, handmade West Indian dolls, hand-painted calabashes, and framed artwork. The large grass mats can be rolled and folded for easy transport home. No credit cards are accepted.

BEQUIA

Bequia's shops are mostly on Front Street and Belmont Walkway, its waterfront extension, just steps from the jetty where the ferry arrives in Port Elizabeth. North of the jetty there's an open-air market and farther along the road are the model-boat builders' shops. Opposite the jetty, at Bayshore Mall, shops sell ice cream, baked goods, stationery, gifts, and clothing; a liquor store, pharmacy, travel agent, and bank are also here. On Belmont Walkway, south of the jetty, shops and studios showcase gifts and handmade articles. Shops here are open weekdays from 8 to 5, Saturday 8 to noon. At **Banana Patch Studio** (⊠ Paget Farm ☎ 784/458–3865), you can view and purchase paintings and scrimshaw work by artist Sam McDowell and shellcraft created by his wife Donna, by appointment only. You can visit the studio of French artist **Claude Victorine** (⊠ Lower Bay, ☎ 784/458–3150) and admire her delicate hand-painted silk wall hangings and scarves. Large wall hangings cost $100, scarves $50. Her studio is open from noon to 7 PM; it's closed Fridays. **Mauvin's Model Boat Shop** (⊠ Front St., Port Elizabeth, ☎ no phone) is where you can purchase the handmade model boats for which Bequia is known. You can even special-order a replica of your own yacht. They're incredibly detailed and quite expensive—from a few hundred to several thousand dollars. The simplest ones take about a week to make. **Sargeant Brothers Model Boat Shop** (⊠ Front St., Port Elizabeth, ☎ 758/458–3312) sells handmade model boats and will build special requests on commission. Housed in the ruins of an old sugar mill, **Spring Pottery & Studios** (✉ Spring, ☎ 784/457–3757) is the working pottery of Mike Goddard and Maggie Overal, with gallery exhibits of ceramics, paintings, and crafts—their own and those of other local artists. All works are for sale.

Outdoor Activities & Sports

ST. VINCENT

➤ BOATING, FISHING, AND SAILING: From St. Vincent you can charter a monohull or catamaran (bareboat or complete with captain, crew, and cook) to weave you through the Grenadines for a day or a week of sailing—or a half-day, full-day, or overnight fishing trip. Boats of all sizes and degrees of luxury are available. Charter rates start at around $250 per day.

Blue Water Charters (✉ Aquatic Club, Villa Beach, St. Vincent, ☎ 784/456–1232, FAX 784/456–2382) will take you on fishing or sightseeing excursions on its modern, 55-ft Sport Fisherman. **Crystal Blue Charters** (✉ Indian Bay, St. Vincent, ☎ 784/457–4532, FAX 784/456–2232) offers sportfishing charters on a 34-ft pirogue for amateur and serious fishermen. **Sunsail** (✉ Blue Lagoon, Ratho Mill, St. Vincent, ☎ FAX 784/458–4308) charters bareboat and crewed yachts ranging in length from 30 ft to 50 ft.

➤ HIKING: St. Vincent offers hikers and trekkers a choice of experiences: easy, picturesque walks near Kingstown; moderate-effort nature trails in the central valleys; and exhilarating climbs through a rain forest to the rim of an active volcano. Bring a hat, long pants, and insect repellent if you plan to hike in the bush.

A hike up **Dorsetshire Hill,** about 3 mi (5 km) from Kingstown, rewards you with a sweeping view of city and harbor. You can also see the monument to Black Carib chief Chatoyer, who lost his life in a duel at this site.

La Soufrière, the queen of climbs, is St. Vincent's active volcano (which last erupted, appropriately enough, on Friday the 13th, April 1979). Approachable from either the windward or leeward coast, this is *not* a casual excursion for inexperienced walkers—the massive mountain covers nearly the entire northern third of the island. Climbs are all-day excursions. You'll need stamina and sturdy shoes to reach the top and peep into the mile-wide crater, which is just over 4,000 ft above sea level. Be sure to check the weather before you leave; hikers have been sorely disappointed to find a cloud-obscured view at the summit. A guide ($25–$30) can be arranged through the Ministry of Tourism & Culture, or tour operators. The eastern approach is more popular. In a four-wheel-drive vehicle you pass through Rabacca Dry River, north of Georgetown, and the Bamboo Forest; then it's a two-hour, 3½-mi (5½-km) hike to the summit. Approaching from the west, near Châteaubelair, the climb is longer—10–12 mi (6–7 km)—and rougher, but even more scenic. If you hike up one side and down the other, arrangements must be made in advance to pick you up at the end.

Trinity Falls, in the north, requires a trip by four-wheel-drive vehicle from Richmond to the interior, then a steep two-hour climb to a crystal-clear river and three waterfalls, one of which forms a whirlpool where you can take a refreshing swim.

Vermont Nature Trails are two hiking trails that start near the top of the Buccament Valley, 5 mi (8 km) north of Kingstown. A network of 1½-mi (2½-km) loops passes through bamboo, evergreen forest, and rain forest. In the late afternoon you may be lucky enough to see the rare St. Vincent parrot, *Amazona guildingii.*

➤ SCUBA DIVING & SNORKELING: Novices and advanced divers alike will be impressed by the marine life in St. Vincent's waters—brilliant sponges, huge deepwater coral trees, and shallow reefs teeming with colorful fish. The best dive spots on St. Vincent are in the small bays along the coast between Kingstown and Layou; many are within 20 yards of shore and only 20 ft to 30 ft down. About 35 dive sites around Bequia and nearby islands are accessible within 15 minutes by boat. The leeward side of the 7-mi (11-km) reef that fringes Bequia has been designated a marine park.

Anchor Reef has excellent visibility for viewing a deep-black coral garden, schools of squid, seahorses, and maybe a small octopus. **The Forest,** a shallow dive, is still dramatic, with soft corals in pastel colors and schools of small fish. **New Guinea Reef** slopes to 90 ft (28 m) and can't be matched for its quantity of corals and sponges. **Young Island** is also a good place for snorkeling, but you need to phone for permission to take the ferry from Villa Beach over to the island and rent snorkeling equipment from the resort's water-sports center. The pristine waters surrounding the **Tobago Cays,** in the Southern Grenadines, will give you a world-class diving experience.

Dive Fantasea (⊠ Villa Beach, St. Vincent, ☎ 784/457–5560 or 784/457–5577) offers dive and snorkeling trips to the St. Vincent coast and the Tobago Cays. **Dive St. Vincent** (⊠ Young Island Dock, Villa Beach, St. Vincent, ☎ 784/457–4714 or 784/547–4928) is where NAUI- and PADI-certified instructor Bill Tewes and his staff offer beginner and certification courses and dive trips to the St. Vincent coast and the southern Grenadines.

BEQUIA

➤ BOATING & SAILING: With regular trade winds, visibility for 30 mi (48 km), and generally calm seas, Bequia is a center for some of the best blue-water sailing you'll find anywhere in the world, with all kinds of options: day sails or weekly charters, bareboat or fully crewed, monohulls or catamarans—whatever's your pleasure. Prices for day trips run $50–$75 per person, depending on the destination.

Friendship Rose (⊠ Port Elizabeth, ☎ FAX 784/458–3373), an 80-ft schooner that spent its first 25 years as a mail boat, was subsequently refitted to take passengers on day trips from Bequia to Mustique and the Tobago Cays. The 60-ft catamaran **Passion** (⊠ Belmont ☎ 784/458–3884), custom-built for day sailing, offers all-inclusive daylong snorkeling and/or sportfishing trips from Bequia to Mustique, the Tobago Cays, and St. Vincent's Falls of Baleine. It's also available for private charter. The Frangipani Hotel owns the **S. Y. Pelangi** (⊠ Port Elizabeth, ☎ 784/458–3255), a 44-ft cutter, for day sails or longer charters; four people can be accommodated comfortably, and the cost is $200 per day.

➤ SCUBA DIVING & SNORKELING: About 35 dive sites around Bequia and nearby islands are accessible within 15 minutes by boat. The leeward side of the 7-mi (11-km) reef that fringes Bequia has been designated a marine park. **The Bullet,** off Bequia's north point, is a good spot for spotting rays, barracuda, and the occasional nurse shark. **Devil's Table** is a shallow dive that's rich in fish and coral and has a sailboat wreck nearby at 90 ft. **Moonhole** is shallow enough in places for snorkelers to enjoy. **The Wall** is a 90-ft drop off West Cay. Expect to pay dive operators $50 for a one-tank and $95 for a two-tank dive. Dive boats welcome snorkelers, but for the best snorkeling in Bequia, take a water taxi to the bay at Moonhole and arrange a pickup time.

Bequia Dive Adventures (⊠ Belmont Walkway, Admiralty Bay, Port Elizabeth, ☎ 784/458–3826 FAX 784/458–3964) offers PADI instruction courses and takes small groups on three dives daily. **Dive Bequia** (✉ Belmont Walkway, Admiralty Bay, Port Elizabeth ☎ 784/458–3504, FAX 784/458–3886), at the Gingerbread complex, offers dive and snorkel tours, night dives, and full equipment rental. Resort and certification courses are available. **Dive Paradise** (✉ Friendship Bay, ☎ 784/458–3563, FAX 784/457–3115) has two modern dive boats and offers dive packages and certified instruction for beginners and advanced divers, equipment rental, wreck dives, and snorkeling packages (but it doesn't take credit cards). **Friendship Divers** (✉ Friendship Bay, ☎ FAX 784/458–3422), near the Bequia Beach Club, offers one- and two-tank dives, instruction, and equipment rental; the dive boat accommodates up to 16 people.

Beaches

ST. VINCENT

St. Vincent's origin is volcanic, so its beaches range in color from golden-brown to black. Swimming is recommended only in the lagoons and bays along the leeward coast. By contrast, beaches on the Bequia and the rest of the Grenadines have pure white sand, palm trees, and crystal-clear aquamarine water; some are even within walking distance of the jetty. **Buccament Bay** is good for swimming. This tiny black-sand beach is 20 minutes north of Kingstown. South of Kingstown, **Indian Bay** has golden sand but is slightly rocky; it's a good place for snorkeling. **Questelle's Bay** (pronounced keet-*ells*), north of Kingstown and next to Campden Park, has a black-sand beach. **Villa Beach,** opposite Young Island and 10 minutes south of Kingstown, is the island's main beach (although it's hardly big enough to merit such a title). Boats bob at anchor in the channel; dive shops and restaurants line the shore.

BEQUIA

Bequia's **Friendship Bay** can be reached by land taxi. You can rent windsurfing and snorkeling equipment at Friendship Bay Resort and also grab a bite to eat or a cool drink. Getting to **Hope Beach,** on the Atlantic side, involves a long taxi ride (about $7.50) and a mile-long (1½-km-long) walk downhill on a semi-paved path. Your reward is a magnificent crescent of white sand, total seclusion, and—if you prefer—nude bathing. Be sure to ask your taxi driver to return at a prearranged time. Bring your own lunch and drinks; there are no facilities. Even though the surf is fairly shallow, swimming can be dangerous because of the undertow. **Industry Bay,** a nearly secluded beach fringed with towering palms, is on the northeast side of the island and requires transportation from Port Elizabeth. This is a good beach for snorkelers, but there could be a strong undertow. Bring a picnic; the nearest facilities are at Spring on Bequia resort, a 10- to 15-minute walk from the beach. Wide, palm-fringed **Lower Bay** is reachable by taxi or by hiking beyond Princess Margaret Beach and is an excellent location for swimming and snorkeling. There are facilities to rent water-sports equipment here, as well as De Reef restaurant. Quiet and wide, with a natural stone arch at one end, **Princess Margaret Beach** is a half-hour hike over rocky bluffs from Belmont Walkway—or you can take a water or land taxi. Though it has no facilities, it's a popular spot for swimming, snorkeling, or snoozing under the palm and sea grape trees.

Where to Eat

A 7% government tax is applicable to your bill, and most restaurants add a 10% service charge in lieu of tip. If they do not, leave an appropriate tip; otherwise, anything additional is expected only for special service.

ST. VINCENT

$–$$$ ✕ **Lime Restaurant & Pub.** Named for the *pursuit* of liming, this sprawling waterfront restaurant also includes a great deal of green in its decor. An extensive all-day menu caters to beachgoers and boaters, who drop by for a roti and a bottle of Hairoun—or burgers, curries, sandwiches, gourmet pizzas, pastas, soups, and salads. Dinner choices include fresh seafood, volcano chicken (with a creole sauce that's as spicy as lava is hot), curried goat, and pepper steak. Casual and congenial by day, it's candlelit and romantic at night—enhanced by the twinkling lights of anchored boats and the soft sound of waves quietly breaking against the seawall. ⊠ *Young Island Channel, Villa Harbour,* ☎ 784/458–4227. *AE, D, DC, MC, V.*

$–$$ ✗ **Basil's Bar and Restaurant.** It's not just the air-conditioning that makes this restaurant cool. Downstairs at the Cobblestone Inn, it is owned by Basil Charles, whose Basil's Beach Bar on Mustique is a hangout for the vacationing rich and famous. This is the Kingstown power-lunch venue. Local businesspeople gather for the daily buffet or a full menu of salads, sandwiches, barbecued chicken, or fresh seafood platters. ⊠ *Cobblestone Inn, Upper Bay St., Kingstown,* ☎ 784/457–2713. *AE, MC, V.*

¢–$$ ✗ **Vee Jay's Rooftop Diner & Pub.** This eatery above Roger's Photo Studios (have your pix developed while you eat) and opposite the Cobblestone Inn offers downtown Kingstown's best harbor view from beneath a green corrugated-plastic roof. Among the "authentic Vincy cuisine" specials chalked on the blackboard are mutton or fish stew, chicken or vegetable rotis, curried goat, souse, and *buljol* (sautéed codfish, breadfruit, and vegetables). Not-so-Vincy sandwiches, fish-and-chips, and burgers can be authentically washed down with *mauby,* a bittersweet drink made from tree bark; linseed, peanut, passion-fruit, or sorrel punch; locally produced Hairoun beer; or cocktails. Lunch is buffet style. ⊠ *Upper Bay St., Kingstown,* ☎ 784/457–2845. *Reservations essential. AE, MC, V. Closed Sun.*

BEQUIA

$$–$$$ ✗ **Gingerbread.** The airy dining room verandah at the Gingerbread Apartments overlooks Admiralty Bay and the waterfront activity. The lunch crowd can enjoy barbecued beef kebabs or chicken with fried potatoes or onions, grilled fish, homemade soups, salads, and sandwiches. In the evening, steaks, seafood, and curries are specialties of the house. Save room for warm, fresh gingerbread—served here with lemon sauce. In season, dinner is often accompanied by live music. ⊠ *Gingerbread Apartments, Belmont Walkway, Admiralty Bay, Port Elizabeth,* ☎ 784/458–3800. *Reservations essential. AE, MC, V.*

$ ✗ **Mac's Pizzeria.** Overheard at the dock in Mustique: "We're sailing over to Bequia for pizza." The two-hour sunset sail to Admiralty Bay is worth the trip for Mac's pizza. Choose from 14 mouthwatering toppings (including lobster), or select quiche, pita sandwiches, lasagna, or soups and salads. Mac's home-baked cookies and muffins are great for dessert or a snack. The outdoor terrace offers fuchsia bougainvillea and water views. ⊠ *Belmont Walkway, Admiralty Bay, Port Elizabeth,* ☎ 784/458–3474. *Reservations essential. No credit cards.*

San Juan, Puerto Rico

Although Puerto Rico is a commonwealth of the United States, few cities in the Caribbean are as steeped in Spanish tradition as San Juan. Within a seven-block neighborhood in Old San Juan are restored 16th-century buildings, museums, art galleries, bookstores, and 200-year-old houses with balustraded balconies overlooking narrow, cobblestone streets. In contrast, San Juan's sophisticated Condado and Isla Verde areas have glittering hotels, Latin music shows, casinos, and discos. Out in the countryside is the 28,000-acre El Yunque rain forest, with more than 240 species of trees growing at least 100 ft high. You can stretch your sea legs on dramatic mountain ranges, numerous trails, vast caves, coffee plantations, old sugar mills, and hundreds of beaches. No wonder San Juan is one of the busiest ports of call in the Caribbean.

Like any other big city, San Juan has its share of crime. Guard your wallet or purse, and avoid walking in the area between Old San Juan and the Condado.

CURRENCY
The U.S. dollar is the official currency of Puerto Rico.

TELEPHONES
Calling the United States from Puerto Rico is the same as calling within the U.S. You can use the long-distance telephone service office in the cruise-ship terminal, or you can use your calling card by dialing the toll-free access number of your long-distance provider from any pay phone. You'll find a phone center by the Paseo de la Princesa.

SHORE EXCURSIONS
The following are good choices in San Juan. They may not be offered by all cruise lines. Times and prices are approximate.

El Yunque Rain Forest. A 45-minute drive heads east to the Caribbean National Forest, where you can walk unguided along various trails, see waterfalls, and climb the observation tower. Includes a stop at Coca waterfalls. ☉ *5 hrs,* 💳 *$29.*

Kayaking. You kayak along the coastline, along white-sand beaches. ☉ *4½ hrs,* 💳 *$75.*

Old San Juan Walking Tour. After a tour of Fort San Felipe del Morro, you walk the narrow streets of Old San Juan and soak up the history, ending at Christo's Chapel. ☉ *2½ hrs,* 💳 *$29.*

Rain Forest Nature Hike. After a 45-minute drive to the forest, you take a guided walk along selected nature trails. ☉ *5 hrs,* 💳 *$49.*

San Juan and the Bacardi Rum Distillery. After seeing how it is made, you can sample and buy some Bacardi rum. Then you take a bus tour of the city. ☉ *3½ hrs,* 💳 *$31.*

Coming Ashore
Cruise ships dock within a couple of blocks of Old San Juan. The Paseo de la Princesa, a tree-lined promenade beneath the city wall, is a nice place for a stroll—you can admire the local crafts and stop at the re-freshment kiosks. A tourist information booth is in the cruise-termi-nal area. Major sights in the Old San Juan area are mere blocks from the piers, but be aware that the streets are narrow and steeply inclined in places.

To get to Cataño and the Bacardi Rum Plant, take the ferry (50¢) that leaves from the cruise piers every half hour. Your best bet to reach Puerta de Tierra, Santurce, and Caparra (still within the San Juan metro area), other than an organized ship excursion, is to take a taxi. Taxis line up to meet ships. White taxis labeled TAXI TURISTICO charge set fares of $6 to $16. Metered cabs authorized by the Public Service Commission charge an initial $1; after that, it's about 10¢ for each additional ⅓ mi. If you take a metered taxi, insist that the meter be turned on, and pay only what is shown, plus a tip of 10% to 15%. You can negoti-ate with taxi drivers for specific trips, and you can hire a taxi for as little as $20 per hour for sightseeing tours.

Exploring San Juan
Numbers in the margin correspond to points of interest on the Old San Juan map.

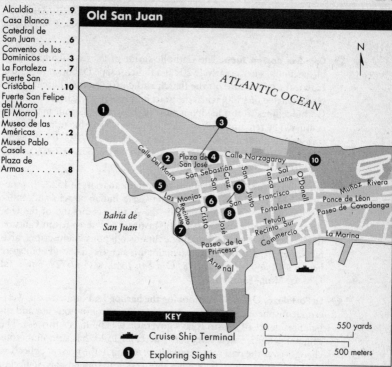

OLD SAN JUAN

Old San Juan, the original city founded in 1521, contains authentic and carefully preserved examples of 16th- and 17th-century Spanish-colonial architecture. Graceful wrought-iron balconies decorated with lush hanging plants extend over narrow, cobblestone streets. Seventeenth-century walls still partially enclose the old city. Designated a U.S. National Historic Zone in 1950, Old San Juan is packed with shops, open-air cafés, private homes, tree-shaded squares, monuments, plaques, pigeons, people, and traffic jams. It's faster to walk than to take a cab. Nightlife can be quiet, but even during the low season you'll find some action on Calle San Sebastián, which has a row of restaurants, bars, and dance clubs. If your feet fail you in Old San Juan, climb aboard the free open-air trolleys that rumble through the narrow streets. Take one from the docks or board anywhere along the route.

❾ Alcaldía. The city hall was built between 1604 and 1789. In 1841 extensive renovations were done to make it resemble Madrid's city hall; it has arcades, towers, balconies, and a lovely inner courtyard. A tourist information center and an art gallery are on the first floor. ✉ *Calle San Francisco 153, Plaza de Armas, Old San Juan,* ☎ *787/724–7171 Ext. 2391.* ▭ *Free.* ☉ *Weekdays 8–4.*

❺ Casa Blanca. The original structure on this site, not far from the ramparts of El Morro, was a frame house built in 1521 for Juan Ponce de León. But the Spanish explorer died in Cuba without ever having lived in it, and it was virtually destroyed by a hurricane in 1523, after which his son-in-law had the present masonry home built. Ponce de León's descendants occupied it for 250 years. From the end of the Spanish-American War in 1898 to 1966 it was the home of the U.S. Army commander in Puerto Rico. There's an archaeology exhibit inside, and several rooms are decorated with colonial-era furnishings. The lush garden, cooled by spraying fountains, is a tranquil spot. ⊠ *Calle San Sebastián 1, Old San Juan,* ☎ *787/724–4102.* 🖾 *$2.* ☺ *Tues.–Sat. 9–noon and 1–4:30.*

❻ Catedral de San Juan. The Catholic shrine of Puerto Rico had humble beginnings in the early 1520s as a thatch-topped wooden structure. Hurricane winds tore off the thatch and destroyed the church. It was reconstructed in 1540, when the graceful circular staircase and vaulted Gothic ceilings were added, but most of the work was done in the 19th century. The remains of Ponce de León are in a marble tomb near the transept. ⊠ *Calle Cristo 153, Old San Juan,* ☎ *787/722–0861.* 🖾 *$1 donation suggested.* ☺ *Weekdays 8:30–4; masses Sat. at 7 PM, Sun. at 9 and 11 AM, weekdays at 12:15 PM.*

❸ Convento de los Dominicos. Built by Dominican friars in 1523, this convent often served as a shelter during Carib Indian attacks and, more recently, was the headquarters for the Antilles command of the U.S. Army. Now home to offices of the Institute of Puerto Rican Culture, the beautifully restored building contains religious manuscripts, artifacts, and art. The institute also maintains a crafts store and bookstore here. ⊠ *Calle Norzagaray 98, Old San Juan,* ☎ *787/721–6866.* 🖾 *Free.* ☺ *Mon.–Sat. 9–5.*

❼ La Fortaleza. On a hill overlooking the harbor, La Fortaleza, the Western Hemisphere's oldest executive mansion in continuous use and official residence of Puerto Rico's governor, was built as a fortress. The original primitive structure, constructed in 1540, has seen numerous changes over the past four centuries, resulting in the present collection of marble and mahogany, medieval towers, and stained-glass galleries. Guided tours are conducted every hour on the hour in English, and on the half hour in Spanish. ⊠ *Calle Recinto Oeste, Old San Juan,* ☎ *787/ 721–7000 Ext. 2211 or 2358.* 🖾 *Free.* ☺ *Weekdays 9–4.*

☝ ❿ Fuerte San Cristóbal. This 18th-century fortress guarded the city from land attacks. Even larger than El Morro, San Cristóbal was known in its heyday as the Gibraltar of the West Indies. ⊠ *Calle Norzagaray, Old San Juan,* ☎ *787/729–6960,* WEB *www.nps.gov/saju.* 🖾 *$2.* ☺ *Daily 9–5.*

☝ ❶ Fuerte San Felipe del Morro. On a rocky promontory at the Old City's northwestern tip is El Morro, which was built by the Spaniards between 1540 and 1783. Rising 140 ft above the sea, the six-level fortress covers enough territory to accommodate a 9-hole golf course. It's a labyrinth of dungeons, barracks, turrets, towers, and tunnels. A small, air-conditioned museum traces the history of the fortress. Tours and a video show are available in English. ⊠ *Calle Norzagaray, Old San Juan,* ☎ *787/729–6960,* WEB *www.nps.gov/saju.* 🖾 *$2.* ☺ *Daily 9–5*

❷ Museo de las Américas. The Museum of the Americas is on the second floor of the imposing former military barracks, Cuartel de Ballajá. Most exhibits rotate, but the focus is on the popular and folk art of Latin America. The permanent exhibit, "Las Artes Populares en las Américas," has religious figures, musical instruments, basketwork, costumes, and farming and other implements of the Americas. ⊠ *Calle Norzagaray and Calle del Morro, Old San Juan,* ☎ *787/724–5052,* WEB *www. museolasamericas.org.* 🖾 *Free.* ☺ *Tues.–Fri. 10–4, weekends 11–5.*

❹ Museo Pablo Casals. The small, two-story Pablo Casals Museum contains memorabilia of the famed cellist, who made his home in Puerto Rico from 1956 until his death in 1973. Manuscripts, photographs, and his favorite cellos are on display, in addition to recordings and videotapes (shown on request) of Casals Festival concerts, which he instituted in 1957. The festival is held annually in June. ⊠ *101 Calle San Sebastián, Plaza de San José, Old San Juan,* ☎ *787/723–9185.* ☎ *$1.* ☉ *Tues.–Sat. 9:30–5:30*

❽ Plaza de Armas. This is the original main square of Old San Juan. The plaza, bordered by Calles San Francisco, Fortaleza, San José, and Cruz, has a lovely fountain with 19th-century statues representing the four seasons.

NEW SAN JUAN

In **Puerta de Tierra,** ½ mi (1 km) east of the pier, is **El Capitolio,** Puerto Rico's white-marble capitol, dating from the 1920s. Another ½ mi east, at the tip of Puerta de Tierra, tiny **Fort San Jerónimo** perches over the Atlantic like an afterthought. Added to San Juan's fortifications in the late 18th century, the structure barely survived the British attack of 1797.

Santurce, the district between Miramar on the west and the Laguna San José on the east, is a busy mixture of shops, markets, and offices. The classically designed Universidad del Sagrado Corazón (Sacred Heart University) is home of the **Museo Contemporáneo del Arte de Puerto Rico** (Museum of Contemporary Puerto Rican Art; ⊠ Barat Bldg., Av. Ponce de León, corner of Av. R. H. Todd, Santurce, ☎ 787/268–0049 or 787/727–5249, WEB www.museocontemporaneopr.org). The former San Juan Municipal Hospital is now the **Museo de Arte de Puerto Rico** (Museum of Puerto Rican Art; ⊠ Av. José de Diego 300, Santurce, ☎ 787/977–6277, WEB www.mapr.org), which displays a permanent collection of Puerto Rican art and changing exhibits.

SAN JUAN ENVIRONS

Bacardí Rum Plant. The first Bacardí rum distillery was built in 1862 in Cuba, but it was confiscated by the Castro regime in 1960, and the Bacardí family was exiled. The Puerto Rico plant was built in the 1950s and is one of the world's largest, with the capacity to produce 100,000 gallons of spirits a day and 221 million cases a year. You can take a 45-minute tour of the bottling plant, museum (called the Cathedral of Rum), and distillery, and there's a gift shop. Yes, you'll be offered a sample. ⊠ *Bay View Industrial Park, Rte. 888, Km 2.6, Cataño,* ☎ *787/788–1500 or 787/788–8400.* ☎ *Free.* ☉ *Tours every 30 mins Mon.–Sat. 9–10:30 and noon–4.*

Caparra Ruins. In 1508 Ponce de León established the island's first settlement here. The ruins—a few crumbling walls—are what remains of an ancient fort, and the small Museo de la Conquista y Colonización de Puerto Rico (Museum of the Conquest and Colonization of Puerto Rico) contains historical documents, exhibits, and excavated artifacts, though you can see the museum's contents in less time than it takes to say its name. ⊠ *Rte. 2, Km 6.6, Guaynabo,* ☎ *787/781–4795,* WEB *www. icp.gobierno.pr.* ☎ *Free.* ☉ *Tues.–Sat. 8:30–4:30.*

Shopping

San Juan is not a free port, so you won't find bargains on electronics and perfumes. However, shopping for native crafts can be fun. Popular souvenirs and gifts include santos (small, hand-carved figures of saints or religious scenes), hand-rolled cigars, handmade lace, carnival masks, Puerto Rican rum, and fancy men's shirts called guayaberas.

Aetna Gold (⊠ Calle Gilberto Concepción de Gracia 111, Old San Juan, San Juan, ☎ 787/721–4756), adjacent to the Wyndham Old San Juan Hotel, sells exquisite gold jewelry designed in Greece. Look for vendors selling crafts from kiosks at the **Artesanía Puertorriqueña** (⊠ Plaza Dársenas, Old San Juan, San Juan, ☎ 787/722–1709) in the tourism company's La Casita near Pier 1. Several vendors also set up shop to sell articles such as belts, handbags, and toys along Calle San Justo in front of Plaza Dársenas. At the **Convento de los Dominicos** (⊠ Calle Norzagaray 98, Old San Juan, San Juan, ☎ 787/721–6866)—the Dominican Convent on the north side of the old city that houses the offices of the Instituto de Cultura Puertorriqueña—you'll find baskets, masks, the famous *cuatro* guitars, santos, and reproductions of Taíno artifacts. **Galería Botello** (⊠ Av. Franklin Delano Roosevelt 314, Hato Rey, San Juan, ☎ 787/250–8274, WEB www.botello.com) offers a broad range of works, from traditional santos to pieces by such up-and-coming Puerto Rican artists as María del Mater O'Neill, whose large formats and bold strokes and colors give familiar home-and-garden themes a twist. **Matahari** (⊠ Calle San Justo 202, Old San Juan, San Juan, ☎ 787/724–5869) sells unusual clothes for men and women as well as accessories, jewelry, and trinkets that proprietor Fernando Sosa collects during his trips around the world.

Outdoor Activities & Sports

BOATING AND SAILING

Eco Action Tours (⊠ Condado Plaza Hotel, Av. Ashford 999, Laguna Wing, Condado, San Juan, ☎ 787/791–7509 or 787/640–7385) rents kayaks, Sunfish, and Jet Skis and offers kayaking trips to other parts of the island.

CYCLING

Selected areas lend themselves to bike travel. In general, however, the roads are congested and distances are vast. Avoid main thoroughfares in San Juan: the traffic is heavy and the fumes are thick. The Paseo Piñones is an 11-mi (18-km) bike path that skirts the ocean east of San Juan. **Hot Dog Cycling** (⊠ Av. Isla Verde 5916, Isla Verde, San Juan, ☎ 787/982–5344, WEB www.hotdogcycling.com) rents Cannondale bicycles for $30 a day and organizes group excursions to El Yunque and other places out on the island.

GOLF

Though there are no courses in San Juan proper, it's possible to do a golf outing to one of Puerto Rico's stellar courses as a day trip. There are four attractive Robert Trent Jones–designed 18-hole courses shared by the **Hyatt Dorado Beach Resort and the Hyatt Regency Cerromar Beach** (⊠ Rte. 693, Km 10.8 and Km 11.8, Dorado, ☎ 787/796–1234 Ext. 3238). With El Yunque as a backdrop, the two 18-hole courses at the **Westin Río Mar Beach Resort** (⊠ Río Mar Blvd. 6000, Río Grande, ☎ 787/888–6000) are inspirational. The River Course was designed by Greg Norman, the Ocean course by George and Tom Fazio. The 18-hole Arthur Hills–designed course at **Wyndham El Conquistador Resort and Country Club** (⊠ Av. El Conquistador 1000, Fajardo, ☎ 787/863–6784) is famous for its 200-ft changes in elevation. The trade winds make every shot challenging.

Beaches

By law, all of Puerto Rico's beaches are open to the public (except for the Caribe Hilton's artificial beach in San Juan). Like Condado to its west, **Playa de Isla Verde** is bordered by resorts and has plenty of places to rent chairs and sports equipment or grab a bite to eat. There aren't any lifeguards, but the sands are white, and the snorkeling is good. East of Old San Juan and west of Ocean Park and Isla Verde, the long, wide **Playa del Condado** is often full of guests from the hotels that tower over it. Beach bars, sports outfitters, and chair-rental places abound, but there are no lifeguards. A residential neighborhood just east of Condado and west of Isla Verde is home to **Playa de Ocean Park,** a wide, 1-mi-long (2-km-long) stretch of golden sand. The waters are often choppy but still swimmable—take care, however, as there are no lifeguards.

Coconut palms line crescent-shaped **Balneario de Luquillo,** and coral reefs protect its crystal-clear lagoon from Atlantic waters, making it an ideal place to swim. Amenities include changing rooms, lockers, showers, picnic tables, tent sites, and stands that sell cocktails and island savories. This beach, on Route 3 east of San Juan, is perhaps the most photographed on the island.

Where to Eat

Tips of 15% to 20% are expected, and appreciated, by restaurant waitstaff if a service charge is not included in the bill.

$$–$$$ ✕ **Casa Borinquen.** A portrait of independence leader Pedro Albizu Campos adorns the building's facade, a holdover from before restoration work, when a group of artists turned the crumbling walls into the "Museo sin Techo" ("Roofless Museum"). Today it's a bright, attractive restaurant serving radically delicious local cuisine. The vegetarian dishes are made with local produce, shrimp is served with acerola (a locally grown fruit similar to a cherry but not as sweet) sauce and mashed casava, and pork loin comes with fresh corn relish. ✉ *Calle San Sebastián 109, Old San Juan,* ☎ *787/725–0888. AE, D, MC, V. Closed Mon.*

$$–$$$ ✕ **Parrot Club.** The cuisine is inventive, the decor is colorful, and the staff is casual but efficient. Stop by the bar for the specialty passion-fruit drink before moving to the adjacent dining room or the back courtyard. The menu has contemporary variations of Cuban and Puerto Rican classics. You might start with mouthwatering crabcakes or tamarind-barbecued ribs, followed by blackened tuna in a dark-rum sauce or churrasco with *chimichurri* (a green sauce made with herbs, garlic, and tomatoes). ✉ *Calle Fortaleza 363, Old San Juan,* ☎ *787/725–7370. Reservations not accepted. AE, DC, MC, V.*

$–$$ ✕ **La Fonda del Jibarito.** Sanjuaneros have favored this casual, family-run restaurant for years. The back porch is filled with plants, the dining room is filled with fanciful depictions of Calle Sol (the street outside), and the ever-present owner, Pedro J. Ruiz, is filled with the desire to ensure that everyone's happy. Conch ceviche and chicken fricassee are among the specialties. ✉ *Calle Sol 280, Old San Juan,* ☎ *787/725–8375. Reservations not accepted. AE, MC, V.*

Nightlife

Almost every ship stays in San Juan late or even overnight to give passengers an opportunity to revel in the nightlife—the most sophisticated in the Caribbean.

CASINOS

By law, all casinos are in hotels. The atmosphere is refined, and many patrons dress to the nines, but informal attire is usually fine. Casinos set their own hours, which change seasonally, but generally operate from noon to 4 AM, although the casino in the Condado Plaza is open 24 hours. Other hotels with casinos include the Wyndham Old San Juan, Wyndham El San Juan, the San Juan Marriott, the Inter-Continental San Juan Resort & Casino, and the Ritz-Carlton San Juan.

DANCE AND MUSIC CLUBS

A long line of well-heeled patrons usually runs out the door of **Babylon** (✉ Wyndham El San Juan Hotel, Av. Isla Verde 6063, Isla Verde, San Juan, ☎ 787/791–1000). Those with the staying power to make it inside step out of the Caribbean and into the ancient Middle East. Those who tire of waiting often head to El Chico Lounge, a small room with live entertainment right off the hotel lobby. **Café Bohemio** (✉ El Convento Hotel, Calle Cristo 100, Old San Juan, San Juan, ☎ 787/723–9200), a Latin restaurant, turns into a jazz and bohemian music club from 11 PM to 2 AM Tuesday through Friday (after the kitchen closes); Thursday night is best. An older, dressy crowd frequents **Martini's** (⊠ Inter-Continental San Juan Resort & Casino, Av. Isla Verde 187, Isla Verde, San Juan, ☎ 787/791–6100 Ext. 356), which is known for its Las Vegas–style reviews; acts have included celebrity impersonators and flamenco music and dance troupes. Record parties and fashion shows are also held here from time to time. With a large dance and stage area and smokin' Afro-Cuban bands, **Rumba** (⊠ Calle San Sebastián 152, Old San Juan, San Juan, ☎ 787/725–4407) is one of the best parties in town.

Tobago

Tobago is the sleepy and beautiful little-sister isle of Trinidad. Though ruled by the central government in Port of Spain, Tobago has a measure of self governance under the Tobago House of Assembly, a sort of mini-parliament.

With very little in the way of nightlife and no casinos, Tobago's attractions are its beautiful beaches, crystal-clear waters, and rain forest–covered interior. The pace of life here is slow, and the people are friendly and welcoming.

Tobago calls itself the Crusoe Isle because, as the locals claim, it was the setting for Daniel Defoe's *Robinson Crusoe*. It was also the location for the Disney film *Swiss Family Robinson* and a hangout for stars like Rita Hayworth and Robert Mitchum in the 1950s.

CURRENCY
Tobago uses the Trinidadian dollar (TT$). At this writing, the exchange rate was about TT$6.20 to US$1. Most businesses on the island will accept U.S. currency if you're in a pinch. In addition to the banks in Scarborough and Tobago's airport, a couple of grocery stores in the southwest part of Tobago have ATMs. Prices quoted in this chapter are in U.S. dollars unless otherwise noted.

TELEPHONES
A digital phone system is in place, bringing with it direct-dial service, a comprehensive cell-phone network, and easy Internet access. Pay phones take phone cards or "companion" cards (which you will need to make an international call); these can be purchased at gift shops and newsagents. To dial a number in North America or the Caribbean, simply dial 1 and the number with area code.

SHORE EXCURSIONS
The following are good choices on Tobago. They may not be offered by all cruise lines. Times and prices are approximate.

Buccoo Reef Boat Ride and Snorkel. After a ride to Pigeon Point, you board a glass-bottom boat for a ride over the Buccoo Reef, with plenty of time to snorkel and see the tropical fish close up. ⊙ *3 hrs,* ⊡ *$45.*

Rain-forest Hike. This easy hike goes through one of Tobago's virgin rain forests, which is among the oldest protected forests in the world. ⊙ *5 hrs,* ⊡ *$60.*

Coming Ashore
Ships pull into the port of Scarborough, the tiny but bustling capital. From here it's possible to walk straight off the dock into downtown and explore. Unfortunately, since the best beaches and restaurants are in Crown Point, a taxi or car rental may be necessary. Taxis are not metered, so agree on the fare before hopping in (it pays to shop around). Braver souls may want to try one of the minibuses, which have a blue stripe on the side, that ply the roads. The trip to Crown Point will cost around $1.50 by minibus.

Tobago drivers are somewhat less aggressive than their Trinidad counterparts, and the roads are not as congested, so renting a jeep is not a bad idea. You can usually rent a car for $40 to $60, depending on the season, but prices jump tremendously from Carnival time through Easter.

Exploring Tobago

A driving tour of Tobago, from Scarborough to Charlotteville and back, can be done in about four hours, but you'd never want to undertake this spectacular, and very hilly, ride in that time. The switchbacks can make you wish you had motion-sickness pills (take some along if you're prone).

Numbers in the margin correspond to points of interest on the Tobago map.

❹ **Flagstaff Hill.** One of the highest points of the island sits at the northern tip of Tobago. Surrounded by ocean on three sides and with a view of other hills, Charlotteville, and St. Giles Island, this was the site of an American military lookout and radio tower during World War II. It's an ideal spot for a sunset picnic. The turnoff to the hill is at the major bend on the road from Speyside to Charlotteville. It is largely unpaved, so the going may be a bit rough.

❷ **Fort King George.** On Mt. St. George, a short drive up the hill from Scarborough, Tobago's best-preserved historic monument clings to a cliff high above the ocean. Fort King George was built in the 1770s and operated until 1854. It's hard to imagine that this lovely, tranquil spot, commanding sweeping views of the bay and landscaped with lush tropical foliage, was ever the site of any military action, but the prison, officers' mess, and several stabilized cannons attest otherwise. Just to the left of the tall wooden figures dancing a traditional Tobagonian jig is the former barrack guardhouse, now housing the small **Tobago Museum.** Exhibits include weapons and other pre-Columbian artifacts found in the area; the fertility figures are especially interesting. Upstairs are maps and photographs of Tobago's past. Be sure to check out the gift display cases for the perversely fascinating jewelry made from embalmed and painted lizards and sea creatures; you might find it hard to resist a pair of bright-yellow shrimp earrings. The **Fine Arts Centre** at the foot of the Fort King George complex shows the work of local artists. ✉ *84 Fort St., Scarborough,* ☎ *868/639–3970.* ☞ *Fort free, museum TT$5.* ☉ *Weekdays 9–5.*

❶ **Scarborough.** Around Rockley Bay on the island's hilly, leeward side, this town is both the capital of Tobago and a popular cruise-ship port, but it conveys the feeling that not much has changed since the area was settled two centuries ago. It may not be one of the delightful pastel-colored cities of the Caribbean, but Scarborough does have its charms, including several interesting shops. Be sure to check out the busy Scarborough Market, an indoor and outdoor affair featuring everything from fresh vegetables to live chickens and clothing. Note the red-and-yellow Methodist church on the hill, one of Tobago's oldest churches.

❸ **Speyside.** At the far reach of Tobago's windward coast, this small fishing village has a few lodgings and restaurants. Divers are drawn to the unspoiled reefs in the area and to the strong possibility of spotting giant manta rays. The approach to Speyside from the south affords one of the most spectacular vistas of the island. Glass-bottom boats operate between Speyside and **Little Tobago Island,** one of the most important seabird sanctuaries in the Caribbean.

Shopping

Shopping isn't a major activity in Tobago, but determined shoppers should manage to ferret out some things to take home. Scarborough

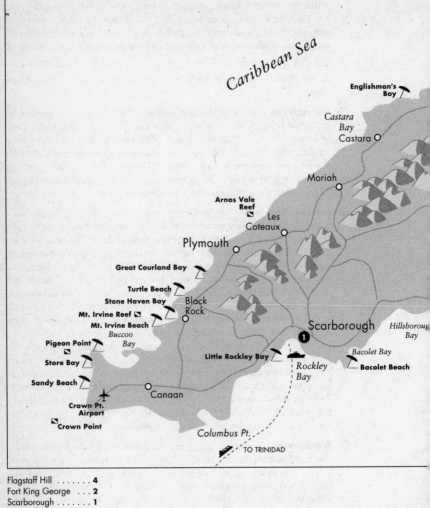

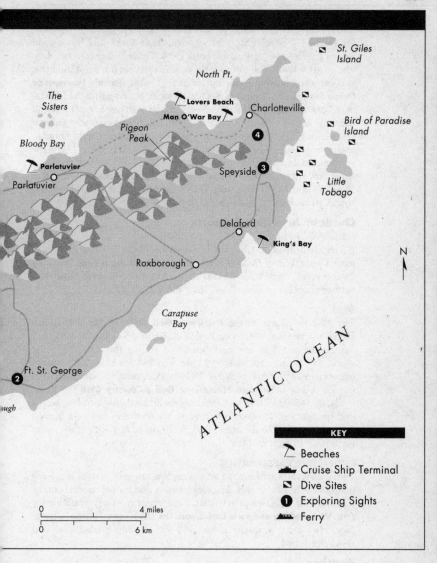

The Sisters

North Pt.

Lovers Beach

Man O'War Bay

Charlotteville

St. Giles Island

Bird of Paradise Island

Pigeon Peak

Bloody Bay

Parlatuvier

Parlatuvier

Speyside

4

3

Little Tobago

Delaford

King's Bay

Roxborough

Carapuse Bay

Ft. St. George

2

ATLANTIC OCEAN

N

KEY
Beaches
Cruise Ship Terminal
Dive Sites
Exploring Sights
Ferry

0   4 miles

0   6 km

has the largest collection of shops, and Burnett Street, which climbs sharply from the port to St. James Park, is a good place to browse. **Cotton House** (⊠ Bacolet St., Scarborough, ☎ 868/639–2727) is a good bet for jewelry and imaginative batik work. Paula Young runs her shop like an art school. You can visit the upstairs studio; if it's not too busy, you can even make a batik square at no charge. **Forro's Homemade Delicacies** (⊠ The Andrew's Rectory, Bacolet St., opposite the fire station, Scarborough, ☎ 868/639–2485) sells its own fine line of tamarind chutney, lemon or lime marmalade, hot sauce, and guava or golden-apple jelly. Eileen Forrester, wife of the Anglican archdeacon of Trinidad and Tobago, supervises a kitchen full of cooks who boil and bottle the condiments and pack them in little straw baskets—or even in bamboo. Most jars are small, easy to carry, and inexpensive. **Souvenir and Gift Shop** (⊠ Port Mall, Wrightson Rd., Scarborough, ☎ 868/639–5632) stocks straw baskets and other crafts.

Outdoor Activities & Sports

BOATING

No trip to Tobago would be complete without the requisite glass-bottomed boat tour of Buccoo Reef. **Hew's Glass Bottom Boat Tours** (⊠ Pigeon Point, ☎ 868/639–9058) are perfect excursions for those who neither snorkel nor dive. Boats leave daily at 11:30 AM.

GOLF

The 18-hole course at the **Mt. Irvine Golf Club** (⊠ Mt. Irvine Bay Hotel, Shirvan Rd., Mt. Irvine Bay, ☎ 868/639–8871) has been ranked among the top 5 in the Caribbean and among the top 100 in the world. Greens fees are $30 for 9 holes and $48 for 18 holes (rates are subject to a 15% V.A.T. tax). The 18-hole, PGA-designed, championship par-72 course at **Tobago Plantations Golf &Country Club** (⊠ Lowlands, ☎ 868/631–0875) is spanking new and set amidst rolling greens and mangroves. It offers amazing views of the ocean as a bonus. Greens fees are $95 for one round, $150 for two rounds (these rates include cart rental and taxes).

SNORKELING/SCUBA DIVING

Tobago's waters are home to an astounding range of marine life, from manta rays to parrot fish. The clear waters and numerous reefs make it perfect for underwater activities. Equipment is widely available for rent. **World of Water Sports Caribbean, Ltd.** (⊠ Hilton Tobago, Claude Noel Hwy., Scarborough, ☎ 868/660–7234) offers guided dives and snorkeling trips.

Beaches

You won't find manicured country-club sand here. But those who enjoy feeling as though they've landed on a desert island will relish the untouched quality of these shores. **Bacolet Beach,** a dark-sand beach, was the setting for the films *Swiss Family Robinson* and *Heaven Knows, Mr. Allison.* Near Fort Bennett, **Great Courland Bay** has clear, tranquil waters. Along the sandy beach—one of Tobago's longest—you'll find several glitzy hotels. A marina attracts the yachting crowd. Surrounded by steep green hills, **King's Bay** is the most visually satisfying of the swimming sites off the road from Scarborough to Speyside—the bay hooks around so severely you'll feel like you're in a lake. The crescent-shape beach is easy to find because it's marked by a sign about halfway between the two towns. Just before you reach the bay there's a bridge with an unmarked turnoff that leads to a gravel parking lot; beyond that, a landscaped path leads to a waterfall with a rocky pool. You may meet locals who'll offer to guide you to the top of the falls; however, you may find the climb not worth the effort. **Pigeon Point,** a stunning locale, is often displayed on Tobago travel brochures. Although the beach is public, it abuts part of what was once a large co-conut estate, and you must pay a token admission (about TT$10) to enter the grounds and use the facilities. The beach is lined with tow-ering royal palms, and there are food stands, gift shops, a diving con-cession, and paddleboats for rent. The waters are calm. **Store Bay,** where boats depart for Buccoo Reef, is little more than a small sandy cove between two rocky breakwaters, but the food stands here are divine: six huts licensed by the tourist board to local ladies who sell roti, pelau, and the world's messiest dish—crab and dumplings. Miss Jean's is the most popular, but you should try Miss Esmie's crab.

Where to Eat

Most restaurants include a 10% service charge, which is considered standard on these islands. If it isn't on the bill, tip according to ser-vice: 10% to 15% is fine.

$$–$$$ ✕ **Kariwak Village.** Recorded steel-band music plays gently in the back-ground at this romantic, candlelit spot in the Kariwak Village complex. In a bamboo pavilion that resembles an Amerindian round hut, Cyn-thia Clovis orchestrates an original four-course menu. Whatever the dish, it will be full of herbs and vegetables picked from Cynthia's or-ganic garden. Saturday buffets, with live jazz or calypso, are a Tobago-nian highlight. ⊠ *Crown Point,* ☎ *868/639–8442. AE, DC, MC, V.*

$–$$$ ✕ **Blue Crab.** Alison Sardinha is Tobago's most ebullient and kindest hostess, and her husband, Ken, one of its best chefs. The menu may include kingfish, curried chicken, or suckling pig. You'll always find callaloo, rotis, and *cou-cou* (a cornmeal dish); sometimes you may find a "cookup"—a pelau-type rice dish with *everything* in it. The place is officially open only on Wednesday and Friday nights, but Miss Alison will open the restaurant on other evenings and for weekend lunches if you call in the morning. ⊠ *Robinson and Main Sts., Scarborough* ☎ *868/639–2737 AE, MC, V Closed weekends. No dinner Mon.–Tues. and Thurs.*

$–$$$ ✕ **Bonkers.** Despite the rather odd name, this restaurant at the Tou-can Inn is atmospheric and excellent. Designed by expatriate British co-owner Chris James, the architecture is a blend of Kenyan and Caribbean styles, executed entirely in local teak and open on all sides. The menu is huge; Chris claims it pains him to remove any items, so he just keeps adding more. You can savor your lobster Rockefeller while enjoying the nightly entertainment. Open for breakfast and lunch seven days a week, this is the busiest eatery on the island. ⊠ *Toucan Inn, Store Bay Local Rd., Crown Point,* ☎ *868/639–7173,* FAX *868/ 639–8933. AE, MC, V.*

Trinidad

Trinidad is the most southerly island in the Caribbean and a melting pot of African and Asian cultures. Though it is not a typical tourist paradise with sparkling waters and large hotels, it offers a tremendously diverse ecosystem. Trinidad is justifiably famous for its Carnival, steel-band music, and calypso.

Although it is a fairly large island, most of the significant attractions are in the north. The capital, Port of Spain, is a bustling economic cen-ter, complete with traffic, crowds, and some urban crime. Just behind the capital is the Northern Range, a wall of mountains covered in pris-tine rain forest that separates the city from the many beaches on the north coast.

Trinidad's ethnically diverse population of just over a million means that cultural and culinary adventures abound.

CURRENCY

The Trinidadian dollar (TT$) is the legal currency here. Banks (many with ATMs that accept international cards) are plentiful in towns and cities all over the island (branches of Republic Bank and the Royal Bank are a common sight, though much less so in the countryside. Prices quoted in this chapter are in U.S. dollars unless otherwise noted.

TELEPHONES

A digital phone system is in place, bringing with it direct-dial service, a comprehensive cell-phone network, and easy Internet access. Pay phones take phone cards or "companion" cards (which you will need to make an international call); these can be purchased at gift shops and newsagents. To dial a number in North America or the Caribbean, simply dial 1 and the number with area code.

SHORE EXCURSIONS

The following are good choices on Tobago. They may not be offered by all cruise lines. Times and prices are approximate.

Caroni Bird Sanctuary. Take a bus to the sanctuary, one of the best birding spots in the world, and then take a birdwatching boat tour through the mangroves. ☉ 3½ hrs, 🖃 $45.

Island Tour. Take a tour of Port of Spain, including the Queen's Park Savannah and the Houses of Parliament, and then venture out to the countryside, ending up at Maracas Bay for a refreshing swim. ☉ 3½ hrs, 🖃 $48.

Coming Ashore

Ships pull into the Cruise Ship Complex in downtown Port of Spain. There are a few shops in the complex itself and numerous local artisans hawking their wares just outside. To get to the downtown core, just look for the imposing twin towers of the Eric Williams Financial complex and walk in that direction.

The tourism authority has introduced "tourism ambassadors" to meet visitors and advise you on how to get around: look for their distinctive jackets. Taxis here will take you to see local sights, but as there is no set fare, you should always ask for a price before getting into a taxi. Generally, a taxi ride to the beach should cost around $30 per carload. Don't bother to take a taxi to the shopping area, since it is only a short walk away, and you will get there faster on foot. Renting a car isn't advisable, as Trinidadians regard driving as a daredevil sport, and only the truly brave would want to tangle with them on the roads. If you do decide to drive, remember that all driving is on the left, as in Britain.

Exploring Trinidad

If you wish to go farther afield than Port of Spain itself, it's probably best to take one of your ship's shore excursions. As distances are sometimes long, it's a good feeling to know that the ship isn't going to leave without you.

Numbers in the margin correspond to points of interest on the Trinidad map.

❷ **Maracas Bay.** This long stretch of sand has a cove and a fishing village at one end. It's *the* local favorite, so it can get crowded on weekends. Lifeguards will guide you away from strong currents. Parking sites are ample, and there are snack bars and rest rooms. Try a shark-and-bake ($2, to which you can add any of dozens of toppings, such as tamarind sauce and coleslaw) at one of the huts at the beach or in the nearby car park. Richard's is by far the most popular shark-and-bake stand.

❶ Port-of-Spain. Most tours begin at the port. If you're planning to explore on foot, which will take two to four hours, start early in the day; by midday the port area can be as hot and crowded as Calcutta. It's best to end your tour on a bench in the Queen's Park Savannah, sipping a cool coconut water bought from one of the vendors operating out of flatbed trucks. For about 35¢ he'll lop the top off a green coconut with a deft swing of the machete and, when you've finished drinking, lop again, making a bowl and spoon of coconut shell for you to eat the young pulp. As in most cities, take extra care at night; women should not walk alone.

The town's main dock, **King's Wharf,** entertains a steady parade of cruise and cargo ships, a reminder that the city started from this strategic harbor. When hurricanes threaten other islands it's not unusual to see as many as five large cruise ships taking advantage of the safety of the harbor. It's on Wrightson Road, the main street along the water on the southwest side of town.

Across Wrightson Road and a few minutes' walk from the south side of King's Wharf, busy **Independence Square** has been the focus of the downtown area's major gentrification efforts. Flanked by government buildings and the familiar twin towers of the Financial Complex (they adorn all T&T dollar bills), the square (really a long rectangle) is a lovely park with trees, flagstone walkways, chess tables, and the Brian Lara Promenade (named after Trinidad's world-famous cricketer). On its south side the Cruise Ship Complex, full of duty-free shops, forms an enclave of international anonymity with the Crowne Plaza Trinidad. On the eastern end of the square is the Cathedral of the Immaculate Conception; it was by the sea when it was built in 1832, but subsequent landfill around the port gave it an inland location. The imposing Roman Catholic structure is made of blue limestone from nearby Laventille.

Frederick Street, Port-of-Spain's main shopping drag, starting north from the midpoint of Independence Square, is a market street of scents and sounds—perfumed oils sold by sidewalk vendors and music tapes being played from vending carts—and crowded shops.

At Prince and Frederick streets, **Woodford Square** has served as the site of political meetings, speeches, public protests, and occasional violence. It's dominated by the magnificent Red House, a Renaissance-style building that takes up an entire city block. Trinidad's House of Parliament takes its name from a paint job done in anticipation of Queen Victoria's Diamond Jubilee in 1897. The original Red House was burned to the ground in a 1903 riot, and the present structure was built four years later. The chambers are open to the public.

The view of the south side of the square is framed by the Gothic spires of Trinity, the city's Anglican cathedral, consecrated in 1823; its mahogany-beam roof is modeled after that of Westminster Hall in London. On the north are the impressive Public Library, the Hall of Justice, and City Hall.

If the downtown port area is the pulse of Port-of-Spain, the great green expanse of **Queen's Park Savannah,** roughly bounded by Maraval Road, Queen's Park West, Charlotte Street, and Saddle Road, is the city's soul. You can walk straight north on Frederick Street and get there within 20 minutes. Its 2-mi (3-km) circumference is a popular jogger's track. The grandstand on the southern end is a popular venue for Calypso and cultural shows. The northern end of the Savannah is devoted to plants. A rock garden, known as The Hollows, and a fishpond add to the rusticity. In the middle of the Savannah you will find

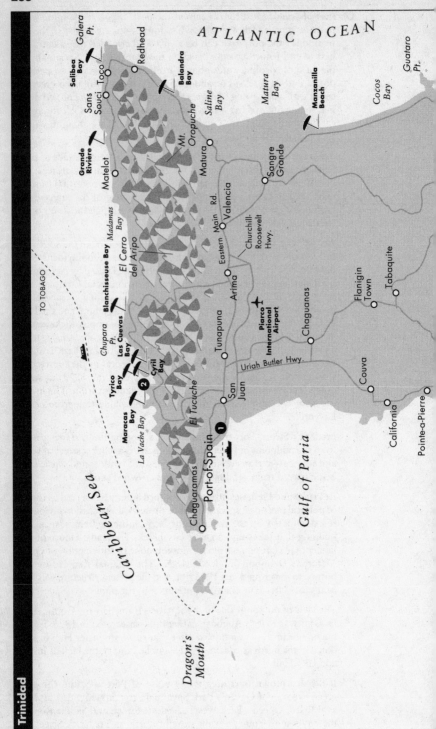

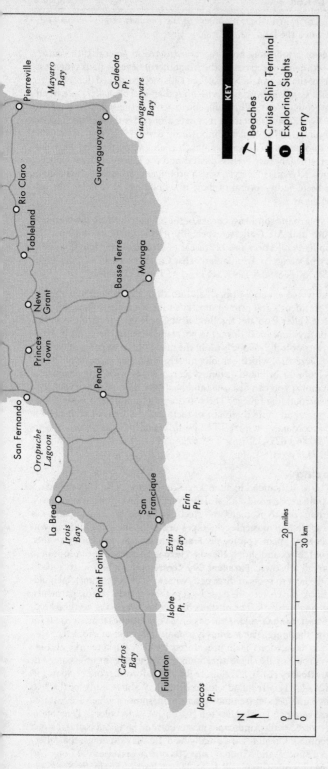

KEY

📷 Beaches

⚓ Cruise Ship Terminal

❶ Exploring Sights

⛴ Ferry

Maracas Bay **2**
Port-of-Spain **1**

20 miles

30 km

N

a small graveyard where members of the Peschier family—who originally owned the land—are buried.

A series of astonishing buildings constructed in several 19th-century styles—known collectively as the **Magnificent Seven**—flanks the western side of the Savannah. Notable are Killarney, patterned (loosely) after Balmoral Castle in Scotland, with an Italian-marble gallery surrounding the ground floor; Whitehall, constructed in the style of a Venetian palace by a cacao-plantation magnate and currently the office of the prime minister; Roomor, a flamboyantly Baroque colonial house with a preponderance of towers, pinnacles, and wrought-iron trim that suggests an elaborate French pastry; and the Queen's Royal College, in German Renaissance style, with a prominent tower clock that chimes on the hour. Sadly, several of these fine buildings have fallen into advanced decay.

Head over to the southeast corner of the Savannah to see the **National Museum and Art Gallery,** especially its Carnival exhibitions, the Amerindian collection and historical re-creations, and the fine 19th-century paintings of Trinidadian artist Cazabon. ⊠ *117 Upper Frederick St.,* ☎ *868/623–5941.* ⊡ *Free.* ⊙ *Tues.–Sat. 10–6.*

The cultivated expanse of parkland north of the Savannah is the site of the president's and prime minister's official residences and also the **Emperor Valley Zoo** and the **Botanical Gardens.** A meticulous lattice of walkways and local flora, the parkland was first laid out in 1820 for Governor Ralph Woodford. In the midst of the serene wonderland is the 8-acre zoo, which exhibits mostly birds and animals of the region—from the brilliantly plumed scarlet ibis to slithering anacondas and pythons; you can also see (and hear) the wild parrots that breed in the surrounding foliage. The zoo draws a quarter of a million visitors a year, and more than half of them are children, so admission is priced accordingly—a mere TT$2 for folks under 12. ⊠ *Botanical Gardens,* ☎ *868/622–3530 or 868/622–5343.* ⊡ *Zoo TT$4, gardens free.* ⊙ *Daily 9:30–5:30.*

Shopping

Good buys in Trinidad include Angostura bitters, Old Oak or Vat 19 rum, and leather goods, all widely available throughout the country. Recordings of calypsonians and steel-pan bands as well as *chutney* (a local East Indian musical style) tapes or CDs make great gifts. Downtown Port-of-Spain, specifically **Frederick, Queen,** and **Henry streets,** is full of fabrics and shoes. **Ellerslie Plaza** is an attractive outdoor mall well worth a browse. **Excellent City Centre** is set in an old-style oasis under the lantern roofs of three of downtown's oldest commercial buildings. Look for cleverly designed keepsakes, trendy cotton garments, and original artwork. The upstairs food court overlooks bustling Frederick Street. **Long Circular Mall** has upscale boutiques that are great for window-shopping. The **Market** is a small collection of shops that specialize in indigenous fashions, crafts, jewelry, basketwork, and ceramics. You can also have afternoon tea in the elegant little café. The **101 Art Gallery** (⊠ 101 Tragarete Rd., Woodbrook, Port-of-Spain, ☎ 868/628–4081) is Trinidad's foremost gallery, showcasing local artists such as Sarah Beckett (semi-abstracts in oil, some of which are featured on local stamps); Jackie Hinkson (figurative watercolors); Peter Sheppard (stylized realist landscapes in acrylic); and Sundiata (semi-abstract watercolors). Openings are usually held Tuesday evenings; the gallery is closed Sunday and Monday. **Just CDs and Accessories** (⊠ Long Circular Mall, Long Circular Rd., St. James, Port-of-Spain, ☎ 868/622–7516) has a good selection of recordings by popular local musicians; other genres are also represented. A fine designer clothing shop, **Meil-**

ing (⊠ Kapok Hotel, Maraval, Port-of-Spain, ☎ 868/627–6975), sells classically detailed Caribbean resort clothing.

Outdoor Activities & Sports

GOLF

The best course in Trinidad is the 18-hole **St. Andrew's Golf Club** (⊠ Moka, Saddle Rd., Maraval, Port-of-Spain, ☎ 868/629–2314), just outside Port-of-Spain. Greens fees are approximately $35 for 18 holes. The most convenient tee times are available on weekdays.

TENNIS

Several establishments allow nonmembers or nonguests to play tennis on their courts, but you will need to call to make reservations. The **Sheraton Trinidad and Conference Centre** (⊠ Lady Young Rd., Port-of-Spain, ☎ 868/624–3211) has two asphalt courts. The **Trinidad Country Club** (⊠ Long Circular Rd., Maraval, Port-of-Spain, ☎ 868/622–3470) has six asphalt courts. The **Tranquility Square Lawn Tennis Club** (⊠ Victoria Ave., Port-of-Spain, ☎ 868/625–4182) has four asphalt courts.

Beaches

Although Trinidad is not the beach destination Tobago is, it has its share of fine shoreline along the North Coast Road, within an hour's drive of Port-of-Spain. Trinidad's beaches are all open to the public and free of charge. In addition to Maracas Bay Beach (☞ *see its listing in* Exploring Trinidad, *above*), the following are worth the trip. On the North Coast Road you'll find **Blanchisseuse Bay**, a narrow, palm-fringed beach. Facilities are nonexistent, but it's an ideal spot for a romantic picnic. You can haggle with local fishermen who take you out in their boats to explore the coast. Narrow, picturesque **Las Cuevas Bay**, on North Coast Road, is named for the series of partially submerged and explorable caves that ring the beach. A food stand offers tasty snacks, and vendors hawk fresh fruit across the road. You can also buy fresh fish and lobster from the fishing depot near the beach. There are basic changing and toilet facilities. It's less crowded here than at nearby Maracas Bay and seemingly serene, although, as at Maracas, the current can be treacherous. Small **Tyrico Bay** is right next door to Maracas Beach. The strong undertow may be too much for some swimmers. Be sure to pack insect repellent, as the sand flies and mosquitoes can be a nuisance in the rainy season.

WHERE TO EAT

Most restaurants include a 10% service charge, which is considered standard on these islands. If it isn't on the bill, tip according to service: 10% to 15% is fine.

$$–$$$ ✕ **Tiki Village.** Port-of-Spainers in the know flock to the eighth floor of the Kapok Hotel, where the views of the city day and night are spectacular. The dining room is lined with teak, and the menu includes the best of Polynesian and Chinese fare. The dim sum—tasting-size portions of dishes such as pepper squid and tofu-stuffed fish—is popular. ⊠ *Kapok Hotel, 16–18 Cotton Hill, St. Clair, Port-of-Spain,* ☎ *868/ 622–5765. AE, MC, V.*

$–$$ ✕ **Veni Mangé.** The best lunches in town are served upstairs in this traditional West Indian house decorated with local art. Credit Allyson Hennessy—a Cordon Bleu–trained chef and local television celebrity— and her friendly, flamboyant sister and partner, Rosemary (Roses) Hezekiah. The creative creole menu changes regularly, and there's always an unusual and delicious vegetarian entrée. This place is popular, so reservations are advised; dinner is served only on Wednesday from 7:30 to 10. The bar area is a fun hangout on a Friday evening (5 to midnight), when Allyson and Roses hold court. ⊠ *67A Ariapita Ave.,*

Woodbrook, Port-of-Spain, ☎ *868/624–4597. Reservations essential. AE, MC, V. Closed weekends. No dinner Thurs.–Tues.*

¢ **The Breakfast Shed.** This Port of Spain institution draws downtown workers like pilgrims to a shrine. Literally a large shed with plenty of wooden tables and benches, it's run by a women's collective, and each woman runs her own kitchen. Choose one (each cook will call to you as you walk by) and place your order. Be prepared for well-prepared, large portions of such local favorites as callaloo, crab and dumpling, and a variety of stewed meats. Despite the name, it's open for both breakfast and lunch. It's noisy, cheap, fun, and delicious—and best of all it is at the Cruise Ship Complex. ⊠ *Cruise Ship Complex, Wrightson Rd., Port of Spain,* ☎ *no phone. No credit cards. Closed Sun.*

INDEX

FODOR'S KEY TO THE GUIDES

America's guidebook leader publishes guides for every kind of traveler.
Check out our many series and find your perfect match.

FODOR'S GOLD GUIDES
America's favorite travel-guide series
offers the most detailed insider reviews
of hotels, restaurants, and attractions
in all price ranges, plus great background information, smart tips, and
useful maps.

COMPASS AMERICAN GUIDES
Stunning guides from top local writers
and photographers, with gorgeous
photos, literary excerpts, and colorful
anecdotes. A must-have for culture
mavens, history buffs, and new
residents.

FODOR'S CITYPACKS
Concise city coverage in a guide plus a
foldout map. The right choice for urban
travelers who want everything under
one cover.

FODOR'S EXPLORING GUIDES
Hundreds of color photos bring your
destination to life. Lively stories lend
insight into the culture, history, and
people.

FODOR'S TRAVEL HISTORIC AMERICA
For travelers who want to experience
history firsthand, this series gives in-
depth coverage of historic sights, plus
nearby restaurants and hotels. Themes
include the Thirteen Colonies, the Old
West, and the Lewis and Clark Trail.

FODOR'S POCKET GUIDES
For travelers who need only the
essentials. The best of Fodor's in
pocket-size packages for just $9.95.

FODOR'S FLASHMAPS
Every resident's map guide, with 60
easy-to-follow maps of public transit,
parks, museums, zip codes, and more.

FODOR'S CITYGUIDES
Sourcebooks for living in the city:
thousands of in-the-know listings for
restaurants, shops, sports, nightlife,
and other city resources.

FODOR'S AROUND THE CITY WITH KIDS
Up to 68 great ideas for family days,
recommended by resident parents.
Perfect for exploring in your own
backyard or on the road.

FODOR'S HOW TO GUIDES
Get tips from the pros on planning the
perfect trip. Learn how to pack, fly
hassle-free, plan a honeymoon or cruise,
stay healthy on the road, and travel
with your baby.

FODOR'S LANGUAGES FOR TRAVELERS
Practice the local language before you
hit the road. Available in phrase books,
cassette sets, and CD sets.

KAREN BROWN'S GUIDES
Engaging guides—many with easy-to-
follow inn-to-inn itineraries—to the
most charming inns and B&Bs in the
U.S.A. and Europe.

BAEDEKER'S GUIDES
Comprehensive guides, trusted since
1829, packed with A–Z reviews and
star ratings.

OTHER GREAT TITLES FROM FODOR'S
Baseball Vacations, The Complete
Guide to the National Parks, Family
Vacations, Golf Digest's Places to Play,
Great American Drives of the East,
Great American Drives of the West,
Great American Vacations, Healthy
Escapes, National Parks of the West,
Skiing USA.